THE HAYDN YEARBOOK
DAS HAYDN JAHRBUCH

XVIII

GENERAL EDITOR:
H. C. ROBBINS LANDON

THE HAYDN YEARBOOK
DAS HAYDN JAHRBUCH
XVIII

General Editor:
H. C. Robbins Landon

Editors:
Otto Biba and David Wyn Jones

1993
Distributed by Thames and Hudson
30 Bloomsbury Street
London
WC1B 3QP

This is volume XVIII in the series of Haydn Yearbooks. Previous volumes (subject to availability) may be attained from Joseph Haydn Stiftung, Schloss Esterházy, A-7000 Eisenstadt, Austria (Fax no. (0)26 82 61 805) in respect of volumes I-XVI, and from Thames and Hudson in respect of volume XVII.

Articles, correspondence and material for review should be addressed to
David Wyn Jones, Department of Music, University of Cardiff, Corbett Road, Cardiff, CF1 3EB, UK.

© 1993 H. C. Robbins Landon, Foncoussières, 81800 Rabastens, France.
All rights reserved; no part of this publication may be reproduced, stored in a retrieval system, or transmittted in any form or by any means, electronic, mechanical, photocopying, recording or otherwise without the prior permission of the General Editor, H. C. Robbins Landon.
ISBN 0-952-16270-9

Computer setting by Rebecca Ball and Petra Illnar
Printed in France by Société de l'Imprimerie Artistique - 81500 Lavaur.

CONTENTS

Two Haydn Portraits		vi
Preface	H. C. Robbins Landon	ix
Documents from the Archives of János Hárich		1
János Hárich	Otto Biba	111
The Acta Musicalia of the Esterházy Archives (Nos. 201-279)	Else Radant	115
An Englishman in Vienna and Eisenstadt Castle in 1748 and 1749 Transcribed and Edited by	H. C. Robbins Landon	197
Rhetoric in Haydn's Applausus	William A. Kumbier	213
Reviews		
Joseph Haydn Werke	H. C. Robbins Landon	267
James Webster, *Haydn's Farewell Symphony*	Tim Rhys Jones	269
Robert N. Freeman, *The Practices of Music at Melk Abbey.*	Dorothea Schröder	277
Marc Vignal, *Joseph Haydn*	A. Peter Brown	283
La Création (avec discographie)	Marc Vignal	289
Haydn News	H. C. Robbins Landon	297
Facsimiles of Haydn's *Armida* and *La fedeltà premiata*		300

Plate 1 Joseph Haydn: Portrait in oils on ivory, 5.5 x 4.5 cm. On reverse a lock of Haydn's hair and the inscription 'J. Haydn'. Pelham Gallery, London.

* * *

Plate 2. Supposed portrait of Joseph Haydn. Oil on canvas. Herbert Huber, Babenhausen (Germany).

Commentary

The miniature of Joseph Haydn, which appears to be authentic, was found some years ago in Amsterdam in antiquarian circles. The coat is light brown in colour and Haydn's eyes are brown. In the other painting, which on the reverse is described as being Haydn's portrait, the wearer has a black coat and hat with gold braid, a pink waistcoat, yellow breeches and black boots with red tops. The identification of the castle or church in the background is difficult. The owner would be happy to receive any information regarding the portrait.

Haydn Yearbook; Preface to Volume XVIII

When the *Haydn Yearbook* was begun in 1962, it was primarily considered as an outlet for the publication of documents from the Esterházy Archives. After some years it was clear that these documents were in every way outstanding for historians. Nothing like them existed for any other major composer in the eighteenth century -- not for Bach in his various ecclesiastical and secular posts, not for Mozart while in the service of the archiepiscopal court at Salzburg, and certainly not for the 'freelance' composers Handel and Beethoven. In fact, it is probably true that the Esterházy Archives -- now located in two principal countries, Hungary (National Széchényi Library) and Austria (Princely Esterházy Archives, Eisenstadt and Forchtenstein) -- are altogether a uniquely valuable source for musicologists, social historians and in general for students of eighteenth-century life and mores.

It is obvious that our knowledge of Haydn's life from 1761 to 1809 -- the period when he was princely *Capellmeister* or, in eighteenth-century translation 'Chapel Master' -- has been, and is still being, totally revolutionized as a result of the publication of these documents, which has been, of course, not limited to the *Haydn Yearbook*, but in which journal the larger part has thus far been published. (Other major sources of publication have been the *Haydn-Studien*, not published for some years now, and in the works of Ulrich Tank -- see the abbreviations for the literature, below). Before 1962, our perception of Haydn's role in the Esterházy establishment was largely limited to generalizations. Now, with the ongoing publication of the *Acta Musicalia* and the Harich *Nachlass*, we are in a position for the first time to write a serious and detailed history of Haydn's complicated and developing relationship with the various Princes Esterházy and the structure in which he gradually became a leading figure, at least culturally.

Imagine if we had detailed descriptions of the costumes in Mozart's major operas -- *Die Entführung aus dem Serail, Le nozze di Figaro, Don Giovanni, Così fan tutte, Die Zauberflöte, La clemenza di Tito*. Well, we have such details for the costumes for all Haydn's operas produced at Eisenstadt and Eszterháza, and in the present *Yearbook* the reader may find elaborate lists of the costumes for Haydn's first Italian opera, *Acide e Galatea*, as well as for the partially lost opera *La Marchesa Nespola*.

Personalities whom we never associated with the Esterházy court suddenly make their appearance, albeit sometimes tantalizingly briefly -- e.g., the fascinating horn-player of Mozartian fame, Joseph Leutgeb, who, it now seems, was the most highly-paid member of Haydn's orchestra at the beginning of 1763. Altogether, Prince Nicolaus Esterházy now appears to have had a real passion for horns, which explains Haydn's many virtuoso parts, even in 'ordinary' works such as Nos. 48 and 51 (as opposed to special 'horn' symphonies such as Nos. 31 and 72). Apparently, too, Prince Nicolaus liked to have a pair of horns to amuse him even when he was in Vienna, and engaged a pair of horn-players who were *apart* from the Capelle and paid separately, as the documents in Harich show.

Turning to the *Acta Musicalia* of the Esterházy Archives, which we have been publishing in their numerical (not chronological) order, we now enter a section in which there are many documents of the era post 1804, when Haydn ceased to be an active administrator for the Esterházys. Although these documents are of interest to the musician and even the general historian (what a graphic tale they provide of the crushing Austrian inflation during the Napoleonic Wars, even from the mole's-eye view of Eisenstadt), they are of limited interest to the Haydn scholar. Hence we have decided to publish them in abbreviated form, giving their contents in sufficient detail to enable scholars to evaluate their content without citing them *in extensis*. Duplicate files of earlier periods, and documents published before in the *Haydn Yearbook* or elsewhere, have been treated similarly.

In the very first document of the new Harich series is a description of what would later become Eszterháza Castle. It is clear from this document that the existing 'country house' of Süttör (as it was called) was, even as early as 1760, a substantial building which already included the present music room, the sala terrena, and so on. The extent to which the bulk of Eszterháza already existed in 1760 was unknown until the publication of this evidence.

It is, however, ultimately the social position of Haydn and his orchestra and singers that appear with such brilliant clarity in these documents. We are very far from the eighteenth century, and these documents seem to push us even further away. The rigid rules, the pattern of life superimposed by the signory, all seem light years away from life at the end of the twentieth century. Here for the first time we begin to understand what it meant to be employed by a great princely court -- the crippling limitations but also the advantages, of which latter the foremost was, quite simply, the pay: Prince Esterházy paid his musicians well and socially they were not treated worse than in any comparable situation -- probably better, because otherwise how can one explain the fact that many of the singers and orchestral players remained for years, indeed all their working life? Esterházy's pension system was also an incentive to remain, particularly as the eighteenth century waned.

We shall have recovered many of the lost Esterházy librettos by the time this documentation has been completed. Dr Harich had already provided us with one vital missing one -- that for *La Circe*, a pasticcio of 1789, without which we could never have reconstituted Haydn's massive 'editing' of the work, which in this case included at least three major new insertions by Haydn himself, all of which were only published after World War II, one (the Terzetto 'Lavatevi presto') not until the 1970s: the reader is referred to Landon II, pp. 713ff. and HYB XVII, p. 192.

There are even several unpublished Haydn letters among the forthcoming Harich material: the first, dealing with a minor administrative problem, has been included here, towards the end of the article, the contents of which Harich arranged in chronological order

***

Otherwise, we shall continue, in this and forthcoming *Yearbooks*, to include other material which we believe to be of interest to lovers of Haydn. In this issue, we print unpublished descriptions of Vienna when Haydn was eking out a living, in the late 1740s, and a fascinating description of Eisenstadt Castle by a travelling Englishman.

A word about our reviews of gramophone records. With the quantity of CDs of music by Haydn appearing on the market -- about twenty a month on average -- we cannot hope to review these adequately. There are many specialist magazines to do this. But what we have done is to start a series of summary, comprehensive reviews: for this issue we are fortunate in having France's leading Haydn scholar, Marc Vignal, to do a survey of available CDs of *The Creation*. This will be followed, in a forthcoming issue, by a survey of *The Seasons*.

H.C.R.L.
Château de Foncoussières
December 1992

Dokumente aus den Esterházy-Archiven in Eisenstadt und Forchtenstein, herausgegeben aus dem Nachlaß von János Hárich. I.

Documents from the Esterházy Archives in Eisenstadt and Forchtenstein, edited from János Hárich's papers. I.

Kommentar/Commentary: Else Radant und H.C. Robbins Landon

Archiv der Gesellschaft der Musikfreunde in Wien, Nachlaß Hárich. Chronologische Reihe, Mappen 1760-1770 (die fortlaufende Zählung der Dokumente stammt von den beiden Kommentatoren).

Archives of the Society of Friends of Music in Vienna, Hárich papers; chronological order, files 1760-1770. The numbering of the documents was provided by the editors.

1. Beschreibung des Schlosses Süttör zu Lebzeiten des Fürsten Paul Anton.
   Description of the castle Süttör during the reign of Prince Paul Anton.
2. Ausgaben, Besoldungen etc. aus den Ausgabenbüchern des Haushofmeisters Züsser.
   Expenses, monies paid, etc., from the account books of Major Domo Züsser.
3. Gesuch des Oboisten und Schulmeisters von Müllendorf, Thomas Ernst Mühlner, ihm ein Gehalt für seine Dienste bei den Grenadierparaden anzuweisen.
   Petition by the oboist and schoolmaster Thomas Ernst Mühlner from Müllendorf, for a salary to compensate for playing at the Grenadiers' parades.
4. Joseph Haydn quittiert das Kostgeld für die Musiker Kapfer, Schwenda und Hinterberger.
   Joseph Haydn signs a receipt for the per diem monies of the musicians Kapfer, Schwenda and Hinterberger.
5. Fürstliche Resolution die Theatermaler, die im großen Saal gearbeitet hatten, zu entlohnen.
   Prince Nicolaus's resolution to pay the painter who had worked for the theatre in the great hall.

6. Notizen über Reisen des Fürsten Nicolaus Esterházy nach Italien aus dem Handbuch des Haushofmeister Züsser.
   Prince Nicolaus travels to Italy, as recorded in the Haushofmeister's Handbuch.
7. Auftrag des Fürsten Nikolaus an seine Hauptkasse die Musiker Dichtler und Leitgeb auszuzahlen und Haydns Quittung, die Gehälter erhalten zu haben.
   Prince Nicolaus commissions his Chief Cashier to pay Dichtler's and Leitgeb's salary. Haydn's receipt.
8. Faksimilie der letzten Seite des Kontrakts mit dem Direktor der Brenner'schen Schauspieltruppe, sowie die Quittung über den Empfang der vereinbarten Bezahlung durch Direktor Brenner.
   End of the contract ('Accord') between Prince Nicolaus Esterházy and Johann Michael Brenner. Facsimilie of the same.
9. Aufstellung verschiedener Ausgaben für Theateraufführungen.
   Various bills for the theatre.
10. Fürst Nicolaus Esterházy schreibt aus Padua an seinen Baumeister Jakoby um sich über den Fortschritt der Bauarbeiten in Süttör zu erkundigen..
    Prince Esterházy writes from Padua to Ing. Jacoby. concerning the progress of work at Süttör.
11. Heirat des Grafen Anton Esterházy: Liste des angelieferten Proviants zur Feier der Hochzeit.
    The marriage of Count Anton Esterházy. List of the food delivered for the marriage festivities.
12/1. Ausgaben für das Theater während der Hochzeitsfeier in Eisenstadt.
    List of various items for the theatre during the marriage festivities.
12/2. Abrechnung des Theaterschusters.
    Bill of the theatre cobbler.
12/3. Zusätzliches Personal wird anläßlich der Hochzeitsfeierlichkeiten für die Bälle engagiert.
    More personnel were engaged for the marriage of Count Anton.
12/4. Auslagen für die Unterhaltung der Hochzeitsgäste und die Festbeleuchtung.
    Expenses for entertaining the guests during the marriage festivities and for the illumination.
12/5 Abrechnung des Kupferstechers für die Ballkarten.
    Engraver's bill for the ball cards.

12/6. Die Morgengabe an die Braut.
Gift to the bride.

12/7. Abrechnung des Maskenverleihers.
Bill for the rented masks.

12/8. Abrechnung des Landkutschers, der einen Musiker zur Druckerei nach Wien brachte.
Bill from the coachman who took a musician to the printer's office in Vienna.

13. Auslagen für die Aufführung von Haydns Oper *Acide e Galatea*.
Expenses for Haydn's opera Acide e Galatea.

14. Rechnung für das Binden des Librettos zur Oper *Acide*.
Bill for binding the libretto of the opera Acide.

15. Schneiderrechnung für Kostüme zu den Opern *Il mercato di Malmantile*, und Haydns *La Marchesa Nespola*.
Bills for the costumes for the opera Il Mercato di Malmantile and Haydn's La Marchesa Nespola.

16. Fürstliche Resolution Peter Ludwig Rahier zum Güterregenten zu bestellen.
Princely resolution to make Peter Ludwig Rahier the regent.

17. Schneiderrechnung von Johann Georg Röck für vier Bauernkostüme zu einer unbekannten Oper.
Bill for four costumes for an unknown opera.

18. Auszug aus den Rentamtsrechnungen über Buchbinderarbeiten.
Bills for book-binding.

19. Fürst Nicolaus Esterházy übersendet seinem Güterdirektor Rahier die Textbücher zu zwei "welschen Comaedien".
Prince Nicolaus sends Rahier the textbooks of two Italian comedies.

20. Rechnung und Quittung des Buchdrucker Sieß für das Drucken und Binden von 100 Operntextbüchern.
Bill from the printer Sieß for printing and binding 100 opera librettos.

21. Tischler- und Malerrechnungen für Arbeiten im Theater.
Carpenter and painter's bills for the theatre.

22. Johann Michael Schuster wird mit seinem Ballorchester nach Eisenstadt engagiert.
Contract for Johann Michael Schuster and his musicians to play at the balls in Eisenstadt.

23. Aus den Haushofmeister Rechnungen. Fürst Nicolaus' Aufenthalt in Innsbruck.
From the Major Domo's account books when Prince Nicolaus was in Innsbruck.

24. Die Theatertruppe spielt zum Geburtstag des Grafen Nicolaus.
Theatre performance to celebrate Count Nicolaus's birthday.
25. Güterdirektor Rahier unterrichtet die Esterházyschen Verwalter, daß Schloß Süttör in Eszterháza umbenannt wird.
Regent Rahier informs the administration that castle Süttör will be called Eszterháza.
26. Ausgaben für Ballmusiker und Theatermaler im Juli.
Bills for the musicians playing at the ball and the theatre painters.
27. Zahlungsauftrag an die Buchhaltung zwei neue Oboen für das Orchester zu bezahlen.
The Chief Cashier is ordered to pay for the two new oboes for the orchestra.
28. Faksimilie von Haydns Brief an einen unbenannten Hausoffizier.
Facsimile of Haydn's letter to an unknown official.
29. Ausgaben für Sommerfeste in Eszterháza aus dem Ausgabenbuch des Haushofmeisters.
Bills for festivities in summer at Eszterháza.
30. Reisekosten für neuengagierte Sänger.
Travelling expenses for newly engaged singers.
31. Abrechnung für die Beförderung von Musikern und Sängern nach Eszterháza.
Bills for carriage charges to bring musicians and singers to Eszterháza.
32. Auszüge aus den Rechnungsbüchern der Baucasse für Blumen und andere Kleinigkeiten für das Theater.
Extracts from the bills of the Baucassa for flowers and other items.
33/34. Abrechnungen für den Ball und die Festlichkeiten anläßlich des Besuches von Erzherzogin Marie Christine und ihrem Gemahl in Eszterháza.
Bills for the ball and festivities during the visit of Archduchess Marie Christine and her consort at Eszterháza. .
35. Eszterházaer Baukosten. Schloßinspektor Kleinrath beanstandet die Kosten der eisernen Kassa.
Eszterháza building costs. Observations about the costs of an iron strong box by Michael Kleinrath, Castle Inspector.
36. Verpflegung für drei italienische Sänger.
Food for three Italian singers.

37. Ausgaben des Haushofmeisters anlässlich des Besuches des kaiserlichen Hofes in Kittsee.
Expenses from the account book of the Major Domo during the stay of the Emperor and his suite in Kittsee.
38. Ausgaben anläßlich der Hochzeit der Gräfin Lamberg, einer Nichte des Fürsten, mit Grafen Pocci.
Bills paid for the festivities during the marriage of Countess Lamberg, a niece of the Prince, to Count Pocci.
39. Vertrag mit den Wiener Theatermalern Herling, Goldman und Spiegel, Kulissen für das Esterházaer Opernhaus zu malen.
Contract with the Vienna painters Herling, Goldman and Spiegel to paint scenery for the Eszterháza opera house.
40. Ausgaben des Haushofmeisters anlässlich der Hochzeitsfeiern.
Expenses paid by the Major Domo for the marriage.
41. Rechnung des Tischlers Haunold für Arbeiten zur Oper *Le pescatrici*.
Carpenter Haunold's bills for work on decoration for Haydn's Le pescatrici.
42. Rechnung des Anton Kerner für gelieferte Waldhörner.
Bill of Anton Kerner for a pair of hunting horns.
43. Rechnung des Kammermalers Grundmann für Materialien und Arbeitstunden.
Bill of the painter Grundmann for material and working hours.
44. Haydn schreibt an Verwalter Schlanstein die Reisekosten seiner Musiker zu begleichen.
Haydn writes to the administrator Schlanstein concerning travelling expenses for his musicians.
45. Dienstvertrag des Kammerpagen Friedrich de Auguste und Anweisung des Fürsten Nicolaus I. Esterházy seinen Kammerpagen mehr Kostgeld anzuweisen.
Contract of the page Friedrich de Auguste and Princely commission to raise his money in kind.

Abkürzungen

Br = Baron
Cab. mahler = Cabinetmaler
Cent = Zentner
d, D = Denar
ds = dass
Durchl(t) = Durchlaucht
duk = Dukaten

Erzhg(in) = Erzherzog(in)
el(n) = Elle, a measurement
F, f, fo, fl = Florin
ftl., flen, fstl = fürstlich(en)
G, gf(in), gfn = Graf, Gräfin
Gr, gr = Groschen
gn = gnädig(ste)
Grhg(in) = Grossherzog(in)
Gralkassa = Generalkassa
Hey. Röm. Reich = Heiliges Römisches Reich
Haus Hofm. = Haushofmeister
Herr. = Herrschaft
Hochged. = Hochgedacht
H^r = Hr. = Herr
Kupferst = Kupferstecher
Kayl. Königl. = Kayserlich-Königlich
Landon I, II, III, IV, V = H. C. Robbins Landon, *Haydn, Chronicle and Works:*
I: *Haydn, The Early Years*, 1732-1765, London 1980
II: *Haydn at Eszterháza*, 1766-1790, London 1978
III: *Haydn in England*, 1791-1795, London 1976
IV: *Haydn: The Years of the Creation*, 1796-1800, London 1977
V: *Haydn: The late Years,* 1801-1809, London 1977
mpria = manu propria
Mst. = Meister
m, n = mm, nn
ord.ri = ordinari
s.g. = so genannt
S^r = Sr = Seiner
Schuh = foot. From: *Nathan Bailey's Dictionary English-German and German-English...*, gänzlich umgearbeitet von D. Johann Anton Fahrenkrüger, Zweiter Theil. Deutsch-Englisch, Elfte, verbesserte und vermehrte Auflage, Leipzig and Jena, Friedrich Fromann, 1810.
19^t = 19t = 19ten
tit = titular
ÿ = y
v. = von
WW = Wiener Währung (currency during Napoleonic period)
Zoll = inch from Bailey (*vide supra*)
xr = Kreuzer

1. Beschreibung des Schlosses Süttör zu Lebzeiten des Fürsten Paul Anton 1760

Generall=Conscription von dem Hoch Gräfl. Nicolas Esterhazischen Dominio Szent Miklóss oder Süttör Anno 1760 in Decembri volbracht durch J: B: D: W: (Herrschaft Süttör fasc. 32. No 1.)

Haupt=Observation von dem Sütörer Schloßl und dabey befindlichem Weesen.
    Das Schoß selbst, und die Gelegenheit darinen betref.
Dieses mehr als gräfliche Schloß Sütör, auf deutsch aber Schütern genent, zeuget seine vortrefliche Lage, und dem Situm, derer Menschen Augen, zum Vergnügen ohnedem genugsam, durch den daran liegend schönen Lust, und Zier, oder mehr zu sagen unvergleichlichen Blumengarthen, samt denen 3 Hauptaléen, welche sich durch den, nahe vor dem Schloß liegenden Wald Lesch, über eine halbe Stunde weit, grad gegen den Markht flekhen Szent Miklos extendiren, und kan durch die mittere, oder grosse Haubt alée, des Markhflekhen Kürchen Thurn, aus des Schlosses Salle à Terren, gantz deutlich gesehen werden. Welches nicht eine geringe Sache ist.

Die Wohnungen und Zimmer im Schloß betr.
Zu Ebner Erde seynd von beyden Seithen 13. unterschiedliche schöne Zimmer, die nicht nur allein mit schönen grossen Wandt Spiegeln, und Henkh Leuchtern gieziehret, sondern auch vortreflich meubiliret, und ziehrlich gemahlen seynd, besonders zu Ebner Erde die Salle á Terren, in welchem Sommerzeit gespeiset wird, und kan ein jede, an der Tafel sietzende Person, in dem schönen Garten, und durch diesen auch durch die Alléen, dem schönen prospect, bis auch nach dem Markht Szentmiklos, und dessen Kürchen Thurn, mit dem grösten Vergnügen sehen.
In dem anderten Condignation, oder anderten Stokh, seynd ebenfals von beyden Seithen 14 Zimmer, welche auch nicht ohne Bewunderung ihrer Meublirung halber, Spiegeln und Mahlereyen anzusehen seynd, sambt einem schönen, hoch und grossen Saal, einer gleichsam fürstlichen Logirung.
In dem dritten Tract, oder Condignation seyn abermahl von beyden seithen 14 Zimmer, in welchen meistentheils die Hauß officianten, und andere Hof Bediente ihre Logierungen haben, und obschon diese denen vorbenenten Zimmern nicht gleich seynd, nichts destoweniger seynd sie alle regulair, und in allen Stukhen gut eingerichtet.

In Summa, wiewohl dieses Schloß nicht alzu groß außsiehet, hat es doch in allem 41 Zimmer, 2 schöne Saale und auch einen passablen Keller, wie auch ein Zimmer, pr modum einer Hof Capelle, in welcher durch den, in diesem Schloß haltenden HofCaplan alle Täge Meß gelesen wird.
Es hat auch dieses Schloß eine Uhre, mit zweyen Glokhen, welche Uhre sowohl viertel, alß auch gantze Stunden schlaget, übrigens ist dieses Schloß an dem Bauwesen, in allem noch in guttem Stand.

Die Gebäue in dießes Schlosses Vorhof betr.
Der Antrag ist, daß in dem Vorhof 2 Tracte von Gebäuen seyn sollen, deren aber dato mirr noch nicht gemachet ist, sonder erst von nun an, gebauet werden wird. Ein Tract aber ist fertig, worinnen erstlich untenher die Hofkuchel, welche schön und sehr Comode ist, dabey befindet sich ein schön Zimmer, worinnen die Hausofficiere Tafel halten, von der Kuchel hinaus nicht weit, seynd die Stallungen auf 40 Pferde. Sehenswürdig gebäuet, mit grossen Fenstern, und gutte Pferde Ständen. Der gantze Stall ist gewölbet und ruhet das Gewölbe auf schönen steinernen Säulen.
Ober der Kuchel ist ein Gebäue mit 2 Zimmern und einen Kuchel, worinnen der Schloßpfleger wohnet, an dieser Wohnung ist auch die herrsch. Dispens, weiterhin ober der Stallung ist eine Gelegenheit zum Frucht schitten, auch wohl auf 1000 Metzen, doch ist dieser Boden so eingerichtet, daß man auch noch etliche Zimmer darauß machen könne.
Der Hof bei diesem Schloße ist wegen seiner Größe, Gleicheit und sauberkeit, auch schön anzusehen, und wird erst noch zierlicher werden, wen der 2te Tract, so wird gebauet stehen, wie der erste Tract, wonembli die herrschl. Kuchel ist. Neben des Hofes Haupt Thor, seynd rechts und links 2 verdekhet kleine Zimmer, worinnen die Thortrabanten logiren, in dem Hofe ist auch eine verdekhter gunpen Brun, mit gutem Wasser.

Gebäue vor dem Schloß draußen.
Seitenwerts rechter Hand auser dem Schloß, ist das Gärtner Haus, welches von guten Zeuge gebauet, und noch in einem guten Stande ist, die Gelegenheit darinnen bestehet aus 2 Zimmern, 1 Kuchel, 1 Kammer und zwey einsatzen, zu dem grünen Garten weesen, wie auch ein Kühe Stall auf 2 stükhel Viech, kein Keller ist bei diesem Hause nicht.
Von diesem Gärtner hause gegen Lesch Wald hinaus, ist der Kuchelgarten, welcher mit einer Mauer umgeben ist, und auch 2

Brunnen mit anpern, samt eisernen Ketten hat, dieser Garten ist so groß, das wan auch die Herrschaft das gantze Jahr hier wohnete, die Kuchel gleichwohl mit genugsamen Kuchelsachen versehen kan, es seynd auch in diesem Garten ein Anzahl von Zwergl Bäumen aber noch jung, jedoch von unterschiedlichen guten Obst Sorten. Es befindet sich auch in diesem Kuchel Garten ein ordinari Glashaus, allein an dem Dachwerk baufällig, es seynd darinnen nichts mehrer als 6 Orangerie Bäume und einige junge Bäumel, das übrige Wesen seynd unterschidlich ausländische Baumer und andere Gewächse.

Schloß Zier Garten betr.
Diesen kan man billig einen Lust und Zier Garten nennen, weilen derselbe aus nichts anderes, als schönen Blumen, parterren, Spallier zieraden und anderen schönen waasen auch Buchbaum Rabateln, bestehet und die schönsten Gänge durch und durch hat, nicht minder 2 verdekhete pumpenbrunen, so seynd auch in diesem so grossen Garten, die grünen Bogengänge, welche an dem Gemauer um und um zu sehen, 1300 Schritt außmachen und mit Weinreben bedekhet seynd, so eine schöne sache, und dabey höchst nützlich, daß auch, wenn die Weinstökhe, die noch nicht lange, bey diesen Bogengängen ausgesetzet seynd, zu ihrer Volkomenheit gelangen, von solchen wohl mehr als 100 Eymer Wein, manches Jahr können gefechstet werden. Auswerts dieses Gartens und nun das gantze Schloß herum seynd schöne breite Gänge, welche von beyden Seiten, rechts u. links mit Castanien Bäumen gezieret seynd, daß diese grüne Spalliere, im Sommer eine Freud, anzuschauen, und ist sowohl dieser schöne Garten, als auch das herrlich Schloß, ein vollkommene Ergötzung der Menschen Augen.

Conscription.
Gesammte Zahl der Einwohner: 93, (Söhne 67.) Davon Hauswirte mit Grundstücken: 51, Kleinhäusler 13, Inwohner 13. Zigeuner u. Juden waren keine. Von Profession waren: 16. Darunter 3 Maurer, 3 Weber, 2 Schuster, 2 Schmid, je 1 Glaser, Schneider, Tischler, Zimmermann u. Berufsmusiker, ein Cimbalist.

Extra ordinare observationes.
Süttör ist ein gemeines Dorf, ausser einiger Landstrasse, im Ödenburger Komitat, hat keine Compossession, ausser zwei eintzige klein Hausel Pauren befinden sich hier, welche sich von einem gewißen H. Bezeredi, unterthanen nennen, wie sie aber nach Süttör

kommen, muß erst untersuchet werden, weilen dieselbe auch einige Grundstücke besitzen.

Die Leute seynd hier insgesambt alte catholischer Religion, von Nation aber Hungarn, doch gibt es auch einige deutsche unter ihnen, besonder in denen s. g. Schloßklein Häuseln.

Was nun dieses Dorf an Unterthanen hat, zeigt die Conscriptions-Tabelle.

Statum Ecclesiae betreffend.

Die Kirche heißet ad S. Andream, sie ist in einem guten Stand, von Gemauer u. hat auch bis an dem Spitz, einen gemauerten Thurn, mit 2 Glocken, auch einen gemauerten Friedhof, aber mit etwas ruinirten Gemauer, und hat diese Kirche als Mater, zu einer Filial, die Kirche von Endröd, item das Capellel an denen Schloß Klein Häuseln, bei dem Dorf Sütör.

Capelle an denen Schloß Kleinhäuslern betr.

Wer diese allen Anfangs gestiftet, oder gebaut hat, ist niemanden bewußt, man glaubet aber, daß diese von den Vorfahrnen der Sütörer Pauren, wegen sehr oft gewesenen Viehumfal, dem Heyl. Leonardo zu Ehren, wegen Führlibitte der Viech Seuchen abwendung, müße seyn erbauet worden, so gehöret zwar zu dem Dorfe, allein sie hat in dem geringesten kein Beneficium, ausser was etwan seltsame Guthäter, zu diese Capelle unterhaltung beytragen. Wie den auch die Schloß Klein hausler, dieses 760ste Jahr ein holtzernes Türmel mit einem blechenen Creutz u. ein Glöckhel beigeschaffet haben.

Jus gladii

Von diesem hat zwar tempore conscriptionis dem Conscriptorem der Utherthanen nicht informieren können, doch ist nicht zu negiren, weilen Sütör u. das ganze Dominium Szt. Miklós zur Herrschaft Kapuvár vorzeiten gehöret hat, daß als auch hier das Jus gladii sein recht hat, kann das eisenstädter Archiv erklären. Die Kriminal delinquenten werden lieber nach Kapuvár führen lassen.

Sztmiklós (in einem Protocoll Nr. 90.)

Diese Herrschaft ist eine Appertinenz und zu dem Schloß und Herrschaft Kapuvár zugehöriges Gut, welches im Ödenburger Komitat liget, und zwar der ausser der Rabau, scheinet als ob es von Natur von solchen Schloß Kapuvár abgesondert wäre, nicht destoweniger ist es darzu ein ware Appertinenz. Welches Gut vor vielen Jahren in verschiedene Handen in Versatz gewesen und zwar leztlichen hatten es in Versatz die PP Benedictini des Fürstl. Stifts und Klosters St Lamperg, oder vielmehr das Kloster zu Maria Zell in Steiermark. Welche Herrschaft sodann Weyl. Fürst Josephus E. anno 1719. mit allen und jeden dazumalen darbei gefundenen Mobilien, Vieh, Körner, Wein und Anbauung, als Erbherr dieser Herrschaft an sich geleset hätte und ihnnen dem darauf gehabten Versatz Schilling par bezahlet und erleget hatte mit 50.000f.

Kommentar

Diese detaillierte Beschreibung des Schlosses, das später Eszterháza (siehe Dok. Nr.25) werden sollte, zeigt, daß das Haus in Süttör viel größer war, als bis jetzt vermutet wurde und auch, daß vieles bei den Umbauten erhalten blieb.

1. Description of the castle Süttör during the reign of Prince Paul Anton

Generall = Conscription of the Count Nicolas Esterhazi's property Szent Miklóss or Süttör Anno 1760, drawn up in December by J: B: D: W:

Principal study of the little castle at Süttör and its characteristics.

The castle itself and its contents.
This castle, nobler than its title 'country castle Süttör', in German Schütern, is distinguished by its fine position . . . and its pleasure garden with its ornaments, or rather, incomparable flower gardens, its three principal allées which traverse, at a distance of more than half-an-hour's walk, the nearby 'Lesch' wood, and extend to the market town of Szent Miklos. The central or principal allée leads to the town's church tower which is clearly visible from the castle's salle à terre. This is no mean thing.

Concerning the appartments and rooms in the castle.
On the ground floor, with both wings there are thirteen different fine rooms, which are distinguished not only by their fine large mirrors on the walls and their chandeliers, but also by their excellent furniture and their delicate frescos, especially the latter in the salle à terre, where one dines in the summer. There, everyone sitting at table can gaze with pleasure at the beautiful garden, and the allées which offer pleasant views up to the village of Szent Miklos and its church tower.
In the other, or second [U.S. first] floor, are with both wings fourteen rooms, in which may be admired their furniture, mirrors and frescos, especially a fine, large and spacious hall, worthy of a princely apartment.
In the third [U.S. second] floor are, with both wings, fourteen rooms, in which live mostly house officials and other court servants, and although these quarters are not the equal of those on the floor below, they are nevertheless all regularly shaped and in all respects well furnished.
In summa, although this castle does not appear to be very large, it contains no less than forty-one rooms, two fine halls and a passable cellar, also a room which serves as a court chapel in which the castle chaplain celebrates mass every day.

The castle also contains a clock with two bells which ring the quarter-hours as well as the hour. Moreover this castle is structurally in good condition.

Concerning the buildings in this castle's outer-court.
The proposal is to add two wings to this outer-court, but the date for this construction has not been made known to me and will begin as of the present. One wing, however, is already completed and contains the court kitchen, which is fine and very convenient; hard by the kitchen are the stables for forty horses. Excellently constructed, with large windows, and good horse stalls. The whole stables are vaulted, and the vaults rest on fine stone pillars. Above the kitchen is a building with two rooms and a kitchen, wherein the castle inspector lives, and next to this apartment is also their lordship's *dispensum* and also above the stables is an attic to store fruit, measuring about 1000 *metzen* [1 metzen = 3.44 litres (miller's dry measure)]; but this attic is so constructed that several more rooms can be made of it.

The court of this castle is because of its size, regularity and cleanliness, pleasant to observe and will be even more elegant when the second wing, which is to be constructed, is completed. It is to be like the first wing where the lordships' kitchen is found. Next to the principal gate of the main courtyard are right and left two small covered rooms where the guards live. In the courtyard is also a covered well, with good water.

Buildings facing the castle.
Outside the castle to the right is the gardener's house, constructed of good materials, and still in good condition. it contains two rooms, one kitchen, one closet and two sheds for garden tools, a cow-stall for two cows. It has no cellar.

In front of the gardener's house towards Lesch wood is a kitchen garden surrounded by a wall, also two wells with pulleys and chains. This garden is so large that if their lordships were to live here all year round, the kitchen could be provided with enough material. In this kitchen garden is also an ordinary green-house, but the roof needs repairing: within are only six orange trees and some young saplings, the rest are various foreign trees and other plants.

Concerning the castle's pleasure garden.
This may be rightly called a pleasure or ornamental garden, since its consists only of beautiful flowers, beds, éspaliers and other beautiful objects, also boxwood hedges which enclose the most attractive paths. Moreover, there are no less than two covered wells. In this large garden, the paths roofed with greenery which follow the enclosing wall consist of 1300 feet and are covered with grapevines - beautiful and useful at the same time. When these vines, which have only recently been planted along the path, reach maturity, they will yield some 100 *Eymer* [Eimer = a liquid measure keg of wine] p.a. if not more. Outside this garden and running round the whole castle are fine wide paths which are graced by chestnut trees, which make a green espalier in summer, a joy to the eye. The beautiful garden and the magnificent castle are a pleasure to behold.

Conscription.
Total number of inhabitants 93 (67 sons). Of these householders with land: 51, inhabitants of small houses, 13; persons renting, 13; gypsies and jews, none. Professions include 16, among which 3 masons, 3 weavers, 2 cobblers, 2 blacksmiths, 1 glazer, tailor, carpenter, joiner and professional musician, a cimbalom player.

Extra ordinaire observations.
Süttör is an ordinary village, except for a single turnpike belonging to the county of Ödenburg; it contains no property except for two single peasant houses which are owned by a certain Herr Bezeredi and can hardly be considered a fief, but how they came to be in Süttör

must be investigated because they also contain some land. The people here are on the whole of the old Catholic religion, of Hungarian nationality, but there are also Germans among them, especially in the so-called Schloßklein houses. The subjects of this village are shown on the conscription table.

Concerning the Statum Ecclesiae.
The church is called Saint Andrew and is in good condition; the tower is walled up to the very top and has two bells. There is also a walled-in cemetery but the masonry is somewhat defective. This mother church has a filial church at Endröd, item the chapel next to the castle in the village of Süttör.

Concerning the chapel next to the castle.
No one knows any longer who consecrated or built it, but they think it was built by the predecessors of the Süttör peasants on account of many accidents with the animals, hence it was dedicated to Saint Leonard, to protect the animals against infection. Thus the chapel belongs to the village but has no beneficium whatever except for the occasional necessity to keep it in order, as for instance in this year 1760 the inhabitants of the castle outbuildings added a small wooden tower with a metal cross to it.

Jus gladii.
Of this the conscriptorum of the subjects has tempore conscriptionis been unable to inform us, but it is not to be ignored because Sütör and the whole dominium Szt. Miklós used to be subject to the signory of Kapuvár, and it is there that the Jus gladii has its rightful place, as the archives in Eisenstadt can explain. Criminal delinquents will better be delivered to Kapuvár.

Sztmiklós [in a protocol no. 90]
This signory is a property belonging to the castle and signory of Kapuvár, in the county of Ödenburg . . . This property has been of late pledged to various owners, the last of whom were the Benedictine Fathers of the princely monastery and abbey of St Lamperg, or rather the monastery of Maria Zell in Styria. Which signory was then redeemed by the late Prince Joseph in the year 1719, with all the then present properties, animals, produce, wine and lands, as hereditary owner of this signory, for which redemption he paid in cash the sum of 50,000 fl.

Commentary
This is a valuable document, giving us details of what would later become Eszterháza (see below document No. 25). It also shows that Süttör Castle was much larger than we suspected and that much of it was retained in the reconstruction.

2. Ausgaben, Besoldungen etc. aus den Büchern des Hauschofmeisters Züsser, 1761

Ausgaab Besoldung und Monath Gelder:
    Waldhornisten: Theodor Liebscher und Jos. Teicher à 15.-f
Ausgaab auf Conto und Zahlungen:
    Nr. 13. dem Nottisten Sadler vor 27 stuk Musicalien à 15gr 20f 15xr

15. dem Sadtler Nottisten vor 26. Bogen Musig: Coupiren samt Pappier a 7xr, 3f.
16. dem Wilhelm Kasta Coupisten vor 27 1/2 bogen Parthyen von Monn in 5 St 3f 9xr
17. dem Buchführer Baader vor 7.Vol. Philosophe Angloise 7f.
20. dem Geigenmacher Conto mit 2f 47xr
25. Empfangt der Mahler Westermayr vor 6 Wanderl mahlen a 1f 30xr
32. dem Mahler Grundermann vor ein neues Farben Castl. Item 16. lection: Vergolte Leisten und Farben 25f 34xr
33. vor 5. Marioneten dem Ferdinand Hofmann von Sr. Excell. selbst
    accordirt à 1. Duc[aten]: 20f 37xr.
36. denen Mahlern welche das Theateur verferttiget 7f.
38. den Anton Adolph lehen bedienten vor 22. tagigen Dienst à 30xr.
    Item 15 Bogen Notten schreiben 12f 15xr

Extra Hauß Außgaab
    den 17. (Jan) vor 4 Rähmel zum Sr Excellencz selbst gemahlnen Bilteln 1f 36xr; denen Leuthen, welche daß Theater gebracht 1f 42xr
1 Wagen umb den Comaedianten 24xr [19. Jan.]
29 stukh zur Comaedi Figurn 2f 15xr
2 grosse, 7 kleine gemahlne deto 33xr
8 Landtschafft von Weigl à 6xr 5 deto von Hertl mit der Zeichnung
30xr
4 Figurn zum Theater 20xr
2 feine Kreyden Glösser [Gläser] zu Sr Excellencz selbst gemahlnen Bildern 30xr
Item 2 deto zum klinen Bildeln 17xr - 1 Eln Adlaß Bandt zu den
Bildern 20xr
6 Ringl mit schrauffel hierzu 6xr
4 Figuren zum Theateur 20xr
Vor ein Miniatas Landschaft den Mahler 1f 8xr
Auf die Opera und 2 Simphonien von Notisten Charppe bezahlt 2f 27xr
Den Mahler Grundner Mann 2 Bilder 24f 30xr
1 Pischel Säitten 4xr
den 30ten vor Parthyen von Sardini 1f 30xr

Item vor disen (t. i. dem Buch Binter) vor 4 Bilder aufziehen und 3 Musig Büchel einbinten 24xr

Dem Tischler geseln von Machinisten welcher beym Theateur gearbeitet 34xr

1 grossen Verschlag zum Theater 2f

Februar.

2 Hornisten wie Januar. - Comödiant Joh.Michl Brenner vor das Mo: Febr. an Gage 36 f

Nr. 12. Empfangt Ferdinand Hofman Comödiant in wienn vor 4 St. Marionet Figurn 16f

Extra Hauß Außgab

febr.1. Denen Comödianten auf hohen anschaffung 2. Tag Diurna 1f 8xr

Den 3t do Sr Excell: in der Comödy gebe 7 St. 17ner 1f 59xr

Denen Musicanten auf den Officirs Fasching bez: 1f 59xr

10ten 6 Büschl A: und D: Saiten à 4xr: 5 Büschl E: 2.Büschl überssponnen erh. 50f

Marcius.

Pater Morocz Kostgeld 90 Tage à 17xr - 2 Hornisten wie vorher. - Brenner weibl. Rollen. Hat P. Morocz auf der Reiß nach Raab umb erlaubnus in dem Schloß Capeln weithers Meß zu lesen.

Nr. 31. den Machinist Retschini vor das kleine Theaterl richten 12f

36. den Mahler Piemontesi vor eine Decoration neü zu machen zum kleinen Theaterl 16f

Aprilis.

Waldhornisten, wie bisher. -

Majus.

Morocz 14ten ausgetreten.- Waldhornisten, wie bisher.

Nr. 24. dem Mahler Grundmann vor Ein Monath Lection geben 6d [Ducaten]: und

2 Bilder, einen Schuster, und Kesten Braderin pr 6 Ducaten in Suma 50f 20xr

48. dem Speckh Hansl vor Perso anstreichen 3f 30xr

Junius.

Livrebediente darunter 2 Hornisten.

Nr. 20. dem Boye (Kammerdiener) vor ein Harpfe bez. 4f 12xr

Julius.

Waldhornisten Th. Liescher, Jos. Teicher, diesen gebührenden vor das ganze Monath 30f: Nach deme sie aber den 30. July Nachts in Wienn heimblich entwichen und nicht mehr als der ersten 1f 8xr: den anderten aber 1f: antizipiret worden so komen diese pr ausgab 28f

    Nr. 18. H. HbM: v: Rahier die erkaufften Bücher zuruck bezahlt mit 2f 33xr

      62. Buchbinder Schatten, vor eine Landkarten reparirn und auf neüe Leinwath zu ziehen 3f.

Augustus.

September.

Nr. 59. Dem Bildhauer von Oedenburg, Meister Kössler, vor ein geschnidenes Tischl in das neu Marmorirte Cabinet pr accord 9f.

    60. Vor ein 20 Clafter lang übertragenes Sail, zum Machin brunn den Veith Conrath

    39. Maurer Arbeith den Veith Conrath pro 7bri 28f.

den 4t denen zwey Waldhornisten welche Sr Excell: nicht anständig auf hohen Befelch vor die Reis nach Wienn und vor sich hören zu lassen geben 2 Ducaten, 8f 19 1/2xr

Die Fuhr von Ocdenburg hieher vor die 2 Waldhornisten zahlt mit 21xr

Oktober.

den 12. bezahle H. Pollhammer Vergolder in Wienn, da dieser mit 2 Gesellen auf S. E: befelch (Nr.20) hiehero beruffen, das Marmorirte Cabinet zu vergolten; weillen es aber inzwischen mit dem Sedlmayr accordirt worden: vor Fuhr Versambnus und Unkosten 21f.

    Nr. 24. den 15. dem ThurnerMst von Oedenburg welcher mit 6 Persohn alhier Mussig gemacht 12f.

    Nr. 25. den 16. Bezahle H: Abdankh burgerl: Stockadorer vor das Cabinet zu marmoriren lauth Contract 180f.

    32. Erkauffe in Wienn von Mster Joh. Michl Weinhart Einen Neüen mit Grinen Tuch gefutterten 4 Sizigen Raißwaagen, und bezahle hievor 280f.

Denen 3. Zigeunern welche am Theresia Tag zur Musig bestellt worden, weillen dise die Würthische Hochzeit verseumbt bezahlt 51xr

November.

Unter den Livere Bediente: Bedienter et Musicus Andre Krempl 10f

Nr. 23-25. Dem H. Sedlmayr Vergolter in Oedenburg, vor Vergoltung des Cabinets 100f Item vor die Spiegl Ram, Spiegl Tisch 1 Canape, 4 Taboret Sessel zu vergolten, und weiß Planiren in eben dises Cabinet 50f zusammen 150f.
45. den 15. dem Buchbinder lauth auszügl 2f 43xr vor das Buch der Granat Apfl bezahlt 1f 51xr.

December.
Musicus Bedienter Andre Krampl [*sic*] 10f.
Nr. 20. den 17. bezahle dem Tischler Mster Conrad Nürnberger in Oedenburg vermög Contrac wegen Austafelung des kleinen Bilder Cabinets 27f.

Kommentar

Jan.: Die beiden Hornisten Liebscher und Teicher scheinen nicht in der 1761er Orchesterliste auf, dort waren Johann Knoblauch und Thaddeus Steinmüller als Hornspieler verzeichnet. Es ist daher eher anzunehmen, daß die beiden bei Jagden spielten und ev. bei Kammermusiken, was ihre Anwesenheit in Wien erklären würde. Die Namen der verschiedenen Kopisten waren uns nur teilweise bekannt. Charppe = Bonifacius Carl Champée. Weitere Informationen über Anton Adolph siehe unten und auch Landon I, S. 646 f.

Im Eisenstädter Musikalienkatalog finden sich Parthien oder Symphonien von M. G. Monn und Sardini. Marionetten spielten im Eisenstädter Theaterleben eine große Rolle.
Feb.: Brenner kam mit einer ganzen Truppe von Schauspielern.
März: es wurden in Eisenstadt ein großes und ein kleines Theater bespielt.
Juni: es wäre interessant zu wissen, wofür die Harfe gebraucht wurde.
Sept.: Nach der Flucht der beiden Hornisten Liebscher und Teicher, wurden Hornisten zum Vorspielen nach Wien beordert.
Okt.: Reisewagen waren so teuer wie heute Automobile, mehr als ein Halbjahresgehalt Haydns. Der Thurnermeister spielte mit seinen Gehilfen Trompeten und Pauken bei Feuerwerken und anderen Gelegenheiten, siehe Landon I, S. 651. Die Zigeuner gaben Festen die exotische Note. Es gab ein Zymbal in Süttör, siehe oben, Dokument 1.
Nov.: Wahrscheinlich Cestis Oper *Il pomo d'oro* (1667). Das Libretto wurde 1666 und 1668 gedruckt, eine deutsche Übersetzung 1672. Es könnte aber auch ein damals sehr modernes und gefragtes Haushalts-

und Kochbuch gewesen sein, wie dieses der Herzogin von Troppau, das viele Auflagen hatte. Es erschien das erste Mal 1695 unter dem Titel: Eleonora Maria Rosalia, Herzogin zu Troppau. *Freywilling-Auffgesprungener Granat-Apffel, . . . Oder Geheimbnuß viler . . . bewärten Mitteln und Wunder-heylsamen Artzneyen . . . Auffs neue vermehrt, sambt einer kleinen Diaeta,* . . . Der Ausgabe von 1697 war auch ein Kochbuch beigegeben und Heilrezepte für zahlreiche Krankheiten.

Interessant ist, daß Fürst Paul Anton ein Amateurmaler war siehe Extra Haus Ausgaben (Jan.).

Partial translation

From Chief Cashier Züsser's Records for 1761.

[January]

Monies disbursed and monthly salaries:

Hunting-horn players Theodor Liebscher and Jos. Teicher à 15-.

Money from accounts and payments.

No. 13 The music copyist Sadler for 27 pieces of music à 15gr. 20f. 15xr.

No. 15 Sadtler music copist for 26 sheets [4 sheets] of music, copying and paper a 7 x 3f.

No. 16 Wilhelm Kasta copyist for 27 1/2 sheets Parthyen by Monn in 5 pts. 3f 9xr.

No. 17 Book-keeper Baader for 7 vols. Philosophe Anglaise 7f.

No. 20 Violin maker's account 2f. 47xr.

No. 33 Five marionettes arranged by H. Ex. personally to Ferdinand Hofmann at 1 duc.

No. 36 The painters who completed the theatre 7f.

No. 38 Anton Adolph liveried servant for 22 days' service at 30xr.

Item 15 sheets of music copied 12f 15xr.

Extra house expenses.

On 17 [Jan] for 4 little frames for pictures painted by H. Ex. personally 1f 36xr.

For the people who brought the theatre 1f. 42xr.

1 carriage for the actors 24xr. [19 Jan]

29 pieces for figures in the theatre 2f 15xr.

2 large, 7 small painted ditto 33xr.

----

4 figures for the theatre 2xr.

----

4 figures for the theatre 20xr.

For the opera and 2 symphonies furnished by copyist Chappe paid 2f 27xr. [27 Jan]

The painter Grunder Mann [Grundmann] 2 pictures 24f 30xr.

1 bundle of strings 4xr [28 Jan.]

On the 30th [Jan.] for Parthyen by Sardini 24f 30xr.

Item for him [Bookbinder] preparing 4 pictures for framing and 3 music books bound 24xr.

The carpenter apprentice who worked for the stage-hand in the theatre 34xr.

1 large locker for the theatre 2f [30 Jan.]

February
Actor Joh. Michael Brenner for month February, salary 36f
No. 12 Actor Ferdinand Hofman from Vienna for four marionette figures 16f.
Extra house expenses:
   1 Feb. The actors, by princely command, 2 per diem 1f 8xr.
   3 ditto H. Ex. distributed [tips of] 7 17teen pieces 1f 59xr.
   Musicians for the officers' carnival 1f 59xr
   10 ditto 6 bundles A and D strings at 4x, 5 bundles E, 2 bundles overspun str. 50x.

March

No. 31 stage-hand Retschini for putting in order the small theatre 12f.
No: 36 painter Piemontesi for a new decoration [stage-set] in the little theatre.

April
Hunting-horn players [as in Jan.].

May
Hunting-horn players [as in Jan.].

June
No; 20 [The servant] Boÿe for a harp 4f 12xr.

July
Hunting-horn players Th. Liescher [*sic*], Jos. Teicher, they should receive for the whole month 30f; but since they secretly fled on the night of 30 July in Vienna and the first had received an advance of 1f 8xr, the other 1f, the total arrives at 2f 8xr.
No. 18 Cptn. v. Rahier repaid for books he had purchased 2f 33xr.

August

September

On the 4th two hunting-horn players who by princely order travelled to Vienna to give an audition 2 ducats 8f 19 1/2 xr.
Travel of the two hunting-horn players from Oedenburg to here 21xr.

October

No. 24 The 15th for the *Thurnermeister* of Oedenburg who arrived with six persons to play music here 12f
----
No. 32. bought from Viennese Master Joh. Michl Weinhart a new 4-seated travelling coach fitted with green material for which paid 280f.
The three gypsies who on St. Theresa's Day were ordered to play music, because they missed the Würth marriage 51xr.

November
Among the liveried servants, the servant and musician Andre Krempl 10f.

---
45. The 15th to the bookbinder according to his account 2f 43 xr.
For the libretti *der Granat Apfel* [*Il pomo d'oro*]] 1f 51xr.

December
Musician servant Andre Krampl [*sic*] 10f.

Commentary

The horn players Liebscher and Teicher do not figure in the lists of Haydn's orchestra of 1761; the orchestral players were, at this time, Johann Knoblauch and Thaddeus Steinmüller. Liebscher and Teicher were possibly used for the hunt and/or for chamber music; the latter function may explain their presence in Vienna in July (q.v.)

The various music copyists were only partially known from hitherto documents. Chappe = Bonifacius Carl Champée.

Note that Eisenstadt Castle had two theatres, a larger and a smaller one.

Concerning the fate of Anton Adolph, see below and also Landon, I pp. 646 f.

Among the repertoire of music at Eisentadt were *Parthyen* (Partitas or Symphonies) by M. G. Monn and Sardini. There were also marionettes which, it can be seen, figured prominently in Esterházy court theatrical life.

After the two horn players fled from Esterházy service in July 1761, the Prince immediately called for two others, who gave auditions in Vienna.

The *Thurnermeister* of Oedenburg supplied, usually, trumpets and timpani for fireworks and, possibly, other services too. See Landon I p. 651 for an interesting receipt.

We notice that Prince Paul Anton Esterházy was an amateur painter (Jan., Extra house expenses).

Feb. 1761: Brenner arrived with a whole troupe of actors and actresses.

June 1761: It would be nice to know why a harp was needed.

Note the large sum (280f.) needed for a travelling coach - as expensive as an automobile today (more than six months wages for Haydn).

October; gypsies were often required to play (note the cimbalon that was in Süttör (see above) Document 1, *Conscription*.

November: Possibly Cesti's opera *Il pomo d'oro* of 1667 of which a libretti was printed in 1666 and 1668, while in 1672 a German libretti was published.

It could also be the then very modern and popular household cookbook such as the one by the Duchess of Troppau, which ran into many editions. It appeared for the first time in 1965 with the title Eleonora Maria Rosalia, Herzogin zu Troppau. *Freywilling-Auffgesprungener Granat-Apffel, . . . Oder Geheimbnuß viler . . . bewärten Mitteln und Wunder-heylsamen Artzneyen . . . Auffs neue vermehrt, samt einer kleinen Diaeta, . . .* The edition of 1697 also included a cookbook as well as receipes for healing all sorts of illnesses.

3. Gesuch des Oboisten Thomas Ernst Mühlner, Schulmeister in Müllendorf, ihm ein Gehalt für seine Dienste bei den Grenadierparaden anzuweisen

Gralcassa, 1761. Rubr. VIII. Nr. 87.

Durchlauchtig Hoch und Wohl Gebohrner
des Hey: Röm: Reichs Fürst

Gnädigst Hochgebiettender Herr Herr
Nachdem ich als ein Unwürdiges Unterthans Kind, und dermahliger Schulmeister in Müllendorff die Ehre gehabt bey Euer Hochfürstlichen Durchlaucht Grenadier-Banda seith den 2ten Aug: des abgewichenen 760ten Jahrs die Stelle des Secunday Hoboisten zu versehen, und bey all denen bißher gewesten Paraden zu Paradieren, muß mir dieses vor eine Sonderlich Grosse Gnade gereichen lassen. Gleichwie dann der Klein- und Groß höffleiner Schulmeister als 2 Fagotisten ihr G[nä]digst ausgeworffenes Solarium viertl-jährig richtig erhoben, ich aber, da mir pur dieserwegen eine neue Hobo samt darzu gehörigen Röhrn einschaffen, auch andere verschiedene Unkösten bestreiten, und dem entlegensten Weege dahin gehen müssen, habe biß Dato nichtes erhalten. Derowegen
Gelanget an Euer Hochfürstliche Durchlaucht mein Unterthänigst- demüthigstes Bitten Höchstdieselbe geruhen mir von diese Zeit allergnädigst etwas zu resolviren. Vor welche hohe Gnad ich Lebenslang verharren werde.
Euer Hochfürstlichen Durchlaucht
Allerdemüthigster Diener
Thomas Ernestus Mühlner
Schulmeister in Müllendorff

Commission
Unßeren Obern Einnehmer Johann Zoller Befehlen Wür hiermit, daß der dem Supplicanten eben jenen Gehalt wie die zwey Fagotisten von Groß, und Kleinhöfflein wehrend ihrer geleisteten Diensten vermög Unserer resolution zu empfangen gehabt haben, pro rato temporis bezahlen, und in Rechnung alß richtige außgaab Bringen solle. Eisenstadt den 14 Juny 1761.
Antoni Fürst Esterhasy

Kommentar

Das Gesuch zeigt uns, daß die Grenadier-Banda aus Amateurmusikern bestand. Zoller ließ am 30. Juni 45f 50xr anweisen, die am 2. August 1761 ausgezahlt wurden.

3. Schoolmaster Mühlner petitions for a salary
Summary Translation

The unworthy subject, at present schoolmaster in Müllendorf, has had the honour of being 2nd oboist in the princely grenadiers' band since 2 Aug. of last year, 1760, and appeared in all parades. The schoolmasters of Klein and Großhöflein, like the two bassoon-players, receive their salary correctly in quarterly payments whereas 'I, despite having purchased a new oboe

and having other expenses, and having gone to the most remote places, have received nothing'. Therefore he begs for a princely dispensation.
The Prince orders his Chief Cashier Johann Zoller to pay Mühlner the same salary as the two bassoon players. Eisenstadt 14 June 1761.

Commentary
It is evident that the grenadiers' band consisted of part-time amateur musicians. On 30 June 1761 Zoller authorized the sum of 45fl. 50xr. which was paid on 2 August 1761.

4. Quittungen Joseph Haydns über Kostgeld für die Musiker Kapfer, Schwenda und Hinterberger.

Gralcassa 1761 Rubr. VIII. Nr. 77/75.

S p e c i f i c a t i o n
Des vor nachstehende 4 Musicis von 3ten Bis 30ten Juny dieses Jahrs Betragenden Kost=geldes:

Des Michael Kapfers betrag ist vor 28 Täg à 17Xr	7f 56Xr
Des Georg Kapfers eben	7f 56X
Des Johann Hinterberger	7f 56X
Des Georg Schwente	7f 56X:

Summa	31f 44X:

Daß obige 4 Musici aus Handen Herrn Ober Einnehmers Johann Zoller besagte Dreyßig Ein Gulden 44Xr empfangen haben, bezeüge hiemit. Eisenstadt den 30ten Juny [1]761:
Joseph Haydn mpria
Was die zwey Herrn Kapfer, Georg Schwenda und Johannes Hinterberger des verflossenen Monaths July 1761 das Kost geld vor 10 täg ein Jeder des Tags 17xr zusammen 11F. 20xr von Herrn Obereinnehmer Richtig empfangen haben bescheine hiemit Wienn den 4t. Aug. 1761
Joseph Haydn
Vice Capel Meister mpria

4. Per diem monies for the horn players
Summary translation.
Per diem monies paid to four musicians for 3 - 30 June 1761, 28 days at 17 xr = 7f 56xr. Countersigned by Haydn, who acknowledges payment in full. A second document, signed by Haydn, acknowledges payment of per diem monies for 10 days in July 1761.

5. Fürstliche Resolution vom Dezember 1762 die Theatermaler zu bezahlen, die im großen Saal gearbeitet hatten (Buchhaltung Eisenstadt 99/1, 99/45)

Commission
Vermög welcher die zu Ausmahlung des Theatri in grossen Saal arbeithende Mahler /:gleichwie vorhin:/ aus Unseren Rändt-Amt Bezahlet, auch die übrige sowohl zu dem Theatro, und Auszierung des Saals und Schloß erforderliche Leüthe, und nothwendigkeiten /:wie es unser Ingenier Jacoby veranstalten wird:/ ebenfalls aus Unserem Rändt-Amt gegen quittungen ausgezahlt werden sollen. Eisenstadt den 25.Xbris [1762]
Nicolaus Fürst Esterhazy

Wolf Kepp 1762, dec. 14-18. vermög angegebener Arbeit von Mons. Bon, bei dem Theatro im großen Saal täglich 1f.
Zu Abstaubung deren Malereien im großen Saal bei dem Theatro 2 Fuchsschweif a 9xr.
Wanweg für das Theater: 2 große Plän auf Leinwand in Felt rahmen. 4f 26 1/2xr. 1762 dec. 1.

Kommentar

Aus diesen beiden Dokumenten ist zu ersehen, daß im großen Saal des Eisenstädter Schlosses (jetzt Haydnsaal) ein Theater installiert worden war. Wolf Kepp ist der Sohn des Malermeisters Christian Köpp, der aus Eisenstadt stammte. Wolfgang und sein Bruder Georg führten beide das Gewerbe des Vaters weiter. Von ihnen stammt das Deckengemälde in der Bergkirche in Eisenstadt. Wolfgang Köpp beendet sein Leben als wohlhabender Mann in Wien. Sein Sohn war ein bekannter Buchillustrator. [Burgenländische Heimatblätter, Sonderheft 1948: *Eisenstadt 300 Jahre Freistadt, p.58*]

5. Prince Nicolaus's resolution to pay the painters who had worked for the theatre in the great hall

Commission, according to which the painters working on decorations for the theatre in the great hall (as before) are to be paid by our Rent-Cashier, also other people responsible for the theatre and the decoration of the hall in the castle (as indicated to *Ingénieur* Jacoby) are also to be paid by our Rent-Cashier against receipts. Eisenstadt 25 Xbris [Dec. 1762].

Summary translation

[14 - 18 Dec. 1762 Wolf Kepp]. Work for Mons Bon at the theatre in the great hall 1 [fl.]... for dusting the paintings in the great hall in the theatre 2 fox-tails a 9xr.

Commentary

From these documents it can be seen that the new theatre had been built in the great hall (now Haydnsaal) of Eisenstadt Castle. The painter Wolf Kepp was the son of the Princely painter Christian Köpp [*recte*] who was born in Eisenstadt. Both sons took up the same craft, they painted the ceiling of the Mountain church in Eisenstadt. Wolfgang Köpp moved later to Vienna where he died a wealthy man. His son was a well known book illustrator. [Burgenländische Heimatblätter Sonderheft *Eisenstadt 300 Jahre Freistadt*, Eisenstadt 1948,p.58].

6. Notizen im Haushofmeister Handbuch über Reisen von Fürst Nicolaus 1763.

Jan: 16, Eisenstadt
     22, Wien
     31, Süttör
März: 3, 29 Süttör
Apr: 13, Süttör
Empfang in Italien
Mai: 13, 21 Venedig
Jun: 6, 12 Bologna, 18, 20, 30 Padua
Jul: 11, 17 Padua

6. Prince Nicolaus travels to Italy 1763, as recorded in the *Haushofmeister's Handbuch*
Jan 16: Eisenstadt
Jan 22: Vienna
Jan 31: Süttör
March 3, 29, April 13: Süttör
Reception in Italy
13 May: Venice
21 May: Venice
6 June: Bologna
12 June: Bologna
18, 20, 30 June: Padua
11, 17 July: Padua

7. Auftrag des Fürsten Nikolaus an seine Hauptkasse Musikergehälter (Dichtler und Leitgeb) auszuzahlen und Haydns Quittung darüber

Gralcassa, 1763. Rubr. VIII. Nr. 120

Commission
Vermög Unser Ober Einehmer Johann Zoller dem Joseph Leidtgeeb Waldt Hornist! Wie auch dem Leopold Dichtler, Tenorist: Beyde zu

der Hochfürstliche music dependiren Ihren Jährigen Behalt: inclusive vom Ersten des Monaths Februarii des Lauffendes Jahr. Nemblich dem Joseph Leidtgeeb mit 400 Gulden und dem Leopoldt Dichtler mit 150 Gulden Jahr Besoltung! Wie gewöhnlich alle Monath aus unserer Haubt Cassa richtig Bezahlt werden Wienn Den 12tn Marty 1763
       Nicolaus Fürst Esterhazy

Daß mir von dem: zu anfang des Monaths Februarii von Sr Hochflen Durchl: Neu:aufgenohmenen Camerwalthornisten Joseph Leitgeb /:So zu Ende Besagten Monaths widerum entlassen worden:/ Sein Monathlicher Gehalt mit 33 f 20 xr, dann vor dem Tenoristen Joseph Dichtler vor Besagtes Monaths Sein gehalt mit 12f 30x in Suma also Viertzig Fünff Gulden, 50 xr durch den Hochften OberEinehmer Herrn Johann Zoller seynd überantworthet worden, quittire hiemit. Schloß Eisenstadt, den 1ten Marty 1763:
Id e 45f 50Xr   Joseph Haydn

Kommentar

Haydn und seine Frau hatten zu den Leitgebs bereits in Wien freundschaftliche Beziehungen. Frau Haydn war auch während Haydns Abwesenheit die Taufpatin von einer der Leitgeb Töchter (siehe Landon I, S. 372) am 3. Juli 1762; Es schien Haydn gelungen zu sein den Fürsten zu überreden Leutgeb mit einem wahrhaft 'fürstlichen' Gehalt von 400 Gulden zu engagieren (Haydn erhielt die gleiche Summe als Vicekapellmeister!). Ein Monat später war Leutgeb wieder entlassen. Vielleicht hat Haydn sein Hornkonzert von 1762 für Leutgebs Antrittskonzert komponiert (Februar 1763? oder sogar früher?). Siehe auch Daniel Heartz: 'Leutgeb and the 1762 horn concertos of Joseph and Johann Michael Haydn' in *Mozart Jahrbuch 1987-8*, D. 59ff.

7. Prince Nicolaus commissions his Chief Cashier to pay Dichtler's and Leitgeb's salary. Haydn's receipt
Summary translation
Commission, according to which Chief Cashier Johann Zoller is to pay Joseph Leidtgeeb [Leutgeb] hunting-horn player and Leopold Dichtler, tenor, both in princely musical service, a yearly salary including the beginning of the month of February of this year. Namely Joseph Leidtgeeb with 400 gulden and Leopold Dichtler with 150 gulden p.a. . . .
Vienna, 12 March 1763 Nicolaus Fürst Esterházy.

The chamber hunting-horn player Joseph Leitgeb, newly engaged by H. S. H. at the beginning of the month of February (who was dismissed at the end of the said month), his monthly salary of 33f 20xr and that of the tenor Joseph Dichtler for the said month 12f 30xr in summer therefore forty-five gulden 50xr has been paid by the Princely Chief Cashier Herr Johann Zoller, for which I take responsibility and hereby do receipt.
 Schloß Eisenstadt, 1 March 1763;

Joseph Haydn.

Commentary

We have seen that Haydn's wife was a witness at the baptism of Leutgeb's daughter (Landon, I p. 372) on 3 July 1762 at Vienna, in the absence of Haydn. Now we see that Haydn persuaded the Prince to engage Leutgeb at a gigantic salary, the equal of Haydn's, only to be dismissed the same month. (Does this tell us something of Leutgeb's character?) Perhaps the Haydn Horn Concerto of 1762 was designed to be Leutgeb's 'entrance piece' at the Esterházy court in February 1763, or even earlier. See Daniel Heartz: 'Leutgeb and the 1762 horn concertos of Joseph and Johann Michael Haydn' in *Mozart-Jahrbuch* 1987-8, pp. 59ff.

8. Faksimile der letzten Seite des Kontraktes mit dem Direktor der Brennerschen Schauspieltruppe sowie die Quittung über den Empfang der akkordierten Summe durch Direktor Brenner.

... von meiner künftig zu verdienen habenden Bezahlung zwey ord.ri Ducaten anticipato heraus gegeben worden. Bescheine hiemit. Wienn ut supra id est 8 F 15 xr:
   Joh: Michael Brenner
   S: T. Comitg

Daß mir H: Hoffmaister Züsser die vermög Accord versprochene 64 F: über oben Empfangene 8F 15 xr heute Dato richtig und paar bezahlet hat Bescheinige Hiemit Suttor den 22 Marty [1] 763.
 Johan Michael Brenner
 Comoediant
[andere Handschrift:]
Item 2 F: vor die Figuren zurichten

Kommentar

In dem Kontrakt verpflichtete sich Johann Michael Brenner vom 21. Februar (seine Abreise von Wien) bis zum 21. März in Süttör (später Eszterháza) deutsche Schauspiele und Marionettenstücke aufzuführen. Dafür erhielt er 64 Gulden,

vermittelst künftig Gehundener hebenden Bezahlung Ihrerig ord.⁼ Ducaten anticipato hinausgegeben werden. Bescheine hiemit Estimen et fors
id est 8 fl 15 xr.   Joh: Michael Brunner
                          H: L: Comicq

Daß mir H: Hofmeister Lußer die Vermög Accord versprochener 6 fl. über oben Empfangene 8 fl 15 x: heüte Dato richtig und gaar bezahlet hat bescheinige hiermit Suttor den 22 Marty 763.
                          Johan Michael Brunner
                          Comoediant.

Man sehe hier die figura zwischen

Quartier und Brennholz für sich und drei Schauspieler und Schauspielerinnen. Unterzeichnet wurde der Vertrag in Wien am 20. Februar 1763 und Brenner ein Vorschuß von zwei Dukaten (8f. 15xr) gewährt. Am 22. März wurde in Süttör die restliche Summe ausbezahlt, samt zusätzlich 2 Gulden für Reparaturen an den Marionetten. Siehe *Haydn Studien IV* (1980), S. 176f, für das ganze Dokument.

8. Commentary

Facsimile of the end of an agreement ('Accord') between Prince Nicolaus Esterházy and Johann Michael Brenner, whereby the latter agrees to stage German plays and marionette players at Süttör (later Eszterháza) from 21 February when he leaves Vienna to 21 March for a total fee of sixty-four gulden with lodgings and free firewood for himself and three other actors and actresses. The contract was signed in Vienna on 20 February 1763, and two ducats (8f 15xr) were given as an advance.

The final reckoning was made at Süttör on 22 March 1763, with '2f for repairing the figures' (i.e. marionettes). See *Haydn - Studien IV* (1980), pp. 176f, for complete document.

9. Aufstellung verschiedener Ausgaben für Theateraufführungen im Jahr 1763

Eisenstädter Rentamts-Rechnung Nr. 141/FF [Jan.]

Zahlung vor einiges zu dem Theatrum nöthiges Geschier 4 Höffen, 1 Krug, 3 Höffel u. 1 Kriegl, 6 große Höffen - 50xr.
Auszigl was dem Monsi[eur] le Bon zum Teatro an Schlosserarbeit verrichtet worden pro 1763: 20 Häckl mit Schraufen gemacht a 3xr (Friedrich Schieller Schloßermeister).
Eisenstädter Rentamts Rechnungen No. 99/4 A - K:
Auslaag vor verschidne auf das Theatrum zur neuen Opera beigeschafte Notwendigkeiten:
1. Oberauer Kaufmann, aug. 5. Specifiaction der Material Farben, so zu dem Hochfürstl. Deadro allhier in Schloß, als nemblich zu der Cavalieurs Comoedie, et Markch Obera, Malerey richtig mit accord. 76f.
2. Wolf Kepp Maler, was auf dem herrschaftl. Theater zur Cavalier Comoedie und neuer Markt-Oper an Malerei verfertiget: vom 15.Juni bis 8.Aug. 39 Tag ohne Feier u. Sonntag besteht 39 Tag = 39f. - Dann vom 9. bis 13. 4 Tag 4f. Magdalena Köppin von 15 Juni bis 20.

auf dem Theater die Leinwath zusammennähen pro 6 Tag a 18 xr = 1f 48xr, Summa 44f 48xr.
3. Flach Tischler und 2 Gehilfen jul. 17., 22., 24 - 26., 29.

9. Various bills for the theatre 1763
Translation

1763. Payment for some table utensils necessary for the theatre, 4 pots, 1 pitcher, 3 small pots, and 1 jug, 6 large pots - 50xr;

Extract [from a bill] by Monsi[eur] le Bon for locksmith work in the theatre for 1763: 20 hooks with screws, done a 3xr (Friedr. Schieller, master locksmith).

Expenses for various necessities for the new opera in the theatre.
1. Oberauer, merchant, Aug. 5 Specification of painting materials for the princely theatre here in the castle, specifically for the Cavalier's play and Market operas, painting [backdrop?] 76f.
2. Wolf Kepp, painter reckoned painting in the cavalier's play and new market opera: from 15 June to 8 Aug. 39 days without holidays and Sundays = 39f. then from 9 to 13 [Aug] 4 days 4f. Magdalena Köpp sewed the canvas for the theatre from 15 June to 20th pro 6 days a 18xr = 1f. 48 Summa 44f. 48x.
3. Carl Flach, master carpenter, and 2 helpers had duties on 17, 22, 24-6 and 29 July.

10. Fürst Nikolaus Esterházy schreibt an seinen Baumeister Jakoby von Padua am 2. Juli 1763

J'ai vû par vôtre detail du 19me du mois passé jusqu' aù Vous étes parvenu avec les traveaux d'Eisenstadt et le Süttör: Vous dites que Vous avez tracé hier /:c'est à dire le 18me Juin:/ la seconde partie ou l'aile gauche; je comprend que Vous entendez par l'aile gauche le Batiment, qui se doit faire du côté des remises, et que l'autre côté ou Batiment ou est le Chapelle serat actuelment en état à y pouvoir poser la toiture. Je voudrois savoir aussi, si la cave dessous à y pouvoir, poser le toiture. Je voudrois Le maitre d'Hotel n'a point accordé, ni ordonné de travailler à la Cave de Cuivre, qui doit servir de reservoir dans la Machinne, ainsi Vous n'avéz qu' à l'accorder le mieux qu' il Vous serat possible et d'y faire travailler; et d'y poser entre tems le Cave de bois, dont vous parlez, pourque je puisse à mon rétour, qui serat vers la fin de ce mois, voir aller le Machinne. au reste factes en sorte, que non seulement cette Machinne, mais encore le Pont, la place et le chemin devant le Chateau d'Eisenstadt soient en état et achevé pour ce tems, et que le Catalogue de la biblioteque de Süttör ne Vous en arrete pas, qui pourat toujours se faire à la suite.

Les bois, la toille et les couleurs emploiés au theatre pour le nouvel opera Vous seront passé en ligne Comptes.
Padove ce 2me Juillet 1763.   Nicolas P: D'Esterhazy
pour le moitié de ce que la Cave de Cuivre conterat, j'écri à Zoller de la payer, quand Vous en auréz fait l'accord.

... aus Ihrem Brief vom 19. v. M. kann ich entnehmen wie weit die Arbeiten in Eisenstadt und Süttör fortgeschritten sind. Sie schreiben, daß Sie gestern, d.h. am 18. Juni, den zweiten Teil des linken Flügel abgesteckt haben; ich denke Sie meinen bei 'linken Flügel' den Bau, der bei der Remise stehen wird und daß die andere Seite des Bauwerks wo die Kapelle ist, bereits so weit ist, daß das Dach aufgesetzt werden kann. Ich möchte auch gerne wissen, ob der Keller schon so weit ist .... [Der Fürst möchte im Keller die 'Maschine' installiert sehen und möchte den best möglichen Preis für die Arbeiten aushandeln] ..... alles übrige kann warten bis zu meiner Rückkehr gegen Ende des Monats .... doch möchte ich die Brücke, den Platz und die Straße vor dem Schloß in Eisenstadt fertig sehen; beschäftigen Sie sich nicht mit dem Bibliothekskatalog von Süttör, der kann immer noch später gemacht werden. . . für Holz, Leinwand und Farben zur neuer Oper im Theater wird die Buchhaltung die Zahlungsanweisung erhalten.

Padua, 2 Juli 1763   Nicolaus P: D' Esterhazy
P.S. Die Hälfte der Kosten für den Kupferkeller habe ich Zoller [Hauptbuchhalter] zur Bezahlung angewiesen, sobald Sie den Baukostenvertrag abgeschlossen haben.

10. [2 July 1763 Prince Esterházy in Padua to Ing. Jacoby]
Summary Translation.
From your letter of 19 ult. I see you have traced the left wing of [Süttör Castle], by which I take it you mean the new wing to be constructed next to the coach-house, and that the other wing where the Chapel is, is in a condition where you can roof it....[discusses the cellar, the copper-lining for the 'machine'], 'the rest can wait for my return which will be towards the end of this month . . .' . . .'As for the rest, see to it that the bridge and the road in front of Eisenstadt Castle are finished within this period, and don't be held up because of the cataloguing of the library in Süttör, which can always be done afterwards'.
'The wood, the roof and the paint used in the theatre for the new opera will be paid by the cashier . . . P.S. For half the cost of the copper cellar I have written to [Chief Cashier] Zoller to pay it, as soon as you have made the contract'.

11. Graf Anton, ältester Sohn des Fürsten Nicolaus, heiratet Gräfin Marie Therese Erdödy im Januar 1763

Proviant für die Hochzeitsgäste. (Haushofmeisterliste) Jan. 8 - 15. hochgräfliche Hochzeit in Eisenstadt: Samstag den 8. Jan. haben alle Köche angefangen zu arbeiten. 1113 Pfund Rindfleisch, 22 1/2 ganze Kälber (gewogen, 2039 Pfund), 326 Pfund Hammelfleisch, 50 Pf. Nierenfett, 24 Stuck Ochsenmäuler, 13 Stück Ochsenschweif, 7 1/2 Mark, 24 Stück Ochsenfüsse, 3 1/2 Pf. Amoureten [Gustostück auch Pfaffen-stückl genannt], 39 St. Kalbszungen, 40 paar Kalbbrüstel, 47 St. Kalbsohren, 24 St. Kalbsschweife, 80 St. Kalbshirn, 4 Spanferkel, 23 1/2 Pf. Schweinefleisch, 30 St. Schweinenetz, 32 Kilo Darm, 17 Pf. Schweinefett, 22 Pf. Schweineschmalz, 45 St. Schweinsohren, 69 Dt. detto füssl, 4 Maaß Blut, 60 St. Hammelzüngl, 14 ganze Lämmer, 44 Hammelschwänze, 40 paar Lämmerhirne, 6 geputzte Lammköpfe, 8 Lammnetze, 84 Lammfüsse, 20 Lammbriese, 250 Cervelatwürste, 60 Pf. Schinken, 103 St. Blutwürste, 40 Leberwürste, 221 Bratwürste, 200 St. Bratwürste von Münkerdorfer Wirt, 46 Lammschweife, 25 Kalbschweife, 3 Pf. Amouret, 24 paar Lammsohren, 20 St. Ochsenmauler, 12 paar Kalbsbrüste. Vom Fleischselcher aus Wien: 318 Pf. Schinken, 510 Pf. Speck, 47 Pf. Kann [Kamm], 20 Pf. Kaiserfleisch, 10 Pf. ord. Fleisch, 50 St. Pöcklzungen, 237 Pf. Pöckelfleisch, 44 Schweinszungen, 12 geselchte Ochsenzungen, 60 Schweinsfüsse, 30 detto Ohren. Rest in Eisenstadt in der Speis: 100 Pf. Schinken, 125 Pf. Speck, 18 Pf. Kamm. Geflügel von Neustadt: 20 Truthähne, 76 Kapaune, 173 Poularden, 78 fette Hühner, 30 alte Hühner, 8 Nest Hühner, 4 alte Gänse, 2 junge Truthähne, 5 junge Gänse, 9 junge Enten, 9 Dutzend Hahnenkämme, 28 steirische Kapaune, 1 Gemse, 2 Lagel mit 800 Austern, das Hundert a 2.30, 6000 Muscheln. Von Wien: 23 Paar Tauben, 6 Paar Nesthühner, 13 paar grössere. Die Judten [Juden?] Rössl zu Eisenstadt hat zur Hochzeit verehrt: 18 ganze fette Gänse, 18 fette Ganslebern.- 10 Wildschweine - 150 Pf. Butter. Weiters aus Wien: Champignon, Pertram, Zuckerwurz, Scorgonerer Würze [Schwarzwurzel], kleine Zwiebel, Rockambol [Lauch], Thöres Kreitl, vom Schweizer in Höflein: 60 Maaß Milch, 58 Obers und Rahm - von Wien: 1 Flasche Provenceöl, 8 Pf. Parmesan, 2 Schachtel Pumellen [Grapefruit], 2 Pf. Sardellen, 1 Pf. Zitronat, 50 St. Zitronen, 11 Pf. Vanille, 8 Pf. Genueser Macaroni, 100 Zitronen, 24 Pomerancen di Porto, Schokolade. Lachs, Hausen, Aeschen [ombre], Schill, Rohrhühner, 227 Krebse, 400 Eier von Kapuvár.

11. To feed the wedding guests
(Translation)

1763 8- 15 January: marriage in Eisenstadt. All the cooks started work on Saturday 8 January.

1113 pounds of beef, 22 1/2 whole calves (weighed 2039 pounds), 326 pounds of mutton, 50 pounds kidney fat, 24 pieces of oxen muzzles, 13 pieces of ox-tails, 7 1/2 marrow, 24 pieces of ox feet, 3 1/2 pounds amoureten = choicest pieces of meat also called *Pfaffenstückel*, 39 pieces calves tongues, 40 pairs of calves breasts, 47 pieces of calves ears, 24 pieces of calves tails, 80 pieces of calves brains, 4 suckling pigs, 23 1/2 pounds of pork, 30 pieces of pork stomach nets, 32 kilogrammes of guts, 17 pounds pork fat, 22 pounds of pork dripping, 43 pieces of porks' ears, 69 pieces of pork trotters, 4 measures of blood, 60 pieces of mutton tongues, 14 whole lambs, 44 mutton tails, 40 pairs of lambs' brains, 6 cleaned and prepared lambs' heads, 8 lambs' nets, 84 lambs' feet, 20 lambs' sweetbreads, 250 Bologna sausages, 60 pounds of ham, 103 pieces of black pudding, 40 liver sausages, 221 frying sausages, 200 pieces of frying sausage from the innkeeper in Minkendorf, 46 lambs' tails, 25 calves tails, 3 pounds of amourets, 24 pairs of lambs' ears, 20 pieces of oxen muzzles, 12 pairs of calves breasts. From the meat-smokery in Vienna: 318 pounds of ham, 510 pounds of bacon, 47 pounds of oxen necks [Kamm], 20 pounds of smoked and roasted pork breast [Kaiserfleisch], 10 pounds ordinary meat, 50 pieces of salt tongue [Pöckelzunge], 237 pounds salted beef, 44 pork tongues, 12 smoked oxen tongues, 60 pork trotters, 30 ditto ears. Remains are in the larder in Eisenstadt: 100 pounds of ham, 125 pounds bacon, 18 pounds of oxen necks [Kamm]. Poultry from [Wiener] Neustadt: 20 turkeys, 76 capons, 173 poulets (grain-fed chickens), 78 roasting chickens, 30 old hens, 8 nest-chickens, 4 old geese, 2 young turkeys, 5 young geese, 9 young ducks, 9 dozen cockscombs, 28 capons from Styria, 1 chamois, 2 boxes with 800 oysters, hundred at 2f 30xr, 6000 mussels. From Vienna: 23 pigeons, 6 nest-chickens, 3 pairs older ones. The Jewess Rössel from Eisenstadt offered for the marriage: 18 fat geese, 18 foies gras, 10 wild boars - 150 pounds of butter. Other things from Vienna: mushrooms, marigold, parsnips, Scorgonere roots [salsify], little onions, leeks, dried spices; from the dairy farm in Höfflein: 60 Maß [liquid measure] milk, 58 of cream, 8 sour cream - from Vienna: 1 bottle of oil from Provence, 8 pounds of Parmesan cheese, 1 box Pumellen [grapefruit], 2 pounds of anchovies, 1 pound candied lemon peel, 50 lemons, 11 pounds of vanilla, 8 pounds of macaroons from Genua, 100 lemons, 24 bitter oranges (from Porto), chocolate, salmon, sturgeon, umber [salmo thymallus], pike-perch, moor-hens, 227 craw-fish, 400 eggs from Kapuvár.

12/1. Ausgaben für das Theater während der Hochzeitsfeier in Eisenstadt

Gralcassa, 1763. Rubr. VIII. Fasc. XI.

L i s t a

Delle cose diverse comprate, e fatte per Sua altezza il Principe Esterasi, ed inviate in Eisenstatt. [F. Xr.]

1° 100 Sraufen per Illuminare il Trasparente, costano,
    secondo che appare dalla qui anessa del Mercante
      di ferro, fiorini   8: 20

2° Una pezza di Tela, e filo per il sudetto Trasparente,
  costa, secondo che appare dalla lista qui anessa del
  Mercante   14: --
3° Lista di diversi Colori e Cose provista del Sig. Babicg;
  parte digià consegnate a mio Figlio Carlo, e parte da
  mè a lui Inviate in Eisenstott, in diverse volte, Importano
  tutto, secondo detta lista   121: 44
4° L'Acordo fatto dà sua Ecellenza Il Sig. Conte Durazzo,
  con il Sig. Mildorfer, per la Pittura del sudetto
  Trasparente, e di fiorini   80: --
                                                224: 4

5° Più, per Lavoranti, e Sarti impiegati a cucire la tela
  del Trasparente, per tirarla, e fare il Vixen; cera per
  farlo, candelle di seno per lavorarci alla sera, legna
  per scaldare la Stuffa; Lavoro per il sudetto, come
  ancora altri piccoli Ferslocht, brochette, e chiodi,
  Importano   28: 23

                 Somma del tutto fiorini 252: 27
                         Gio: Maria Quaglio
                       Ingegniere delli Teatri di Vienna.
C. Durazzo   Nicolaus Fürst Esterhazy

1) Eisenlager zur Golden Schaufel, Wien.
2) Mathias Schwimmer, Wien.
3) Johann Babitsch, Wien.
4) Josephus Ignatius Milldorffer.
5) 1763 li 13 Febraio in Vienna.
     Attesto Jo ssottoscritto d'aver ricevuto dalla Cassa di Sua Altezza il Sig. Principe Esterhasy, per diverse cose fatte fare in Vienna, ed inviate in Heisenstatt, come appare della lista gia datta, per ornare la Sala e Teatro, In occasione del sposalizzio seguito colà li 10 Genajo, fiorini 28: 23
                       Gio: Maria Quaglio
                Ingegniere delli Teatri di Vienna

Übersetzung

L i s t e
der verschiedenen gekauften oder angefertigten Sachen für seine
Hoheit den Fürsten Esterasi, die nach Eisenstadt geschickt wurden.
                                                        [F.   Xr.]
1° Schrauben [Leuchter] um die Transparente zu beleuch-
    ten,Kosten siehe beiliegendes Konto des Eisenhändlers,
                              Gulden: 8:   20
2° Ein Stück Leinwand und Faden für das obengenannte
    Transparent, Kosten siehe beiliegende
              Liste des Händlers   14:   --
3° Liste der verschiedenen Farben und Sachen, die Herr
    Babicg benötigte, die ich teils schon meine Sohn Carlo
    übergeben hatte oder die von mir an ihn nach
    Eisenstott gesendet wurden, machen im ganzen laut
                    Liste   121:   44
4° Vertrag zwischen Seine Excellenz Herrn Grafen Durazzo
    und Herrn Mildorfer abgeschlossen für die Malerei des
    Transparentes, beträgt F.   80:   --
                                             _____
                                             224
5° Dazu für Arbeiter, Schneider, Näherinnen zum Nähen der
    Leinwand für das Transparent, spannen und wachsen,
    Wachs dafür, Kerzen, um abends arbeiten zu können,
    Holz für den Ofen: weiters Tischlerarbeiten um den
    grossen Ferlocht [= Verschlag?], für dieses, sowie
    andere kleine Krügerln und Nägel,
    betragen   28:   23
                                             _____
         Summa Sumarum Gulden   252:   27
           Gio: Maria Quaglio
             Theateringenieur der Theater in Wien
     Durazzo   Nicolaus Fürst Esterhazy
1) Eisenlager zur Goldenen Schaufel, Wien.
2) Mathias Schwimmer, Wien.
3) Johann Babitsch, Wien.
4) Josephus Ignatius Milldorffer.
5) 1763, den 13 Februar in Wien
   Ich Unterschriebener bestätige von der Buchhaltung
   Seiner Fürstl.Durchlaucht Fürst Esterhazy für
   verschiedene Sachen, die in Wien hergestellt und

nach Heisenstatt [sic] geschickt wurden (laut bereits abgelieferter Liste) um den Saal und das Theater anlässlich der Hochzeit am 10. Januar auszuschmücken,
 Gulden 28: 23 erhalten zu haben.
Gio. Maria Quaglio
Ingenieur der Theater in Wien.

Kommentar

Für die Theateraufführungen anlässlich der Hochzeitsfeierlichkeiten wurde von Graf Giacomo Durazzo (damals Direktor der Wiener Hoftheater) der berühmte Wiener Theaterregisseur Giovanni Maria Quaglio nach Eisenstadt geschickt.

12/1. List of various items purchased and made for His Highness the Prince Esterhasi, and sent to Eisenstadt

		f.	xr.
1.	100 Screw-lamps to illuminate the transparent screen, cost, according to the annex by the iron monger, Florins	8:	20
2.	A piece of canvas and thread to sew it together, costs, according to attached list by the merchant	14:	-
3.	List of diverse colours and material provided by Sig. Babicg [Johann Babitsch], some already delivered by my son Carlo, some sent by me to him in Eisenstott [sic] total as follow, according to annex	121:	44
4.	Agreement made by H. E. Si. Count Durazzo with Sig. Mildorfer for the painting of the above transparent screen	80:	-
		224:	4
5.	Moreover for workers and tailors engaged to sew the canvas of the transparent screen, to mount it and stretch it, wax for doing so, candles to be able to work at night, wood to heat the stove; work by carpenters to make the big locker for the same and also other small lockers, little bowls [for illumination], nails, add up to	28:	23
	Sum total Florins	252:	27

Gio: Maria Quaglio
Theatrical Designer of the Vienna Theatres
C. Durazzo   Nicolaus Fürst Esterházy

[Translation of receipt for item 5]
1763, 13 Feb. in Vienna. I the undersigned attest to have received from the Cashiers of the Prince Esterhazy, for having made various things in Vienna and having sent them to Heisenstadt [sic], as appears on the list already submitted, for adorning the hall and theatre, on the occasion of the marriage celebrations following the ceremony on 10 January. Florins 28: 23
Gio: Maria Quaglio...

Commentary

The famous Quaglio was employed by Count Durazzo, director of the Vienna Court Theatre to work on the Eisenstadt Theatre.

12/2. Eisenstädter-Rentamt. 1763. Nr. 99/1/43

S p e c i f f i c a t [i] o n
Was ich zur Oberä an Schuemacher Arbeith gemacht und Erfolgen
Lassen wie folgt   f: Xer
Erst: Vorn Herrn 1 par schuech gemacht   1   18
Item vor die Frau ein par Mans schue   1   15
und ein par Frauenzimer schuech gemacht   1   6
Mehr vor ein Jungfrau ein par Mans schuech   1   15
Mehr vor Eine Jungfrau ein par Frauenzimer Schue
gemacht   1   --
Item ein par Manß Schuech vor einen Franzoßen
gemacht   1   25

                 S u m a   7f: 19

Das obstehende Schuch mit meinen   Antony Stumpf
Vorwissen zur Oppera Puffa   Schuemacher Meister
gemacht worden attestire   Alhier
Eisenstatt den 22n Febr. [1]763
Züsser Haushofm.   Bon

Kommentar

Die Schuhe waren für eine uns unbekannte *opera buffa* (von Haydn?) bestimmt, die anläßlich der Hochzeitsfeier im Januar 1763 in Eisenstadt aufgeführt wurde.

12/2. Specification
Translation

What I did for the Obrä [sic] by way of cobbler's work and delivered,
viz   f   xr
First: 1 pair of mens' shoes   1   18
item 1 pair of mens' shoes for the woman   1   15
and a pair of womens' shoes   1   6
more for a maiden a pair of men's shoes   1   15
more for a maiden a pair of lady's shoes   1   -
item a pair of men's shoes for a Frenchman   1   25

                Suma   7f   19

The above shoes made with my knowledge Antony Stumpf
for the opera Puffa Master Cobbler
Eisenstatt 22 Feb. 1763 Here
Züsser Major Domo

Commentary
The shoes were for an unknown *opera buffa* (Haydn?), performed during the wedding festivities in January 1763 at Eisenstadt.

12/3. Zusätzliches Personal wird anläßlich der Hochzeitsfeierlichkeiten für die Bälle engagiert

Gralcassa, 1763. Rubr. V. Nr. 1.
C o m m i s s i o n
Vermög welcher, vor drey tägige Ball-Musig vor 24. Persohn accordirter masse Vier Hundert Gulden aus unserer Gral: Cassa durch dem OberEinnehmer Zoller Bezahlet, und in seiner Rechnung als eine richtige Ausgaab angeführet werden solle.
Eisenstatt den 14t January 1763.   Nicolaus Fürst Esterhazy

Quittung
Über Vierhundert Gulden Rhein, welche Ich Ends unterschriebener vor die durch 3 Täg gemachte Ball-music accordirter massen von dem Hochftlen OberEinnehmer Herrn Johann Zoller richtig empfangen habe.
Eisenstadt den 14ten Jan: 1763.
Id e: 400 f   J: V: R: Schuster
                   Stadt Musicus

Eisenstädter-Rentamt. 1763. Nr. 99/1/15.
S p e c i f i c a t i o n
Waß für die Wiennerische Musicanten so bey Beylager Sr Graflichen Gnaden Antoni Esterhasi gedient, an Kost und Zimmer accordirter massen auf gegangen

[1]763			f	Xr
den 9ten	24 Personen 1 a 24 Xr		9	36
den 10ten	24	"	9	36
den 11ten	24	"	9	36
den 12ten	24	"	9	36
den 13ten	24	"	9	36
für 6 Täg das Zimer			3	—
		S u m m a	51f	--

Das obige Kost und Zimmer von Stephan Joseph Esch
mir accordirt worden attestire Jacob Ursch
Eisenstadt den 17n Jenner [1]763.
   Züsser Haus Hofm.

                                                            Gral-Cassa
Vor die fremden Mundköche, Zuckerbacher u. Gehilfen 973f 56 xr
Mundkoch Charles Petis vom Hof a duk. 7 Tage 115f 30xr
Zuckerbacker Franc. Mouchette a 2d 5
Suppen(koch) Kuhrner v. Liechtenstein 2d 5
Backerei Leopold von Batthyany 3d
Gehilf Antoni vom Hof 2d
Bratmeister Georg Guine 2d 5
Gehilf Strizek 2d
Suppenkochgehilfe Zwerger 2d
Mundkoch von der 2. Tafel Schotl v. Erdödy 3d
2 Gehilfe a 2d, 7 Jungen a 2f
Zuckerbäcker waren 3 (Friedrich v. Canal, Fleischer v. Zobor und von Russischem Botschafter) bereits dec.31 und eigentlich ständig bis zum 13.
a 4 F.   Summa   87f 56 1/4xr.
Denen Luftspringern und Gauklern   100 duk.
Commissioniert 14. Jan. Eisenstadt
Aufgenommen Giov. Bat. Rossi

12/3. More personnel are engaged for the marriage of Count Anton

                                Commission
According by which, for three days of ball music with 24 persons, the agreed price of four hundred gulden to be paid by our General Cashier's Office by Chief-Cashier Zoller and placed in the file as a proper expense.
Eisenstatt, 14 January 1763   Nicolaus Fürst Esterházy
                                Receipt
For four-hundred Rhein Gulden which I undersigned have received, as agreed, for 3 days of ball music, from the princely Chief Cashier Herr Johann Zoller. Eisenstadt 14 Jan. 1763.
Id e: 400 f   J: V: R: Schuster
                                Stadt Musicus
                              Specification
The food and lodgings required for the Viennese musicians who played for his Grace Count Antoni Esterhasi.

1763	f	xr
the 9th 24 persons 1 a 24xr	9	36
the 10th 24 persons 1 a 24xr	9	36
the 11th 24 persons 1 a 24xr	9	36
the 12th 24 persons 1 a 24xr	9	36

the 13th 24 persons 1 a 24	9	36
for 6 days the rooms	3	-
Summa	51f.-	

Above food and lodgings agreed by me, I attest   Stephan Joseph Esch
Eisenstadt 17 January 1763   Jacob Ursch
Züsser Major Domo

for the master-cooks, confectioners and assistants, not in our service: 973f. 56xr.
Master-cook Charles Petis from the Court a duk. 7 days 115f. 30xr.
confectioner Franc. Mouchette a 2d. 5.
Soup cook Kuhrner from Liechtenstein's 2d.5.
baker Leopold from Batthyany 3d
assistant Antoni from the Court 2d
roasting master Georg Guine 2d.5.
assistant Strizek 2d
soup-cook assistant Zwerger 2d
master-cook for the second table Schotl from Erdödy 3d
2 assistants a 2d, 7 boys a 2f
3 confectioners: Friedrich from Canal, Fleischer from Zobor and from the Russian Ambassador, already from December 31 and remaining there until January 13 a 4f,
　　　　　　　　　　　　Summa 873f 56xr 1/4
the acrobats and jugglers 100 ducats
Eisenstadt 14 Jan. commissioned, Giov. Bat. Rossi.

12/4. Auslagen für die Unterhaltung der Hochzeitsgäste und die Festbeleuchtung

Eisenstädter-Rentamts Rechnungen Jan. 1763 No. 99, 99/1:
Sail-Täntzer in dem Greiffen Würtshaus:
　　Jan.8 [abends Ankunft]Nachtmahl 2f 52xr
　　　　　2 Zimmer und Heizung 2f -
　　9.-13. Kost 4f 46xr, Zimmer 2f - Summa 37f 33 1/2xr.
Die Kleider vor die gesamte Balgeiger gebrämt worden
　　　　　21 Kleider gebrämt a 51xr
　　　　　(reg. 42xr)
　　　　　2 Kleider ungebrämt, wird birt
　　　　　[breit] gebrämt a 3f (2f 15xr)
Anton Höld Thurnermeister: für gemachte Musik vor all u. Jedes 4 Dukaten (16f 40xr)

Bei der Illumination in Hofgarten sind den 13. Jan. 1763 folgende Tagwerk verrichtet worden, als von 12 Uhr mittags bis nachts 3 Uhr 5 Maurer a 1 1/2 Tagwerk, welche nur a 12xr wie die Taglöhner zu bezahlen sind.

1763. 99/1 Zur Illumination bei der Hochzeit:
Specification deren under 3ten und 4ten Jan. 1763 bei mir zugestellten leeren Lampen Degeln: welche sein 4800 St., so gewogen 1317 pfund, habe also gegossen gewogen 5453 pf. Nach Abzug dessen sind zu bezahlen 4136 pfund, jedes accordirtermass 22 Ung. ertragt zusammen 909f 92 den

     Item 300 St. Fakeln jedes pr. 15d 45.-

  Macht zusammen in allen [*sic*]   909 f 92 d
controlliert Jacoby, empfangen Jan. 24
Jos. Swoboda, Seyfensieder

5300 Tiegeln von Stoober Hafnermeister Hans Mandl und Georg Schumberger 1 Stück 1 d empfangen dec. 31. Jacoby

Zu Beleuchtung des Saals u. Teatri Seitz, Witwe: Jan 6., 464 pf. weiße Wachskerzen a 54xr = 417f 49xr mit gebeizten Tächtern
Item gelbe Wachskerzen mit Baumwollenen
Tacht a 45xr, 66 3/4 pf = 50 f 3/4 d
150 st. Gläser mit gelben Wachs gefüllt,
40 1/4 pf a 44 xr = 29 f 31 xr.
398 Tögl mit gelbem Wachs gegossen a 44xr = 110f 44 den. Zum Aufzeiten einen gelben Zuch mit 1/2 pf. = 22 den. Das übrige Wachs, das ist die Trimmel u. überbliebene Körtzen seynd ins Künftige aufbehalten worden.
Summa 608f 30xr 1/4 den.

12/4 Expenses for entertaining the guests during the marriage festivities and for the illumination.

Tightrope-walkers in the Griffin inn: Jan. 8 (arriving in the evening), dinner 2f. 52xr
2 rooms and firewood 2f.-. 9.-- 13. maintenance costs 4f. 46xr, rooms 2f.-.
Summa 37f. 33 1/2xr
The costumes for all the musicians in the dance orchestra trimmed: 21 trimmed a 51xr (42xr), 2 costumes untrimmed, will be done with large trimmings a 3f. (2f. 15)
Anton Höld *Thurnermeister*: for all the music done 4 ducats (16f. 40xr)
For the illumination in the castle gardens on 13 Jan. 1763 the following working hours were observed, viz. from 12 o'clock noon to 3 o'clock a.m., 5 masons at 1 1/2 working days, who will receive the same as ordinary day labourers only 12xr.
For illumination during the marriage
Specification for 3 and 4 Jan. 1763, empty lamp-pots delivered by me: which numbered 4800 pieces, when weighed 1317 pounds, when filled with wax they weighed 5453 pf. Subtracting these two sums there remains 4136 pounds, each at agreed price 22 Hungarian [florins], makes   909f. 92 dena[ri]
Item 300 torches each pr. 15 d[enari]   45 -

  Makes together in all   909f. 92 d [sic]

Countersigned by Jacoby, received 24 Jan. 1763 by Jos. Swoboda, Soap-maker.

Further documents

Hans Mandl and Georg Schumberger, master-potters from Stoob delivered 5300 lamp-pots on 31 Dec. 1762, countersigned by Jacoby.
Further: For the lighting of the hall and theatre the widow Seitz sent a bill on 6 January 1763 for 464 pf white wax candles a 54xr = 417f. 49xr with soaked wicks.
Item yellow wax candles with cotton wicks a 45x, 66 3/4pf = 50f. 3xr 3/4 d
150 glasses filled with yellow wax 40 1/4pf. a 44xr = 29f. 31xr.
398 pots filled with yellow wax a 44xr = 110f. 44xr.
Then to light them a yellow taper with 1/2pf = 22 den.
The rest of the wax, i.e. the remains and remaining candles have been kept for the future.
Summa 608f. 30xr. 1/4 den.

12/5.

Grl-Cassa

Georg David Nicolai, acad. Kupferst.
Jan.5.W.[ien] 1500 Baal Zettel dem Kartenmacher
         "   "   " abzudrucken
per Buchbinder die Ballzettel zu pressen
summa 16 f 34 xr

12/5. Translation.

1763. Georg David Nicolai, academic engraver.
Vienna 5 Jan. 1500 ball cards to the map-maker
    1500 ball cards to be printed
      for the book-binder to have the ball sheets pressed
        Summa 16f 34xr
        Grl-Cassa

12/6. Auszug aus Fürst Nicolaus Esterházys 'Haus und Kuchlausgaben 1763'

Gral-Cassa 93.754.

. . . 4200f - xr Morgengabe an die Freile Braut Theresia Gfin v. Erdödy unseres Älteren Sohns Antony . . .

12/6. From Nicolaus Esterházy house and kitchen expenses 1763

. . .4200f. - xr gift to the bride Freile Theresia Countess v. Erdödy on the part of our eldest son Antony. . .

12/7.

Grl-Cassa

Masquer Ausleiher 1763. Bei der Hochzeit,
Jan.12. 2 schwartze Domino a 2f - xr

13. 1 gelb, 1 grün a 2f - xr
11., 12., 13., 2 ord. detto a 1f 30xr
                          Summa 17f - xr Math.Fischer.
Denen Comödianten in Ei[senstadt] nach hoher
Anschaffung 4f 12xr

12/7. Masks rented 1763 during the wedding fesivities
12 Jan. 2 black dominos a 2f - xr
13. Jan. 1 yellow, 1 green a 2f. - xr
11., 12., 13. 2 ordinary ditto a 1f. 30xr
                summa 17f. - xr Mathias Fischer
For the actors and actresses in Eisenstadt, as ordered by their Lordships 4f. 12xr.

12/8.

Jan.7. Auslag wegen einem um die Opera Büchl drucken zu lassen nacher Wien abgeführten Musicum betr. (2f an den Landkutscher)

Kommentar

Der Musiker wurde mit einem Landkutscher nach Wien in die Druckerei geschickt, um die Arbeiten an den Textbüchern zu Haydns Oper *Acide e Galatea* zu überwachen.

12/8. Translation
Expenses of sending a musician to Vienna because of printing the opera libretto (7 Jan. 1763).

Commentary
The musician took the *Landkutscher* (travelling carriage) for which he was paid 2 gulden for this service, to Vienna, where he supervised the publication of *Acide e Galatea* by Haydn.

13. Auslagen für die Aufführung von Haydns Oper
Acide e Galatea

Gralcassa, 1763. Rubr. VIII. Nr. 28.

V e r z e i c h n u s
Was für Ihro Durchlt den Fürsten zu Verfertigung deren Opera Kleydungen nacher Eisenstadt erkaufft und verarbeitet worden ist,

	f	Xr
T e t i d e		
6. Elen feine weiße glantz Leinwand zum Rock a 21xr	2	6
6 1/2 - Boloneser Düntuch zum Rock und Corsette a 24Gr:	7	48
5 1/2 - glantz Leinwand zu Corsette und Schürtzel a 7Gr:	1	55 1/2
6 1/2 - Meer grünen Tafet a 26Gr:	8	9
7 1/2 - grünen silber Docc a 34xr	4	15
3 - weißen silber Docc zum Schürtzel a 24xr	1	12
Düntuch zu Halß Streif und Datzel	-	20
Bandel und Düntuch zum Gresel	-	20
Zwey weiße Federn daß Stuck a: 40xr	1	20
Ein Reigerl	-	30
Flinterl	-	51 1/2
4 Grosse Muscheln auf den Rock		
6 Kleinere auf den Schlep		
1 Stuck auf die Brust		
2 - auf die Aufschläg		
2 - zur Eintheilung		
Ist für Flinterl, Silber, Draps d'argent, Meergrünen Silber Docc, schwartze Schürr, Seiden und weiße Leinwand zum einspannen, und für Sticken Arbeit alles zusammen veraccordirt mit	19	-
NB: rauchen Zeich zu denen Corallen wie auch zu der Rohrkühl.		
Macherlohn	6	--
	55	23
Latus herüber mit	55	23
G a l a t h e a		
6 Elen feine weiße glantz Leinwand zu Rock a: 21xr	2	6
6 1/2 - Boloneser Düntuch auf den Rock und Corsette a: 24 Gr:	7	48
7 - glantz Leinwand zu Corsette und Schürtzel a: 7 Gr:	2	27
7 1/2 - roten Dafet a 26 Gr:	9	45
13 - silber Docc a: 24xr	5	12
84 - rosenfarbe Dafet Band a: 3xr	4	12
10 - silberne Bördel zum einfassen a: 3xr	-	30

1/2 - weißen Dafet a: 3 Gr:	-	39
2 1/2 Marg Flinterl a: 51xr	2	8
Düntuch zu Halß Streif und Datzel	-	20
Detto zum Halß Gresel samt Bandel	-	20
2 weiße Federn daß Stuck a: 40xr	1	20
1 Reigerl	-	30
Macherlohn	8	24
	45	53

Glauce

6 Elen feine weiße glantz Leinwand zu Rock a 21xr	2	6
6 1/2 - Boloneser Düntuch zu Rock und Corsette a: 24 Gr:	7	49
6 - glantz Leinwand zum Corsette und Schürtzel a: 7 Gr:	2	6
6 1/2 - blauen Dafet a: 26 Gr:	8	24
13 1/2 - silber Docc a: 24xr	5	24
10 - silberne Bördel	-	30
Adlaß zu 13 Duzend Blumen und soviel Lauber nebst Macherlohn a: 45xr daß Duzend	11	3
3 1/2 Marg Flinterl	2	59
2 weiße Federn	1	20
1 Reigerl	-	30
Düntuch zu Halß Streif und Datzel	-	20
Detto zum Gresel samt Bandel	-	20
Machelohn	8	24
	55	59
Latus herüber mit	55	59

Acide

8 1/2 Eln rosenfarbe glantz Leinwand a: 14 Gr:	5	57
3 - Blaue glantz Leinwand a: 30xr	1	30
4 - Siegel Leinwand zum Schurtz a: 14xr	-	56
3 1/2 - raucher Barget a: 13 Gr:	2	16 1/2
9 1/2 silber docc a: 24xr	3	48
5 Marg Flinterl	4	15
22 Elen Bördel a: 3xr	1	6
Fuderleinwand zum Casquet	-	5
5 Große weiße Federn a: 18 Gr: daß Stück	4	30

1 Kleine Detto a: 34xr	-	34
2 Fiancket [Hüftpolster]	-	34
Schnür Riemen	-	2
Bugran zum Casquet	-	3
Stiefel samt Schnür Riemen	2	-
Haar Maschen und Halß Band	-	18
Macherlohn	6	30
	34	24

Polifemo

9 Eln Leinwand zum Kleyd a: 24xr	3	30
5 - gelbe detto zur Tigerey a: 21xr	1	45
2 1/2 - raucher Barget a: 13 Gr:	1	37 1/2
2 - Fuder Leinwand	-	14
6 - silber Docc	2	24
12 - Bördel	-	36
Stiefel samt Schnur Riemen	2	-
2 Rote Lange Federn daß Stuck a: 1f: 15xr	2	30
1 schwartze Detto	1	-
2 Elen feine gelbe Leinwand zur Tieger Haut a 12 Gr:	1	12
4 - Siegel Leinwand a 14xr	-	56
2 Kiancketen [sic]	-	34
Bugran zum Casquet, Bard, Laruen, und Kolben	2	12
Die Tiegerey zu mahlen	1	42
Für die Borden auf zu nähen auf daß Musio Kleyd	1	30
Macherlohn	6	-
Latus hinüber	29	48 1/2
Latus herüber mit	29	48

Borden so in die Eisenstadt geschicket worden		
624 Elen breite a: 3xr	31	12
336 - Schmale a: 2 1/2xr	14	-
3 Große Strück Röck	9	58
1 Kleiner Detto	1	55
	86	53

Ein Braunes Manns Kleid

10 Elen Braunen Zeich zu Rock und Hosen a: 16 Gr:	8	-
2 1/2 - weißen zur Veste gedruckten Consent a: 14 Gr:	1	45
3 - rauchen Barget auf Leibl und Hosen a: 13 Gr:	1	57
6 1/2 - braune glantz Leinwand zum Rock a: 19xr	2	3 1/2
2 - weiße glantz Leinwand zur Veste a: 19xr	-	38
3 - Siegl Leinwand	-	30
3 1/2 Duzend Knöpf zum Rock a: 18xr	1	6
2 1/2 Detto zur Veste a: 9xr	-	22 1/2
35 Elen Borden a: 5xr	2	55
41 - Detto a: 3xr	2	3
46 - Detto a: 2 1/2xr	1	55
45 - Spitzel a: 2 1/2xr	1	52
2 Marg gelbe Flinterl a: 51xr	1	42
Sieb und Watten	-	18
Näh-Seiden	-	7
Macherlohn	8	-
	35	14

Ein rotes Detto

8 Eln roten Zeich zum Rock a: 22 Gr:	8	48
2 1/2 - blauen zur Veste a: 14 Gr:	1	45
2 1/2 - schwartzen zur Hosen a: 14 Gr:	1	45
6 1/2 - weiße glantz Leinwand zu Rock a: 19xr	2	3
2 - glantz Leinwand zur Veste a: 19xr	-	38
3 - rauchen Barget a: 13 Gr:	1	57
3 - Siegl Leinwand	-	30
3 1/2 Duzend Knöpf zum Rock	1	6
1 1/2 Detto zur Veste	-	13 1/2
1 Duzend auf die Hogen	-	7
20 1/2 Elen silberne Borden a: 15 Gr	15	22 1/2
Sieb und Watten	-	18
Näh-Seiden	-	7
Macherlohn	6	-
	40	40
Latus herüber mit	40	40

                Ein blaues
8 Elen blauen Zeich zum Rock a: 14 Gr:	5	36
2 1/2 - roten zur Veste a: 22 Gr:	2	45
2 1/2 - schwartzen zur Hosen a: 14 Gr:	1	45
3 - rauchen Barget a: 13 Gr:	1	57
2 - weiße glantz Leinwand zur Veste a: 19xr	-	38
6 1/2 - glantz Leinwand zum Rock a: 19xr	2	3
3 - Siegl Leinwand	-	30
3 1/2 Duzend Knöpf zum Rock	1	6
1 - auf die Hosen	-	7
1 1/2 Detto zur Veste	-	13 1/2
36 Elen Bördel a: 3xr	1	48
45 - Spitzel a: 2 1/2xr	1	52
3 Marg Flinterl	2	33
Sieb und Watten	-	12
Näh Seiden	-	7
Macherlohn	7	-
	30	19

                Livree
9 Elen Silberfarben Zeich zu Rock und Hosen a: 16 Gr:	7	12
4 - grünen zur Veste a: 14 Gr:	2	48
3 - rauchen Barget	1	57
6 1/2 - glantz Leinwand zum Rock	2	3
3 1/2 Duzend Knöpf zum Rock	1	6
2 1/2 Detto zur Veste und Hosen	-	22 1/2
54 Elen Bördl a: 2 1/2xr	2	15
28 - Cöllnische rote Band a 4xr	1	52
Rothe Woll zu Quastel	-	24
Plasch [Plüsch] zu Detto 1 1/1 Elen	-	45
2 Elen weiße glantz Leinwand zur Veste	-	38
Machelohn	5	30
	26	52

                Frauen Kleyd
14 1/2 Elen feine weiße glantz Leinwand zu Rock a: 12 Gr	8	42
1 - Fuder Leinwand a: 19xr	-	19

1/2 - rauchen Barget a: 13 Gr:	-	19 1/2
10 - Gold docc zur Garnirung a 24xr	4	-
Latus hinüber	13	20 1/2
Latus herüber mit	13	20 1/2
Bandel und Haftel	-	12
Macherlohn	6	-
	19	32

Blauer Sack		
14 1/2 Elen feine blaue glantz Leinwand a: 30xr	7	15
1 - Fuder Leinwand a: 19xr	-	19
1/2 - rauchen Barget	-	19 1/2
9 - silber Docc zur Garnirung	3	36
Bandel und Haftel	-	12
Macherlohn	6	-
	17	41

Gelber Sack		
15 Elen feine glantz Leinwand a: 12 Gr:	9	-
1 - Fuder Leinwand	-	19
1/2 - rauchen Barget	-	19 1/2
9 - Silber Docc	3	36
Bandel und Haftel	-	12
Macherlohn	6	-
	19	26
Summa Sumarum	468	26

Vorstehenter Konto samt der Ester aus gab ist Mihr von herr Ober einnemer Zoller mit 448 f. vor alles und Jedes Richtig bezallet worden Wienn den 15 Märtzi [1] 763   (L.S.) Johan Georg Spöck
qatterober

Extra Ausgaben	f	Xr
Für daß Maut Zettel auf der Haupt Maut	-	32
Linien Geld	-	24
Weg Maut	2	8
Für Zimmer und Kost in der Eissenstadt		

für 3 Personen	7	24
Summa	10	28

Kommentar

Die eleganten und zum Teil sehr teuren Kostüme für Haydns erste italienische Oper zeigen wie professionell die Esterházy Oper geleitet wurde. Die Rechnungen sind wertvolle Dokumente zur Veranschaulichung der Theaterpraxis des 18. Jahrhunderts.

13. Expenses for Haydn's opera *Acide e Galatea*
List

What was purchased and sent to Eisenstadt and worked on, for preparing the opera costumes for H. H. the Prince.

Tetide

6 elen [ells; an ell = 27 inches, Flemish measure] fine white glazed linen for skirt a 21xr	2	6
6 1/2 thin bolognese material for petticoat and *corsette* a 24 Gr:	7	48
5 1/2 glazed linen for *corsette* and apron a 7 Gr:	1	55 1/2
6 1/2 sea green tafetta a 26 Gr:	8	9
7 1/2 green and silver *toque* a 34xr	4	15
3 white and silver *toque* for apron a 24xr	1	12
Thin material for neck-cloth and tassel	-	20
Ribbon and thin material for curling	-	20
Two white feathers each a 40xr	1	20
A little heron feather	-	30
Spangles [Flinterl = Flitter]	-	51 1/2
4 large shells on the skirt		
6 smaller ones on the train		
1 piece on the breast		
2 pieces on the lapels		
2 pieces for distributing		
For spangles, silver, draps d'argent, sea-green toque, black cord, silk and white linen to be stretched for embroidery work as agreed, total	19	-
N.B. Hairy material to make corals and reed-mace Tailor's bill	6	-
	55	23
Carried over	55	23

49

Galathea

6 elen fine white glazed linen for skirt a 21xr	2	6
6 1/2 thin bolognese material for the skirt and corsette a 24 Gr:	7	48
7 glazed linen for *corsette* and apron a 7 Gr:	2	27
7 1/2 red tafetta a 26 Gr:	9	45
13 silver *toque* a 24xr	5	12
84 rose coloured taffeta ribbon a 3xr	4	12
10 silver edging for trimming a 3xr	-	30
1/2 white trimming a 3 Gr:	-	39
2 1/2 marks [weight] spangles a 51xr	2	8
Thin material for neck-cloth and tassel	-	20
Ditto for a ruff with ribbon for the collar	-	20
2 white feathers each a 40xr	1	20
1 heron feather	-	30
Tailor's bill	8	24
	45	53

Glauce

6 elen fine white glazed linen for skirt a 21xr	2	6
6 1/2 thin Bolognese material for skirt and *corsette* a 24 Gr:	7	49
6 glazed linen for *corsette* and apron a 7 Gr:	2	6
6 1/2 blue tafeta a 26 Gr:	8	24
13 1/2 silver *togue* a 24xr	5	24
10 silver edging	-	30
Satin for 13 dozen flowers and as many leaves plus tailor's fee a 45xr the dozen	1	3
3 1/2 marks spangles	2	59
2 white feathers	1	20
1 heron feather	-	30
Thin material for neck-cloth and tassel	-	20
Ditto for a ruff with ribbon	-	20
Tailor's bill	8	24
	55	59
Carried over	55	59

Acide

8 1/2 Eln rose coloured glazed linen a 14 Gr:	5	57
3 blue glazed linen a 30xr	1	30
4 sailcloth linen for apron a 14xr	-	56
3 1/2 rough fustian a 13 Gr:	2	16 1/2
9 1/2 silver *toque* a 24xr	3	48

5 marks spangles	4	15
22 Elen edging a 3xr	1	6
Lining linen for head-piece	-	5
5 large white feathers a 18 Gr: a piece	4	30
1 small ditto a 34xr	-	34
2 pieces of stuffing [round the hips]	-	34
Laces	-	2
Buckram for head-piece	-	3
Boots with shoelaces	2	-
Hairnet and neck-cloth	-	18
Tailor's bill	6	30
	34	24

Polifemo

9 Eln green linen for costume a 24xr	3	30
5 yellow ditto for Tiger costume a 21xr	1	45
2 1/2 rough fustian a 13 Gr:	1	37 1/2
2 linen for lining	-	14
6 silver *toque*	2	24
12 edging	-	36
Boots with shoelaces	2	-
2 long red feathers a piece a 1f 15xr	2	30
1 black ditto	1	-
2 Eln fine yellow for tiger-skin a 12 Gr:	1	12
4 sailcloth linen a 14xr	-	56
2 pieces of stuffing [round the hips]	-	34
Buckram for head-piece, beard, masque and club	2	12
For painting the tiger	1	42
To sew the edgings on the costume of the 'Musio' [Monsieur] dress	1	30
Tailor's bill	6	-
	29	48 1/2
carried over	29	48 [sic]

Edging sent to Eisenstadt

624 Elen broad a 3xr	31	12
336 Elen small a 2 1/2xr	14	-
3 large knitted skirts	9	58
1 small ditto	1	55
	86	53

One man's brown suit

10 Elen brown cloth for coat and breeches a 16 Gr:	8	-
2 1/2 a similar tinted white one for the waistcoat a 14 Gr: 1	45	
3 rough fustian for bodice and hose a 13 Gr:	1	57
6 1/2 blue glazed linen for coat a 19xr	2	3 1/2
2 white glazed linen for waistcoat a 19xr	-	38
3 sailcloth linen	-	30
3 1/2 dozen buttons for coat a 18xr	1	6
3 1/2 Ditto for waistcoat a 9xr	-	22 1/2
35 Elen edging a 5xr	2	55
41 ditto a 3xr	2	3
46 ditto a 2 1/2xr	1	55
45 lace a 2 1/2xr	1	52
2 marks yellow spangles a 51xr	1	42
Lining and padding	-	18
Sewing thread	-	7
Tailor's bill	-	8
	35	14

1 red ditto

8 Eln red cloth for coat a 22 Gr:	8	48
2 1/2 blue [cloth] for waistcoat a 14 Gr:	1	45
2 1/2 black ditto for breeches a 14 Gr:	1	45
6 1/2 white glazed linen for coat a 19 Gr:	2	3
2 glazed linen for waistcoat a 19xr	-	38
3 rough fustian a 13 Gr:	1	57
3 sailcloth linen	-	30
3 1/2 dozen buttons for coat	1	6
1 ditto for the breeches	-	7
1 1/2 ditto for waistcoat	-	13 1/2
20 1/2 Elen silver edging a 15 Gr:	15	22 1/2
Lining and padding	-	18
Sewing thread	-	7
Tailor's bill	6	
	40	40
carried over	40	40

One [man's] blue suit

8 Elen blue cloth for coat a 14 Gr:	5	36
2 1/2 red ditto for waistcoat a 22 Gr:	2	45
2 1/2 black ditto for breeches a 14 Gr:	1	45
3 rough fustian a 13 Gr:	1	57
2 white glazed linen for waistcoat a 1xr	-	38
6 1/2 glazed linen for coat a 19xr	2	3

3 sailcloth linen	-	30
3 1/2 dozen buttons for coat	1	6
1 ditto for breeches	-	7
1 1/2 ditto for waistcoat	-	13 1/2
36 Elen edging a 3xr	1	48
45 lace a 2 1/2xr	1	52
3 marks spangles	2	33
Lining and padding	-	12
Sewing thread	-	7
Tailor's bill	7	-
	30	19

Livrée

9 Elen silver coloured cloth for coat and breeches a 16 Gr:	7	12
4 green [cloth] for waistcoat a 14 gr:	2	48
3 rough fustian	1	57
6 1/2 glazed linen for coat	2	3
3 1/2 dozen buttons for coat	1	6
2 1/2 ditto for waistcoat and breeches	-	22 1/2
54 Elen edging a 2 1/2xr	2	15
28 Cologne red edging a 4xr	1	52
Red wool for tassel	-	24
Shag for ditto 1 1/2 Elen	-	45
2 Elen white glazed linen for waistcoat	-	38
Tailor's bill	5	30
	26	52

Woman's dress

14 1/2 Elen fine white glazed linen for skirt a 12 Gr:	8	42
1 linen for lining	-	19
1/2 rough furstian a 13 Gr:	-	19 1/2
10 gold *toque* for trimming a 24xr	4	-
	13	20 1/2
carried over	13	20 1/2
Ribbons and hooks	-	12
Tailor's bill	6	-
	19	32

Blue sack dress

14 1/2 Elen fine blue glazed linen a 30xr	7	15

1 linen for lining a 19xr	-	19
1/2 rough fustian	-	19 1/2
9 silver *toque* for trimming	3	36
Ribbons and hooks	-	12
Tailor's bill	6	-
	17	41 [sic]

Yellow sack dress

15 Elen fine [yellow] glazed linen a 12 Gr:	9	-
1 linen for lining	-	19
1/2 rough furstian	-	19 1/2
9 silver *toque*	3	36
Ribbons and hooks		12
Tailor's bill	6	-
	19	26 [sic]
Summa Sumarum	468	26

The above bill together with the extra expenses was paid in full and correctly to me by Chief Cashier Zoller with 448f [sic] Vienna 15 March 1763

Johan Georg Spöck
Garderobier

Extra expenses

For the customs sheet at the Main Customs Office	-	32
Toll at the Line [city walls]	-	24
Toll en route	2	8
For room and board in Eisenstadt for 3 persons	7	24
Summa	10	28

Commentary

The elaborate and in part costly costumes for Haydn's first Italian opera show the high standard that would be the mark of all Esterházy opera productions. As evidence of eighteenth-century theatrical practice, the bill (and others) are valuable and instructive.

14. Buchdruckerrechnung für das Binden des Librettos der Oper *Acide*

Gralcassa, 1763. Rubr. VIII. Nr. 121.

S p e c i f i c a t i o n   f   X

1. Den Buchdrucker vor die Opern Büchel	21	-
2. Den Buch Binder	28	18
Vor die Saiten und zurichtung deren Geigen	34	6
Vor die Copisten	25	10
Vor Wellisches Notten Papier	5	42
Vor den eignen Botten die Opern Büchel zu holen mit allen Unkosten	8	27
Ein neues Dach auf die Geigen gemacht	3	-
Vor S: Durchl: dem Fürsten einen neuen Bogen	3	-
dem Mons. Bon seine Ausgaben	11	7
dem schlosser	-	18
Röhr vor Englische Horn, Oboe und Fagott 36 stuck eines zu 10Xr	6	-
Summa	146f	8Xr

Diese obbenandte Conto werden von Herrn OberEinnehmer Joan Zoller aus der Eisenstädter General Cassa Bezahlet werden Wienn den 17ten Marty [1]763. Nicolaus Fürst Esterhazy

Zu Bezahlung vorstehender Conto seynd mir von herrn OberEinnehmer Zoller obige 146 f 8 Xr richtig und Baar zu meinen Handen gestellet worden. Wienn den 16 (!) Marty [1]763
Joseph Haydn
Fürstlicher Capell Maister
[Mit Ausnahme der Unterschrift des Fürsten von Haydns Hand]

Nr.1. Auf Anordnung Sr Hochfürstl: Durchlaucht Herrn, Herrn Fürsten Esterhasy ist nachfolgende Opera Acide, bestehend in 3 1/2 Bogen gedruckt und geliefert worden, auf jedem Bogen 150. Exemplar auf feinem Postpapier, der Bogen pr. 6f.
macht zusammen   21f.

Summa per se Accordirt   21f(Haydn)
Johann Parth
der von Ghelischen [sic] Buchdruckerey Factor.
Obige Summa ist von 18. Marty 1763 richtig bezahlt worden, durch den Hochfürstl. Ober-Einnehmer H. Zoller.

Nr.2.
[1]763. Le 19. Janua [sic]:   flo: X:
     M e m o i r e

Ein opera in 4to Eingebunden
12. in roden taffat a 51x   10   12
a 12 x. 24. in silberpapir steif Ein Gebunden a 17x   6   48
a 7 x. 114 glat iber zogen a 10x   19   -

                                        Soladi: 36   -

Regulirt à 28 f 18 Xr. Haydn.   Joseph Walch
                                Maiter Relieur a la française
Diese 28f. 18x seind mir durch den hochfirstlichen herrn ober Einnemmer Zoller Richtig bezohllet worden, den 18. Marzi [1]763.

Kommentar

Bis jetzt konnte kein Exemplar dieses gedruckten Librettos gefunden werden. Die Gesellschaft der Musikfreunde in Wien besitzt eine handschriftliche Kopie von Pohl (10957/Textb.).

14. Printer's bill for Haydn's opera *Acide* (libretto)
Specification

		f	x
1.	The printer for the opera librettos	21	-
2.	The bookbinder	28	18
	For the strings and repair of the violins	34	6
	For the copyist	25	10
	For Italian music paper	5	42
	For our own messager to fetch the opera libretti with all expenses	8	27
	A new top plate made for the violins	3	-
	For H. H. The Prince a new bow	3	-
	For the expenses of Mons Bon	1	7
	The locksmith	-	18
	Reeds for cor anglais, oboe and bassoon 36 pieces each at 10xr	6	-
	Summa	146f	8xr

This above account will be paid by Chief Cashier Joan Zoller from the General Pay-Office at Eisenstadt, Vienna, 17 March 1763.   Nicolaus Fürst Esterhazy
For payment of the above account Herr Chief Cashier Zoller has given me the above 146f 8xr in full and cash.
Vienna 16 [sic] March 1763
                                    Joseph Haydn
                            Fürstlicher Capell Meister
[The above all in Haydn's hand - except the Prince's signature.]

No. 1. On the orders of His Serene Highness Herr Fürst Esterhazy the following opera Acide, consisting of 3 1/2 Bogen printed and delivered, 150 copies of each Bogen on fine post-paper, the Bogen pr. 6f

Makes a total of 21f

Summa per se
[Haydn's hand]
Accordirt 21f   Johann Parth
           Agent in the Ghelen Publishing Office
Above sum has been correctly paid 18 March 1763, through the Princely Chief Cashier H. Zoller

No. 2. 1763, 19 January   f   xr
          Memoire
   An opera in 4to bound
   12 in red taffeta a 51x   10   12
   a 12x 24 bound in stiff silver paper covers a 17x   6   48
   a 7x 114 simply bound   19   -

          Soladi: 36   -
Regulated à 28f 18xr Haydn [mpria]
           Joseph Walch
           Maiter [sic] Relieur a la française
This 28f 18x have been correctly paid to me by the Princely Herr Chief Cashier Zoller 18 March 1763.

Commentary
No copy of this printed libretto for *Acide* has survived. A MS copy by Pohl is in the Gesellschaft der Musikfreunde, Vienna (10957/Textb).

15. Schneiderrechnung für Kostüme zu den Opern *Il mercato di Malmantile*, und Haydns *La Marchesa Nespola*

Gralcassa, 1763. Rubr. VIII. Nr. 27.

S p e c i f i c a z i o n e
Delle Spese fatte per Li Abiti Dell'Opera il Mercato, e per La Comedia La Marchesa, oltre La nota del Mercante

	fno	Xr
Fattura de sarti	16	30
Due paruche	4	-
Due Capelli neri	-	27
Lustrini d'oro	3	20
Un paro Calzette di color rosso	1	-
Un paro di Scarpe	1	18
Filo, Camelo, Bottoni, et altre cose	3	21
Suma fni	29	56

Unser OberEinnehmer Zoller hat obspecificirte Zwanzig Neun Gulden 56Xr dem le Bon zu bezahlen und in Anrechnung zu bringen.
Kittsee den 7ten 8bris [1]763.   Nicolaus Fürst Esterhazy
                                  Jo Girolamo Bon
Hò ricevuto La Somma de ventinove Fiorini, e cinquanta sei Xr Dal Sigr De Zoller.

Gralcassa, 1763, Rubr.VIII, Nr.27.

Aufstellung der Ausgaben für die Kostüme zur Oper *Il Mercato* und die Komödie *La Marchesa* zusätzlich zur Rechnung über den *Mercante* [sic]

	F	xr
Schneiderlohn	16	30
2 Perrücken	4	-
2 schwarze Hüte	-	27
Goldene Glanzseide	3	20
1 Ein Paar rote Socken	1	28
Nähfaden, Camelo [?] Knöpfe und anderes	3	21
Suma Fni.	29	56

[Zahlungsbestätigung von Girolamo Bon]
Ich habe von Herrn De Zoller die Summe von neunundzwanzig Gulden sechsundfünfzig Kreuzern erhalten.

Kommentar

Rechnungen für die Aufführung der zwei Opern *Il mercato di Malmantile* (G. Scarlatti oder D. Fischietti ?) von Goldoni und Haydns teilweise verschollene Komödie *La Marchesa Nespola*, die man jetzt mit 1763 datieren kann (siehe Landon I, S. 646, ref. p. 371f).

15. Bills for the costumes for the opera *Il Mercato* and la comedie *La Marchesa.*
Specification
Of expenses for the costumes of the Opera Il Mercato and for the comedy La Marchese apart from the note regarding Mercante [sic].

	f	xr
Tailor's bill	16	30
Two wigs	4	-
Two black hats	-	27
glazed golden silk	3	20

a pair of red stockings	1	-
a pair of shoes	1	28
Thread, camelo, buttons and other things	3	21
Summa	29	56

Our Chief Cashier Zoller has to pay the above sum of twenty nine gulden 56xr to Le Bon and to file it. Kittsee, 7 Oct. 1763. Nicolaus Fürst Esterházy. I, Girolamo Bon have received the sum of twenty-nine florins and fifty-six xr from Sigr. De Zoller.

Commentary

Bills for the two operas *Il mércato di Malmantile* (G. Scarlatti or D. Fischietti?) by Carlo Goldoni and Haydn's partially lost comedy *La Marchesa Nespola* now to be dated 1763 (see Landon, I p. 646, referring to p. 371f).

16. Fürstliche Resolution Peter Ludwig Rahier zum Güterregenten zu bestellen
Prot. 6625, S. 152. Kurrental. Herr. Eisenstadt

Rahier Peter Ludwig, K. K. Hauptmann.
nachdeme der Kays.- Königl. Haubtmann H: Peter Ludwig von Rachier [sic] gegen Sr. Hochfürstl. Durchlaucht tragende Devotion Kriegsgebrächigermassen quittiret hat, so haben Hochdieselbste besagten Hrn. Haubtmann in Betracht dessen, und seines bekannten Eyfers zum Regenten in herobere Herrschaften erwählet, an und aufgenohmen, daher ist auch Sr. Hochfürstl. Durchlaucht austrücklicher und ernstlicher Befehl ...... ihm alle Schuldige Ehren geben u. Parition leisten sollen.
An die Schloß u. Buchhalterey 1763, Nov. 9.

Kommentar

Mit der Bestellung Rahiers zum Güterregenten hatte der Fürst einen guten Griff getan. Der ehemalige Hauptmann neigte zwar zu einem militärisch ausgerichteten Regime und war ob seines Jähzorns gefürchtet, hatte aber andererseits ein offenes Ohr für die Nöte seiner Untergebenen. Haydn hatte einige Mißhelligkeiten mit Rahier, bis er sich den Respekt verschafft hatte, der seinem Rang als Kapellmeister und Operndirektor gebührte.

16. Princely resolution to make Peter Ludwig Rahier the regent
Translation

Herrschaft Eisenstadt, kurrental 1763, Prot. 6625, p. 152 Rahier, Peter Ludwig I. R. Captain.
Since the I. R. Captain H. Peter Ludwig von Rahier, who displayed such valuable devotion to his Princely Highness [in the Esterházy Regiment in the Seven Years' War] in the form of

being wounded in the war and forced to quit the service that his Highness, in consideration thereof, and because of his further diligence, has nominated said captain to be Regent of the above *Herrschaften* [Northeastern signories], hence also his Princely Highness's express and serious order to show him [Rahier] all due respect and submission. [9 Nov. 1763, protocol to castle bookkeeper].

Commentary

With Rahier's nomination as Regent, the signory of Eisenstadt began to run like a military machine. The former captain favoured a kind of barrack-style with his underlings and was feared because of his short temper; but he also cared for the poor people and was decent and just. Haydn had many run-ins with the overpowering Regent, until such time as he could gain Rahier's respect and was treated in a fashion befitting a Princely Kapellmeister and opera director.

17. Schneiderrechnung von Johann Georg Röck für vier Bauernkostüme zu einer unbekannten Oper vom 12. Oktober 1763

Süttör. Opera. 1763. Gral-Cassa

Okt. 12. W. Joh. Georg Röck Oppera Schneider Conto 102 f.
Verzeichnis Was zu Verfertigung zweyer Manns u. zwey Frauen
Bauern Kleidung erkauft worden ist:

	f	xr
39 el. Rothe rosenfarbe glantz Leinwath a 39xr	25	21
37 Ellen grüne Leinwat a 21xr	12	57
18 Elln Futter Leinwat a 19xr	5	42
38 " silber Dak a 27xr	17	6
32 " breite silberne Bördel a 6xr	3	12
229 " schmale Bördel a 3xr	11	27
4 " Sigel Leinwat a 14xr	-	56
Zwey Mannes Hüt	1	48
Frauen Hütel	-	24
Tafet zum Hutfüteren	-	54
6 Ellen Tafet Bandel zu den Hoosen a 7xr	-	42
Für das Aushacken der Lauber und Garnirung	2	30
Boloneser Dünn Tuch 2 1/2 Ellen a 1f 15xr	3	7
Geblumtes Dünntuch 5 Ellen a 1f 9xr	5	45
Roosenfarbe Band 4 Ellen a 7xr	-	28
Für Macherlohn und aller zugehörung	43	-
Summa	135	19
(bezahlt 102f. -)		
Vor 4 Weinleser Kleider	121	-

Kommentar

In Eszterháza (Süttör) wurden seit 1763 Opern gespielt, anfangs wahrscheinlich auf einer Behelfsbühne; so kann diese Rechnung sowohl für eine Opernaufführung in Eszterháza als auch in Eisenstadt gewesen sein, vielleicht für eine von Haydns verlorenen Komödien, *La vedova, Il dottore,* oder *Il Scanarello.*

17. Bill for four costumes to an unknown opera 1763

Süttör Opera 1763 Generalkassa
   Oct. 12 W. Joh. Georg Rück, operatic tailor, conto 102f.
List of items purchased for the preparation of two men's and two women's peasant costumes

	f	xr
39 Elen red rosy-coloured glazed linen a 39xr	25	21
37 Eln green linen a 19xr	15	21
18 Eln linen for lining a 19xr	5	42
38 Eln silver *toque* [Dak] a 27xr	17	6
32 eln broad silver *bordures* a 6xr	3	12
229 eln small *bordures* a 3xr	11	27
4 eln sailcloth a 14xr	-	56
Two hats for men	1	48
Lady's bonnet	-	24
Taffeta for lining hat	-	54
6 ellen taffeta for trousers a7xr	-	42
For cutting up foliage and decorations	2	30
Thin Bolognese linen 2 1/2 ellen a 1f 15xr	3	7
Flowered thin linen 5 ellen a 1f 9xr	5	45
Rose-coloured ribbon 4 ellen a7xr	-	28
For tailoring and everything else pertaining there to	43	-
Summa	135	19
(Paid 102f.	-	)

[In a parallel file] 4 costumes for vintagers 121.-

Commentary

Opera was being given at Eszterháza as early as 1763, probably on a temporary stage; or the bill may be for a performance in Eisenstadt. It is not known for which opera the costumes were made - possibly for one of Haydn's lost *commedie, La Vedova, Il dottore* or *Il Scanarello.*

18. Auszug aus den Rentamtsrechungen über Buchbinderarbeiten 1763

Eisenstädter-Rentamt. 1764. Nr. 132. D.

A u s   Z i g l

Was ich Endsunter Schriebener vor Ihro Hoch Fürstlichen Durchleicht in Buchbinder arbeit verferdiget habe. wie folget: 2.Messe 2.Verspern. 2.Salve Regina und ein Requiem eingebunden. welche arbeit mit 2f ist accordiret worden.

Eissen Stadt den 16. Decem: 1763   Joannes Widerkorn
   Gregorius Werner   Burgerlicher Buchbinder Ma:
   fürstlr. Capellmeist.

Kommentar

Die Werke sind nicht zu identifizieren, sie waren wahrscheinlich von Gregor Werner.

18. Bills for book-binding 1763
Summary Translation

What I the undersigned completed in bookbinding work for His Serene Highness as follows:
    2 Masses, 2 Vespers, 2 Salve Reginas, and a Requiem bound. Which work was agreed to at 2f.

Eisenstadt 16 Dec. 1763   Johannes Widerkorn
   Gregorius Werner   Bürgerlicher Master
   Princely Capellmeist.   Bookbinder

Commentary
The works can no longer be identified, but they were probably by Gregor Werner.

19. Acta Musicalia Nr.4336
Fürst Nicolaus Esterházy übersendet seinem Güterdirektor Rahier die Textbücher zu zwei 'welschen Comaedien'

Wohl Edl Gebohrner
Hochgeehrter Herr v Rahier!
... Übrigens überschicke Ihnen auch zweyfache welsche Comaedie unterhandlungen, damit Sie von jeder Sorte 50 Exemplaria mit guten Leßbaren Character in 4to zu Oedenburg sollen druckhen, und mit Gold-Papier einbinden lassen. Wormit verharre
Euer Wohl Edl Gebohrn
Wien den 29tn Xbris 1764.   Bereitwilliger
                             Nicolaus Fürst Esterhazy

Kommentar

Diese Eisenstädter Rentamts-Rechnungen unterrichten uns über Opern, Bälle und Schauspiele des Jahres 1765, geben uns aber keine

Titel der aufgeführten Opern und Schauspiele. Haydns *Acide* wurde zwar 1764 wieder aufgeführt, aber das Textbuch dafür war allein 3 1/2 Bogen lang, während Buchdrucker Sieß (siehe Dok. Nr. 20) 3 1/2 Bogen für zwei Operntextbücher verrechnet.

19. Prince Nicolaus sends Rahier the textbooks of two Italian comedies.
[Partial translation]

Moreover I send you as well two Italian comedy librettos, so that you can have them printed in 50 copies each in good readable type in 4to in Oedenburg and have them bound in gold paper...
Vienna 29 Dec. 1764

Commentary
We are unable to identify these two opera librettos of 1764/5. It should be noted, however, that Haydn's *Acide* was revived in 1764; but *Acide* was 3 1/2 Bogen and the two operas for 1764/5 were also the same length (see document No. 10). Here is a mystery which can not be solved.

20. Eisenstädter-Rentamt. 1764. Nr. 132. WW

C o m m i s s i o n

Vermög welcher der Eisenstädter Rändtmeister Herr Frantz Nigst dem Oedenburger Buchdrucker für, vor Sr Durchlaucht dem Fürsten getruckte 2. Opera Bichl welche in 3 1/2 Bögen Bestehen, und derenselben 100. Stuck getrucket worden, accordirter massen für diese getruckte Büchl Vierzehen Gulden Bezahlen solle. Schloß Eisenstadt den 5n Jenner [1]765:
    Idest: 14f.   P. L. Rahier
Daß mir diese Vierzehen Gulden aus dem Eisenstädter Ränt-Amt bezahlet worden, quittire. Edenburg. den 6ten Jan: 1765:
    (L. S.) Johann Joseph Sieß Buchdr:

20. Commission
According to which the Eisenstadt Rent Master Herr Frantz Nigst is to pay the Oedenburg printer for 2 opera librettos, which consist of 3 1/2 Bogen and are printed in 100 copies, for His Highness The Prince; the agreed price for these printed libretti was fourteen gulden. Schloß Eisenstadt 5 January 1765.
    Idest: 14f   P. L. Rahier
I attest that these fourteen gulden have been paid to me by the Eisenstadt Rental Office, and this is the receipt therefor. Edenburg [sic]. 6 Jan. 1765
    Johann Joseph Sieß mpria
    and printer.

21. Tischler- und Malerrechnungen für Arbeiten im Theater 1765

Eisenstädter-Rentamt. 1765. Nr. 131. Lit. C.

	Ges.	stund	f		Xr
Feyrums Arbeith welche ych und die Geselen zu Empfangen habe auf den Deadrum					
Zum Ersten den 9ten Juny Mäyster	4	4	1	-	-
den 10 Tato Mäyster und	4	4	1	-	-
den 12 Tato Mäyster und	4	4	1	-	-
Mehr haben wür gearbeitet nach Feirum Zwey Verschlag zur Schne Bergweser Mäyster und	4	4	1	-	-
Also haben wür mehr gearbeitet an denen Kasten Tisch und Tafell So alles nach Prespurg ins Hauß gekommen Vor Mitag von 4 Uhr bis 5 und Nachmitag von 7 Uhr bis 8 also haben Sie Dag an gearbeitet Mäyster und	6	2	9	-	48
Gantze 14 Teg von 14ten Juny bis 5ten July	4	2	-	-	30
Mehr den 18ten 9bris Mäyster und	4	2	-	-	30
den 19 Tato Mayster und	3	-	1	-	12
Von Neu Jahr wider den 1ten Jenuary habe Maister wider den 2t Mayster und	3	3	-	-	36
also haben die Geselen auf meiner weg stadt gearbeitet in der Firstlichen wergstadt den 3ten Jenuarj von 8 ohr vormitag bis 12 und nachmitag 1 ohr bis 7	3	10	1	-	30
den 5ten dato Nachmitag von 1 ohr bis 6	3	5	-	-	45
den 3ten der Mäyster mit	11	9	5	-	24
den 6ten der Meister Dag und nacht mit	11⸳	19	11	-	24
den 7ten dato der Mäister mit	6	9	3	-	9
S u m a f			37		48
Latus Heryber Tragen			37		48
den 8ten dato der Mäyster mit	6	9	3		9

den 9ten dato der Mäyster mit	6	9	3	9
den 10ten dato der Mäyster mit	6	9	3	9
den 12ten dato der Mayster mit	6	9	3	9
den 13ten dato der Mayster mit Tag und nacht	7	16	6	24

attestire auf die Operen und Ball   f56   48
    Jacoby Ingenieur   Corolus Flach
                                   Hof Tischler
                                   Mäyster

                Eisenstädter-Rentamt. 1765. Nr. 131. Lit. KK.

      S p e c i f i c a t i o n
Was ich in den Hochfürstlichen Theatro an verschiedenen gemähl gemacht habe [1]765.   Alß

In Monath April den   15. 16. 17. 18. 19. 20. 21. 22. Tag
                    f: 1 1 1 1 1 1 1 1
  S u m m a: Tag: 8. F: 8
                               Wolffgang Köpp
                               Hieronymus Bon
Daß mir diese acht gulden aus dem Räntamt bezahlet worden, quittire.
Eisenstadt den 30ten Xbr [1]765:   Wolffgang Köpp

                Eisenstädter-Rentamt. 1765. Nr.131. Lit. O.
      A u s l a a g
Vor extra verrichtete Tischler-stunden Bey denen Commaedien.

Conto for die Feiramstunten Bey der Comedi Alß	f	Xr
den 9ten Apprill ich und 4 Geselen Jeder 6 Stundt macht zu Samen	1	30
den 10 Tato ich und 4 Gesellen Jeder 2 stundt ma:	-	30
den 11 Deto ich und 4 Gesellen Jeder 2 stundt macht also	-	30
den 13 Deto ich und 4 Gesellen Jeder 3 stund macht also	-	45
den 14 Deto ich und 4 Gesellen Jeder 5 stund macht also	1	15
den 16 Deto ich und 4 Gesellen		

Jeder 2 stund macht also	-	30
den 17 Deto ich und 4 Gesellen		
Jeder 2 stund macht also	-	30
den 18 Deto ich und 4 Gesellen		
Jeder 2 stund macht also	-	30
den 20 Deto ich und 4 Gesellen		
Jeder 3 stund macht also	-	45
den 21 Deto ich und 5 Gesellen		
Jeder 4 stund macht also	1	12
den 22 Deto ich und 4 Gesellen		
Jeder 2 stund macht also	-	30
den 23 Täto ich und 5 Gesellen		
Jeder 5 stund macht also	1	30
den 24 Deto ich und 5 Gesellen		
Jeder 5 stund macht also	1	30
den 25 Deto ich und 4 Gesellen		
Jeder 2 stund macht also	-	30
den 27 Deto ich und 4 Gesellen		
Jeder 2 stund macht also	-	30
den 28 Deto ich und 5 Gesellen		
Jeder 8 stund macht also	2	24
den 30 Deto ich und 4 Gesellen		
Jeder 2 stund macht also	-	30
Manath Mäy: Alß		
den 1t: Dato ich und 5 Gesellen		
Jed 5 Stundt macht also	1	30
den 2 Däto ich und 4 Gesellen		
Jeder 2 stund macht also	-	30
S a m a f	17	21
Latus Her yber Tragen	17	21
den 5t May ich und 5 Gesellen		
Jeder 5 stund macht also	1	30
den 6 Dato ich und 4 Gesell		
Jeder 3 stund macht also	-	45
den 7 Deto ich und 4 Gesell		
Jeder 1 stund macht also	-	15
den 8 Deto ich und 4 Gesell		
Jeder 1 stund macht also	-	15
den 9 Deto ich und 4 Gesell		
Jeder 2 stund macht also	-	30

den 11 Deto ich und 4 Gesell
 Jeder 2 stund macht also   -   45
den 12 Deto ich und 4 Gesell
 Jeder 4 stund macht also   1   -
den 13 Deto ich und 4 Gesell
 Jeder 2 stund macht also   -   30
den 16 Deto ich und 4 Gesell
 Jeder 4 stund macht also   1   -
den 18 Deto ich und 4 Gesell
 Jeder 1 stund macht also   -   15
den 19 Deto ich und 4 Gesell
 Jeder 5 stund macht also   1   15
den 20 Deto ich und 6 Gesell
 Jeder 1 stund macht also   -   21
den 21 Deto ich und 3 Gesell
 Jeder 1 stund macht also   -   12
den 25 Deto ich und 2 Gesell
 Jeder 3 stund macht also   -   27
den 26 Deto ich und 4 Gesell
 Jeder 4 stund macht also   1   -
den 27 Deto ich und 4 Gesell
 Jeder 4 stund macht also   1   -
den 28 Deto ich und 3 Gesell
 Jeder 4 stund macht also   -   48
den 29 Deto ich und 4 Gesell
 Jeder 2 stund macht also   -   30
den 30 Deto ich und 3 Gesell
 Jeder 2 stund macht also   -   24
den 1t Juny ich und 4 Gesell
 Jeder 3 stund macht Also   -   45
den 2 Tato ich und 5 Gesell
 Jeder 4 stund macht Also   1   12
         S u m a   f   32   -

Seind Feiram Stundten 640 Also macht zu Samen in Gelt die Soma 32 f

        Corolus Flach hoch Firstl
         Tischler Mäyster
Obige stunten seint richtig verrichtet worten   N. Gout

21. Carpenter and painter's bills for the theatre 1765

In a document (Eisenstadt Rentamts-Rechnungen, Jan 1765, 131/C), a list of 'Opern und Ballen, Tag und Nacht' signed by Ing. Jacoby, is given 3, 5-10, 12-13 Jan. 1765. 'Carpenters' extra hands for the plays 32f.- (see the German for details: 9 April - 2 June, not every day), signed by Gout (131/0).

There is also a bill by Wolf Köpp, approved by Bon (131/KK) for 'painting work in the theatre' during 15 - 22 April at 1 fl. p. d. = 8 fl.

22. Johann Michael Schuster wird mit seinem Ballorchester vom 3. - 13. Januar 1765 engagiert

Gralcassa, 1765. Rubr. VIII. Nr. 3.

Heunt zu Ende gesezten Dato ist in Nahmen Sr Durchlaucht Fürstens Nicolai Eszterhazy v Galatha &c &c durch Hochdero selben Camer Diener Michael Kleinrath, dan den Herrn Schuster Music Director folgender Contract verabredet und vest geschlossen worden.

Erstens verspricht Herr Schuster Music Director sich den 3ten Jenner 1765 nebst funpfzehen andere Musicis nach Eysenstadt zu begeben also zwar, daß Sie gleich nach Ihrer ankunft Ihre Function zu verrichten sich bewilligen. Worzu

Zweytens von seiten Herrn Musicae Directoris die benöthigte Instrumenta sambt Musicalien, daß ist Minuet, Steyrisch, und contra-Tänze beyzuschaffen seynd.

Drittens werden Sie verbunden seyn von bemelten Dato an biß den 13te dieses allda zu verbleiben, und alltäglich, wan eß Seine Durchlaucht befehlen werden, Music zu machen, widrigen fahls, wan Sie vor bemelten Termin weg giengen, wurden Sie vor die allda zugebrachte Zeit nichts zu fordern haben.

Viertens Wan eß Seiner Durchlaucht gefallen möchte Sie länger zu behalten, so sollen Sie auch schuldig seyn zu bleiben, und musiciren, wird aber einen jeden täglich wie durch die zehen Täg, seyn außgemachtes Quantum auch ferners applacidirt.

Hingegen wird Ihnen von seiten Sr Durchlaucht passiret.

Erstens, von 3ten Jener an biß 13tn ejusdem einen Jeden täglich 3 f in geld, den H. Director aber 6f: und sobald Sie in loco seynd die tägliche Kost nebst einer Maaß Wein, und Loschirung

Zweytens wird Ihnen die Gelegenheit zu hin, und wider zuführen beygeschaffet werden.

Drittens Weillen Herr Director zukünfftigen Sambstag alß den 5ten dieses wegen denen Redouten zuruckh zu kehren bemüssiget, so wird ihm zwar die erlabnuß hierzu mitgetheilet, jedoch mit diesen

Vorbehalt, daß er vor die täge seiner Abwesenheit nichts praetendire, seinen untergebenen nicht destoweniger die gute Ordnung anbefehle, damit Sr Durchl: auch in Abwesenheit Seiner bestens bedienet werde, und in der Music kein Fehler vorbey gehe, vor welchen obbemelter H. Music Director sich zu verantworten haben würde.

Viertens Wan Sie vor verfliessung bemelter Zehen Tägen auß Befehl Seiner Durchlaucht zuruckh geschicket wurden, sollen Sie vor dieselbe dannoch vollständig bezahlet werden.

Zu Bekräfftigung dessen zwey gleich lautende Exemplaria außgefertigt, und unter beeden Theillen außgewechselt werden. Beschehn Wien den 2tn Jener 1765.
 (L. S.) Johann Michael schuster Musicus.

Gralcassa, 1765. Rubr. VIII.

Unser Ober Einnehmer Johann Zoller wird die Musicanten nach dem Obstehenden Contract bezahlen und in Anrechnung bringen.
Eisenstadt den 14ten Jenner [1]765.
 Nicolaus Fürst Esterhazy
Daß wir Endes gefertigten, vor obig Accortirt und ver richte Paall Music, alß nemblichen, von 3ten biß 14 Jenner alß an dag zu unser Zurickh kunft vor 15 persson à 3f: vor mich Director aber durch drey dag à 6f. in Summa 558f: durch H: Ober Ein nehme Zoller richtig und baar bezahlet worden bescheine hiermit Sig: den 21 Jener [1]765
 Johann Michael schuster director

Kommentar

Haydn und seine Musiker spielten keine Tanzmusik. Für Bälle holte Fürst Nicolaus Musiker aus Wien. Schuster und sein Orchester wurde im Juli 1766 wieder engagiert.

22. Contract for Johann Michael Schuster and his musician to play at the balls from 3 to 13 January 1765

Today, under date appended hereto, is in the name of His Highness Prince Nicolai Eszterhazy v. Galantha etc etc through his Lordship's *Cammer Diener* Michael Kleinrath, the following contract agreed and vouchsafed with Herr Schuster, Music Director.

First, Herr Schuster Music Director agrees to take himself and fifteen other players on 3 January 1765 to Eisenstadt, there to take up their duties at once; to which end

Secondly, on the part of Herr Musicae Directoris the necessary music, that is minuets, styrians and contra-dances will be organised.

Thirdly, they will be obliged from the afore-mentioned date to the 13th to remain there and daily, whenever His Highness orders, to play music; otherwise, if they leave before the end of their sojourn, they will have no recourse to the time heretofore spent.

Fourthly, should His Highness be pleased to keep them longer, they should be willing to remain and to make music, but their services will be remunerated daily beyond the ten appointed days.

For this His Highness agrees:-

First, from 3rd to and including the 13th ejusdem, each musician will be paid 3f in cash, the H. Director however 6f., and, as soon as they are in residence, the daily board together with a Maaß of wine and lodgings.

Secondly, their transport to and from [Vienna] will be arranged.

Thirdly, since Herr Director is required to return on next Saturday the 5th because of the [Imperial Court] Redouten [ball], he is permitted to do so but with the proviso that during the days of his absence he sees to it that order is continued to be observed, so that His Highness also in his [Schuster's] absence will be well served and there are no mistakes in the music [performances], for which responsibility the aforesaid Herr Music Director assumes full responsibility.

Fourthly, should they be sent back, on the orders of His Highness, before the period of ten days is up they will be paid in full for the whole period.

To implement this agreement two identical copies of this contract will be drawn up and signed, and exchanged between each party. Given at Vienna the 2nd January 1765.

Johann Michael Schuster Musicus mpria.

Commentary

Nicolaus Esterházy was always at great pains that his chamber musicians did not play dance music, for the performance of which expensive 'foreign' orchestras were engaged and sent to Eisenstadt or Eszterháza. Evidently dance orchestras were considered to be of a more lowly social status then Esterházys' musicians, who were under contract as 'house officers'.

The orchestra was a great success, as usual, and united again to perform in July 1766 at Eisenstadt Castle.

23. Aus den Haushofmeister Rechnungen von 1765: Fürst Nicolaus Aufenthalt in Innsbruck

aug. 7. Dem Kammerdiener Georg in die Oppra zu frisirn 21xr.

aug. 20. Umb die Sessl von Theateurs zu Hn. Gf. Wolkenstein zu transportiren 7 1/2 tiroli münze xr.

Nr. 71 aug. 20. Dem Pfarr Organisten und Claviermeister Georg Paul Falck vor ein der Fürstin Lamberg entlehntes Flügl u. Reparierung eines, so zerbrochen 4 dukat = 17.48 Innsbruck.

Den 18 Juli habe ich zu I. Hfl. Durchl. ein Passetl geliehen, die Wochen 30xr, haben solches bis 21. Aug. behalten machet also 2.30 - Einen Figl [Fidl] Pogen behärt 12xr - 5 Pischl saiten 20xr - 2 Kreizer Calfany 2xr Summa 3f 4xr

Maria verwittibte Psennerin [Pfennerin], Lauthen u. saiten Macherin allda.

Kommentar

Am 5. August 1765 heiratete Erzherzog Leopold die Spanische Infantin Maria Luisa in Innsbruck. Zu den Feiern war auch Fürst Nicolaus mit einem Teil seines Hofstaats angereist, doch sollte das Fest bereits am 18. August in tiefer Trauer enden, da Kaiser Franz Stephan im Theater einen Herzschlag erlegen war.

23. From the Major Domo's account books from 1765, when Prince Nicolaus was in Innsbruck

Translation

7 Aug: Valet-de-chambre Georg ordered to the opera to dress hair 21xr.

20 Aug: To take the chairs from the theatre to H. Count Wolkenstein, 7 1/2 Tyrolean coins xr.
To the parish organist and clavier teacher Georg Paul Falck for 2 harpsichords, one rented from Princess Lamberg, (one broken and repaired).
Innsbruck, 4 ducats =17f 48xr.

On 18 July I lent H. S. H. a cello, 30x the week, which was kept until 21 August, which makes 2f 30xr.-
Hair for a bow 12xr. - 5 bundles of strings 20xr. -
2 kreuzer rosin 2xr Summa 3f 4xr

Maria widow Psenner [Pfenner?]
Lute and string-maker here
[Innsbruck]

Commentary

On 5 August 1765 Archduke Leopold married the Spanish Infanta Maria Luisa in Innsbruck and Prince Nicolaus came for the festivities, which ended abruptly on 18 August when the Emperor Francis Stephen died of a heart attack in the theatre.

24. Die Theatertruppe spielt zum Geburtstag des Grafen Nicolaus

Eisenstädter-Rentamt. 1765. Nr. 131. Lit. Y.

C o m m i s s i o n

Vermög welcher der Eisenstädter Rendtmeister denen Commedianten für die Commedien so sie am Vorabend des Geburtsfests Tit. Herrn Grafen Niclas v. Esterhazy gespielet Vier Kremnitzer Ducaten geben und diese in seinen Rechnungen alß eine Güldige Auslaag ansetzen solle.

Eisenstadt den 10ten Aug. [1]765

P. L. Rahier

Daß diese 16 f 48 xr denen Comaedianten aus dem Räntamt bezahlet worden, attestire.
Eisenstadt, den 11ten Aug. 1765
De Gout

Kommentar

Graf Nicolaus war der jüngere Sohn des Fürsten.

24. Theatre performance to celebrate Count Nicolaus's birthday
Summary Translation
The players gave a play ('comedie') on 9 August or the evening before Count Nicolaus's birthday. Costs 4 kremnitz ducats. Commission by P. L. Rahier. Count Nicolaus was Prince Nicolaus's younger son.

25. Güterdirektor Rahier an alle Esterházyschen Verwalter

Protokoll 6625, fol.172.

Wohl Edle
Verehrte Herrn Verwalters!
Denenselben wird hiermit zur Wissenschaft, und fernerer Richtschnur mitgetheilet, das das Schloß bey Süttör von Sr Durchl. Esterház benennet worden sey; mithin in Zukunft auf denen dahin gerichten addressen gesetzet werden solle: a Eszterház bey Süttör.
Womit verbleibe Derenselben
Eisenstadt den 3.n Jenner 1766.   Dienstschuldiger
P. L. Rahier

Kommentar

Zu 'Eszterház', 'Estoras', wie Haydn es nannte, gesellte sich 'Eszterháza' und während des kommunistischen Regimes in Ungarn 'Fertöd', um jede Erwähnung der Familie Esterházy auszuschliessen.

25. Regent Rahier to the whole Esterházy administration
... you are herewith informed of the decision of His Highness that the castle at Süttör is henceforth to be called Eszterház, hence in the future this form of address is to be employed: Eszterház at Süttör.... Eisenstadt, 3 January 1766.

Commentary
The spelling varied between 'Eszterház', 'Eszterháza' (now used) and 'Estoras' (Haydn's customary spelling). To avoid the aristocratic name, the Communist Government in Hungary substituted the name 'Fertöd'.

26. Ausgaben für Ballmusiker und Theatermaler im Juli 1766

Gralcassa, 1766. Rubr. VIII.

H: Musig Director Schuster hat zu empfangen vor seine Persohn auf 2 Tag accorditermassen a 6f:	12f -
18. Persohn ordinair à 3f 2 Tag	108f -
Su.	120f -

Quittung
Pr Ein Hundert Zwäntzig Gulden, welche ich Endes Unterschriebenen aus der Eisenstätter General Cassa und Händen des Obereinnemers H. Johann Zoller vor 2. Täg als vor 30tn undt 31tn July vermög accord und vor den gestrigen Baall vor mich und allübrige Wienerische Musicanden baar und richtig Empfangen habe. Schloss Eisenstatt den 31tn July 1766.
Idest 120f - x   Johann Michael schuster
                                 Music Director

Eisenstädter-Rentamt. 1766. Nr. 132. Lit. T.

den 30 Juli 1766 C a n t o [sic]		
stan den Hern Musigänten for 19 bersan for Jete bersan 18x	5f	42x
Den Antern Dag mittag Esen for Jeten 12 x macht	3f	48
Item for daß Zimmer	-	30
	10f	--

Dise Musicy haben die Kost richtig empfangen, wessentwegen auch rechtens zu bezahlen seyn 10f Züsser.
Daß diese zehen Gulden aus dem Räntamt bezahlet worden, quittire. Eisenstadt den 1ten Sept. 1766.
                         Mathias Döltl Greiffen wirth.

Eisenstädter-Rentamt. 1766. Nr. 132. Lit. EE.
Den vergangenen Sommer habe ich Wolfgangus Köpp in den fürstlichen Theatro zwey Scenen ausgebessert ist davor 3f.
Eisenstadt den 22n Xbris [1]766   Hieronymus Bon.
Daß mir 3f aus der Räntmat bezahlet worden, quittire.
Eisenstadt, den 22ten Xbr [1]766
                         Wolfgangus Köpp Mahler

Kommentar

Im Juli wurde der Namenstag des Grafen Anton, ältesten Sohn von Fürst Nicolaus, gefeiert. Malermeister Köpp wird wahrscheinlich die Kulissen von Haydns *La canterina,* die am 27. Juli aufgeführt wurde, ausgebessert haben. Siehe Landon II, S. 123.

26. Bills for the musicians playing at the ball and the theatre painters, July 1766

H. Music Director is to receive for his person, as agreed,
6f: for 2 days   12f   -
18 ordinary musicians à 3f per 2 days   108f -

                                                          Su[mma]   120f   -

Receipt
for one hundred twenty gulden which I the undersigned received correctly and in cash from the Eisenstadt General Pay-Office at the hands of Chief Cashier H. Johann Zoller for 2 days, viz the 30th and 31st July as agreed for yesterday's ball for me and all the other Viennese musicians. Schloß Eisenstadt 31 July 1766.
            Idest 120f - x   Johann Michael Schuster
                                                       Music Director

The 30th July 1766   Canto [sic]
For the Herr musicians, 19 persons
      for each person 18x   5f   42x
The next day a lunch for
      each at 12x makes   3f   48x
Item for the room 30

                                                                                          10f   -

These musicians have in fact received their board, hence it is correct to pay the 10f. Züsser. I attest and offer receipt that these ten gulden have been paid by the Eisenstadt Rental Office.

Eisenstadt 1 Sept. 1766   Mathias Döltl Greiffen Wirth
Last summer Wolfgang Köpp repaired two scenes in he princely
theatre   3f.
Eisenstadt, 22 Dec. 1766   Hieronymus Bon
I attest and offer receipt that these 3f have been paid to me by the Rental Office.
Eisenstadt, 22 Dec 1766.   Wolfgang Köpp
                                                              Painter

Commentary

In July fell the name day of Count Anton, eldest son to Prince Nicolaus. The painter Köpp may have provided the last touches to the scenery of Haydn's *La canterina* which was performed on 27 July. See Landon, II, p.123.

27. Auftrag an die Buchhaltung zwei neue Oboen, die Haydn für das Orchester wünschte, zu bezahlen

Gralcassa, 1766. Rubr. VIII. Nr. 39.

C o m m i s s i o n
Vermög welcher Unser Ober Einnehmer Johann Zoller die zu Unserer Musique neu gemachte zwey Hautboi mit Acht Dugaten bezahlen, und in Anrechnung bringen solle. Prespurg den 30ten Jener 1767.
Nicolaus Fürst Esterhazy

werde es in Wienn Berwerfen lassen. Die 2 Hautboi aber kann Er aufrimmen [bestellen], und durch den Zoller gegen Vorzeigung dieses mit 8. Ducaten Bezahlen lassen, welcher hernach zu seiner Zeit die gehörige Commission schon anverlangen wird. Eszterhaz den 5n Xber 1766.
Nicolaus Fürst Esterhazy
Obstehende 8 Ducaten habe Richtig empfangen
Josephus Haydn mppria

Q u i t t u n g
Pr: Zwey Huboe eine VerAgutiert pr Vier dugatten zwey mahen 8 Dugathen welches ih von den Wohl Kunstreichen Musi, Heyden alß Capelmeister richtig empfangen Habe
Rihtig und bar bezahlt   Mathias Rockhubauer
Instramentmaher

Kommentar

Am 5. Dezember 1766 schrieb Haydn seinem Fürsten, daß Instrumentenmacher Rockobauer in Wien extralange Oboen, herstellte, die er für das Orchester gerne bestellen würde. Siehe Landon II, S.126, Bartha, *Briefe* 6. Bis jetzt fehlte uns jeder Beweis, daß Haydns Bitte erfolgreich war; erst dieses Dokument zeigt uns, daß der Fürst sofort nach Erhalt von Haydns Brief die zwei Oboen in Auftrag geben ließ.

27. Prince Nicolaus orders his Chief Cashier to pay for two new oboes, which Haydn wished to procure for his orchestra

Commission

According to which our Chief Cashier Johann Zoller should pay for two new oboes for our musique, price eight ducats, and to enter the sum on the files. Prespurg [Pressburg] 30th January 1767.

                                                                       Nicolaus Fürst Esterhazy

... I will order payment in Vienna; the 2 oboes he can commission at once and upon displaying this letter to Zoller receive 8 ducats, after which, when the time comes, the required commission can be drawn up. Eszterhaz 5th Dec. 1766.

[Haydn's hand]   Nicolaus Fürst Esterhazy
Above-listed 8 ducats received correctly
Josephus Haydn mpria

Receipt

Pr: two oboes as agreed for four ducats twice makes 8 ducats which I have received from the excellent musician Heyden as Capelmeister correctly
    Correctly paid in cash   Mathias Rockhubauer
                                           Instramentmaker [sic]

Commentary

On 5 Dec. 1766 Haydn wrote a letter to Prince Nicolaus Esterházy requesting *inter alia* oboes of extra length from Mathias Rockobauer in Vienna: Landon, II, p.126, Bartha letter 6. It was always thought that Haydn was not given the oboes, but now, a new series of documents reveals the contrary. On the very day Esterházy received the letter, he authorised the purchase for Haydn's suggested price to Rockobauer of 8 ducats.

28. Faksimile nach einer Photokopie von Haydns Brief vom 17. July 1768 an einen unbenannten Hausoffizier

Kommentar

Für weitere Details see Landon II, S.149; ganzer Text des Briefes siehe *Haydn-Studien* IV, Heft 1 (1976).

28. Facsimilie from a photograph of Haydn's letter of 17 July 1768 to an unknown official

For details see Landon II, S.149. *Haydn-Studien* IV, Heft 1 (1976).

HochEdel gebohren

Insonders Hochgeehrtester Herr!

Vermög Comißion des Fromgisten und Ehrwürdigen Herr Habts ... den Herren Thurn Meister von ... praeceß seinem Sinn gezogen umb 3 Species Ducaten ... Accordiert, so hätte dieser Dienst ... 2 Ducaten ... wenn er nicht ... ... in den nachmittägigen Gottes Dienst bey ... Closter ... zu ... in vermöglich ... ... bestehen bezahlen müste. ... Hierob nembich die Gürst hab ich in den Fürst ... den 26 dies Monaths um 4 uhr nachmittag ... ... meiner Comißion gnad

Anliegen zu haben, um eine Schwägerin und übrige
Freundschaft zu sehn, eine Schwägerin Respect
zu machen, ich soll meiner Schwägerin Respect
zu Zeigen, die Herrn Secretairs und übrigen Herrn
Officiers Empfehlen.

Thomas Vosstellen

Fayerbach, dem 17. ten July
1708.

Fayerbachischer Cramer
Gottfried Hauptmann

29. Ausgaben für Sommerfeste in Eszterháza aus dem Ausgabenbuch des Haushofmeisters

1768. Julius. Monatliche Ausgaben.
Denen extraord. bei dem Anna Fest in Eszterhaz gehabten Köchen. (Aug.5) 2 Köche. Dem Rauchfangkehrer von Güns mit 4 Gesellen abends 16F 30xr zu dem producirten Feuerwerk 'bin berufen worden, als seint hier gewest in 23. Juli 1 Gesell, der 24. detto, 25. detto, 26. vier Geselle[n], 27. zwei, 28. zwei Gesellen, täglich 1[F.] 30[xr], vor 6 Täge 16F. 30xr.'
Den 26. Dem Thurnermeister Plankh in Sopron vor ein Chor Trompeten und Pauken bei dem Feuerwerk.
Dem Maler Wenzl Decorations Mallerey 2F.- (Ohne Beleg)
 Auszug aus den Büchern der General-Cassa.
Feuerwerk in Eszterháza. 1768.
Joh. Jos. Siess 24. [Juli] - Aug. 12. wegen ein gedruckten Bücheln vom Feuerwerk. Anweisung Aug. 11. vor die Druckung der neulichen Feuerwerksbeschreibung.

1768. Oktober. Monatliche Ausgaben.
Schrott: was ich vor dem Zuckerbacher Jos. Ziegegeist an Gipsformen verfertigt habe:

Einen Elefanten per		2	-f.
" Atler (Adler)		2	-
" Elent Thier		1	-
" Affen		1	-
" Mohren		1	-
" Fisch		1	-
	Summa	8f	

okt. 22. ausbezahlt 6f.

Kommentar

Im Juli wurde das Annenfest (26. Juli) und gleichzeitig der Namenstag der Schwägerin des Fürsten gefeiert. Im September kam Erzherzogin Marie Christine mit ihrem Gemahl, dem Herzog Albert von Sachsen-Teschen, nach Eszterháza. Ihnen zu Ehren wurde am 28. September Haydns Oper *Lo speziale* erstmals aufgeführt.

29. Bills for festivities in summer at Eszterháza
Partial translation

July 1768

For the feast of St Anne [26 July] at Esterhaz extraordinary cooks...

The chimney-sweep of Güns with 4 apprentices for the protection of fireworks which occured on 23 July (1 apprentice). 24 (ditto), 25 (ditto), 26 (4 apprentices), 27 (2 app.) 28 (2 app.).

Daily 1f 30xr., for 6 days 16f 30xr.

On the 26th the Thurnermeister Plankh from Sopron [Oedenburg] for a choir of trumpets and timpani during the fireworks.

The painter Wenzel for painting decorations [no receipt attached].

[J. J. Siess's bill of 12 August 1768] for a printed booklet of fireworks [11 Aug. authorization] for the printing of a new description of the fireworks display [Gral-cassa].

Schrott: what I have created for the pastry-cook Jos. Ziegengeist in plaster forms:

an elephant for	2f.
an eagle	2f.
a moose [deer]	1f.
an ape	1f.
a blackamoor	1f.
a fish	1f.
Summa	8f.

paid 6f. 22 Oct. 1768

Commentary

In July St Anne's Day and at the same time the name day of Prince Nicolaus's sister-in-law was celebrated on 26 July. In September Archduchess Marie Christine and her consort, Duke Albert von Sachsen-Teschen, came to Eszterháza. In their honour Haydn's opera *Lo speziale* was first performed on 28 September.

30. Reisekosten für neuengagierte Sänger

Gralcassa, 1768. Rubr. VIII. Nr. 31.

S p e c i f i c a t i o n .

Nachstehendes hab auf allerhöchste Ordre Sr Dhl: Außlegen müssen.

	f:	Xr:
Alß die Singerin Magdalena Spanglerin		
alleinig nach Eisenstadt abgegangen Fuhrlohn	6	-
Mauth und Futterey	2	49
Mittagmahl in Windpässing	2	48
accordirtes Tring-geldt	1	-
Alß ich auf Befehl mit der singerin Francisca		
Ulmanin nach Esterhaz abgegangen Fuhrlohn	6	-
Mauth und Futterey	1	-
Mittagmahl in Windpässing	3	-

accordirtes Trinnkgeld	1	-
Mauth vor dem Wagen zuruckh	-	51
Abendt-mahl in Eisenstadt	1	46
in Eisenstadt Mittagmahl und nachtmahl	5	-
Alß die Singerin nach Esterhaz Beruffen worden daß erstemal Fuhrlohn Biß Eisenstadt	6	
Mauth Futterey Mittagmahl	5	18
	42	32
Latus	42	32
Ein Mittagmahl in Edenburg	4	48
Bey der Retour von Esterhaz zu Edenburg	-	40
Vor Ein Mittagmahl und zwey nachtmahl in Eisenstadt	5	55
In Eisenstadt ein nachtmahl	2	58
In Wienn vor Wägen außgeben	2	-
vor der hinunter Reiß nach Esterhaz 2 Mittagmahl und 1 nachtmahl	6	30
Bey der Zuruckh Kumpft vor ein nachtmahl	1	30
S u m m a	67	51
Christian Specht Suma	66	53

Carlo Friberth [Haydns Schrift]
Obstehende Summa pr 66f 53xr hat Unser Ober-Einnehmer zu zahlen und in Anrechung zu bringen, Eisenstadt den 27ten 8bris [1]768
                                          Nicolaus Fürst Esterhazy
Obstehende 66f 53Xr seyndt uns richtig bezahlet worden
                                               Carl Friberth
                                             Christian Specht

Kommentar

Am 28. September 1768 wurde das neue Theater in Eszterháza mit Haydns Oper *Lo speziale* eröffnet, in der die zehn Tage vorher engagierte Sängerin Magdalena Spangler die Rolle der 'Grilletta' sang. Die Altistin Franziska Ullman wurde zur gleichen Zeit für den Eisenstädter Kirchenchor engagiert, wie auch der Baßsänger Christian Specht, der bei der Operntruppe und auch bei Kammermusiken verwendet wurde.

30. Travelling expenses for newly engaged singers
Specification
The list below concerns sums for matters ordered by His Highness and advanced by me:

	f	xr
When the singer Magdalena Spangler had to leave alone to Eisenstadt; travel costs	6	-
Customs and fodder	2	49
Lunch in Windpässing [Wimpassing]	2	48
Tip, as agreed	1	-
Where on order I went with the singer Francisca Ulmanin to Esterhaz; travel costs	6	-
Customs and fodder	1	-
Lunch in Windpässing	3	-
Tip, as agreed	1	-
Customs for waggon's return journey	-	51
Dinner in Eisenstadt	1	46
In Eisenstadt lunch and dinner	5	-
When the lady singer was called to Esterhaz the first time, travel costs to Eisenstadt	6	-
Customs, fodder, lunch	5	18
	42	32
carried over	42	32
A lunch in Edenburg [Oedenburg]	4	48
Return from Esterhaz to Edenburg	-	40
For a lunch and two dinners in Eisenstadt	5	55
In Eisenstadt a dinner	2	58
In Vienna, money for carriages	2	-
For the trip down to Esterhaz 2 lunches and 1 dinner	6	30
On the return journey for a dinner	1	30
Summa	67	51
Summa	66	53
	[corrected total]	

Christian Specht
[Haydn's hand:]
Carlo Friberth

Above-listed sum of 66f. 53xr. is to be paid by chief Cashier and entered in the books, Eisenstadt the 27th Oct. 1768

Nicolaus Fürst Esterházy

Above listed 66f. 53xr. are paid correctly and in full
Carl Friberth
Christian Specht

Commentary

Probably last-minute alterations for the festivities at Eszterháza in October 1768 when the new theatre had opened with Haydn's *Lo Speziale* on 28 September 1768, with Magdalena Spangler, who had just ten days before been engaged by the Prince. Francisca

Ullmann, alto, was also engaged at this time, as was Christian Specht, bass singer. Ullmann was to sing in the Eisenstadt choir, Specht in the chamber and opera ensemble.

31. Aus dem Eisenstädter Rentamts-Rechnungen für 1769

Nr. 128. Lit. C

Herr Rentmeister wird dreyen Kleinhöffleiner bauren, welche mit drey gedeckten wagen 12 Musici nach Esterhaz gefihret haben, das accordirte Fuhrlohn mit 13f: bezahlen. Schloß Eusenstadt den 18: Febr. [1]769.
            Edmund Schlanstein Verw.
Daß diese 13 f aus dem Räntamt bezahlt worden, quittire.
Eisenstadt, den 22ten Febr. [1]769
       Andre Kleinrat

Nr. 128. Lit. J

Der Joseph Gabriel hat den Musicum Früebert und seine Frau auff Esterhaz geführet, und ist derenselben 4f. accordiret worden, weillen aber H. Frübert zu denen anderen Musicis sich hätte zu setzen sollen, da Er aber mit seiner Frau des anderten tags alleine gefahren, so wird Hr Rentmeister diesem Fuhrmann nur 2f: bezahlen, die anderen 2f: aber wird Hr Frübert selbsten zu zahlen haben. Schloß Eisenstadt den 1: May [1]769.
            Edmund Schlanstein Verw.

Nr. 128. Lit. K

Hr Rentmeister wird dem Pollauf wegen deme: daß derselbe den H. Capelmeister und noch 3 Musicos auf Esterhaz ge-führet hat an fuhr lohn 4 f. bezahlen. Schloß Eusenstadt den 1 May [1]769.
            Edmund Schlanstein Verw.

Nr. 128. Lit. M

Herr Rentmeister wird dem land Kutscher Glaßer wegen deme daß Er auff hochen Befehl Sr hochfürstlen Durchl. die Singerin Tüchtlerinn auff Esterhaz geführet hat, accordirter massen für das Fuhrlohn bezahlen.
4f: 12x. Schloß Eisenstadt den 20: May [1]769.
            Edmund Schlanstein Verw.

Nr. 128. Lit. O

Herr Rentmeister wird dem Landkutscher Pollauf wegen deme, daß derselbe dem Fürstl: Musicum Hr Diechtler, seine Frau, und dem Dapacirer [*sic*] nach Eszterhaz geführet, 4f: Fuhrlohn bezallen. Schloß Eisenstadt den 5tn Juny [1]769.

Edmund Schlanstein Verw.

Kommentar

Ende Januar war Güterdirektor Rahier zu Ohren gekommen, daß Frieberth seine Kollegin Magdalena Spangler heiraten wollte und dies ohne die Erlaubnis des Fürsten. Die Heirat sollte außerhalb Eisenstadts, in Weigelsdorf, stattfinden. Rahier wollte die beiden sofort entlassen und es bedurfte Haydns diplomatischen Geschicks seine beiden Sänger in der Opertruppe zu halten und des Fürsten Vergebung für Frieberths Eigenmächtigkeit zu erreichen.

31. Bills of the Rentamt in Eisenstadt for 1769.

Herr Rent-Master will pay the agreed carriage charges to three Kleinhöffein peasants who with three covered wagons transported 12 musicians to Esterhaz.
Schloß Eisenstadt, 18 Feb. 1769

Edmund Schlanstein
Administrator

I acknowledge receipt of these 13f from the Rental Office
Eisenstadt, 22 Feb. 1763

Andre Kleinrat;

Joseph Gabriel drove the musician Früebert [Friberth] and his wife to Esterhaz for which it was agreed to pay him 4f., but since H. Frübert was supposed to be seated with the other musicians whereas in fact he and his wife went alone the next day, Hr Rent-Master will pay only 2f: to this driver, the other 2f. will be paid by Hr Fribert himself. Schloß Eisenstadt, 1 May 1769

Edmund Schlanstein
Administrator

Hr. Rent-Master will pay driver's fee of 4f. to Pollauf who drove H. Capelmeister [sic] and 3 other musicians to Esterhaz. Schloß Eusenstadt [sic], 1 May 1769

Edmund Schlanstein
Administrator

Herr Rent-Master will pay to the agreed the driver's fee of 4f. 12x. to the land-driver Glaßer for having driven the lady singer Tüchler [Dichtler] to Esterhaz. Schloß Eisenstadt 20 May 1769

Edmund Schlanstein
Administrator

Herr Rent-Master will pay to the land-driver Pollauf the sum of 4f. driver's fee for having driven the princely musician H. Diechtler, his wife, and upholsterer to Esterhaz.
Schloß Eisenstadt, 5 June 1769

Edmund Schlanstein
Administrator

Commentary

Regent Rahier heard at the end of January that Frieberth wanted to marry his colleague Magdalena Spangler without the permission of the Prince; therefore the marriage was planned to take place in the village of Weigelsdorf, far away from Eisenstadt. Rahier wanted to dismiss both for their breach of discipline and it took all of Haydn's diplomatic skill with the Prince to retain the two singers.

32. Auszüge aus den Rechnungsbüchern der Baucasse für 1769

Baucassa-Rechnungen, 1769. Nr. 34.

             f   Xr.

Im Berechnungs-Buch: Nr. 34. Dem
  Kaufmann von Oedenburg
vor Blumen, welche zur Opera gebraucht worden   3   50

Dokument:

         den 23. aug. Ao. 1769 in Wienn.
vor die Cometianten nach Esterhass ist verabfolgt worden
  1 grosses Pouquet Blumen   f. 1 42 x
  2 Kleinere detto   2 16
            ―――――
            f. 3 58

Ao: 1769 den 30n 8bris
durch Hrn Michael Kleinrath
Inspecteur, zur Höfl: Dankh
Richtig Bezalt worden, mit
3f: 50x

Baucassa-Rechnungen, 1769. Nr. 35.

             f   Xr.

Im Berechnungs-Buch: Nr.35.
  Dem Galanterie handler Gruber
vor falsche Haar Nadeln zur Opera   3   12

Dokument:
Herr Cleerat Inspeckder bey Tietl. First Esterhasy beliebet zu geben nur empfang

6 Stock Har Nahl vom stein eine	a 15x	1f	30
deto 6 Stock	a 12x	1f	12
deto 6 Stock	a 5x	-	30

          Sama 3f 12x

Wien den 14 Saul (!) [1]769
       Joh Mihel Rueber
ist dur (!) Clerat Inspektor
Richtig bezalt den 30 Oct. [1]769

    Baucassa-Rechnungen, 1769. Nov. Nr. 1.

Im Rechnungs-Buch: Nr. 1. Dem Buchhandler vor Meßbücher nach Eszterház 9f 59Xr.
Dokument:
        Wienn den 21t Octbr 1769.
Bey Joh.Thomas Edlen v. Trattnern, K. K. Hofbuchdrucker und Buchhändler, auf dem Kohlmarkt im Grosserischen Hause

	f	Xr
1 Missale Romanum cum proprio Hungariae, et Missae defunctorum	6	-
vor das Missale und Missae defunctorum einzubinden	3	59
Summa	9	59

  Pr: K. K. Hofbuchhandlung Joann Thomas Edl v. Trattnern

    Baucassa-Rechnungen, 1769. Nov. Nr. 10.

Im Berechnungs-Buch: Nr. 10. Dem Lautenmacher Stadlmann vor öftere Veränderung und Besaitung des Fürstens Durchl. Pariton   f 20-

Dokument:

		f	xr
	Was vor Ihro Hochfürstliche Durchlaucht Fürst von Esterhazy		
d: 23.Juni.	In Lauten macher Arbeit gelifferet worden Ein Pariton oben unt unten ney besait	2	23
d:27.July.	Ein Pariton Oben auf 7 und unten auf 10 Saiten gericht, ein neyes baul oben gemacht die Saiten anderst ausgetheilet, den Hals weider hinaufgestehen 3 neye		

Item	Schrauffen, etliche briche geleimt 3 neye Pas unten aufgezogen den stäch briche mit Ebenholz umleget	6	30
	Ein ibersponene weitleischig auf die Gampa	-	10
d:21.Nov.	Ein Pariton unten und Oben ney besait stärker ein neye auflache gemacht den stähe breter mit Ebenholz unterlegt, und durchaus weiter ausgetheilet die Briche geleimt, und ein bakl[1] geleimt	6	30
	Ein Pasetl ney besait den Griff abgericht, und geleimt	1	30
Item	Ein Langen Indianischen geschrauften Gampa bogen mit goldenen und Seitenen schnirl umgewiklet	4	30
Item	Ein schwöheres Pariton C:	-	24
	Summa	22	7

Joann Joseph Stadlmann
Kayl. Könil. Hofflauten macher

Daß durch den Herrn Inspektor Michael Gleinrath Richtig ist bezalt worden mit zwantzig Gulten dto 29 Novem. 1769 Johann Joseph Statlman

Kommentar

Zur Aufführung der Oper *La contadina in corte (La contadina ingentilita)* im Sommer 1769, deren Komponist nicht zu eruieren ist, wurden Haarnadeln und Blumen gebraucht.

32. Various items from the books of the Baucassa for the year 1769

In expenses book No; 34: The merchant from Oedenburg for flowers

	f	xr
which were needed for the opera	3	50

Document;

23 Aug. Ao. 1769 in Vienna

---

[1] In einem anderen Dokument 'Päkln', wahrscheinlich Sattel für die Saiten unter dem Griffbrett, die gezupft werden. *Haydn-Studien* IV (1980), S. 286

The following were sent to Esterhass
                              for the actresses [singers]
    1 large bouquet of flowers   1   42
    2 smaller ones ditto   2   16
                                                                                         3f   58
                                  Ignati Jos.Sigmund

Ao: 1769 the 30th Oct.
Paid and received with
grateful thanks through
H. Michael Kleinrath
Inspecteur, the sum of
3f. 50x [sic]

In expenses book No. 35 the Galanterie seller Gruber   f   xr
    false hairpins for opera   3   12
Document:
    Herr Clerat Inspector at Prince Esterhazy
        is requested to settle below account
    6 boxes hairpins of false gems each a 15x   1   30
    ditto 6 a 12x   1   12
    ditto 6 a 5x   -   30

Vienna 14 Saul [sic] 1769   Summa   3f   12x.
                                     Joh.Michel Roeber
Has been paid in full through
Clerat Inspector 30 Oct. 1769

Document: In accounts book No. 1: Bookseller for mass books sent to Eszterház 9f 59xr.

                                                                                 Vienna, 21 Oct. 1769
At Joh. Thomas Edler v. Trattern, I.R. Count printer and bookseller on the Coal Market in the Grosser House.
                                                                                   f   xr
1.   Missale Romanum cum proprio
        Hungariae et Missae defunctorum   6   -
        for binding the Missale and
        missae defunctorum   3   59

                                                                     Summa   9   59
                                                       Pr: I. R. Court bookseller
                                                       Joan Thomas Edl v. Trattern

In account book No. 10: Lute-maker Stadlmann for frequent alterations
    to and stringing of the princely baryton   f   20   -
Document : For Prince von Esterhazy for lute-maker
    work delivered
23 June a baryton newly stringed above and below   2   23
27 July a baryton, repairs to 7 strings above and 10 below,
    a new scroll on top constructed the strings laid
    differently, to the neck 3 pegs attached, several cracks

88

	repaired, 3 new bass strings on the bottom attached and the fret changed to ebony wood	6	30
Item	on overspun long string for the gamba	-	10
	21 Nov., a baryton strung more strongly on the top and bottom, a new tail piece prepared and the fret made wider with ebony wood and altogether widened, the cracks repaired and a corner block [2] glued	6	30
	A cello newly strung, the neck repaired and glued	1	30
Item	A long Indian turned gamba bow wound with gold and silk thread	4	30
Item	A heavy Baryton C: [string]	-	24
	Summa	22	7

Johann Joseph Stadlmann
I. R. Court Lute-maker

which has been correctly paid through
Herr Inspecktor Michael Gleinrath
[Kleinrath] with twenty gulden [sic] 29 Nov. 1769   Johann Joseph Stadlman [sic]

Commentary
The ladies were offered flowers and ornamental hairpins for their performances in *La cantadina in corte* (*La contadina ingentilita*), composer unknown, in the summer of 1769 at Eszterháza.

33. Abrechnung des Ing. Jacoby für den Ball und die Festlichkeiten im August 1769

Baucassa-Rechnungen 1770. Febr. Nr. 24.

Ausgaaben von dem 1769igstes Jahr wie folgt

Erstens dem Traxler meister v S. Nicolas [unweit Eszterháza]
Welcher von dorthen weck gezogen vor 22 stuck
carterollen zu denen Scenes in daß Comoedie=hauß
a 9 x stuck macht   3f 18
vor die Extra stunden deren arbeither den oval platz zu
Illuminiren und auszulöschen und abnehmen   4 -
In dem Comoedie hauß bey zwey ball die henck leuchter
wie die andere Illumination zu bewachten   2 36

               S u m m a   9f 54x

---

[2] Or (in another document) Päkln, probably supported the plucked string below the finger-board. *Haydn-Studien* IV (1980), p.286.

Die Summa von Neun Gulden 54 xr seindt mir richtig Durch Herren Kleinrath Inspector bezahlt worden

Eszterhaz den 9ten mertz 1770
Jacoby
Ingenieur

33. Bill for the ball and festivity in August 1769

Expenses for the year 1769 as follows:
First the Master-Turner of Saint Nicolaus [near Eszterháza] who moved from there, 22 rolls of cardboard for the scenes in the opera house a 9xr each 3f. 18xr. For extra hours of the workers for lighting and extinguishing the illuminations in the oval square [before the castle] 4f. In the opera house during two balls [24 August and autumn].

34. Aus dem Rechnungsbuch des Haushofmeisters August und September 1769

Rechnungen für den Ball in Eszterháza am 24. August :

Conto

Über die gegen denen Billietten ausgefolgten Masquera alß: 87. St: Billietter à 1f	87f	-X
Dann auf Anschaffung Sr Hochfürstl D: dem Satl-Knecht 1. paar Handsschuch 1. Larven	1	8
Dann gegen 1. Billiet sind erfolgt worden 2. Domino Larven mit Barth	1	8
mehr dem H: Capell Meister abermahl erfolgt worden zur Opera gehörige 2. Dom: Larven	1	42
abermahl durch einen Fürstl: Lauffer gehollet worden 2. Larven mit Barth	1	42

Summa 93f 40X

mit 92f Richti[g] bezahlt worden von H: Hoffmeister

Mathias Fischer
Burgl Stadt Tandler
in Wienn

Vor die Comödianten Nachstehendes.
16 paa[r] Handschuch a 34Xr macht   9f   4
14 larfen anche [*sic*] bartt a 34Xr   7   56
2 dto mit bartt a 51Xr   1   42
Haa[r] - und Huet Maschen a   1   25

                        Suma   20   7
mit 18f Richti[g] bezahlt worden   Mathias Fischer
von H Hoffmeister   Burgl Statt Tandler

Monatliche Ausgaben. September:
17. und 18. 2 Extra Koch von Sopron.
Frantz Wrabetz, Maler 30 Tage Dekorationsarbeit in der Zuckerbäckerei 37f 30xr
Joh. Leop. Planckh Oedenburger Turnermeister 88,- wegen in Eszterhaza verrichtete Ballmusic, als den 24. Aug. mit 16 Personen 40f, Sept. 17. eben vor 16 Personen 48f -xr
Fischer Math. Stadttandler, Liste:
Gr. Windischgrätz 1 p. Handschuh
Vor den Hn Kammerdiener v. Holländischen Gesandten Larven u. Handschuh
Vor die Kammerjungfrau u. Stubenmädl bei der gfin Weissenwolf 2 Larfen u. Handschuhe
Kammerdiener Mor. u. gfin v. Windischgrätz Larfen u. Handschuh
Kammerdiener des Gf. Nik. Esterházy, die Kammerjungfer von detto Larfen u. Handschuh
Kammerjungfer von Holl. Gesandten.

Kommentar

Im August besuchten Erzherzogin Marie Christine und ihr Gemahl Herzog Albert von Sachsen-Teschen Eszterháza. Ihnen zu Ehren wurde ein großer Ball veranstaltet. Weitere Details siehe *Haydn-Studien* IV, S.289 und Landon I, S.653f.

34. Bills the Major Domo paid for the ball at Eszterháza on August 24 1769
(Summary and/or partial translation)

Aug. 24: Mathias Fischer town haberdasher in Vienna concerning the Masquera [ball] and the tickets issued for it.
87 tickets a 1f   87f.   -
On orders of H. H. the saddle-groom 1 pair of gloves, 1 mask   1f   8xr

Then against one ticket were issued 2 Domino masks with beard		1	8
More, H. Capell Meister once again issued for the opera 2 Domino masks		1	42
Again issued to princely footman 2 costumes with masks		1	42
	Summa	93f	40xr

Correctly paid 92f by H. Hoffmeister [court major-domo]

For the comedians following 16 pairs of gloves a 34xr makes		9f	4xr
14 masks without [?] beards a 34xr		7	56
2 ditto with beards a 51xr		1	42
Hair and hat ribbons at		1	25
	Summa	20f	7xr

Correctly paid 18f. by H. Hoffmeister [court major-domo]

1769 Monthly expenses.
17, 18 Sept. 2 extra cooks from Sopron
Frantz Wrabetz painter 30 days decoration work at the patisserie 37f. 30xr.
Joh. Leop. Planckh 88f. to the *Thurnermeister* in Oedenburg who played the dance music for the masked ball at Esterháza. 'For the ball music on 24 August, performed with 16 musicians 40f. and 17. Sept. also with 16 musicians 48f.' [bill 17 Sept. 1769]
Mathias Fischer's (haberdasher) list:
Count Windischgrätz 1 pair gloves
Spanish Ambassador, valet-de-chambre masks and gloves
for the valet-de-chambre of the Dutch Ambassador, mask and gloves
For the gentle-woman and the chambermaid of Countess Weissenwolf, 2 masks and gloves
Valet-de-chambre Mor and Countess Windischgrätz, masks and gloves
Valet-de-chambre of Count Nicolaus Esterhazy, the gentle-woman of the same, masks and gloves
Gentle-woman of the Dutch Ambassador, [ditto].

Commentary

Archduchess Marie Christine and her consort Duke Albert Sachsen-Teschen visited Eszterháza in August and for their entertainment a masked ball was given. *Haydn-Studien* IV, p.289. For the period of summer and autumn 1769, festivities at Esterháza, see also Landon, I, 653f.

35. Esterházaer Baukosten von 1. Oktober bis Ende Dezember 1769. Schloßinspektor Kleinrath beanstandet die Kosten der eisernen Kassa

Baucassa-Rechnungen, 1769.
Observationes über des Herrn Michael Kleinrath Schloß Inspectors geführte Eszterházer Bau-Rechnung von 1. Okt. bis lezten Xbris 1769.
Bey dieser eisernen Cassae trugen, haben gantz sicher ihre drey, nemlich erstens der Schloßer, zweytens der Mahler, und drittens der Kaufmann jeder seinen Profit gesuchet, wurde also beßer gewesen

seyn mit beeden erstern ihre Arbeit wegen zu accordiren, so hätte wenigstens des Dritten sein Profit darbey ersparet werden können.

Replique: Ohne Profit arbeith niemand in der Welt, und wann man auch accordiret hätte, so wurde keine von diesen dreyen seinen Profit zuruck gelassen haben. Übrigens wird eine Hochftl. Buchhalterey nicht wissen, das derley Gattungen Truchen, aus dem Magazin oder Niederlaag nach dem Gewicht wie dem Becker eine Kreutzer Semmel erkauft, und mithin nicht angefriemet [bestellt] werden.

Kommentar

Unter Fürst Nicolaus und dem Güterregenten Rahier wurde das Esterházysche Vermögen ausgezeichnet verwaltet und die Kosten für Bauten und Theater niedrig gehalten.

35. Eszterháza building costs from 1st October till the end of 1769. Observations about the costs of an iron strong box by Michael Kleinrath, Castle Inspector.

Observations about the costs of an iron safe [cassa] as prepared by Herr Michael Kleinrath, Castle Inspector, from 1 Oct. to end Dec. 1769.

In this account, quite obviously three persons - first the locksmith, secondly the painter and thirdly the merchant - each sought to make a profit; hence it would have been better if one had made prior agreements for their work, with the first two, thus avoiding the profit of the third party.

Replique: No one in this world works without profit and even if we had made agreements beforehand, none would have avoided making a profit. Moreover, a princely bookkeeper can not know that such a kind of strong-box is bought from the shop or warehouse according to weight in the way that a baker sells his Kreutzer buns, and hence does not need to be specially ordered.

Commentary

The Esterházy administration always sought to preserve a certain economy in their enormous expenses - often with considerable success.

36. Aus dem Ausgabenbuch des Haushofmeisters 1770

1770. Junius, monatliche Ausgaben

20ten. Nota für 3 wellische Singer u. Singerinnen.
    Vor das Essen. 1f 56xr, Wein 56xr., Käse 2f 34xr
    Zimmer 2f Summa 7f 26xr
        Martin Leopold
        Würth in Esterhaz

Kommentar

Es handelt sich hier wahrscheinlich um Gertruda Cellini und Giacomo Lambertini, die im August, beziehungsweise September 1769 engagiert worden waren; wer die dritte Person war, wissen wir nicht. Sie könnten zur Probe für Haydns Oper *Le pescatrici* in Eszterháza gewesen sein.

36. Monthly expenses from the hand book of the Major Domo 1770

June 1770
    20th. Nota for 3 Italian lady and gentleman singers.
For the food 1f. 56xr., wine 56xr., cheese 2F. 34xr. Room 2f.- Summa 7f. 26xr.

Martin Leopold
Innkeeper at Esterhaz

Commentary

Probably Gertruda Cellini (engaged Aug. 1769), Giacomo Lambertini (engaged Sept. 1769) and an unidentified third person - rehearsals for *Le pescatrici*?

37. Ausgaben für die Festlichkeit in Kittsee im Juli 1770

Auszug aus den Ausgabenbuch des Haushofmeisters:
1770, Monatliche Ausgaben. Festin Kittsee.
Juli 22. Springer, Mahler u. Francoise Koch von Wien nach Kittsee.
Jul. 25. Kittseer Schutzjud Bänder für das Ballhaus.
Für den Rauchfangkehrer einen Gehilfen zu Beachtung des Feuers Juli 19-20, zwei Tag mit 1 Gesell, 21-24. mit zwei Gesellen.
Dem Turnermeister für Musik mit 20 Personen a 3f, 'meine Person doppelt macht 63f', Vor 1 Chor Trompeten u. Pauken 4 f. Math. Otzlsberger Stadtturnermeister.
Specification deren frembden Bedienten, welche beim Fest den 25. Juli die fürstl. Galalivré angezogen u. bedient haben a 1 f :1 Laufer von Br. Sischan, 1 detto von Gr. Grassalkovics, 4 Bediente von detto, 2 von Gfin Antoni Esterhazy, 3 von jungen Gr. Balassa, 2 Gr. Jos. Erdödy, 2 Gr. Jos. Csáky, 3 Gr. Apponyi, 1 Gfin Stahrenberg, 1 Gr. Aspremont, 4 Gf. Sützy 2 gr Szunyogh, 2 gr Illésházy, 1 grin Thun, 2 Gfin Starey, 1 Elexandr. Erdödy, 1 G[ene]ral Casrola, 2 Prinz Nassau, 2 Gr.Weissenwolf. summa 39f.
Denen Bedienten von Kay. Hof: Bei dem Kayser u. Kayserin 2-2 Leiblaquein, detto 2 beim Erzhg Ferdinand Maximilian, Bei Großherzog u. Grhgin 4.- Bei Princess Charlott 2, Printz Karl 2 -

Bei Ihro königl. Hochheit Herzog Albert, den 25 Juli in Kittsee 4 Leiblaqueien, 9 Postillions

Kommentar

Am 25. Juli kam der kaiserliche Hof zu Besuch nach Kittsee. Joseph II, Maria Theresia, Leopold von Toskana mit seiner Gemahlin, die Erzherzöge Ferdinand und Maximilian, sowie die Prinzessin Charlotte von Lothringen, und ihr Bruder Herzog Carl von Lothringen. 200 Mann fürstliche Garde, 56 Diener in Galalivrée, 24 Hausoffiziere in hechtgrauer Uniform und das ganze Musikkorps (36 Musiker), ebenfalls in Hechtgrau, standen an beiden Seiten des Ehrenhofes und an den Seiten der grossen Freitreppe die hohen Herrschaften zu begrüssen.

37. Extracts from the account book of the Major Domo.

1770 Monthly expenses, fête in Kittsee.
22 July Springer, Mahler and Françoise Koch from Vienna to Kittsee. 25 July the protected Jew from Kittsee, ribbons for the ball room.
For the chimney sweep and one assistant to watch the fire 19/20 July, 2 days with one apprentice, 21/24 with two apprentices.
The *Turnenmeister* with 20 musicians for music a 3f., 'my person double fee' is 63f. For 1 choir of trumpets and timpani 4f. Math. Otzlsberger Town *Thurnermeister*.

Specification

concerning foreign [i.e. not family] servants who on 25 July wore the princely gala livrée and served a 1f. - 1 runner-footman from Baron Sischan, 1 ditto Count Grassalkovics, 4 servants of the same, 2 from Countess Antoni Esterhazy, 3 from the young Count Balassa, 2 Count Joseph Erdödy, 2 Count Joseph Csáky, 3 Count Apponyi, 1 Countess Stahrenberg, 1 Count Aspremont, 4 Count Sûtzy [Zichy], 2 Count Szunyogh, 2 Count Illésházy, 1 Countess Thun, 2 Countess Starey, 1 Alexander Erdödy, 1 gral [sic] Casrola, 2 Prince Nassau, 2 Count Weissenwolf. Summa 39f.
The servants from the Imperial Court - Emperor and Empress 2 each - 2 body-lackeys, 2 ditto Archduke Ferdinand Maximilian, for Grand Duke and Grand Duchess 4, for Princess Charlott[e] 2, Prince Karl 2.
For H. R. H. Duke Albert [von Sachsen-Teschen] on 25 July in Kittsee, 4 body lackeys, 9 postillions.

Commentary

One can see that the Kittsee festivities were among the largest ever mounted by Prince Nicolaus, involving 55 'foreign' servants. 200 men from the princely guard, 56 servants in gala livrée, 24 house officers in silver grey uniform and the whole music corps were ranged in the court yard and on the stairs. On 25 July the Imperial Court arrived at Kittsee - Joseph II, Maria Theresia, Leopold of Tuscany and his consort, Archduchess Ferdinand and Maximillian, Princess Charlotte of Lorraine and her brother, Charles.

38. Ausgaben anläßlich der Hochzeit der Gräfin Lamberg, einer Nichte des Fürsten, mit Grafen Pocci im September 1770

Baucassa-Rechnungen 1770. August Nr. 19.

Bey Aufbrechung des Tüppelbodens in der alten Stallung ....
Item die extrastunden bey denen Comaedien
1770 aug. 5-18. 15 Zimmermanstagwerke
extrastunden aug

5.	28
6.	28
7.	7
8.	18
9.	6
10.	8
11.	21
12.	10
13.	7
14.	-
16-8	-

Baucassa-Rechnungen 1770. September Nr.12.

Extrastunden bey die Comaedien

sept.	30.	7
	31.	6
sept.	1.	18

Baucassa-Rechnungen 1770. September Nr.30.

S p e c i f i c a t i o n

Deren Tagwercken, welche bey der Machin von der Illumin-ation deren Grenaden von denen Grenadiern in Esterhaz seyn verricht worden als

Sept.	Tagwerck	f:	Xr
den 13. Erstl: Tagwerck	12	3	-
14. Mehr deto	10	2	30
15. Abermahlen deto	22	5	30
16. Item deto	13	3	15
17. Dann deto	6	1	30
S u m m a	63	15	45

Nicolaus Fürst Esterhazy

Sig Esterhaz den 19tn Septem. [1]770.
Obige zehen fünf gulden 45 Xr sind durch Herrn Schlößer Inspector
Michael Kleinrath Richtig bezahlet worden; wird hiemit bescheinet.
Eszterház den 19n 7bris [1]770.
    Id est 15f 45Xr   Joh: Hammer
                                      Fourier.

        Baucassa-Rechnungen 1770. September Nr.31.

   C o n s i g n a t i o n
Deren Tagwercken, welche durch die Grenadiers von 16tn bis 18tn 7b:
[1] 770. bey den Theatro und Feüerwerck verricht worden: als
    Erstl: seind Tagwerck beschehn   13.
    Item extra stunden   18.
Jedes Tagwerck à 15xr
Jede extra stund à 1 1/2 xr betragen   [Summa:] 3f: 42x
        Anton Kühnel
Obige drey gulden 42 xr seynd durch Hn Schlößer Bausch. Inspector
Michael Kleinrath Richtig bezahlet worden; wird hiemit bescheinet.
Eszterház den 19n 7bris [1]770
    Id est 3 f 42 xr   Caspar Marmor
                                Granatir

        Baucassa-Rechnungen 1770. September Nr.34.

Daß dem Jacob Doll schneider Gesell vom 8ten 7bris bis 16ten
Inclusive an den Scenen der Neuen Opera gearbeithet hat und ihme
täglich Neun Groschen des Täg verwilliget vor acht Täg ihme bezahlt
kan werden
[3f 36xr. 9 Groschen = 27xr] atestire
        Esterhaz den 20ten 7bris 1770
            Jacoby
            Ingenieur

Kommentar

Zur Feier der Hochzeit wurde Haydns neue Oper *Le pescatrici*
aufgeführt.

38. Bills paid for the festivities during the marriage of Countess Lamberg, a niece of the Prince, to Count Pocci.
Festivities at Eszterháza Castle, September 1770
Partial translations;
Grenadiers daily services 13-17 Sept. : 12, 10, 22, 13,
6 days' work a 15xr 63 days work 15f 45xr.
Consignation of daily services performed by the grenadiers from 16 through 18 Sept. at the theatre and fireworks, viz:

First the days' work: 13
Item extra hours: 18
Every days' work a 15xr
Every extra hour at 1 1/2xr.   Total 3f 42xr.
Anton Kühnel

[Ingenier Jacoby's bill] Tailor apprentice Jacob Doll worked from 8th to 16th incl. for scenes for the new opera, for an agreed fee of nine groschen per diem, eight days work paid to him, attested: Esterhas. 20 Sept. 1770 Jacoby Ing. 3f. 36xr. [9gr. = 27xr.]

Commentary

Haydn's new opera was *Le pescatrici*, part of the festivities in honour of the gala marriage between Countess Lamberg, Prince Nicolaus Esterházy's niece, and Count Pocci.

39. Vertrag mit den Wiener Theatermalern Herling, Goldman und Spiegel, Kulissen für das Eszterházaer Opernhaus zu malen

Baucassa-Rechnungen 1770. September Nr. 29.

A c c o r d.

Es verobligiren sich die 3 Herrn Mahler als Carl Herling, Jacob Goldman, und Johann Spiegl nach dem Fürst Esterhasischen Schlos Esterhas in Ungarn abzugehen, um aldorten die benöthigte Theatral arbeith zu verfertigen, und wie gewöhnlich um 7 uhr frühe zur arbeith zu gehen bis 12. uhr Mittag, den von 2 uhr bis widerum 6 uhr abends, und den Tag fleissig zu seyn! Vorgegen dan in Nahmen Sr Durchlaucht verspreche ein Jeden und zwar von dem Tag ihrer Abreise bis zur widerkunft inclusive, mit inbegrif das sich Selbe selbst verkösten müessen Drey Gulden bezahlen zu lassen. Dan werden obige Herrn Mahler mit Hochfürstl: Gelegenheit hin und wider Transportiret, und denen selben in Esterhas Zimmer und licht gegeben werden! Beschlossen Wien d: 8ten 7br: 1770.
Michael Kleinrath Inspector.

C o n s i g n a t i o n
Deren Tagwercken, welche durch die Theatral Mahler Bey Verfertigung deren neüen Scaenen, und verschiedenen andern stucken zur neüen Opera in Esterhaz, seind verricht worden:

                                          Tagw: f:
Erstl: seind vermög schriftl: accord von
Tag ihrer Abreiss von Wien, Jedes Tagwerck
pr: 3f zu zahlen Contrahiret worden, mithin
von 8tn bis 17tn 7b:[1]770. seind Tagwerck
beschehen, samt einigen Nächten

Mahler Herrling hat   17
      Goldman   17
      Spiegl   17
      Unterttal   13 1/2
      Mörck   13 1/2
                                          ─────────
                       S u m m a   78:   234
                       Anton Kühnel
                       Bausch [reiber]:
Obaufgesezte zwey hundert vier und dreyssig gulden seynd durch
herrn Schlösser Inspector Michael Kleinrath Richtig bezahlet worden;
bescheinen hiemit. Schlos Eszterház den 1ten 7b: 1770
         Id est: 234f - Xr: Carl Herling in Nahmen
                                        aller übrigen

              Baucassa-Rechnungen 1770. September Nr. 32.

Denen Theatral=Mahlern seind zum Farben Reiben folgende
Taglöhner geholfen worden:
      in 7b: [1]770. den 10. 11. 12. 13. 14. 15. 16.
Anna Bauerin   1   1   1   1   1   1   -
Theresia Mayrin   1   1   1   1   1   1   -
grenadir   2   2   2   2   2   2   2
                         ─────────────────────────────────
              facit   4   4   4   4   4   4   2
Summa 26 Tagwerck à 15xr betr.   6f: 30xr
N: diese Tagwerck seind den Mahler Conto beyzulegen.
              Anton Kühnel
              Bauschr:

39. Contract with the Vienna painters Herling, Goldman and Spiegel to paint scenery in Eszterháza opera house
Summary translation
Accord

Three painters to leave for the Esterházy Castle, Esterhas in Hungary, to work in the theatre there, beginning as usual at 7 a.m. to 12 noon and then from 2 o'clock p.m. to 6 p.m. Their transport and lodgings/board and light to be at princely expense. Vienna 8 Sept. 1770.
Michael Kleinrath
Inspector

Consignation
Daily work at opera house, Esterhaz...

Above mentioned two hundred four and thirty gulden have been paid correctly and in full..
Carl Herling in the name
of the others.

40. Ausgaben des Haushofmeisters anlässlich der Hochzeitsfeiern

1770. September, monatliche Ausgaben.
Math. Fischer, Tandler, am 17. nach Eszterház geliefert: 106 verschiedene Masken a 1.-
Plank, Turnermeister und Personal, 17. und 18. Ballmusik u. 1 Chor Trompeten u. Pauken beim Feuerwerk 48f.
Lorenz, Rauchfangkehrer 16., 17., u. 18. zum Feuerwerk.

40. Expenses paid by the Major Domo for the marriage
Mathias Fischer delivered 106 various masks to Eszterháza at 1f. each. Bill 17 Sept. 1770. Plank, *Thurnermeister* and assistants, 17/18 music for ball, choir trumpets and timpani for fireworks 48f. Lorenz, chimney sweep for fireworks on 16, 17 and 18 [Sept.].

41. Rechnung des Tischlers Haunold für Arbeiten für die Oper *Le pescatrici*

1771. Haunold.   Eisenstädter Bau-Cassa

Jan. 10. In die neu gemachte Zimmer einen Uhrkasten von Lindenholz, geschweift u. zum Bildhauer gericht 25f.
Zur Illumination 200st Latten geschnitten, solche alle gespitzt, oben Bretl darauf gemacht, alle die Drat einschraufen geholfen die Gläser eingehenckt u. anzünden geholfen zusammen 24 Tag a 1f.
Im Komödiehaus zur neuen Opera verschiedene Arbeit gemacht, 16 Tallarwägen, 4 Wafen Canape, auch ein Schif mit einer Brucken samt denen Rödern, mit Rueder u. Segelbaum u. andere verschieden Kleinigkeiten, auch einige Figurn u. Tauben Kobel, auch die Blumen gehäng aufgemacht. 63 Taglohn. [August bis Ende September] 219f.
1770 Oktober: Zum Teatro 3 verleimte Wänd, 4 Piramider von weichem Holz. 93f 21xr.

41. Haunold's bills for work on decoration for Haydn's
Le pescatrici **Eszterháza 1770**

In the theatre for the new opera, various work undertaken, 16 *Tallar wägen,* 4 *Wafen Canape,* also a ship with a bridge together with its wheels [to move it], also rudder and mast and various others minutiae, also some figures and a dovecot, also mounted the garlands of flowers, 63 days' work, 219f. Aug - Sept. 1770.
Oct. 1770: For the theatre 3 walls glued, 4 pyramids of soft wood.

42. Rechnung des Anton Kerner für gelieferte Waldhörner

Gralcassa. 1770. Rubr. VIII. Fasc. XVIII. Nr.
Wienn, 8ten Decemb. 1770.

Um verfertige und Lüfere mit accord
1. Paar. D: Wald-horn pr: 10. Ducaten
1. gefüttertes Futtral pr: 3. Ducaten
                                   ─────────
         S (umm)a: 13. Ducaten
                  Anton Kerner Kay. König:
         Hof: Trompeten und Wald-horn macher
Obstehende Zehen drey Ducaten wird Unser Ober Einnehmer Johan Zoller bezahlen, und in Anrechnung bringen. Wienn den 16ten Xbr [1]770.
                              Nicolaus Fürst Esterhazy
Obstehende 13. Ord: ducaten ist mir durch Herrn Johann Zoller. Richtig bezallet worden.   Anton Kerner
Fürst Essterhaischer Ober Einnehmer. Den 17tn Xb: [1]770:

Kommentar

Was das Wort 'D' vor dem Wort Waldhorn bedeutet, ist unklar. Es könnte sich um ein Horn in D handeln, was kaum auzunehmen ist, da Kerner sicher die üblichen Bogen von C alto bis B basso lieferte.

42. Bill of Anton Kerner for a pair of hunting horns
                                      1770 8 Dec. in Vienna
For manufacture of and delivery as agreed.
1 pair D hunting horns at   10 ducats
1 lined case at   3 ducats
                                 ─────────
         S(umm)a   13 ducats
                         Anton Kerner I. R.
             Court trumpet and hunting-horn maker
Above thirteen ducats are to be paid by our Chief Cashier Zoller and entered in the accounts
Vienna 16 Dec. 1770   Nicolaus Fürst Esterhazy

Above 13 ordinary ducats have been paid to me by Herr Johann Zoller, Chief Cashier to Prince Esterhazy
17 Dec. 1770 Paid in full

                                    Anton Kerner.

Commentary

A new pair of horns. The meaning of 'D:' before the 'hunting-horns' is unclear. It may mean the pitch of D, but this is unlikely as Kerner probably delivered crooks for all the usual keys (from C alto to B flat basso).

43. Rechnung des Kammermalers Grundmann für Materalien und Arbeitstunden 1773 in Eszterháza

Ausgabe derer Maderialien, Mahlen und Tagwerck, welche Esterhas 1773 auf verschiedene Mahler Arbeit verwendet worden.

Nr.			
1. Farben Conto		486F	39 xr
2. -----		463	14
3. -----		130	23
4. Berggrün		187	30
5. Spiridus Viny		67	4
6. -----		52	15
7. Farben		89	28
8. Leim		32	30
9. Pemsel		20	--
10. Farben		20	9
11. von der Hand erkauffet		84	6
12. Mahler und Tagwerck		2009	35
	Summa	3642F	53xr

Empfangen von Herrn Ober Einnehmer
Züßer vermög Fürstl. Commission   3542F   53xr
aus der Bau Cassa von Sütörer Verwalter
H. Stumpff   100   --

                                                       3642F   53xr
                        Grundmann Cab. mahler

Verfertigt ist worden von 1 Februar bis 3. September 1773. wie folgt.
Nr   1. der große Chinöser Saal
       2. Zwey Rediraten und Stiegen

3. das Große Comedien Hauß mit einer großen Cordine
4. daß kleine Comedienhauß mit einer Cordine
5. vier Decoration zur Kleinen Obera
6. die Heremitage
7. das Ringerl Spiel
8. 12. Zimmer in denen seiten Gebäu, nebst 13 Cabinetter
9. 24 Transparenten, mit 24. Trilage Rahmen und 24 Transparente Blumen Körbe
10. Gloriette auf dem Oval Platz
11. Decoration auf dem Oval Platz mit 8. Fronde Spitz
12. Zwey Decoration zu der Opera
13. 6. Cabinetter an dem Chinöser Saal mit 41, Lantschafften.
14. Salee Terren. und dem vor Saal erneuert
15. den Sonnen Tempel auf Gold Blumen gemahlen
16. nach Monpisu drey Zimmer
17. Decoration zu der Comedie und Ballet
18. den Anstreichern 1/2 Cent. Berggrün und 4 Cent. Bleiweiß abgeben
19. Feuerwercks Decoration
20. ein Grotten Hauß in der Ermitage
21. in der Juden Backerey gearbeitet worden
22. alle Herrschafts Zimmer renoviert worden
23. ein Fronde Spitz an dem Kleinen Comedie Hauß.

Haydn bestellt zur besseren Verwahrung der Musikinstrumente Verschläge

	F	K.
Aus Zügel. was aus ansschaffung dafür Herrn Herrn Koböl Meüster [Kapellmeister] an Dischler Arbeit vor die Musi an Verschlöhnen [Verschlägen] gemacht ist worten den 22. et 23. Feb. [1]776 Erstlich ein groser Musicalien Verschlach mit 6 schuh lang, breit 2 schuh 6 zoll, tief 2 schuh und auswentig abgehoblet und zusammenschlosen und mit leisten unten u. oben	2	45
Vor ein neuen löckel mit 3 schuh 5 zol lang breit 3 schuh auch mit leisten darauf	-	30

vor die alten Verschlöch zusamb gericht und mit stüker laten und leisten ausgearbeitet	-	20
vor zwei löckel neie, ein mit 3 schuh lan[g], breit 2 schuh und leisten darauf, auf den anteren mit 2 schuh lan[g] und breit ist	-	42
vor die Verschloch ale zugenagel	-	15
Suma	4f	32x

[Haydns Hand:] Josephus Haydn mpria
          Capell Meister
[Schlansteins Hand:]
mit 3f. 30xr zu bezahlen
Edmund Schlanstein mpria
verwalt.
ob. angewiesene drey gulden 30 xr sind mir aus dem Eisenstätter Rent Amt richtig bezahlet word. Eisenstadt den 24ten Febr. [1]776
          Carl Flach Dischler Meister.

Kommentar

Grundmann, der auch Haydns erstes Portrait in Esterházyscher Uniform malte, das verschollen ist, dekorierte beide Theater, die meisten Zimmer des Schlosses, aber auch kleine Lustgebäude im Park, wie Monbijoux und die Eremitage. Der Sonnentempel wurde von dem kölner Juristen Johann Baptist Fuchs, der 1780 Eszterháza besuchte in seinen Memoiren folgendermassen geschildert: 'Man staunt, wenn der Tempel der Sonne sich öffnet. Das ganze Innere ist von Glanz der Sonne so vergoldet, daß man auf einige Minuten wie geblendet ist.' (Johann Baptist Fuchs, 1757-1827: *Erinnerungen aus dem Leben eines Kölner Juristen,* Köln, 1912, S.157).

Haydn benötigte mehr Verschläge, da sein Orchester größer geworden war und die Musiker für ihre kostbaren Instrumente einen sicheren Aufbewahrungsort benötigten.

43. Bill of the Kammermaler Grundmann for material and working hours in 1773 at Eszterháza
Expenses for the material, painter and work days in Esterhaz 1773 for various painting work.
No. 1.   account for colours, 2 and 3 ditto, No. 4 mountain green, 5. spirit of wine. ditto 6. No. 7. colours, 8. glue, 9. brushes, 10. more colours, 11. bought by myself, 12. painter and days of work

Paid to me by the Chief Cashier Züßer by
Princely permission   3542f   53xr
Paid from the Bau Cassa of the Sütör
administrator H. Stumpf   100   -
                                                                                          ─────────────
                                                                                         3642f   53xr
                            Grundman cabinet painter.

From 1 February until 3 September 1773 the following work was done:
1. the big chinese hall, 2. two toilets and stairs, 3. the big theatre and a big stage curtain, 4. the small theatre and a stage curtain, 5. four decorations for the small opera theatre; 6. the Hermitage, 7. the small merry-go-round, 8. 12 rooms and 13 cabinettes at the side wing, 9. 24 transparencies with 24 frames and 24 transparent flower baskets, 10. Gloriette at the oval square, 11. Decoration at the oval square with eight pointed decorations at the front, 12. two decorations for the opera, 13. six cabinets in the chinese hall with 41 landscapes, 14. Sala terrena and the entrance renovated, 15. temple of the sun painted with gold flowers, 16. at Monbijoux three rooms, 17. Decoration for the comedy [plays] and the ballet, 18. for the painters 1/2 hundred-weight of mountain-green and 4 hundred-weight of pewter white, 19. decorations for the fireworks, 20. a grotto at the Hermitage, 21. work in the bakery of the Jews, 22. all the rooms for people of quality renovated, 23. one pointed decoration on the facade in the theatre.
Carpenter's bill for housing the music instruments.
What Herr Capellmeister ordered for the music and was done on the 22nd and 23rd Feb. 1776.
First a big closet 6 feet long, 2 feet and 6 inches wide, deep 2 feet and the outside planed, nailed together and ledges provided above and down at the bottom   2f   45xr
for a new locker with 3 feet 5 inches long,
3 feet wide, also with ledges   -   30
the old closets repaired ledged and lathed   -   20
2 new lockers, one 3 feet to 2, ledged, the other
2 feet long and wide   -   42
all the closets nailed together   -   15
                                                                                          ─────────────
                                                    Suma   4f   32x
[Haydn's hand:] Josephus Haydn mpria, Chapel Master
[Administrator Edmund Schlanstein's hand:] paid 3f 30xr. Edmund Schlanstein; the above-assigned three gulden and 30 kreutzer were paid in full from the Eisenstadt Rentamt, Eisenstadt 24 Feb. 1776, [signed:] Carl Flach master carpenter.

Commentary
The Esterházy chamber painter Grundmann, who also painted the first (lost) portrait of Haydn in his Esterházy uniform, decorated nearly the whole castle, both theatres, but also little buildings at the park as Monbijoux and the Hermitage. Haydn needed more closets since his orchestra had grown in size and the musicians needed to leave their precious instruments in a secure place.
Johann Baptist Fuchs, a lawyer from Köln, visited Eisenstadt in 1780 where he also saw the Sonnentempel and wrote in his memoirs: 'one gapes when the temple of the sun opens. The golden sun shines so strongly that one is blinded for a few minutes'. (Johann Baptist Fuchs, 1757-1827: *Erinnerungen aus dem Leben eines Kölner Juristen*, Köln, 1912, S.157).

44. Haydn schreibt an Verwalter Schlanstein 1775.

Wohl Edl gebohrner
Insonders Hochzu Ehrender Herr Verwalter!
Da Seine hochfürstliche Durchlaucht befohlen den Herrn Griessler und übrige wegen dem Gottesdienst nach Eisenstadt zu liefern, Herr Stallmeister aber in ermanglung derer Pferden solches nicht befördern kan, waren wür gezwungen
eine Fuhr vor 3F./: welches in der That nicht zu viell:/ aufzunehmen, welche 3F. Sie die Güte haben werden zu bezahlen. Der ich übrigens mit aller Hochachtung verbleibe
                Dero
                      Ergebenster Diener
                      Josephus Haydn mpria
Estoras den 2ten September 1775
[Schlansteins Schrift:]
aus dem Rentamt zu bezahlen diese 3F.
                      Edmund Schlanstein mpria
                      Verwalt.
[Rückseite:]
linke Seite: Inbegriffene, und durch mich bezahlte drey Gulden sind mir aus dem Rent amt Bonificium worden.
Eisenstadt 3 ten 7bris 1775.
Best. 3 - xr   Melchior Griessler mpria
Kanzleischrift: Eisenstädter Rentamt 1775. No. 167/20
rechte Seite: Haydns Schrift: Monsieur Monsieur Schlanstein persl. a Eisenstadt
Kanzleischrift aus der Zeit: Zahlung [1]775 wegen Fuhre nach Eszterhaz. von 3F. Nr. 20 ad. Nr. 167 gehörig dd 3ten 7bris

44. Haydn writes to administrator Schlanstein 1775

Nobly born
Highly respected Herr Administrator!
Since His Serene Highness has ordered Herr Griessler [Griesler] and others to proceed to Eisenstadt for the church service there, but the Herr Stables-Master because of a lack of horses can not oblige, we were obliged to take a waggon and to spend for it 3fl: (which is in fact not too much), which 3f you will have the kindness to pay, otherwise I remain with all respect
                      your
                      most humble servant
                      Josephus Haydn mpria
Estoras 2 September
    1775
[Schlanstein's hand:]
These 3fl. to be paid by the Rent Office ...
[Address in Haydn's hand, see German and facsimile].

Wohl her gebohrner!
Insonders Hochzuehrender Herr Oheim!

CE Deme Hochzu Ehr: Schreibens habe ich heute nebst der
übrigen wegen Sme geldt Sach: mit Freüden zu Händen Herr
sad Ihm, Ihm eher im vermögliche Sorg Schaffer freylich nicht befriedig:
dann, wer wird gefangenen vmb seft. denn Zh nicht in die sprül
auf's Libell! einschreiben wollen?! rechts 3 g Die habe zahl nach
Zu begreif: den auf verlangen über Gestreckung beröftigen
Oheim

Ebers den 26 October   Zeitgebens wie Gund
        1745.   Gruf ... Hayd...
mit der hand Enkel zu dienste Casto:
                                J. v. ... St ...

45. Dienstvertrag des Kammerpagen Friedrich de Auguste und Anweisung des Fürsten Nicolaus I. seinem Kammerpagen mehr Kostgeld anzuweisen

v. J. 1779. No. 15. Dem Mohr namens Friedrich de Auguste wird hiemit als Cammer-Page mit nachstehenden Gehalt in unsere Dienste aufgenohmen, als: an jahres Besoldung 200 Gulden, Kostgeld für ihn und sein Weib alljährlich 150 Gulden, ausser denen wird ihmo von uns seine benöthigte Kleidung von Zeit zu Zeit nach unseren Wohlgefallen angeschaffet werden, und es wird Selber noch über diess für seine Person Quartier, Holz und Licht unentgeltlich zu genüssen haben. Eszterhaz den 19ten July 1779. Nicolaus Fürst Esterhazy.

Acta Varia Fasc. No.191., Archiv Forchtenstein.
No.17. Commission vermög welcher unser controleur jerome unseren Cammer Page vom 1ten Septembris diess Jahrs anzufangen zu seinen bisherigen Kostgeld annoch monatlich drey Gulden als eine Zulage bezahlen, und in Anrechnung bringen solle. Eszterhaz den 25ten Aug. 1780. Nicholaus Fürst Esterhazy.

Kommentar

Friedrich de August war der Vater des zu Beethovens Zeiten sehr berühmten englischen Geigenvirtuosen George Polgreen Bridgetower. Wie und wann er des Fürsten Dienste quittierte, und wann sein Sohn zur Welt kam ist uns bis jetzt noch unbekannt. Laut *New Grove* wurde Bridgetower 1779 in Biala (Polen) geboren. Bridgetower besuchte 1802 seine Mutter in Wien und spielte mit Beethoven zusammen in einem Konzert. Siehe Landon II, S.38 und Landon, *Beethoven*, S.148 f.

45. Contract of the page Friedrich de Auguste and Princely commission to raise his money in kind

Contract of Friedrich de Auguste.
1779 No.15. The blackamoor named Friedrich de Auguste is hereby placed in our service as chamber page for the approved salary, viz. a yearly stipendium of 200 gulden, as well as board and lodging money for him and his wife of 150 gulden; moreover the clothes he requires will be supplied by us from time to time as we see fit, and in addition he is to receive *gratis* for his person lodgings, wood and light. Eszterhaz 19 July 1779
Nicolaus Fürst Esterhazy

No. 12 Commission
According to which our Controleur Jerome will pay an additional three gulden per month to our chamber page as a supplement to his previous board and lodging money and to enter this in the record as a supplement. Eszterhaz, 25 Aug. 1780. Nicolaus Fürst Esterhazy.

Commentary
Friedrich de Auguste was the father of the famous English violin virtuoso George Polgreen Bridgetower. When and how he left the service of Prince Esterházy and when his son was born we do not know. Bridgetower visited his mother in 1802 in Vienna and played together with Beethoven in a concert. For more details see Landon, II, p.38 and Landon, *Beethoven*, p.148f. In the *New Grove*, Bridgetower is listed as born in Biala, Poland in ?1779 (place probably correct, date probably wrong).

Otto Biba
János Hárich (1904-1990)

Am 21. Juli 1990 ist in Eisenstadt Dr. János Hárich verstorben. Sein Name und seine Publikationen sind jedem, der sich mit Haydn beschäftigt, wohlvertraut. Daß sich in diesem Namen ein Teil seiner Biographie widerspiegelt, bedenkt aber kaum jemand. Denn als Ungar hätte sich Harich stets Hárich János nennen müssen, weil in der ungarischen Sprache der Vorname stets nach dem Familiennamen genannt wird. Harich hat aber zeitlebens mit deutschen (und lateinischen) Quellen gearbeitet und wichtige Jahre seines Lebens in Österreich verbracht. Daher verzichtete er bei sinem Namen - in vielem anderem blieb er ein echter, überzeugter Ungar - auf die ungarische Tradition und nannte sich, angepaßt an internationale Usancen, nicht Hárich János, sondern Janos Harich oder Johann Harich.

Harich ist 1904 in Veszprém in Ungarn geboren werden, besuchte das Piaristengymnasium in seiner Heimatstadt, beherrschte schon als Jugendlicher zahlreiche Instrumente (Violine, Viola, Violoncello, Klavier, Orgel, Flöte, Klarinette, Trompete, Horn, Fagott, Gitarre), studierte Geschichte an der Universität Budapest und promovierte dort 1928 zum Doktor der Philosophie. Noch in diesem Jahr wurde er als Hilfsarchivar im Fürstlich Esterházyschen Archiv in Budapest angestellt. Von 1930 bis zur Enteignung des fürstlichen Besitzes im Jahr 1946 war er Leiter des Fürstlich Esterházyschen Archivs und der Fürstlich Esterházyschen Bibliothek in Budapest. Seine besonderen musikalischen Interessen ließen ihn dort die *Acta Musicalia* aus der Registratur-Ordnung des Archivs herauslösen und gesondert aufstellen. Nebstbei begann er auch an einem Werkverzeichnis von Gregor Joseph Werner zu arbeiten - ein Projekt, das ihn zeitlebens beschäftigte, das er aber selbst nicht mehr abschließen konnte. In diesen Jahren als fürstlicher Archivar war Harich vielen Historikern, aber vor allem der Musikwissenschaft ein wichtiger Partner. Besonders enge, kollegiale Kontakte pflegte er mit dem Archiv der Gesellschaft der Musikfreunde in Wien, das für ihn damals die wichtigste wissenschaftliche Adresse außerhalb Ungarns war, wo er auch als Leiter eines ebenfalls privaten, wenn auch anders gewachsenen und strukturierten Archivs vielfache Unterstûtzung von Dr. Karl Geiringer und Dr. Hedwig Kraus und manche kollegiale Privilegien genoß.

1946 begann für Harich eine schwierige Zeit. Er war erst arbeitslos, dann für etwa zwei Jahre im Ungarischen Staatsarchiv angestellt, wo er jedoch 1949 im Zuge der Mindszenty - und Esterházy-Prozesse entlassen wurde. Er war selbst einige Zeit in Haft und wirkte danach bis 1953 als Gelegenheitsmusiker und "Kultur-Arbeiter" in einer Elektrizitätsfabrik. Von 1953 bis 1957 verdiente er als Musiklehrer seinen Lebensunterhalt.

Im Jahr 1958 kam Harich nach Österreich, wo er zum Leiter des Fürstlich Esterháyschen Archivs in Eisenstadt bestellt wurde. Diese Position war ihm vom Fürsten bereits 1945 angeboten worden, doch konnte sich Harich damals nicht entschließen, Budapest zu verlassen, nicht zuletzt auch wegen seiner Gatin, die er in diesem Jahr geheiratet hatte und die als Neurologin in verantwortungsvoller und interesanter Position in einer Budapester Klinik tätig war.

Harich konnte sein wissenschaftliches Arbeitsmaterial nach Österreich mitbringen und hier die 1946 unterbrochene wissenschaftliche Arbeit fortsetzen. Sein umfangreicher, wohlgeordneter Zettelkatalog mit Exzerpten aus dem vormaligen Fürstlichen Archiv zu Budapest und dem ihm nunmehr anvertrauten Fürstlichen Archiv in Eisenstadt sowie aus einigen anderen relevanten Quellenbeständen war die Grundlage für zahlreiche wichtige Publikationen, unter denen die zur Musikgeschichte des Fürstlichen Hauses Esterházy dominieren.

Wer sich in diesen Jahren mit einer Frage an Dr. Harich wandte, bekam auf die liebenswürdigste und selbstloseste Weise Auskunft und Hilfe aus dieser Exzerpten-Sammlung, die Harichs wissenschaftliches Lebenswerk darstellte, von ihm aber nicht eifersüchtig als geistiges Eigentum gehütet wurde, sondern jedem Interessenten offenstand. Ich selbst erinnere mich gerne an Harichs Wiener Wohnung, an die überaus gastfreundliche Aufnahme dort und den immer wieder tiefen Eindruck, den die wohlgeordnete Materialsammlung Harichs und die unter vielen Gesichtspunkten mögliche Abrufbarkeit der darin enthaltenen Informationen auf mich gemacht hat. Es war sein Wunsch, daß sie nach seinem Tod in das Archiv der Gesellschaft der Musikfreunde in Wien gelangt, um dort weiterhin der dokumentarischen Forschung zur Verfügung zu stehen.

1966 trat Harich in den Ruhestand, den er in Eisenstadt verbrachte und, solange ihm dies gesundheitlich möglich war, für seine wissenschaftliche Publikationstätigkeit nützte. 1975 starb seine erste Gattin. Seine zweite Gattin, mit der er seit 1979 vermählt war, schenkte ihm in den letzten Jahren, als er schon von Krankheit gesch-wächt war, eine aufopfernde Pflege und Betreuung.[1]

Es spricht für Harichs begeistertes Aufgehen in seinem Lebenswerk, daß er nicht nur die Fürstlich Esterházyschen Archivbestände bestens betreute und kannte und nicht nur in anderen für seine Themen wichtigen Archiven und Bibliotheken arbeitete, sondern bei Sammlern wie Antiquaren[2] für seine Fragen nach einschlägigen Quellen bekannt war. Es machte ihm große Freude, ein nicht näher bezeichnetes handschriftliches Musikalieninventar zu erwerben, dem ein mit Notizen beschriebenes Folioblatt beigelegt war, in dessen Handschrift er jene Gregor Joseph Werners erkennen konnte, womit der Band als ein Musikinventar des esterházyschen Hofes agnosziert war.[3] Eine abenfalls bei Gilhofer in Wien erworbene Sammlung zeitgenössischer Abschriften von Kompositionen Fürst Paul Esterházys war für ihn ebenfalls eine Trouvaille.[4]

Seine Publikationstätigkeit sah Harich immer im Zusammenhang mit seinem Beruf, sozusagen als Ausfluß seiner Arbeiten als fürstlicher Archivar. Daher dominieren unter seinen Veröffentlichungen Quellen-oder Regesteneditionen[5]

---

[1] Alle Angaben zur Biographie verdanke ich Unterlagen des Fürstlich Esterházyschen Archivs in Eisenstadt und der Familie Dr. J. Harichs.

[2] Herrn Rudolf Hoffmann, bis 1992 Kommanditist des Wiener Antiquarists Gilhofer, verdanke ich anschauliche diesbezügliche Erinnerungen.

[3] Publiziert im Haydn-Jahrbuch IX (1975), S.31-66. Mit Harichs Nachlaß das Archiv der Gesellschaft der Musikfreunde in Wien übernommen.

[4]. Heute ebenfalls im Archiv der Gesellschaft der Musikfreunde in Wien.

[5] Haydn Documente (I), in: Haydn-Jahrbuch II (1963/64), 2.2-35;

bzw. Darstellungen, die stark auf Quellen aufbauen.[6] Diese Quellen zitiert er mit genauen Quellenangaben aus den Fürstlich Esterházyschen Archiven. Das Verantwortungsgefühl den ihm anvertrauten Archivmaterialien gegenüber, als dessen Sprachrohr er sich geradezu fühlte, ging so weit, daß er bei den Publikationen aus den von ihm betreuten oder betreut gewesenen Arhiven minutiös Signaturen und Provenienzangaben brachte, das Wissen aus anderen Beständen zwar verwertete, mit Abbildungen oder Zitaten auch belegte, aber - fast möchte man sagen geradezu eifersüchtig schweigend - keine Provenienzangaben machte.[7] Die Korrektheit im einem war beruflich-wissenschftliche Pflicht, im anderen sah er wohl das persönliche Finderglück privater Such - und Forschungstätigkeit.

Alle Publikationen Harichs stellen aber nur einen Auschnitt aus seinem Wissen, aus seiner Quellen- und Materialkenntnis und aus seiner Materialsammlung dar. Letztere steht den nachkommenden Wissenschaftler-Generationen im Archiv der Gesellschaft der Musikfreunde in Wien zur Verfügung. Seine Publikationen behalten ihre zeitlose Gültigkeit und Notwendigkeit. Seine Typoskript gebliebenen Archivbehelfe[8] sind heute in der Nationalbibliothek

---

[6] Haydn Documents (II), in Haydn-Jahrbuch III (1965), S.122-152
Haydn Documents (III), in Haydn-Jahrbuch IV (1968), S.39-101
Haydn Documents (IV), in: Haydn-Jahrbuch VII (1970), S.47-168
Haydn Documents (V), in: Haydn-Jahrbuch VIII (1971), S.70-163
Esterházy-Musikgeschichte im Spiegel der zeitgenössischen Textbücher, Burgenländische Forschungen Heft 39, Eisenstadt 1959; Das Repertoire des Opernkapellmeisters Joseph Haydn in Esterháza, in: Haydn-Jahrbuch I (1962), S.9-107; Das fürstlich Esterházy'che Fideikomiß, in: Haydn)Jahrbuch IV (1968), S.5-38, Das Opernensemble zu Eszterháza im Jahr 1780, in: Haydn-Jahrbuch VII (1970), S.5-36; Das Haydn-Orchester im Jahre 1780, in: Haydn-Jahrbuch VIII (1971), S.5-52; Werner Gergely József elöde as Esterházyudvarban, in: Muzika 4/5 (1930); Beethoven in Eisenstadt. Die Beziehungen des Meisters zum Fürsten Nikolaus Esterházy, in: Burgenländische Heimatblätter 21 (1959), S.168-188; Szenische Darstellungen und Oratorien-Aufführungen im 18. Jahrhundert am Esterházy-Hof zu Eisenstadt, in: Burgenländische Heimatblätter 38 (1976), S.112-130; Die Testamente der Musiker Tobias Fritsch und Gregor Josef Werner, in: Burgenländische Heimatblätter 39 (1977), S.119-136.

[7] So befindet sich Haydns Besetzungsliste zu den Opern *Il ratto della sposa* (Pietro Gugielmi) und *La vedova scaltra* (Vincenzi Righini), die Harich in seiner Esterházy-Musikgeschichte im Spiegel der zeitgenössischen Textbücher (vgl. Anm. 6) auf Seite 35 abgebildet hat, in einer traditionsreichen alt-österreichischen Privatsammlung. Ein Exemplar des Anstellungsvertrages für Anton Kraft, den Harich im Haydn-Jahrbuch VIII (1971), Seite 123, veröffentlicht hat, befindet sich im Archiv der Gesellschaft der Musikfreunde in Wien (Briefautographe Anton Kraft 1); da in Harichs Manuskript ganz offensichtlich die Provenienzangabe gefahlt hat, wurde von der Redaktion des Haydn-Jahrbuches in eckigen Klammer *Unter den Personalakten* ergänzt. Da auch beim Haydn-Dokument 133 im Haydn-Jahrbuch IV (1968), Seite 76 ff, als Provenienzangabe - allerdings ohne eckige Klammer - *Personalakten* vermerkt ist, ein solcher Fundorthinweis von Harich aber ansonsten nicht verwendet wird, könnte auch ein Exemplar dieses Anstellungsvertrages noch anderswo überliefert und von Harich verwendet worden sein. Freilich muß in jedem Fall von einem Anstellungsvertrag ein Exemplar auch beim Dienstgeber hinterlegt und überliefert sein.

[8] Vorallem: Szövegkönyvgyüjtemény. Összegyüit, és jegyzékelte dr. Hárich János [Maschinschriftlicher Katalog der Esterházy-Textbuchsammlung von Archivar Dr. Johann Harich]; Werner Gergely József müveinek tématikus katalógusa [Thematisches Verzeichnis der im Fürstlich Esterházyschen Archiv vorhandenen Kompositionen Gregor Joseph Werners]

Szechényi in Budapest ebenso unentbehrlich, wie sie es zuvor im Fürstlichen Archiv waren.

Summary Translation

Dr János Hárich (Johann Harich) died at Eisenstadt on 21 July 1990. Born in Veszprém (Hungary) in 1904, he attended the Piarists in his town and soon mastered the violin, viola, violoncello, piano, organ, flute, clarinet, bassoon, horn, trumpet and guitar. He studied history at Budapest University and in 1928 he received his doctorate in philosophy. In the same year he was enagaged by Prince Esterházy as assistant archivist and in 1930 he became director, which post he retained until the princely administration and goods were confiscated by the Communist authorities in 1946. In this period he reorganized the entire archives, creating the famous Acta Musicalia and Acta Theatralica, in the process of which he discovered a vast quantity of autograph letters and other documents by Haydn. The years 1946-1957 were difficult ones for Hárich, who had meanwhile married a brilliant neurologist. In 1958 he emigrated to Austria, where he again took up his former position as princely archivist at Eisenstadt, Prince Esterházy having also fled Hungary. (Both men were imprisoned for a time by the Communists.)

Hárich began publishing the results of his research as soon as he started living in Austria, and in 1962 the *Haydn Yearbook* was founded, largely to enable Hárich to publish his Haydn findings, which he did in that and forthcoming issues. He wished that his extensive files should, after his death, pass to the Gesellschaft der Musikfreunde, which occured after his death. The *Haydn Yearbook* is happy to publish these files which, as will be seen, include a large amount of hitherto unknown documents from the Esterházy Archives in Hungary and Austria.

ACTA MUSICALIA
Die Acta Musicalia des Esterházy-Archives, herausgegeben und transkribiert von Else Radant.
The Acta Musicalia of the Esterházy Archives, edited and transcribed by Else Radant.

Nr. 201 bis 279
No. 201 to 279

201. Bericht des Güterregenten Szent Gály an den Fürsten Nicolaus II. über die Schwängerung der Tochter Magdalena Polzers durch den Musiker Franz Finger.
Report from Regent Szent Gály to Prince Nicolaus II concerning the pregnancy of Magdalena Polzer's daughter by the musician Franz Finger.

202. Gutachten des Güterregenten Szent Gály das Gesuch der Witwe Elisabeth Dietzl um eine Pension betreffend.
Report by Regent Szent Gály concerning widow Elisabeth Dietzl's petition for a pension.

203. Johann von Szent Gály erbittet von Fürst Nicolaus II. die Bestätigung der Zahlungsanweiung für den Komponisten Joseph Heidenreich.
Johann von Szent Gály asks Prince Nicolaus II to confirm an order for payment to the composer Joseph Heidenreich.

204. Anweisungen des Güterregenten Szent Gály an die verschiedenen Ämter über die Anstellung der Sängerin Elisabeth Schneider und Anfrage an den Fürsten Nicolas II. über die Möblierung ihrer Wohnung.
Orders by Regent Szent Gály to various offices regarding the engagement of the singer Elisabeth Schneider and a query to Prince Nicolaus II.

205. Gutachten des Güterdirektors Szent Gály zur Bittschrift der Sängerin Barbara Pillhofer um eine Zulage.
Report by Regent Szent Gály concerning the petition by the singer Barbara Pillhofer for an increase.

206. Anfrage des Güterdirektors Szent Gály an die fürstliche Domänendirektions-Registratur über Michael Bader.
Query by Regent Szent Gály to the princely Domains-Director Registry concerning Michael Bader.

207. Bericht des Güterregenten Szent Gály an den Fürsten Nicolaus II. über die beiden Söhne des Bassisten Johann Bader.
Report by Regent Szent Gály to Prince Nicolaus II on the two sons of the bass-singer Johann Bader.

208. Fürstliche Resolution den Kapellknaben Religionsunterricht erteilen zu lassen.
Princely resolution to ensure that the boy choristers are given instruction in religion.

209. Fürstliches Intimatum an den Güterregenten Johann von Szent Gály den Kapellmeister Franz Teiber wieder nach Wien zurückzuschicken.
Princely Intimatum to Regent Johann von Szent Gály that Kapellmeister Franz Teiber should return to Vienna.

210. Fürstliche Resolution über die Zuweisung von Wohnungen an die Sängerin Elisabeth Schneider, ihren Kollegen Joseph Treidler und den fürstlichen Buchhalter Ignaz Kühnelt.
Princely resolution concerning the assignment of lodgings for the singers Elisabeth Schneider, Joseph Treidler and the princely bookkeeper Ignaz Kühnelt.

211. Anfrage des Fürsten Nicolaus II. wie Domainendirektionsrat Schubarnegg ausgezeichnet werden könne.
Query by Prince Nicolaus II, in which fashion Domain Director Councillor Schubarnegg could be rewarded.

212. Luigi Tomasini junior bittet Fürst Nicolaus II. um die Heiratserlaubnis.
Luigi Tomasini Jr. requests permission to marry from Prince Nicolaus II.

213. Fürst Nicolaus II. befiehlt die sofortige Ablieferung der unterschriebenen Dienstverpflichtungen aller Musiker und Sänger.
Prince Nicolaus II orders the immediate delivery of the signed contracts for all musicians and singers.

214. Fürstliche Resolution den jungen Luigi Tomasini nicht zu entlassen.
Princely resolution that the young Luigi Tomasini is to be retained in service.

215. Güterregent Szent Gály berichtet Fürst Nicolaus II. über die Wohnungssuche für den Sänger Joseph Treidler und den Buchhalter Ignaz Kühnel.

Regent Szent Gály reports to Prince Nicolaus about finding quarters for the singer Joseph Treidler and the bookkeeper Ignaz Kühnel.

216. Fürst Nicolaus II. wünscht den Domainen-Direktions-Sekretär Fajt und den Bratschisten Johann Treidler standesgemäß unterzubringen.
Prince Nicolaus II wishes that Domain Director Secretary Fajt and the viola player Johann Treidler should be given appropriate lodgings.

217. Gutachten des Güterdirektors Szent Gály über Pietro Travaglias Ansuchen seine fürstliche Pension trotz anderweitiger Anstellung in alter Höhe behalten zu dürfen und die fürstliche Resolution.
Report of the Regent Szent Gály concerning Pietro Travaglia's petition to receive his princely pension.

218. Gutachten des Güterdirektors Szent Gály über ein weiteres Bittgesuch des Sängers Johann Bader seinem Sohn Michael eine Kleiderrechnung zu bezahlen und ihm selbst einen Vorschuß von 400 Gulden zu bewilligen.
Report of Regent Szent Gály on a further petition by the singer Johann Bader to have the tailor's bill for his son Michael paid and for his own person an advance of 400 gulden.

219. Gutachten des Güterregenten Szent Gály über das Gesuch der verwitweten Barbara Tomasini, ihr ein Holzdeputat anzuweisen.
Report by Regent Szent Gály on a petition by the widowed Barbara Tomasini in which she requests firewood.

220, 221, 222 a-d
Furst Nicolaus II. befiehlt seinem Güterregenten Szent Gály die beiden Sängerinnen Vadász und Schneider wegen Abwesenheit und Rollentausch zurechtzuweisen.
Prince Nicolaus II orders his Regent Szent Gály to reprimand the two singers Vadász and Schneider because of absence without leave at rehearsals and switching roles.

223 a-b Gesuch des Vizekapellmeisters Johann Fuchs ihn näher beim Schloß unterzubringen und dessen Ablehnung durch den Fürsten.
Petition by Vice Capellmeister Johann Fuchs to live nearer to the castle and the princely refusal.

224 a-c   Antoinette Dorner, Kostgeberin der Sängerknaben ersucht den Vorschuß von 400 Gulden zur Verpflegung der Knaben nicht zurückzahlen zu müssen.
Antoinette Dorner, landlady of the boy choristers, requests that she need not repay an advance of 400 gulden used for the boys' food.

225 a-d   Bericht des Güterregenten Szent Gály an den Fürsten wer die Sängerknaben im Violinspiel unterrichte und welche Fortschritte sie gemacht hätten.
Report by Regent Szent Gály to the Prince as to which person teaches violin to the boy choristers and how much progress they have made.

225b   Szent Gály erläutert dem Lehrer Rathmayer, wie er sich die Kontrolle der Geigenlehrer vorstelle.
Szent Gály explains to teacher Rathmayer how he imagines the violin teachers may be controlled.

225c   Der Fürst ist mit Szent Gálys Maßnahmen einverstanden.
The Prince agrees with Szent Gály's proposals.

225d   Vizekapellmeister Fuchs erhält die fürstliche Resolution vom 8. Mai.
Vice Capellmeister Fuchs receives the princely resolution of 8 May.

226   Fürst Nicolas II. schreibt seinem Güterregenten über das schlechte Benehmen der Sängerknaben.
Prince Nicolaus II writes to his Regent about the bad behaviour of the boy choristers.

227   Szent Gály weist das Hauptzahlamt an, dem Tenor Joseph Treidler weiter seine Convention zu bezahlen.
Szent Gály indicates to the Chief Cashier's office that they should continue to pay the tenor Joseph Treidler according to the terms of his contract.

228 a-b   Fürst Nicolaus II. befiehlt seinem Güterregenten Szent Gály die Verwaltung der Güter während seiner Abwesenheit weiter zu besorgen.
Prince Nicolaus II orders his Regent Szent Gály to administer in his [the Prince's] absence.

228b   Bericht des Theaterregisseurs Heinrich Schmidt über seine Verhandlungen mit Konzertmeister Müller.
Report by theatre director Heinrich Schmidt concerning his negotiations with Konzertmeister Müller.

229a Die Lebensmittelteuerung in Eisenstadt bedingt eine Erhöhung der Verpflegungskosten der Kapellknaben.
The rise in food prices in Eisenstadt meant a rise in the living costs of the choir boys.

229b Da Madame Dorner um eine Erhöhung des Kostgeldes eingekommen war, referiert Szent Gály im Detail.
Madame Dorner was somehow forgotten in all this and received no rise in her board money for the boys. Szent Gály reports in detail.

229c Brotration genehmigt.
The bread ration is aproved.

229d Der Fürst befiehlt sich um eine andere Kostgeberin umzusehen.
The Prince orders another kitchen director to be found.

229e Kopie eines Briefes von Professor Rathmayer indem er Frau Dorner ersucht ihm eine finanzielle Aushilfe zu gewähren
Copy of a letter by Professor Rathmayer in which he seeks financial assistance from Madame Dorner.

230 a-b Fürst Nicolaus hört in Pest, daß Mitglieder der fürstlichen Kapelle sich in Wien aufhalten.
Prince Nicolaus hears in Pest that members of the princely chapel are living in Vienna.

231 a-e Güterregent Szent Gály übersendet dem Fürsten eine Kostenberechnung der Sängerknaben.
Regent Szent Gály sends to the Prince a list of expenses for the boy choristers.

231a Die Kosten für einen Sangerknaben.
The cost for a boy chorister.

231b Schneiderrechnung für die Einkleidung der Sängerknaben.
Tailor's bill for clothing the boy choristers.

231c Verzeichnis der notwendigen Leibwäsche für die Sängerknaben.
List of the necessary underclothing for the boy choristers.

231d Die Wintekleidung kann beschafft werden.
The winter clothing may be ordered.

232 a-b Ansuchen der Sängerin Theresia Stotz um Kostgeld. Resolution des Fürsten.
Petition of the singer Theresia Stotz for board money. Resolution of the Prince.

233 a-b	Philipp Ludwig Möglich schreibt an Güterdirektor Szent Gály, warum es ihm unmöglich sei, zur angegebenen Frist nach Eisenstadt zu kommen. *Philipp Ludwig Möglich writes to Regent Szent Gály why it is impossible for him to come to Eisenstadt in the given period.*
234a	Barbara Tomasini wird das Holzdeputat gestrichen. *The Prince orders the cancellation of the wood allotment for Barbara Tomasini.*
234b	Güterregent Szent Gály gibt die fürstliche Verfügung an das Schafferamt weiter. *Regent Szent Gály fowards the princely order to the Administration.*
234c	Barbara Tomasini ersucht den Güterregenten sich für sie zu verwenden. *Barbara Tomasini asks the Regent for his assistance.*
234d	Fürstliche Resolution. *Princely resolution.*
234e	Szent Gály weist das Schafferamt an, das Brennholz auszufolgen. *Szent Gály informs the Administration to deliver the wood.*
234f	Szent Gály berichtet dem Fürsten über ein neuerliches Gesuch der Witwe Tomasini. *Szent Gály reports to the Prince about yet another petition by widow Tomasini.*
234g	Gesuch der Barbara Tomasini an den Fürsten um Bewilligung des Holzdeputats. *Petition by Barbara Tomasini to the Prince for permission to receive an allotment for firewood.`*
235a	Anton Polzelli schickt an den Güterregenten die Liste der Sänger. *Anton Polzelli sends to the Regent a list of singers whom he teaches.*
235b	Bericht des Güterdirektors Szent Gály an den Fürsten, daß Polzelli die Korrepetitorstelle im Theater haben möchte. *Report of the Regent Szent Gály to the Prince that Polzelli would like to secure for himself the post of coach in the theatre.*
235c	Fürstliche Resolution. Polzelli erhält 400 Gulden. *Princely Resolution. Polzelli recieves his 400 gulden.*
235d	Szent Gály weist das Hauptzahlamt an, 400 Gulden an Polzelli auszuzahlen.

	Szent Gály instructs the Chief Cashier's Office to pay 400 gulden to Polzelli.
236a	Güterregent Szent Gály wird vom Fürst Nicolaus II. angewiesen dem Kammersänger Joseph Treidler die Fiskal Assistenz zu gewähren.
	Szent Gály is ordered by Prince Nicolaus II to inform Chamber Singer Joseph Treidler to aid and abet the Deputy of the Exchequer.
236b	Szent Gály unterrichtet den Fiskalen Regner, daß er Treidler bei seiner Klage zu vertreten habe.
	Regent Szent Gály informs Deputy of the Exchequer Regner that he is to represent Treidler in his lawsuit.
237a	Nicolaus II. weist Güterregenten Szent Gály an, den Sänger Treidler die Räumung der Wohnung am Berg zu befehlen.
	Nicolaus II indicates to Regent Szent Gály that the singer Treidler must evacuate the lodgings on the hill.
237b	Szent Gály gibt den fürstlichen Befehl an Treidler weiter.
	Szent Gály transmits the princely order to Treidler.
237c	Schreiben des Regisseur Schmidt an Szent Gály, daß Konzertmeister Müller im April nach Eisenstadt kommen wird.
	Letter by Director Schmidt to Szent Gály about the arrival of Concertmaster Müller in Eisenstadt in April.
238	Güterdirektor Szent Gály referiert über das Gesuch des Bratschisten Treidler um ein anderes Quartier.
	Regent Szent Gály informs about the petition of the viola-player Treidler for another lodging.
239a	Hofrat Karner teilt Szent Gály mit, daß der neu engagierte Klarinettist Ignatz Skrabal verheiratet sei.
	Hofrat Karner informs Szent Gály that the newly engaged clarinettist Ignatz Skrabal is married.
239b	Güterdirektor Szent Gály berichtet daß zur Zeit nur zwei Wohnungen für Skrabal in Betracht kämen.
	Regent Szent Gály reports that at the moment only two flats for Skrabal can be considered.
239c	Fürstliche Resolution.
	Princely Resolution.
239d	Szent Gály unterrichtet Vizekapellmeister Fuchs and Hausreferenten Vadatz vom Wunsch des Fürsten.
	Szent Gály informs Vice Capellmeister Fuchs and Lodging-master Vadatz of the Prince's wish.

240a Fürst Nicolaus II. läßt den Sängern Grell, Cornega und Konzertmeister Hummel die Gehälter streichen.
Prince Nicolaus II orders the salaries of the singers Grell and Cornega and Concertmeister Hummel to be docked.

240b Szent Gály berichtet Nicolaus II. über seine Maßnahmen.
Szent Gály informs Nicolaus II about his actions.

241a Fürst Nicolaus II. erteilt seinem Kammersänger Otto Grell einen dreiwöchigen Urlaub.
Prince Nicolaus II permits a three-week vacation for his chamber-singer Otto Grell.

241b Güterdirektor Szent Gály beauftragt das Hauptzahlamt und den Vicekapellmeister Fuchs, den dreiwöchigen Termin im Auge zu behalten.
Regent Szent Gály orders the chief cashier's office and Vice Capellmeister Fuchs to keep in mind the three weeks' limit.

242a Güterdirektor Szent Gály berichtet dem Fürsten über ein Gesuch des Violinisten Franz Lechner um Quartiergeld und Holzdeputat.
Regent Szent Gály reports to the Prince concerning the petition of violinist Franz Lechner for board and lodging money.

242b Der Fürst antwortet.
The Prince answers.

242c Weisung des Güterregenten an die Hauptzahlkassa Lechner für die Klavierstunden zu bezahlen.
Order of the regent to the Chief Cashier to pay Lechner for the piano lessons.

243a Weisung des Fürsten Esterházy an seinen Güterregenten, die Gruft in der Bergkirche in Ordnung zu bringen, da er seinen Kapellmeister Joseph Haydn dort beizusetzen gedenke.
Order by Prince Esterházy to his Regent that the grave vault in the Bergkirche [Mountain church] is to be brought in order, inasmuch as he proposes to bury Kapellmeister Joseph Haydn there.

243b Szent Gály beauftragt das Hofbauamt die Gruft zu säubern, und Probst Seitz dann für die weitere Instandhaltung Sorge zu tragen.
Szent Gály orders the court works department to clean the grave vault and provost Seitz is to be responsible for the future upkeep.

| 244 | Fürst Nicolaus II. gewährt der Witwe des verstorbenen Tenors Thilo ein Holzdeputat. |

Prince Nicolaus II allows the widow of the late tenor Thilo to receive an allotment of firewood.

| 245a | Fürst Nicolaus II. erteilt dem Cancellisten Johann Raichen die Heiratserlaubnis. |

Prince Nicolaus II allows clerk Johann Raichen to marry.

| 245b | Szent Gály hält am selben Tag noch die fürstliche Einwilligung aktenmäßig fest und bereitet die Pensionsverzichtserklärung der eventuellen Witwe vor. |

Szent Gály places a note of the princely permission in the files and prepares a statement that as a widow she renounces all claims to a pension.

| 246a | Fürstliches Intimatum, die von der Herrschaft verliehenen Möbel in den Sängerwohnungen zu kontrollieren. |

Princely intimatum to have an examination of princely furniture lent to the singers.

| 246b | Szent Gály benachrichtigt die Hofbuchhaltung, den Eisenstädter Schloßverwalter Pointer, den Pfleger Lechner und den Musikgebäudepfleger Pack von der fürstlichen Resolution. |

Szent Gály informs the Count Bookkeeping Administration, the Eisenstadt Castle Administrator Pointer, the warden Lechner and the Administrator of the music building Pack of the princely resolution.

| 247a | Güterdirektor Szent Gály berichtet Fürst Nicolaus II. über das Gesuch des Sängers Rotter um Bezahlung der Singlehrstsunden im Jahre 1806 für Ferdinand Gsell. |

Regent Szent Gály reports to Prince Nicolaus II on the petition of the singer Rotter concerning the payment for vocal teaching hours given to Ferdinand Gsell in the year 1806.

| 247b | Rotter wird abgewiesen. |

Rotter's petition is refused.

| 248 | Güterdirektor Szent Gály bittet den Eisenstädter Prefekten Menicoy um Auskunft über Adam List. |

Regent Szent Gály to the Eisenstadt Prefect Menicoy for information about Adam List.

| 249a | Güterdirektor Szent Gály berichtet dem Fürsten über ein Bittgesuch des Joseph Cornega um Kostgeld. |

Regent Szent Gály reports to the Prince concerning a petition of Joseph Cornega concerning board money.

249b   Fürstliche Resolution.
        Princely resolution.
249c   Szent Gály unterrichtet Rotter von der Verfügung des Fürsten und gibt dem Eisenstädter Verwalteramt den Auftrag das Brennholz für Rotter bereitzustellen.
        Szent Gály informs Rotter of the Princely decision and indicates to the Eisenstadt Administration the order to prepare the wood for Rotter.
250a   Kurze Notiz des Fürsten Nicolaus II. für den Güterregenten Szent Gály, ihm mit Vizekapellmeister Fuchs 300 Gulden nachschicken zu lassen.
        Short note by Prince Nicolaus II to the Regent Szent Gály to give Vice Capellmeister Fuchs 300 gulden to take with him.
250b   Szent Gály benachrichtigt das Hauptzahlamt vom Wunsche des Fürsten, und befiehlt die von Fuchs unterschriebene Quittung den fürstlichen Konten beizulegen.
        Szent Gály informs the Chief Cashier's office of the princely wishes and orders the signed receipt by Fuchs to be added to the princely account.
251a   Güterregent Szent Gály verwendet sich bei Distriktingenieur Krantz wegen einer Schuldforderung der Sängerin Barbara Pillhofer.
        Regent Szent Gály turns to District Engineer Krantz on account of a debt registered by singer Barbara Pillhofer.
251b   Szent Gály schreibt erneut an den Distriktingenieur: bis jetzt habe Barbara Pillhofer noch kein Geld gesehen.
        Szent Gály writes again to the District Engineer that Barbara Pillhofer has not yet seen the money.
252   Fürst Nicolaus I. reorganisiert die Kapelle nach dem Tod seines Bruders Paul Anton.
        Prince Nicolaus I reorganizes the Capelle following the death of his brother Paul Anton.
253   Anstellungsvertrag des Theatermalers Hieronymus Le Bon.
        Contract of engagement for the theatrical decorator Hieronymus Le Bon.
254a   Fürst Esterházy verlangt von seinem Güterdirektor Szent Gály einen Bericht über die Zustände im Sängerknabeninstitut.
        Prince Esterházy requires from his Regent Szent Gály a report concerning conditions in the Boys Choir institute.
254b   Szent Gály beauftragt Sakristan Skeley und Vizekapellmeister Fuchs, ihm über die Vorgänge im 'Stift' zu berichten

Szent Gály orders Sacristan Skeley and vice Capellmeister Fuchs to inform him about conditions in the Institute.

255 Anstellungsvertrag des Paukers Johann Adam Sturm.
Contract of engagement for the kettle-drum player Johann Adam Sturm.

256 Anstellungsvertrag des Feldtrompeters Christian Wolfgang Dobmeyer.
Contract of engagement for the field trumpeter Christian Wolfgang Dobmeyer.

257 Anstellungsvertrag des Trompeters Joseph Reisinger.
Contract of engagement for trumpeter Joseph Reisinger.

258 Anstellungskontrakt des Feldtrompeters Joseph Bayer.
Contract of engagement for the field trumpeter Joseph Bayer.

259 Anstellungskontrakt des Trompeters Stephan Sachs.
Contract of engagement for the trumpeter Stephen Sachs.`

260 Anstellungskontrakt des Trompeters Peter Hofbauer.
Contract of engagement for the trumpeter Peter Hofbauer.

261 Anstellungskontrakt des Waldhornisten Franz Kohl.
Contract of engagement for the horn-player Franz Kohl.

262 Anstellungskontrakt des Waldhornisten Mathias Wirth.
Contract of engagement for the hunting-horn player Mathias Wirth.

263 Anstellungskontrakt des Oboisten Carl Joseph Brauner.
Contract of engagement with oboist Carl Joseph Brauner.

264 Anstellungskontrakt des Flötisten Johann Adam Schulz.
Contract fo engagement with the flautist Johann Adam Schulz.

265 Anstellungskontrakt des Geigers Franz Garnier in französischer Sprache.
Contract of engagement with the violinist Franz Garnier in the French language.

266 Anstellungskontrakt des Flötisten Franz Sigl.
Contract of engagement with the flautist Franz Sigl.

267 Anstellungsvertrag des Violoncellisten Joseph Weigl.
Contract of engagement with the violoncellist Joseph Weigl.

268 Anstellungsvertrag des Geigers Johann Georg Heger.
Contract of engagement with the violinst Johann Georg Heger.

269 Anstellungsvertrag des Fagotisten Johann Georg Schwenda.

	Contract of engagement with the bassoonist Johann Georg Schwenda.
270	Anstellungskontrakt mit den Oboisten Johann Michael Kapfer.
	Contract of engagement with the oboist Johann Michael Kapfer.
271	Anstellungsvertrag des Oboisten Johann Georg Kapfer.
	Contract of engagement with the oboist Johann Georg Kapfer.
272	Fürst Paul Anton kauft den Oboisten und Fagottisten ihre Instrumente ab.
	Prince Paul Anton purchases the instruments from the oboists and bassoonists.
273	Anstellungsvertrag mit dem Baßsänger und Violonisten Melchior Griessler.
	Contract of engagement for the bass singer and violinist Melchior Griessler.
274	Anstellungskontrakt des Fagottisten Johann Hinterberger.
	Contract for the bassoon-player Johann Hinterberger.
275	Anstellungsverträge der Waldhornisten Franz Pauer und Joseph Oliva.
	The contracts of engagement for the hunting-horn players Franz Pauer and Joseph Oliva.
276 a-d	Anette Dorner möchte des bezogene Kostgeld für den abwesenden jungen Cornega nicht zurückzahlen.
	Anette Dorner wishes not to refund the board money she has received for the absent young Cornega.
277 a-c	Friedrich Tomasini ersucht um ein Stipendium.
	Friedrich Tomasini requests a stipendium.
279 a-c	Barbara Tomasini bittet den Fürsten, ihren Sohn Friedrich bei einem Wirtschaftsdepartement als Praktikant einzustellen.
	Barbara Tomasini begs the Prince to engage her son Friedrich as a practioner in one of the economic departments.

Anmerkung der Redaktion:
Die Redaktion des Haydn Jahrbuches hat sich entschlossen, alle Dokumente nach 1804 in kurzen Zusammenfassungen zu veröffentlichen.
Editorial Note. The Haydn Yearbook has decided to publish all documents dated post 1804 in abbreviated form.
Abkürzungen: Abbreviations see above, p.6-7

Acta Musicalia Nr.201

Bericht des Güterregenten Szent Gály an den Fürsten Nicolaus II. über die Schwängerung der Tochter Magdalena Polzers durch den Musiker Franz Finger. Eisenstadt, den 5. Juni 1805.

Finger stellt nicht in Abrede mit der Tochter Umgang gehabt zu haben, verneint aber sie zu Fall gebracht zu haben oder ihr die Heirat versprochen zu haben. Die Schuld an der Schwängerung treffe ganz allein die Mutter, da sie die Tochter ohne Aufsicht in Eisenstadt, im Engelswirtshaus oder beim Musiker Hornik, wohnen ließ. Die Rechnung für den Aufenthalt der Tochter habe Finger bezahlt. Finger bekennt auch, daß er Frau Polzer 140F. schulde, worüber er ihr einen Schuldschein habe ausstellen wollen, den sie nie annehmen wollte. Es wäre ihm jedoch ein leichtes seinen Vater um das Geld zu bitten, doch möchte er die Rechnung für den Engelwirt abziehen so daß er nur mehr 86F. zu zahlen hätte. Szent Gály schlägt dem Fürsten vor, dem jungen Mann von seiner jährlichen Besoldung von 400 F. monatlich 6 - 8 Gulden abzuziehen und die Beschwerde wegen der Schwängerung der Tochter abzuweisen.

Kommentar

Franz Finger war am 14. April 1802 zusammen mit Johann Hornik als Klarinettist eingestellt worden, sein Anfangsgehalt betrug 314 Gulden, ab 1805 aber 400 Gulden. Roger Hellyer, HJB XV, 37, 56, 58f.

No.201
Report from Regent Szent Gály to Prince Nicolaus II concerning the pregnancy of Magdalena Polzer's daughter by the musician Franz Finger. Eisenstadt, 5 June 1805.
Summary Translation
Finger did not deny having relations with the daughter, but denied seducing her or offering his hand in marriage. The responsibility for her becoming pregnant is her mother's, who left the daughter unsupervised in Eisenstadt, living either in the Angel Inn or boarding with the musician Hornik. The bill for the daughter's board was paid by Finger, who also admits owing Frau Polzer 140f; he has confirmed this to her by writing an I. O. U. which however she never wanted to accept. It would be easy for him to take the money from his father, but he wants to subtract the bill from the Angel Inn so that he would owe only 86f. Szent Gály suggests to the Prince that the young man pay 6 - 8 gulden monthly from his annual salary of 400f. and to refuse responsibility for the daughter's pregnancy.

Commentary

Franz Finger was engaged on 14 April 1802 together with Johann Hornik as clarinet players. At the beginning he earned 314 gulden p.a., from 1805 400. Roger Hellyer HYB XV, 37, 56, 58f.

Acta Musicalia Nr.202

Gutachten des Güterregenten Szent Gály über das Gesuch der Witwe Elisabeth Dietzl um eine Pension betreffend. Eisenstadt, den 3. März 1806.

Der Güterregent unterstützt die Bitte der Supplikantin, da ihr verstorbener Mann schon bei Fürst Nicolaus I. in Diensten gewesen war, dann zur Hofkapelle in Wien wechselte, wo er eine lebenslängliche Pension gehabt hätte. 1802 sei er wieder in die fürstliche Kapelle gekommen und hätte sich der hoch fürstlichen Gnade würdig gemacht. Daher sollte der Witwe, wie der Pensionistin Pauer 200 oder der großen Theuerung wegen 300 Gulden angewiesen werden. Da ihre Tochter in fürstlichen Diensten in Eisenstadt sei, so solle der Mutter gestattet sein bei der Tochter zu wohnen, ungeachtet des fürstlichen Verbotes, daß sich Pensionisten nicht in Eisenstadt niederlassen dürfen.

Kommentar

Es handelt sich hier um die Witwe des Kontrabassisten Johann Dietzl, dessen Vater Organist und Schulmeister bei Fürsten Nicolaus I. gewesen war; Haydn schätzte die Dietzlfamilie - Johanns Bruder war Hornist - als gute Musiker. Nach der Auflösung der Kapelle war Johann Dietzl nach Wien übersiedelt.

No.202

Report by Regent Szent Gály concerning widow Elisabeth Dietzl's petition for a pension. Eisenstadt, 3 March 1806.

The Regent supports this petition, since her late husband was already in service to Prince Nicolaus I, then went to the Vienna Court Chapel, where he would have enjoyed a life pension. Since 1802 he was again in the princely service and derserves princely grace and favour. Therefore the widow should, like pensioned widow Pauer, receive 200 or because of the severe inflation 300 gulden. Since her daughter is in the princely service, the widow should be allowed to live with her daughter, despite the princely edict that pensioners are not allowed to settle in Eisenstadt.

Commentary

This was the widow of double bass player Johann Dietzl, whose father was organist and schoolmaster under Prince Nicolaus I. Haydn held the Dietzl family in high professional regard: Johann's brother was horn player in the band. After the dissolution of the Capelle Johann Dietzl went to work in Vienna.

Acta Musicalia Nr.203

Johann von Szent Gály erbittet von Fürst Nicolaus II. die Bestätigung der Zahlungsanweisung für den Komponisten Joseph Heidenreich am 27. Mai 1807.
Heidenreich hatte vier Litaneien abgeliefert und sollte dafür von Vizekapellmeister Johann Fuchs 250 Gulden ausbezahlt erhalten, doch fehlte noch die Bestätigung des Fürsten.

Kommentar

Auch Joseph Haydn beschäftigte Heidenreich und gab ihm verschiedene seiner Jugendstücke zur Orchestrierung. Siehe Landon V, 338n, 339.

No.203
Johann von Szent Gály asks Prince Nicolaus II to confirm an order for payment to the composer Joseph Heidenreich, 27 May 1807.
Heidenreich delivered four litanies and should have received 250 gulden from Vice Capellmeister Johann Fuchs, but princely confirmation was lacking.

Commentary
Joseph Haydn also used the services of Heidenreich and entrusted to him the orchestration of various youthful compositions. See Landon V, 338n., 339.

Acta Musicalia Nr.204

Anweisungen des Güterregenten Szent Gály an die verschiedenen Ämter über die Anstellung der Sängerin Elisabeth Schneider und Anfrage an den Fürsten Nicolaus II., wie das Quartier der Sängerin möbliert werden solle. Eisenstadt den 2. Juli 1807.
Buchhalter Schmidt vom Hauptzahlamt: Demoiselle Schneider wurde am 1. Juni auf zwei Jahre mit halbjähriger Kündigungsfrist angestellt und erhält jährlich 300 Dukaten W.W. oder 1350 Rhein. Gulden W.W., samt Freiquartier mit Einrichtung, Holz und Licht.
Verleihamt: freies Brennholz.
Rath Canto: Equipage für den Hofdienst, dies sei auch Schmidt mitzuteilen.
Kapellmeister Hummel und Schmidt: Schneider sei sowohl bei Kirchen- und Kammermusik als im Theater zu verwenden.

Zahlamt: nebst dem Gehalt erhält die Sängerin jährlich 46 Pfund gegossene Unschlitkerzen zum gängigen Preis.
Verwaltersamt: jährlich sechs Klafter Buchenholz durch das hiesige Schafferamt bereitzustellen.
Buchhaltung und Schmidt: Gehalt, Kerzen und Brennholz für zwei Jahre in Evidenz zu halten, ditto die Equipage.
Oberwald und Jägeramt: jährliche Brennholz in Evidenz zu halten.
Regentialvortrag an den Fürsten: Demoiselle Schneider wurde auf hochfürstlichen mündlichen Befehl mit den gleichen Bedingungen wie Demoiselle Croll eingestellt und alle Anweisungen erlassen, doch erbitte er schriftlichen Befehl, ob für die Demoiselle, die gegenwärtig im Schloß wohnt, ein Quartier gemietet und durch den Schloß Pfleger eingerichtet werden solle.

Kommentar

Für Elisabeth Schneider siehe A.M.96, 137, 220.

No.204

Orders by Regent Szent Gály to various offices regarding the engagement of the singer Elisabeth Schneider and a query to Prince Nicolaus II as to how her apartment is to be furnished. Eisenstadt, 2 July 1807. Bookkeeper Schmidt of Chief Cashier's office: Demoiselle Schneider was engaged on 1 June for two years with six months notice and receives 300 ducats p. a. W. W. or 1350 Rhenish gulden W. W. together with free furnished lodgings, wood and light.
To lending depot: free wood.
Rath Canto: Equipage for court service, Schmidt also to be informed. Kapellmeister Hummel and Schmidt: Schneider to be employed in church and chamber music as well as in the theatre.
Cashier's office: apart from salary the singer is to receive 46lbs tallow candles p. a. at the market price.
Administration: p.a. six fathom cords of beech wood is to be prepared by our Transport office.
Bookkeeper and Schmidt: salary, candles and firewood to be kept on books for two years, also equipage.
Forestry and hunting offices: firewood p. a. to be registered.
Regent's proposal to the Prince: Demoiselle Schneider has been engaged, as a result of an oral order, on the same terms as those for Demoiselle Croll, and all necessary orders issued, but he requests that written orders be issued if Demoiselle, who at present lives in the castle, should be given quarters rented and furnished by the castle inspector.

Commentary

For Elisabeth Schneider see A.M.96, 137, 220.

Acta Musicalia Nr.205

Gutachten des Güterdirektors Szent Gály über die Bittschrift der Sängerin Barbara Pillhofer um eine Zulage. Eisenstadt, 3. Juli 1807. Regential Vortrag: die Supplikantin singt bereits 20 Jahre und versieht seit zehn Jahren den Kirchendienst ganz allein. Sie wird auch von Vizekapellmeister Fuchs sehr geschätzt, der eine Zulage von jährlich 100 Gulden vorschlägt, die auch Szent Gály angemessen findet.

Kommentar

Barbara Pillhofer, die Nichte der fürstlichen Sängerin Eleonore Jäger, stammte aus Schottwien und trat als Elevin 1788 in fürstliche Dienste. Sie sang im Eisenstädter Kirchenchor und erhielt 25 Gulden im Jahr. Nach der Auflassung der Kapelle durch den Fürsten Anton war sie eine der wenigen, die nicht entlassen wurde. Sie hatte ihr Debut 1797 in Eisenstadt in Haydns 'Missa in tempore belli', deren Sopranpartie eine virtuose Sängerin voraussetzt. Haydn schätzte seine 'Babette' und vermachte ihr in seinem Testament 50 Gulden. Landon II, 49; IV, 433; V, 380.

No.205
Report by Regent Szent Gály concerning the petition of the singer Barbara Pillhofer for an increase. Eisenstadt, 3 July 1807.
Regent's proposal: The supplicant has been singing for 20 years and for the last ten years provides the church services all by herself. She is much appreciated by Vice Capellmeister Fuchs, who suggests a rise of 100 gulden p.a., with which sum Szent Gály agrees.

Commentary
Barbara Pillhofer, the niece of the princely singer Eleonore Jäger, came from Schottwien and entered the princely service as a pupil (apprentice) in 1788. She sang in the Eisenstadt church choir and earned 25 gulden p.a. After the Capelle's dissolution under Prince Anton she was one of the few who was not dismissed. She made her debut in Eisenstadt in 1797 as soprano solo in Haydn's *Missa in tempore belli* which requires a highly trained virtuoso voice. Haydn was fond of 'Babette' and left her 50 gulden in his will. Landon II, 49, IV, 433; V, 380.

Acta Musicalia Nr.206

Anfrage des Güterdirektors Szent Gály an die fürstliche Domänendirektions- Registratur über Michael, Sohn des fürstlichen Kammersängers Johann Bader. Eisenstadt, 3. Juli 1807.

Der Güterdirektor will wissen, ob Michael tatsächlich in der Registratur so brauchbar sei, als sein Vater in seiner Bittschrift (seinem Sohn eine Kleiderzulage zu gewähren) glauben machen will.

Kommentar

Über Michael Bader siehe A.M.207.

No. 206

Query by Regent Szent Gály to the princely Domains-Director Registry concerning Michael, son of the princely chamber singer Johann Bader. Eisenstadt, 3 July 1807.

The regent wishes to know if Michael is really as useful to the registry as his father suggests in his request (in which he asks for more clothing for his son).

Commentary

For Michael Bader, see A.M.207.

Acta Musicalia Nr.207

Bericht des Güterregenten Szent Gály an den Fürsten Nicolaus II. über die beiden Söhne des Bassisten Johann Bader. Eisenstadt, 10. Juli 1807

Regential Vortrag: 1. der ältere Sohn Michael, Sängerknabe, erhält 90 Gulden, kann nichts, hat keine Schulen, kann weder Latein noch Ungarisch kann daher nie in der Registratur verwendet werden. Vielleicht tauge er für die Wirtschaft und könne beim Verwalteramt praktizieren, muß aber monatlich überwacht werden, ob er Fortschritte mache, sonst müße er zu einem Handwerker in die Lehre. 2. der jüngere Sohn ist Supernumerarius, erhält jährlich 40 Gulden und könnte bis zum Stimmwechsel - sollte sich eine freie Stelle finden - in das Institut der Kapellknaben aufgenommen werden.

Die vom Vater eingereichten Rechnungen des Apothekers in Höhe von 21F 11xr, des Schneiders mit 87F 38xr und des Schusters mit 76F 55xr könnten dieses eine Mal in Gnaden bezahlt werden.

Kommentar

Über Bader und seine Söhne siehe A.M.103, 136, 137, 206, 218.

No.207

Report by Regent Szent Gály to Prince Nicolaus II on the two sons of the bass singer Johann Bader. Eisenstadt, 10 July 1807.

Regent's porposal : 1. The elder son Michael, boy chorister, receives 90 gulden, can do nothing, has no education, can speak neither Latin nor Hungarian, and can therefore never

serve in the Registry. Perhaps he could learn economics and practice in the Administrative offices, but would have to be supervised every month to see if he is making progress, otherwise he must learn a trade. 2. The younger son is supernumerarius, earns 40 gulden and until his voice breaks could be taken into the boys' choir, should a free place be available.
The submitted bills from the apothecary for 21f 11xr, from the tailor for 87f 38xr and from the cobbler for 76f 55xr could be paid this once as an act of mercy.

Commentary

About Bader and his sons, see A.M.103, 136, 137, 206, 218.

Acta Musicalia Nr.208

Fürstliche Resolution den Kapellknaben Religionsunterricht erteilen zu lassen (Wien, 17. Februar 1807). Bericht des Güterregenten an den Fürsten über die dafür getroffenen Maßnahmen (Eisenstadt, 24. Februar 1807).
Fürst Nicolaus schreibt Szent Gály, daß der Eisenstädter Schloßkaplan die Kapellknaben und deren Lehrer Rathmayer in der 'Christenlehre' unterrichten solle, und zwar an Sonn- und Feiertagen. Szent Gály schlägt jedoch vor dies an einem Werktag zu tun, da die Kinder besonders im Winter nach den Gottesdiensten nicht noch eine weitere Stunde in der ungeheizten Kirche zubringen könnten. Daher solle der Kaplan die Buben in ihrer Wohnung unterrichten und für seine Mühe jährlich 100 Gulden erhalten, damit er 'selbsten auch aus Rücksicht dessen, daß er die Gnade hat Schloßkaplan zu seyn, von denen anderen Kaplänen etwas vorhabe'. Szent Gály verständigt dann auch den Probst von Eisenstadt und Lehrer Rathmayer über die Wünsche des Fürsten, daß an Mon- und Samstagen von 11 bis 12 Uhr die Kapellknaben Religionsunterricht erhalten sollen.

No.208

Princely resolution to ensure that the boy choristers are given instruction in religion. Vienna, 17 February 1807. Report by Regent on the measures taken to implement it. Eisenstadt, 24 February 1807.
Prince Nicolaus writes to Szent Gály that the Eisenstadt Castle chaplain should give lessons in catechism to the boy choristers and their teacher Rathmayer; this to be done on Sundays and holidays. Szent Gály however suggests that this be done on a working day, since the children, especially in winter, should not be obliged to spend another hour after the service in the unheated church. Therefore the chaplain should teach catechism to the boys in their quarters and should be recompensed for his troubles with a yearly stipend of 100 gulden, 'in order that, considering his honourable position as castle chaplain, he should be in a position above that of the other chaplains'. Szent Gály then informs the provost of Eisenstadt and the teacher Rathmeyer about the princely wishes, viz. that religious instructions should be given to the boy choristers on Mondays and Saturdays from 11 a.m. to 12 noon.

Acta Musicalia Nr.209

Fürstliche Intimatum an den Güterregenten Johann von Szent Gály den Kapellmeister Franz Teyber, der im Gasthof Adler in Eisenstadt wartete um vom Fürsten engagiert zu werden, wieder nach Wien zurückzuschicken. Kanzleidirektor Karner übermittelt am 17. März 1807 den fürstlichen Befehl an Szent Gály. Dieser weist am 2. April das Hauptzahltamt an, Teyber Reisegeld auszuzahlen und 'ihn mit einer sicheren Gelegenheit nach Wien zurückzusenden'. Seine 'Zehrungskosten' samt dem Reisegeld beliefen sich auf 87 Gulden 20 Kreuzer.

Kommentar

Franz Teyber, 1756 geboren, entstammte einer Wiener Musikerfamilie und war ein viel bewunderter Klavier- und Orgelspieler. Nach jahrelangem Wanderleben durch Deutschland und die Schweiz kam er 1798 wieder nach Wien zurück und ernährte sich von Gelegenheitsarbeiten. 1801 schrieb er für Schikaneder zur Eröffnung des Theaters an der Wien eine erfolgreiche Oper namens *Alexander von Indien* (Libretto von Schikaneder). 1806 komponierte er eine große Messe in Es. Erst 1809 gelang es ihm eine sichere Stelle zu erhalten: er wurde Domorganist von St. Stephan und ein Jahr später Hoforganist. 1811 später starb er gänzlich verschuldet.
HJB V,96; MGG Bd.13, 271.

No.209

Princely *Intimatum* to Regent Johann von Szent Gály that Kapellmeister Franz Teyber, who is waiting in the Eagle Inn at Eisenstadt to be engaged by the Prince, should return to Vienna. Chancery Director Karner forwards this princely order to Szent Gály on 17 March 1807, who in turn, on 2 April, advises the Chief Cashier's Office to issue travelling money to Teyber and 'to find a safe way to have him sent back to Vienna'. His lodging and food, together with his travel expenses, came to 87 gulden 20 kreuzer.

Commentary

Franz Teyber born in 1756, came from a family of Viennese musicians and was much admired as a pianist and organist. After many years travelling in Germany and Switzerland he returned to Vienna in 1798 and lived as a free lance musician. In 1801 he wrote a successful opera *Alexander von Indien*, libretto by Schickaneder, to open that impresario's Theater an der Wien. In 1806 he composed a large-scale mass in E flat. Not until 1809 did he find a regular position - as cathedral organist at St Stephen's and a year later court organist as well. He died improvised in the following year.
HYB V, 96; MGG Vol.13, 271.

Acta Musicalia Nr.210

Fürstliche Resolution über die Zuweisung von Wohnungen für die Sängerin Elisabeth Schneider, ihren Kollegen Joseph Treidler und den fürstlichen Buchhalter Ignaz Kühnelt. Wien, den 12. Februar 1808.
Der Kammer- und Chorsängerin Schneider wird die Wohnung des Actuars Schmid, dem Tenoristen Treidler eine größere im neuerbauten Wimmerischen Haus, Kühnelt hingegen das ehemalige Quartier der Sängerin Schneider im Thurnerischen Haus zugewiesen. Die kleinere Wohnung im Hause Wimmer bleibt leer. Außerdem wird dem Sänger Treidler ein Depot von vier Klaftern Brennholz bewilligt. Szent Gály verständigt am 26. Februar das Waldamt, den Vizekapellmeister und das Verwalteramt über Treidlers Holzdepot, den Verwalter auch über die Summe des vom Actuarius Schmid verlangten Zinses in Höhe von 250 Gulden pro Jahr. Seiner Meinung nach müßte davon etwas abgehandelt werden. Am gleichen Tag schreibt er an Fürst Nicolaus, daß Kühnelt lieber das Quartier 'im Schmidischen Hause' haben möchte, wenn er kein anderes 'geräumigeres erlangen' und die Sängerin in ihrem gegenwartigen Quartier ruhig belassen werden könnte. Zwei Tage später langt die Einwilligung des Fürsten ein. Das Schmidische Quartier wird für Kühnelt auf mehrere Jahre gemietet.

No.210

Princely resolution concerning the assignment of lodgings for the singers Elisabeth Schneider, Joseph Treidler and the princely bookkeeper Ignaz Kühnelt. Vienna, 12 February 1808.
The chamber and choir singer Schneider is assigned quarters in the apartment of the clerk Schmid, the tenor Treidler a large one in the newly built Wimmer House, Kühnelt is to occupy the Thurner house [Thurnermeister]. The smaller flat in the Wimmer House remains empty. Moreover the singer Treidler is to be granted four fathom cords of firewood. Szent Gály informs the forestry office on 26 February, also the Vice Capellmeister and the Administrator about Treidler's wood allotment. The Administrator is informed as well about the amount of rental money asked by clerk Schmid (250 gulden p.a.). He believes that this sum could be reduced. On the same day he writes to Prince Nicolaus that Kühnelt would rather have a flat in the Schmid house if none larger could be located and the lady singer could be left in the quarters she now occupies. Two days later the princely approval arrives. The Schmid quarters are rented for Kühnelt for a period of some years.

Acta Musicalia Nr.211

Anfrage des Fürsten Nicolaus II. wie Domainendirektionsrat Schubarnegg ausgezeichnet werden könne (Wien, 12. Februar 1808) und ausführliche Antwort (19. Februar) des Güterdirektors Szent Gály um die Verdienste Schubarneggs ins rechte Licht zu setzen. Weiters bestätigt Fürst Nicolaus, daß er die unterzeichneten Dienstreverse des Musikpersonales erhalten habe und für jedes Mitglied nach 'Maßgab ihres Verdienstes besorgt sein werde'. Cellist Clameth habe seine lebenslängliche Dienst-Unterzeichnung übergeben, die des Violonisten Luigi Tomasini sei bis jetzt jedoch nicht eingelangt, weshalb Vizekapellmeister Fuchs angehalten werden solle Tomasini den Dienst aufzukündigen.

Kommentar

Die Kinder des alten Konzertmeisters Luigi Tomasini machten dem Vater und dem Fürsten viel Kummer. Alois jun. wurde 1779 in Eszterháza geboren und, wie auch sein älterer Bruder Anton, zum Geiger ausgebildet. Mit 17 Jahren wurde er Mitglied der fürstlichen Kapelle und am 1. Januar 1796 mit einem Gehalt von 450 Gulden angestellt. 1803 erhielt er eine Zulage von 60 Gulden, da Haydn in einem Gutachten ihn als 'seltenes Genie' bezeichnete und eine Zulage von 50 bis 100 Gulden befürwortet hatte. Wie immer, einigte man sich auf die niedrigere Summe und der virtuose Geiger erhielt 60 Gulden, die für seinen flotten Lebensstil nicht ausreichten. So hatte er stets Schulden. 1807 wollte er die Sängerin Sophie Croll heiraten. Er bat den Fürsten um die Heiratserlaubnis und die Bezahlung der aufgelaufenen Schulden, was Nicolaus abschlug. 1808 verlangte der Fürst von seinen Musikern eine lebenslange Dienstverpflichtung, die Tomasini nicht unterschreiben wollte, solange er keine Heiratserlaubnis käme, worauf der Fürst ihn entlassen wollte. Tomasini richtete an den Fürsten noch ein weiteres Gesuch (A.M.212), ehe er endlich den Revers unterzeichnete. Nicolaus nahm die Kündigung zurück (A.M.214), gab aber nie die schriftliche Einwilligung zur am 17. Juli 1808 erfolgten Trauung, was bedeutete, daß seine Frau nicht pensionsberechtigt gewesen wäre. Als der Fürst nach dem Tode Luigi Tomasinis Luigi jun. nicht die Konzertmeisterstelle zugestand, verließ das Ehepaar die fürstliche Kapelle. HJB VIII, 17f.
Domainendirektionsrat Schubarnegg sollte dem Fürsten 1811 noch weitere gute Dienste leisten. Da er verantwortlich für die Schafzucht war, die er, wie Szent Gály in diesem Bericht hervorhebt, durch großen Fleiß verbessert hatte, konnte er mit dem Geld, daß er durch den Verkauf der 'spanischen Wolle' erzielt hatte, dem Fürsten aus einer großen Geldverlegenheit helfen, da Wechsel, die Nicolaus in Paris 1810 in Höhe von 400.000 Dukaten ausgestellt hatte, und die durch Arnstein und Geymüller gedeckt worden waren, fällig wurden.

Schubarnegg kam Anfang Juni mit 185.000 Gulden Conv. Münze in die Wallnerstraße. Hauptkassier Stessel nahm das Geld in Empfang und bezahlte bis 15. Juni die in Paris ausgestellten Wechsel. Am 14. Juni reiste der Fürst nach Eisenstadt, entließ einen großen Teil der Dienerschaft der Fürstin und bedeutete ihr, daß sie nach drei Tagen Eisenstadt verlassen und in Bodendorf residieren müsse. Alle Bauarbeiten am Eisenstädter Schloß wurden eingestellt und eingerissenen Gebäude eingeplankt. Hohe fürstliche Beamte rieten Nicolaus die fürstliche Grenadiergarde auf 70 Mann zu reduzieren, auch Beamte aus der Buchhaltung und Musiker der Kapelle zu entlassen. Der Fürst wartete die Ankunft seines Sohnes Paul aus Dresden ab, um alle Maßnahmen mit ihm besprechen zu können. (Confidentenbericht 1262b/9 vom 15. Juni 1811, Polizeihofstelle, Verwaltungsarchiv, Wien)

No.211
Query by Prince Nicolaus II, in which fashion Domain Director Councillor Schubarnegg could be rewarded (Vienna, 12 February 1808) and lengthy reply (19 February) from Regent Szent Gály on the subject. Further Prince Nicolaus confirms that he has received the signed service receipts of the music personnel and will concern himself to settle on each one the sum he or she deserves according to the quality and length of service. The cellist Clameth handed in his contract for life, but that of the violinist Luigi Tomasini has not yet arrived, hence Vice Capellmeister Fuchs is instructed to dismiss Tomasini from his position.

Commentary
The children of the old leader Luigi Tomasini caused much trouble both to their father and the Prince. Alois Jr. was born at Eszterháza in 1779 and like his elder brother Anton studied the violin. At the age of seventeen he became a member of the princely chapel and on 1 January 1796 was engaged at a salary of 450 gulden p.a. In 1803 he was given a rise of 60 gulden, Haydn in his recommendation having described Alois Jr. as a 'rare genius' and backing a rise of 60-100 gulden. The rise of 60 gulden, although a compromise, was still insufficient to accommodate Alois's lifestyle, which led him into regular debts. In 1807 he wanted to marry the singer Sophie Croll. He asked the Prince for permission to do so and requested that his debts be paid (which Nicolaus refused). In 1808 the Prince wanted lifetime contracts with his musicians, which Tomasini did not wish to sign, so long as no permission to marry was forthcoming, whereupon the Prince prepared to dismiss him. Tomasini then wrote another petition (A. M. 214), before signing the contract. Nicolaus withdrew the dismissal (A. M. 214), but never issued written permission for Tomasini's mariage, which occured on 17 July 1808, which also meant that Tomasini's wife was not entitled to a pension. When the Prince, after the death of old Luigi Tomasini, did not confer the position of leader to Alois (Luigi) Jr., the young couple left the princely chapel. HYB VIII, 17f.
Domain director Councillor Schubarnegg was destined to be of great service to the Prince in 1811. Since he was responsible for the princely lambing operations, he was able through the sale of 'spanish wool' to help the Prince out of an unfortunate economic situation. Prince Nicolaus had borrowed 400,000 ducats in Paris in 1810, insured by Arnstein and Geymüller (the bankers and brokers), and these promissary notes now became due. Schubarnegg arrived at the princely palace in the Wallnerstrasse in Vienna at the beginning of June 1811 with 185,000 gulden in Conv. Münze. Chief Cashier Stessel received the cash and the promissary

notes, due in Paris by 15 June, could be paid. On 14 June the Prince travelled to Eisenstadt, dismissed the greater part of the Princess Maria Hermenegild's servants and told her that she must leave Eisenstadt within three days and reside in Bodendorf. All building activities concerned with the castle (which was being refurbished) were stopped and scaffolding erected around incomplete building sites. The leading princely officials suggested that Nicolaus reduce the princely grenadiers to 70 men, also to dismiss civil servants in the book keeping administration and the Capelle as well. The Prince awaited the arrival of his son from Dresden to discuss all this with him.
(MS. Confidentenbericht 1262b/9 of 15 June 1811, Police court archives, Verwaltungsarchiv, Vienna, unpublished).

Acta Musicalia Nr.212

Luigi Tomasini jun. bittet Fürst Nicolaus II. um die Heiratserlaubnis. (Eisenstadt, 16. Februar 1808).
Luigi Tomasini appelliert an des Fürsten Menschenliebe und Fürstengröße ihm die Erlaubnis zur Heirat mit der Sängerin Sophie Croll zu geben und eine Gehaltsaufbesserung dazu, da beide nichts sehnlicher wünschen als lebenslänglich in fürstlichen Diensten zu bleiben. Den vom Fürsten verlangten Dienstrevers könne er nur für ein Jahr und nicht wie gewünscht für drei Jahre unterschreiben, da Sophie Crolls Kontrakt bereits das kommende Jahr ablaufe. Es fühle seine dreißig Jahre 'am Nacken' und sein heißester Wunsch sei es sich mit einem 'Geschöpf wie Sophie!, welche mir meine Lebenstage mit Ruhe, Zufriedeheit und wahrer Anhänglichkeit !! für mich bezeugt! ehlich zu verbinden!'

Kommentar

Siehe A.M.211, 213, 214.

No.212
Luigi Tomasini Jr. requests permission to marry from Prince Nicolaus II. Eisenstadt, 16 February 1808. Luigi (Alois) Jr. asks humble and gracious permission to marry the singer Sophie Croll and also a rise in salary, both wish nothing more than to remain all their lives in princely service. He can sign the document requested by the Prince for a period of only one year and not as wished for three, since Sophie Croll's contract expires in the coming year. He feels his age of thirty and his dearest wish is to ally himself with 'such a creature as Sophie!, who would grant him peace, contentment and true faithfulness all his life'.

Commentary
See A. M.211, 213, 214.

Acta Musicalia Nr.213

Fürst Nicolaus II. befiehlt die sofortige Ablieferung der unterschriebenen Dienstverpflichtungen aller Musiker und Sänger. Wien, den 17. Februar 1808.
Zweimal hatte der Fürst bereits befohlen die unterschriebenen dreijährigen Dienstverpflichtungen zu ihm nach Wien zu schicken, und immer noch zögerten einige Musiker, voran der Geiger Luigi Tomasini jun., die Unterschrift zu leisten. Güterregent Szent Gály sollte den Zögerern mit sofortiger Entlassung drohen und in den nächsten 24 Stunden die unterfertigten Reverse versiegelt mit Regisseur Schmidt nach Wien schicken. Bemerkung am Aktenumschlag: Ist befolgt und der anbefohlene Revers am 18. Feb. mittels Regisseurs Schmidt eingesendet worden.

No.213
Prince Nicolaus II orders the immediate delivery of the signed contracts for all musicians and singers. Vienna, 17 February 1808.
Prince Nicolaus had ordered twice the immediate delivery of the signed three-year contracts from all musicians and singers, but some musicians hesitated, particularly the violinist Luigi (Alois) Tomasini Jr. Regent Szent Gály should threaten those hesitating with immediate dismissal and within 24 hours the sealed and signed contracts should be taken to Vienna by [theatre] Director Schmidt. Note on cover: has been done and the contracts ordered sent via Director Schmidt on 18 February to Vienna.

Acta Musicalia Nr.214

Fürstliche Resolution den jungen Luigi Tomasini nach Unterschrift des dreijährigen Dienstvertrages weiter im Dienst zu behalten und die am 23. Februar angekündigte Entlassung aufzuheben. Wien, 28. Februar 1808.

Kommentar
Siehe A.M.211

No.214
Princely resolution that the young Luigi Tomasini, after having signed the three-year contract, is to be retained in service and the dismissal of 23 February declared null and void. Vienna, 28 February 1808.

Commentary
See A. M.211

Acta Musicalia Nr.215

Güterregent Szent Gály berichtet Fürst Nicolaus II. über die Wohnungssuche für den Sänger Joseph Treidler und den Buchhalter Ignaz Kühnel. Eisenstadt 17. Januar 1808.
Buchhalter Kühnel muß seine Wohnung räumen und kann trotz angebotener Mehrzahlung kein Quartier finden. Laut Convention muß die fürstliche Verwaltung ihm ein Quartier zur Verfügung stellen und das größere Quartier im Wimmerischen Haus wäre genau das Richtige für ihn, falls der Fürst es nicht jemanden anderen bereits versprochen hätte. Kammersänger Treidler und seine Gattin bewerben sich auch um die gleiche Wohnung und berufen sich auf eine mündliche Zusage des Fürsten. Szent Gály meint, daß Kühnelt das größere und Treidler das kleinere Quartier im Wimmerischen Haus beziehen sollten.

Kommentar

Die Entscheidung des Fürsten siehe A.M.219

No.215
Regent Szent Gály reports to Prince Nicolaus about finding quarters for the singer Joseph Treidler and the bookkeeper Ignaz Kühnel. Eisenstadt, 17 January 1808.
Bookkeeper Kühnel must clear his quarters and despite offering more rent can not find new quarters. According to his contract the princely administration must provide him with lodgings, and the larger flat in the Wimmer house would be just right for him, supposing the Prince has not already promised it to someone else. Chamber singer Treidler and his wife are also applying for the same quarters and refer to an oral agreement with the Prince; Szent Gály thinks that Kühnel could have the larger quarters and Treidler the smaller in the Wimmer house.

Commentary

For the princely decision; see A. M.219.

Acta Musicalia Nr.216

Fürst Nicolaus II. wünscht den Domainen Direktions Sekretär Fajt und den Bratschisten Johann Treidler standesgemäß unterzubringen. Wien, 15. April 1808.
Güterdirektor Szent Gály berichtete am 26. März d.J. dem Fürsten, daß zur Zeit zur herrschaftlichen Disposition nur das Wimmerische Neugebäude stünde, das eine schöne geräumige Küche, davon links ein abgesondertes Zimmer, rechts aber ein Zimmer samt Kabinet habe. Diese Wohnung könne man dem Bratschisten geben, der jetzt

bei seiner Schwiegermutter wohne und samt ihr aus der gemeinsamen Wohnung ausziehen müsse. Die Wohnung im Stefingerischen Haus könne man dann an den Sekretär Fajt weitergeben.

No.216
Prince Nicolaus II wishes that Domain Director Secretary Fajt and the viola player Johann Treidler should be given appropriate lodgings. Vienna, 15 April 1808.
Regent Szent Gály reported on 26 March to the prince that the only princely lodging available were in the new Wimmer house, which includes a nice roomy kitchen, on the left a separate room, and on the right another room with a little room attached. This apartment could be given to the viola player, who is now living with his mother-in-law but who must now evacuate their joint quarters; the flat in the Stefinger house could then be given to Secretary Fajt.

Acta Musicalia Nr.217

Gutachten des Güterdirektors Szent Gály über Pietro Travaglias Ansuchen seine fürstliche Pension trotz anderweitiger Anstellung in alter Höhe behalten zu dürfen und die fürstliche Resolution. Eisenstadt, 16. November 1808.
Als Travaglia 1798 entlassen wurde, erhielt er eine jährliche Pension von 300 Gulden, die ihm bis zur Erlangung einer anderen Stelle bezahlt werden sollte. Diese Regelung focht Travaglia an, da er nachweisen konnte, daß er auf ausdrücklichen Wunsch des Fürsten Anton seine sichere, pensionsberechtigte Stelle bei den kaiserlichen Theatern in Wien aufgegeben habe. Fürst Anton habe ihm ebenfalls eine lebenslängliche Versorgung zugesichert. Daraufhin habe Fürst Nicolaus am 27. Juni 1798 Travaglia die jährliche Pension von 300 Gulden bestätigt, die jedoch auf 200 Gulden vermindert werden sollte, wenn er eine anderweitige Anstellung gefunden habe. Dieser Fall sei nun eingetreten, da Travaglia beim Fürsten Grassalkovich als Hausinspektor angestellt sei. Szent Gály sieht deshalb keine Veranlassung ihm mehr als die zugesicherten 200 Gulden zu zahlen. Fürst Nicolaus ist der gleichen Meinung und Pietro Travaglia wird am 11. Januar 1809 mit seinem Gesuch abgewiesen.

Kommentar

Siehe A.M.83

No. 217
Report of Regent Szent Gály concerning Pietro Travaglia's petition to receive his princely pension in full despite the fact that he has other work elsewhere. Princely Resolution on the subject. Eisenstadt, 16 November 1808.

When Travaglia, the Eszterháza Theatrical designer was dismissed in 1798 he received a yearly pension of 300 gulden, to be paid to him until he found another post. Travaglia objected since he could prove that at the express desire of Prince Anton [reigned 1790-4] he had renounced a sure, pensioned position with the Royal Imperial Theatres in Vienna. Prince Anton also promised him a life-long position with pension. Thereupon Prince Nicolaus ordered a yearly pension of 300 gulden to be paid to Travaglia, effective 27 June 1798, until he could find another position, in which case he would receive 200 gulden pension. This latter has now come to pass, in that Travaglia has found a position as house inspector at Prince Grassalkovich's. Szent Gály therefore sees no reason to pay him more than the 200 gulden promised to him. Prince Nicolaus is of the same opinion and Pietro Travaglia was informed of the decision on 11 January 1809.

Commentary

See A. M.83.

Acta Musicalia Nr.218

Gutachten des Güterdirektors Szent Gály über ein weiteres Bittgesuch des Sängers Johann Bader seinem Sohn Michael eine Kleiderrechnung zu bezahlen und ihm selbst einen Vorschuß von 400 Gulden zu bewilligen. Eisenstadt, 16. November 1808. Fürst Nicolaus weist beide Ansinnen ab. Wien, 2. Januar 1809.

Johann Bader bat um den Vorschuß, da er seinen Sohn Michael, der (siehe A.M.206, 207) in der fürstlichen Verwaltung wegen mangelnder Begabung nicht unterkommen konnte, nach Raab zu einer Ausbildung als Schullehrer bringen und auch mit Kleidern und Wäsche ausstatten mußte. Dort machte der junge Mann, wie Szent Gály berichtet, so geringe Fortschritte, daß er auch für diesen Beruf ungeeignet wäre. Vater Bader war nun in größeren Schulden, da er auch für 'seine Theaterdienste weniger als der kleinste Statist erhalten habe', der Fürst seine 1807 eingereichte Kleiderrechnung für Michael nicht bezahlt hätte, und anderes mehr.

Kommentar

für Michael Bader siehe A.M.206, 207

No.218

Report of Regent Szent Gály on a further petition by the singer Johann Bader to have the tailor's bill for his son Michael paid and for his own person an advance of 400 gulden. Eisenstadt, 16 November 1808.
Prince Nicolaus refuses both petitions, Vienna 2 January 1809.
Johann Bader, whose son Michael (see A. M.206, 207) was not accepted into the Esterházy administration because he showed no aptitude for such work, sent him to Raab (Györ) as an apprentice school teacher, for which he had to provide him with linen and clothes. But there too, as Szent Gály reports, the young man made little progress and was not suited for that

profession either. Father Bader had rung up considerable debts, since he 'earns for this theatrical work less than a minor stage hand', and the Prince had not paid the tailor's bills for Michael submitted in 1807.

Commentary

For Michael Bader, see A. M.206, 207.

Acta Musicalia Nr.219

Gutachten des Güterregenten Szent Gály über das Gesuch der verwitweten Barbara Tomasini, ihr ein Holzdeputat anzuweisen. Eisenstadt, 27. Oktober 1808.
Szent Gály führt aus, daß alle neu verliehenen Pensionen nur mehr Bargeld enthalten und es nicht ratsam sei, Ausnahmen zu machen. Da jedoch die Supplikantin ihre beiden Stieftöchter Josepha und Elisabeth Tomasini bei sich habe, die beide als Chor- und Kammersängerinnen kein Holzdeputat genießen, so könnte der Witwe unentgeltlich jährlich 6 Klafter Brennholz überlassen werden, solange die Töchter bei ihr wohnen.

Kommentar

Die beiden Töchter sangen von 1807 bis 1809 bzw. 1810 in Eisenstadt. Siehe auch A.M.234.

No.219

Report by Regent Szent Gály on a petition by the widowed Barbara Tomasini in which she requests firewood. Eisenstadt, 27 October 1808.
Szent Gály explains that all newly granted pensions include cash money only and it is not advisable to make exceptions. But since the petitioner also lodges her two step daughters Josepha and Elisabeth Tomasini, both of whom as choir and chamber singers are not entitled to firewood, the widow could be granted gratis 6 further cords of wood p.a; as long as the daughters continue to live with her.

Commentary

Both daughters sang from 1807 to, respectively, 1809 and 1810 in Eisenstadt.
See also A. M.234.

Acta Musicalia Nr.220, 221, 222 a-d

Fürst Nicolaus II. befiehlt seinem Güterregenten Szent Gály die beiden Sängerinnen Vadász und Schneider wegen Abwesenheit und Rollentausch zurechtzuweisen (Preßburg, 13. Oktober 1808). Szent Gály unterrichtet Vizekapellmeister Fuchs und Konzertmeister

Hummel von der fürstlichen Resolution. (Eisenstadt, 18. Oktober 1808)

Bei der Durchsicht der Monatsrapporte (A.M.222a) über die dienstliche Verwendung der 'Kapell-Individuen' sah der Fürst, daß die Sängerin Josepha Vadász sich ohne Erlaubnis aus Eisenstadt entfernt hatte und daß sie außerdem die Rolle der Sophie in der Oper *Die Schatzgräber* (Méhul) übernommen hätte, die der Sängerin Elisabeth Schneider übergeben worden war. Solche Eigenmächtigkeiten seien zu vermeiden. Szent Gály gab den fürstlichen Verweis an die Sängerinnen weiter. Elisabeth Schneiders schriftliche Erklärung beinhaltet, daß sie schon drei Rollen zu studieren hatte (nämlich die Elvira in *Don Juan*, die Agnes Sorel in der gleichnamigen Oper von Gyrowetz sowie die Rolle der Gräfin in einer Oper von Kreuzer) und Vadász die Rolle der Sophie schon gesungen hätte. Diese schriftliche Erklärung schickte Konzertmeister Hummel am 25. September (A.M.221) an den Fürsten.

Aus dem 'Theater Proben Dienst' vom 12. September (A.M.222a) sah der Fürst, daß die Sopranistinnen Elisabeth Schneider, Theresia Stotz und Anna Cornega Singproben zu Mozarts *Don Giovanni* hatten und auch den Vermerk über den Rollentausch der Sängerinnen Schneider und Vadász. Krank gemeldet war der Geiger Ludwig Philipp Möglich. Am 8. Oktober gab es eine Klavierprobe von Hummels Oper *Das Haus ist zu verkaufen* um 9 Uhr früh. A.M.222b: Waldhornist Michael Prinster war krank gemeldet und Madame Vadász als 'abwesend ohne zu melden'. Der Kirchendienst am 9. Oktober um 10 Uhr verlief problemlos, Prinster krank und Vadász abwesend. Am 10. Oktober war eine neuerliche Klavierprobe zu Hummels Oper um 3 Uhr. Krank gemeldet war Prinster, abwesend Vadász (A.M.222d). Abgezeichnet waren die Theaterdienste von Theaterregisseur Heinrich Schmidt und Konzertmeister Hummel, die Kirchdienste von Vizekapellmeister Johann Fuchs.

Nos.220, 221, 222 a-d

Prince Nicolaus II orders his Regent Szent Gály to reprimand the two singers Vadász and Schneider because of absence without leave at rehearsals and switching roles. Pressburg, 13 October 1808. Szent Gály informs Vice Capellmeister Fuchs and Konzert Meister Hummel of the princely resolution. Eisenstadt, 18 October 1808.

In examining the monthly reports (A.M.222a) concerning services of the members of the Capelle, the Prince saw that the singer Josepha Vadász left Eisenstadt without permission and moreover that she took on the role of Sophie in Méhul's opera *Die Schatzgäber* which had previously been assigned to Elisabeth Schneider. Such unilateral decisions must be deplored. Szent Gály passed on the reprimand to the two singers. Elisabeth Schneider's written declaration states that she already has three roles to learn, Donna Elvira in Mozart's *Don Giovanni*, Agnes Sorel in the opera of that name by Gyrowetz and the Countess in an opera

by Kreutzer, and that Vadász has already sung the role of Sophie. Konzertmeister Hummel sent this declaration to the Prince on 25 September (A.M.221).
From the list of rehearsals of 12 September (A.M.222a) the Prince saw that the sopranos Elisabeth Schneider, Theresia Stotz and Anna Cornega had vocal rehearsals for *Don Giovanni* and also that the role of Schneider and Vadász were switched. The violinist Ludwig Philipp Möglich was reported sick. On 8 October there was a piano rehearsal of Hummel's opera *Das Haus ist zu verkaufen* scheduled for 9 a. m. A.M.222b: the horn-player Michael Prinster was reported sick and Madame Vadász as absent without leave. The church rehearsal for 9 October at 10 o'clock a. m. was without problems, Prinster ill and Vadász absent. On 10 October there was another piano rehearsal of Hummel's opera at 3.00 p.m., again with Prinster ill and Vadász absent (A.M.222a). The roll call was made by Theatre Director Heinrich Schmidt and Konzertmeister Hummel for operas, and by Johann Fuchs for the church services.

Acta Musicalia Nr.223 a-b

Gesuch des Vizekapellmeisters Johann Fuchs ihn näher beim Schloß unterzubringen und dessen Ablehnung durch den Fürsten (Eisenstadt, 20. Dezember 1808)
Fuchs' "promemoria" trägt kein Datum. Fuchs weist auf seine sechsjährige Dienstzeit hin und auch auf seine Kompositionen, 'worunter doch einige sind, welche eine Achtung verdienen'. Doch wurden andere und auch Untergebene mit Gnaden ausgezeichnet; besonders tief empfand er die Kränkung, daß bei der letzten 'hohen Geburtsmesse' seine Arbeit 'keiner Erinnerung gewürdigt' wurde. Er bitte nun um die Gnade das Quartier des verstorbenen Domainendirektionsrathes Purgarth zu erhalten, da er nur ein heizbares Zimmer habe und die große Kälte ihn zwinge, mit dem Hausgesinde zu sein, was seine Arbeit empfindlich störe, und der heftige Wind auf dem täglichen Weg ins Schloß ihn krank mache. Des Fürsten Antwort an Szent Gály war kurz: von einer neuen Komposition wäre nichts bekannt 'sowie auch jeder Wert seine Composition billigermassen die Schätzung und Beweis der Zufriedenheit erhält'. Das Quartier sei bereits vergeben.

Kommentar

Für Fuchs siehe A.M.108. Die Untergebenen, die ihm vorgezogen wurden, war eine Anspielung auf Konzertmeister Hummel, der den etwas trockenen Fuchs durch seine Ironie stets an die Wand spielte, sodaß Fuchs einmal sich sogar schriftlich beschwerte 'Ich bitte daher E. Wohlgeboren, mir einmal Ruhe vor diesem Menschen zu verschaffen, denn ich bin das Necken wirklich satt'.
Hummelkatalog, Goethe Museum, Düsseldorf 1972, S.15.

No.223 a-b
Petition by Vice Capellmeister Johann Fuchs to live nearer to the castle and the princely refusal. Eisenstadt, 20 December 1808.
Fuch's pro memoria is undated. Fuchs refers to his six years of service and also to his compositions, 'among which are some which deserve notice'. But others, and those below him in rank, have been graciously rewarded; he was especially offended that on the occasion of the last 'high birthday mass', his work 'was not noticed'. He asks for the favour of being given the quarters of the late Domain Director councillor Purgarth, because Fuchs has but one heatable room and the very cold weather forces him to be with the servants which is most disturbing to his work, and the strong winds which blow on his daily walk to the castle make him ill.
The princely answer to Szent Gály was very brief. He was not aware of any new composition and obviously all Fuchs's compositions are properly received and appreciated anyway. The lodging has been otherwise promised.

Commentary
About Fuchs, see A.M. 108. the 'others ...below him in rank' refer to Konzertmeister Hummel, who always got the upper hand of the rather dry Fuchs, so that once he objected in writing that 'I must ask your well-born self to get that man off my back, for I've really had enough of his teasing.'
Hummel Catalogue, Goethe Museum, Düsseldorf 1981. p. 15.

Acta Musicalia Nr.224 a-c

Antoinette Dorner, Kostgeberin der Sängerknaben ersucht den Vorschuß von 400 Gulden zur Verpflegung der Knaben nicht zurückzahlen zu müssen. Eisenstadt, 18. September 1808.

Dorner führt aus, daß sie die Verköstigung der Sängerknaben von Frau Vutkovacz übernommen habe und einige 'Notwendigkeiten beischaffen mußte'. Güterregent Szent Gály berichtet, daß die frühere Kostgeberin schon um eine Erhöhung des Kostgeldes eingekommen sei und die Teuerung der Lebensmittel seither noch mehr angestiegen sei, weshalb er die 'Relaxierung' befürworte, was der Fürst am 27. September genehmigt, weshalb Szent Gály am 9. Oktober das Hauptzahlamt von der Resolution benachrichtigt.

Kommentar

Siehe A.M.229

No.224 a-c
Antoinette Dorner, landlady of the boy choristers, requests that she need not repay an advance of 400 gulden used for the boys' food. Eisenstadt, 18 September 1808.
Dorner explains that she took over feeding the boys from Frau Vutkovacz and had to purchase some necessary items. Regent Szent Gály reports that the previous landlady had already applied for a rise in the money for board; now, the rise in price of food is even

greater, hence he pleads for a 'relaxation' which the Prince approves on 27 September, which decision Szent Gály passes on (9 October) to the Chief Cashier.

Commentary

See A. M. 229.

Acta Musicalia Nr. 225 a-d

Bericht des Güterregenten Szent Gály an den Fürsten wer die Sängerknaben im Violinspiel unterrichte und welche Fortschritte sie gemacht hätten (ohne Datum).
Die Anfrage des Fürsten stammt vom 14. März. Szent Gály ersieht aus den Akten und der am 16. Juli 1804 erlassenen Resolution, daß Tomasini Vater zwei Zöglingen je drei Stunden pro Woche zu erteilen habe, Tomasini junior ebenfalls zwei Knaben drei Stunden wöchentlich, Tomasini Anton wie sein Vater, drei, Clameth einen Knaben drei Stunden und Anton Polzelli zwei Schüler je zwei Stunden in der Woche zu unterrichten habe. Daraufhin referiert er dem Fürsten, daß Anton Tomasini, der nur zwei Knaben unterrichte, einen dritten annehmen solle, entweder den Schüler Hummels oder den von Vizekapellmeister Fuchs. Außerdem wäre es seine 'unterthänigste Meinung' während der Theaterzeit, wo die Zöglinge monatelang keine Lektionen erhalten, die jeweiligen Lehrer abwechselnd von den Proben zu dispensieren, damit die Lektionen weitergehen können. Lehrer Rathmayer werde er anweisen den Unterricht, sollte er außerhalb des Knabeninstituts stattfinden, durch unterschriebene Billets zu kontrollieren.
Tomasini sen.: unterrichtet Johann Uhl, einen Anfänger; und Jacob Leeb, der schon Bratschist und Orchestergeiger ist.
Tomasini jun.: Johann Novotny, Anfänger; Joseph Dezl (Dätzl?) noch nicht ganz fertig, spielt aber schon bei den zweiten Geigen und verspricht sehr gut zu werden.
Polzelli: Ladislaus Rupp; Joseph Langstöger, bereits brauchbarer Orchestergeiger und zuverlässig.
Clameth: Anton Stadler, zeigt beste Anlagen zum Cello, kann schon überall mitspielen.
Tomasini Luigi jun.: Joseph Foidoich ist Anfänger, spielt aber schon kleine Divertimenti. Joseph Kestner wohnt schon im Musikgebäude, ist Orchestergeiger, wird bald Solospieler werden.
Ferdinand Gsell, Ignaz Förstl sind Anfänger. Alle Sängerknaben wurden in Gegenwart von Vizekapellmeister Fuchs befragt wie und wie oft sie unterrichtet werden. Alle sagten übereinstimmend aus, daß sie während der Theatersaison keinen Unterricht bekämen. Die

Schüler des Tomasini sen. erhalten keine Stunden, wenn er krank sei. Luigi Tomasini sei oft abwesend und die Schüler des Anton Tomasini bekommen oft 14 Tage keine Lektion. Über Clameth gibt es keine Klagen. Nun wurden die Lehrer befragt und gaben zu, während der Theatersaison überhaupt keine Zeit für Lektionen zu haben.
Concertmeister Tomasini entschuldigt sich mit vieler Krankheit, Anton Tomasini meint, daß, wenn er unterrichte, dies auch länger als eine Stunde tue und seine Schüler hinreichende Fortschritte machen.

Acta Musicalia Nr.225b

Szent Gály erläutert dem Lehrer Rathmayer, wie er sich die Kontrolle der Geigenlehrer vorstelle: Rahmayer müsse Protokoll führen, damit die 'hohe und milde Absicht Seiner Durchlaucht unseres gn. Fürstens denen sich auf die Musique verlegenden Sängerknaben erzielet und diese nicht vernachlässigt werden'. Jeder Schüler werde in Zukunft zur Unterrichtsstunde ein Billet mitnehmen, daß sein Lehrer zu unterschreiben habe. Sollte er den Lehrer nicht antreffen, so müßte er das Billet zurückbringen und Rathmayer habe 'den Saumseligen' namentlich Szent Gály anzuzeigen, der ihn zuerst in Güte ermahnen und sollte dies nichts fruchten, die Zahlung streichen würde.

Acta Musicalia Nr.225c

8. Mai 1808: Der Fürst ist mit Szent Gálys Maßnahmen einverstanden, doch solle Vizekapellmeister Fuchs, der das ganze Jahr in Eisenstadt sei, die Aufsicht übernehmen und vor allem die beiden Tomasinis kontrollieren, die es mit dem Lektionsgeben nicht so genau nehmen.

Acta Musicalia Nr.225d

Eisenstadt, 27. Mai 1808. Vizekapellmeister Fuchs erhält die fürstliche Resolution vom 8. Mai. Szent Gály schlägt Fuchs auch vor in der Theatersaison die Unterricht gebenden Geiger abwechselnd von den Proben zu dispensieren, damit der Unterricht der Knaben nicht leide. Für die Schüler Uhl und Leeb habe er einen anderen Lehrer zu finden, da Tomasini sen. mittlerweile gestorben wäre und dem einen Tomasini, der nur zwei Schüler habe, einen dritten zuzuweisen. Konzertmeister Hummel und Rathmayer werden über die Probenregelung ebenfalls unterrichtet, daß laut fürstlicher Resolution Fuchs die Lektionen zu kontrollieren hätte.

No.225 a-d
Report by Regent Szent Gály to the Prince as to which person teaches violin to the boy choristers and how much progress they have made (n.d.)
The query of the Prince is dated 14 March. Szent Gály sees from the files and from the resolution of 16 July 1804 that Father Tomasini is to teach 2 pupils for three hours each every week, Tomasini Jr. also 2 pupils for three hours each every week, Anton Tomasini ditto, Clameth has one pupil for three hours weekly and Anton Polzelli two pupils for two hours each weekly. Whereupon he suggests to the Prince that Anton Tomasini, who teaches only two boys, should teach a third, either Hummel's pupil or that of Vice Capellmeister Fuchs. Moreover, in his humble opinion, during the period when the opera/theatre is given, when the pupils receive no lessons whatever for some months, the sundry teachers should be exempted alternatively from the rehearsals so that they can continue to teach. Teacher Rathmayer will be informed that, when the instructions take place outside the boys' halls, the procedure should be controlled by signed cards.
Tomasini Sen.: teaches Johann Uhl, a beginner and Jacob Leeb, already a viola player in the orchestra.
Tomasini Jr.: Johann Novotny, beginner; Joseph Dezl (Dätzl), not yet ready but already plays in the second violins and shows signs of promise.
Polzelli: Ladislaus Rupp; Joseph Langstöger, already a useful musician and reliable.
Clameth: Anton Stadler, is a promising cellist who can already play everywhere;
Luigi Tomasini Jr.: Joseph Foidoich is a beginner but already plays small divertimenti. Joseph Kestner already lives in the musicians' building, is an orchestra musician, will soon be solo player.
Ferdinand Gsell, Ignaz Förstl are beginners.
All the boy choristers were questioned in the presence of Vice Capellmeister Fuchs how and how frequently, they received instruction. All agreed that they had no instruction during the theatrical season. The pupils of Tomasini sen. receive no instruction when he is ill. Luigi Tomasini [Jr.] is very often absent and the pupils of Anton Tomasini often miss instruction for 14 days. Concerning Clameth there are no complaints. Then the teachers were asked and admitted that during the theatre season they have no time to give lessons.
Leader Tomasini excused himself, he is often ill; Anton Tomasini says that when he teaches, it is also for more than an hour and that his pupils show sufficient progress;

No.225b
Szent Gály explains to teacher Rathmayer how he imagines the violin teachers may be controlled. Rathmayer must make a list so that the 'high and mild intentions of H. H. our gracious Lord regarding the musical instruction of the boy choristers may be implemented and not remain neglected'. Every pupil will take a card with him to his lesson, which his teacher is to sign; in this fashion Rathmayer can inform Szent Gály which teachers were being negligent; they will be first reprimanded and should this not prove to be effective, their pay will be docked.

No.225c
8 May 1808. The Prince agrees with Szent Gály's proposals, but Vice Capellmeister Fuchs, who is in Eisenstadt the whole year, should take over the overall control, especially of the two Tomasinis, who do not seem to take their teaching jobs very seriously.

No.225d
Eisenstadt, 27 May 1808. Vice Capellmeister Fuchs receives the princely resolution of 8 May and Szent Gály proposes to Fuchs that during the theatrical season the violin teachers

are to be dispensed alternatively from rehearsals, so that teaching the boys does not suffer. For pupils Uhl and Leeb another teacher must be found, since Tomasini Sen. has died meanwhile and the Tomasini who has only two pupils is to take on a third. Konzertmeister Hummel and Rathmayer will also be told about organizing the rehearsals to this end, and that Fuchs should oversee the lessons.

Acta Musicalia Nr.226

Fürst Nicolaus II. schreibt seinem Güterregenten über das schlechte Benehmen der Sängerknaben. Eisenstadt, 4. Juli 1808.
Der Fürst habe erfahren, daß die Sängerknaben, die aus dem Institut ausgetreten, aber von ihm immer noch unterhalten würden, nicht die beste Coduite zeigten, spät nach Hause kämen, weshalb Lehrer Rathmayer und Corporal Laurent anzuweisen seien auf eine ordentliche Lebensweise zu achten und ev. Anzeige zu erstatten.

No.226
Prince Nicolaus II writes to his Regent about the bad behaviour of the boy choristers. Eisenstadt, 4 July 1808.
The Prince has learned that the choristers who have left the Institute but are still being supported by the Prince, do not behave well. They return home late, to which end teacher Rathmayer and Corporal Laurent are to see that they behave properly, otherwise they may be reported.

Acta Musicalia Nr.227

Szent Gály weist das Hauptzahlamt an dem Tenor Joseph Treidler weiter seine Convention zu bezahlen. Eisenstadt, 30. Juni 1809.
Die Convention sollte zwar aufhören, da Treidler, nachdem er kein Quartier bekam, um seine Entlassung bat, doch habe der Fürst ihm mündlich ein Quartier zugesichert und daher habe Treidler seinen Dienst weiterversehen.

Kommentar

Siehe A.M.210, 215. Quartiersuche.

No.227
Szent Gály indicates to the Chief Cashier's office that they should continue to pay the tenor Joseph Treidler according to the terms of his contract. Eisenstadt, 30 June 1809.
The 'convention' (contract) should expire since Treidler, after having sought in vain for lodgings, asked to be relieved of his duties, but inasmuch as the Prince has promised orally to find lodgings, Treidler will continue in service.

See A. M.210, 215.

Commentary

Acta Musicalia Nr.228 a-b

Fürst Nicolaus II. befiehlt seinem Güterregenten Szent Gály die Verwaltung der Güter während seiner Abwesenheit weiter zu besorgen, Regisseur Schmidt über die Convention des Konzertmeisters Müller zu befragen, und ihn, sowie die Sängerin Schneider nach Eisenstadt zu berufen. Pest, 2. Juli 1809.

Acta Musicalia Nr.228b

Bericht des Theaterregisseurs Heinrich Schmidt über seine Verhandlungen mit Konzertmeister Müller. Eisenstadt, 27. Juli 1809. Er hätte folgende Bedingungen ausgehandelt: Müller als Konzertmeister und seine Frau als Kammersängerin erhalten ein jährliches Gehalt von 2400 Gulden, Freiquartier, Holz- und Kerzendeputat. Als Ersatz für ihren sechswöchigen Aufenthalt in Wien 1808 hätte Fürst Nicolaus ihnen als Entschädigung täglich eine Maß Wein versprochen. Als Gegenleistung seien beide zu allen und jeden gewöhnlichen Dienstleistungen im Theater, Kirche und Konzert verpflichtet. Kündigungsfrist von ihrer Seite zwei Jahre, von Seiten des Fürsten sechs Monate.

Kommentar

Der unglückliche Krieg von 1809 verschonte auch Eisenstadt nicht. Wien kapitulierte am 13. Mai und bereits zwei Tage später kam französische Kavallerie nach Eisenstadt; ein Monat später wurde die Stadt Hauptquartier von Eugène Beauharnais, dem Stiefsohn Napoleons. Der General residierte im Schloß, das die Familie Esterházy mit dem größeren Teil des Hofes geräumt hatte. Fürst Nicolaus wohnte nun in Pest und er sollte dort bis zur Unterzeichnung des Friedens von Schönbrunn (14. Oktober) bleiben.

No.228 a-b

Prince Nicolaus II orders his Regent Szent Gály to administer in his [the Prince's] absence, Director Schmidt is to ask about the contract of Konzertmeister Müller, and to order the lady singer Schneider to come to Eisenstadt. Pest, 2 July 1809.

No.228b
Report by theatre director Heinrich Schmidt concerning his negotiations with Konzertmeister Müller. Eisenstadt, 27 July 1809.
He arrived on the following terms. Müller as Konzertmeister and his wife as chamber singer receive a yearly salary of 2400 gulden, free quarters, firewood and candles. As a substitute for their six weeks' sojourn in Vienna in 1808, Prince Nicolaus proposed a remuneration of a Maß [liquid keg measure] of wine daily. For their side they agree to each and every usual service in theatre, church and concert. For their part they have two years' notice, the Prince six months.

Commentary
The unfortunate war of 1809 did not spare Eisenstadt. Vienna capitulated on 13 May and two days later French cavalry units were already in Eisenstadt. A month later the town became headquarters for Eugène Beauharnais, Napoleon's step son. The general resided in the castle, which the Esterházy family, together with most of the court, had evacuated. Prince Nicolaus now lived in Pest (Budapest) and was to remain there until the signature of the treaty of Schönbrunn (14 October).

Acta Musicalia Nr.229a

Die Lebensmittelteuerung in Eisenstadt bedingt eine Erhöhung der Verpflegungskosten der Kapellknaben. Güterdirektor Szent Gály berichtet den Fürsten am 25. August 1809.
Madame Dorner, die Kostgeberin der Knaben, habe bereits wiederholt um Erhöhung des Kostgeldes gebeten und lasse sich nicht mehr abweisen. Weshalb er nach Rücksprache mit dem Fürsten die Anweisung an das Verwaltungsamt erließ, den im Institut und im Musikgebäude wohnenden Knaben samt dem Professor Rathmayer (der junge Bader esse bei seien Eltern) täglich 16 Pfund Grenadiersbrot auszufolgen. Wäre es nicht besser, die 'kostspieligen Sängerknaben' jetzt nach Hause abzuschieben, und 'bei Eintretung friedlicher Zeiten wiederum einzuberufen?' Er erwarte unterthänigst die hohe 'Willensmeinung', die am gleichen Tag erfolgte, daß die Brotration bewilligt sei.
Bei den Knaben im Institut handelt es sich um Johann Novotni, Ladislaus Augg, Ignatz Förstl, Ferdinand Gsell, Johann Uhl und Joseph Pritschner (Prinster?). Johann Bader werde bei den Eltern verpflegt. Im Musikgebäude befinden sich Anton Steiner, Anton Stadler, Joseph Kastner, Johann Zimmermann.

Acta Musicalia Nr.229b

Da Madame Dorner um eine Erhöhung des Kostgeldes eingekommen war, referiert Szent Gály im Detail: Eisenstadt, 19. September 1809.

Die Höhe des Kostgeldes wurde zu einer Zeit festgesetzt, als das Pfund Rindfleisch 8xr kostete, jetzt hingegen 36. Sie erhält jährlich bar pro Knabe 200 Gulden, 23.20 für ein Frühstück, 5 1/2 Metzen Korn für Brot a 10 Gulden sind 53.20 und 2 6/10 Klafter Holz zum Kochen und Heizen zu 16 Gulden. So erhält sie für die Kost eines Knaben insgesamt 317F 30xr.
Am 27. Juli erhielt sie zur Überbrückung vier Metzen Weizen vom Kastenamt a 10F 30xr (= 54 Gulden) und am 25. August die neue Brotration, so wäre dies alles pro Knabe eine Erhöhung des Kostgeldes von täglich einen Gulden, so lange die Teuerung wäre.

Acta Musicalia Nr.229c

Fürstliche Resolution vom 16. September (Pest): Brotration genehmigt, weitere Verbesserungen des Kostgeldes wären zu besprechen.

Acta Musicalia Nr.229d

Fürstliche Resolution. Pest, 9. Oktober 1809.
Zurückkommend auf den Regentialvortrag vom 19. September befiehlt der Fürst sich um eine andere Kostgeberin umzusehen, falls Antoinette Dorner mit dem bemessenen Kostgeld nicht zufrieden sein sollte.

Acta Musicalia Nr.229e

Kopie eines Briefes von Professor Rathmayer vom 28. Februar 1808, indem er Antoinette Dorner ersucht, ihm eine finanzielle Aushilfe zu gewähren, damit er seine Schulden zahlen könne. Diesen Brief schickte Madame Dorner am 10. Oktober (?) 1809 an Szent Gály mit einer Beschwerde, daß sie beim Fürsten angeklagt sei, sich an dem Kostgeld der Knaben zu bereichern. Ihr Ankläger sei Rathmayer, da sie ihm kein Geld geliehen habe, seine Schulden beim früheren Kostgeber Schaffer Vutkowatz abzuzahlen, wo er immer 200 Gulden oder mehr schuldig war und deshalb auch nicht in der Lage gewesen wäre, gegen die Unzulänglichkeiten (unreine Wäsche, etc,) zu protestieren. Sie habe trotz der höheren Lebenskosten die Knaben rein gehalten und gut versorgt, auch keine Schulden beim Schneider, Schuster oder Hutmacher, wie das früher der Fall war. Eine Liste der Preise von 1804 (als Vutkowatz die Knaben verpflegte), von 1808 (als sie den Posten übernahm) und von 1809, müsse genügen, ihren guten

Ruf wieder herzustellen. Außerdem sei es nur der liederlichste Bursche in Eisenstadt, der Knabe Kastner, der von Rathmayer angestiftet, Lügen über sie verbreite.

	1804	1808	1809
1 Pfund Rindfleisch	9-12xr	- 16xr	34-36xr
1 Mäßl Mehl	24xr	1F 10	2F -
1 Paar Hendeln a	24xr	1F -	2F -
1 Pfund Schweinernes	30xr	1F -	2F -
1 Ei	1xr	- 2xr	- 7xr
1 halbe Milch	3xr	- 11xr	- 12xr
1 Pfund Salz	3xr	- 5xr	- 10xr
1 Pfund Reis	20xr	- 25xr	1F -
1 Pfund Kalbfleisch	20xr	- 30xr	1F 12xr
1 Pfund Seife	16xr	- 24xr	1F 12xr

Zudem erhielt Vutkowatz noch jährlich unentgeltlich von der Herrschaft 100 Pfund Kerzen.

Kommentar

Siehe A.M.224 a-c

No.229a

The rise in food prices in Eisenstadt meant a rise in the living costs of the choir boys. Regent Szent Gály reports to the Prince on 25 August 1809.
Madame Dorner, the head of the kitchen for the boys, has repeatedly asked for a rise in the board money, and can not be put off any longer. Therefore, after conferring with the Prince, he ordered the Administration to supply the boys living in the institute and in the music building, together with Professor Rathmayer (the young Bader ate with his parents), with 16 pounds of grenadiers' bread every day. Would it not be better to send the 'expensive boy choristers' back to their homes and 'to convene them again when a period of peace returns?' He awaits an 'opinion from on high', which was given that same day, permitting the increased bread ration.
The boys in the Institute were Johann Uhl, Joseph Novotni, Ladislaus Augg, Ignatz Förstl, Ferdinand Gisell, Johann Uhl and Joseph Pritschner [Prinster?]. Johann Bader ate with his parents. In the music building there were Anton Steiner, Anton Stadler, Joseph Kastner and Johann Zimmerman.

No. 229b

Madame Dorner was somehow forgotten in all this and received no rise in her board money for the boys. Szent Gály reports in detail, Eisenstadt 19 September 1809.
The amount of board money had been established at a time when the pound of beef cost 8xr, now it is 36. She receives in cash 200 gulden for each boy, 23f. 20xr. for one breakfast, 5 1/2 Metzen [3.44 litres, miller's measure] wheat for bread at 10 gulden makes 53f. 20xr. and 2

6/10 [fathom cords] of wood for cooking and heating at 16 gulden. Thus she receives for boarding each boy a total of 317f. 40xr.

On 27 July she received, to bridge over the period, four metzen of white wheat fom the treasury office at 10f. 30xr. (=54 gulden) and on 25 August a new bread ration, so that all this means a rise of board money of one gulden daily for each boy, so long as the inflation continues.

No.229c

Princely resolution of 16 September 1809 from Pest [Budapest]. The bread ration is approved, further rises in board money are to be discussed.

No. 229d

Princely resolution, Pest, 9 October 1809. In the matter of the Regent's proposals of 19 September, the Prince now orders another landlady to be found, in case Antoinette Dorner should not be satisfied with her board money.

No.229e

Copy of a letter by Professor Rathmayer of 28 February 1808, in which he seeks financial assistance to enable him to pay his bills. Madame Dorner sent this letter on 10 October [?] 1809 to Szent Gály with a complaint that she has been denounced to the Prince as having enriched herself at the expense of the boys' boarding money. Her accuser was Rathmayer, to whom she refused to lend any money to pay off his debts to the previous kitchen director, Administrator Vutkowatz, to whom he is still in debt to the sum of 200 gulden or more, and was thus not in a position to complain of insufficiencies (unclean linen, etc.). Despite inflation she kept the boys clean and properly looked after, and there are no debts with the tailor, cobbler or hat-maker, which was the case before. A list of the prices of 1804 (when Vutkowatz boarded the boys), of 1808 (when she took over the position) and of 1809 must suffice to restore her good name. Moreover, it was only the most wretched of boys in Eisenstadt, that boy Kastner who, egged on by Rathmayer, spread lies about her.

	1804	1808	1809
1 lb. beef	9-12xr	- 16xr	34-36xr
1 Mäßl [measure] of flour	24xr	1f 10xr	2f. -
1 pair of chickens a	24xr	1f -	2f -
1 lb. pork	30xr	1f -	2f -
1 egg	1xr	- 2xr	- 7xr
1 half [litre?] milk	3xr	- 11xr	- 12xr
1 lb. salt	3xr	- 5xr	- 10xr
1 lb. rice	20xr	- 25xr	1f -
1 lb. veal	20xr	- 30xr	1f 12 xr
1 lb. soap	16xr	- 24xr	1f 12 xr

In addition Vutkowatz received gratis 100 pounds of candles from the signory.

Commentary

See A. M.224 a-c.

Acta Musicalia Nr.230 a-b

Fürst Nicolaus hört in Pest (18. Sept. 1809), daß Mitglieder der fürstlichen Kapelle sich in Wien aufhalten und beauftragt den Güterregenten, diese nach Eisenstadt einzuberufen. Güterregent Szent Gály befiehlt den in Wien befindlichen Musikern und Sängern innerhalb von 14 Tagen nach Eisenstadt zurückzukehren, da sonst die Gehälter gestrichen werden. Eisenstadt, den 23. September 1809.

Kommentar

Es handelt sich hier um die Sängerinnen Anna Cornega (Sopran), Elisabeth Sieber (Alt), die Sänger Otto Grell (Tenor), Möglich und Anton Forti (Baß). In der Musikerliste findet sich nur ein Geiger namens Möglich, aber Abbé Bevilaqua als Tenor. Beim Herannahen der französischen Truppen hatte sich der Fürst nach Ungarn, die Sänger und Konzertmeister Hummel nach Wien abgesetzt.

No.230 a-b

Prince Nicolaus hears in Pest (18 September 1809) that members of the princely chapel are living in Vienna. He orders the Regent to have these members return to Eisenstadt. Regent Szent Gály orders the musicians and singers now in Vienna to return to Eisenstadt within 14 days, otherwise their salaries will be docked. Eisenstadt, 23 September 1809.

Commentary

These were the singers Anna Cornega (sop.), Elisabeth Sieber (alto), Otto Grell (ten.) and Anton Forti (bass). Among the list of musicians there is a violinist Möglich Abbé Paolo Bevilaqua (ten.). At the approach of the French troops, the ¨Prince fled to Hungary and the singers and violinist named above as well as Konzertmeister Hummel settled in Vienna.

Acta Musicalia Nr.231a-e

Güterregent Szent Gály übersendet dem Fürsten eine Kostenberechnung der Sängerknaben. Eisenstadt, 18. September 1809.

Acta Musicalia Nr.231a

Laut Berechnung aller Spesen, Kleidung, Verköstigung, Aufsicht usw. kommt ein Sängerknabe jährlich auf 600 Gulden, alle 12 Knaben auf 7.200 Gulden.

Acta Musicalia Nr.231b

Schneiderrechnung für die Einkleidung der Sängerknaben 1735F 6xr, 3/4d. Eisenstadt, 16. September 1809.
Die Knaben erhielt 15 Hemden, 33 Paar Socken (gestrickt), 14 weiße und 6 schwarze Halstücher, 16 blaue Schnupftücher, 11 Chemise, 8 Handtücher, 13 Kompagnieröcke und je zwei Hosen dazu aus hechtgrauem Tuch, 13 Westen, Knöpfe, 13 Hüte und 39 Paar Schuhe. Die Rechnung von Schneider Joseph Ruterich wurde von Vizekapellmeister Fuchs gegengezeichnet.

Acta Musicalia Nr.231c

Verzeichnis der notwendigen Leibwäsche für die Sängerknaben erstellt von Professor Rathmayer. Eisenstadt, 10. August 1809. (identisch mit der Schneiderrechnung).

Acta Musicalia Nr.231d

Resolution des Fürsten. Pest 19. Oktober 1809.
Die Winterkleidung kann beschafft werden; gestrichen wird die Kleidung für Zimmermann, der für den verstorbenen Thilo zur Kapelle wechselt. Was mit den Knaben in Zukunft geschehen soll, wird nach der Rückkunft des Fürsten entschieden werden.

Acta Musicalia Nr.231e

Szent Gály unterrichtet Vizekapellmeister Fuchs und das Dieneramt von der Weisung des Fürsten und befiehlt die Anfertigung der Garderobe für die Sängerknaben.

No.231 a-e
Regent Szent Gály sends to the Prince a list of expenses for the boy choristers. Eisenstadt, 18 September 1809.

No.231a
After adding together all the costs, clothing, board, guardians, etc., a boy chorister costs 600 gulden p.a., all twelve cost 7200 gulden.

No.231b
Tailor's bill for clothing the boy choristers 1735f. 6xr, 3/4d. Eisenstadt, 16 September 1809. The boys received 15 shirts; 33 pairs of socks, knitted; 14 white and 6 black neckerchiefs; 16 blue handkerchiefs; 11 chemises, 8 hand-towels, 13 uniform coats and two pairs of breeches with each one of pike grey cloth, 13 waistcoats, buttons, 13 hats, and 39 pairs of shoes. The bill by the tailor Joseph Ruterich was countersigned by Vice Capellmeister Fuchs.

No.231c
List of the necessary underclothing for the boy choristers, drawn up by Professor Rathmayer. Eisenstadt, 10 August 1809 (identical with the tailor's bill).

No.231d
Resolution by Prince Nicolaus II Esterházy. Pest, 1 October 1809. The winter clothing may be ordered, cancelled are the clothes for Zimmermann, who was engaged instead of the late Thilo. The future of the boys will be decided upon the return of the Prince.

No.231e
Szent Gály instructs Vice Capellmeister Fuchs and the Household service about the princely decision and orders the clothing to be prepared for the boy choristers;

Acta Musicalia Nr.232 a-b
Acta Musicalia Nr.232a

Ansuchen der Sängerin Theresia Stotz um Kostgeld. Eisenstadt, 26. September 1809.
Szent Gály berichtet dem Fürsten nach Pest, daß die Sopranistin aussagt, der Fürst hätte ihr Kostgeld versprochen. Sie hätte von der Familie Traidler zur Familie des Violoncellisten Lorenz gewechselt und wäre die Kost dort noch schuldig. Szent Gály weiß nichts von einem fürstlichen Versprechen, aber davon, daß der Fürst am 19. Mai ihm befohlen hätte, der Sängerin 100 Gulden auszuzahlen; dieses Geld behauptet Stotz der Madame Traidler gegeben zu haben, nun sei sie aber Madame Lorenz 30 Gulden schuldig.

Acta Musicalia Nr.232b

Resolution des Fürsten. Pest 30. September 1809.
Der Sängerin Stotz wurde kein Kostgeld versprochen.

Kommentar

Für Therese Stotz siehe HJB XVI, S.130 f, A.M.157.

Nos. 232 a-b
No.232a
Petition of the singer Theresia Stotz for board money. Eisenstadt, 26 September 1809.
Szent Gály reports to the Prince in Pest that the soprano maintains the Prince promised her board money. She has changed from the family Traidler to the family of the cellist Lorenz and still owes board money to the latter. Szent Gály knows nothing of such a princely promise, only that on 19 May the Prince ordered him to pay 100 gulden to the singer, which money she maintains was given to Madame Traidler. Now she owes Madame Lorenz 30 gulden.

No.232b
Resolution of the Prince. Pest, 30 September 1809. The singer Stotz was not promised any board money.
Commentary
For Theresa Stotz see HYB XVI, p. 130f, A. M.157.

Acta Musicalia Nr.233 a-b

Philipp Ludwig Möglich schreibt an Güterdirektor Szent Gály, warum es ihm unmöglich sei, zur angegebenen Frist nach Eisenstadt zu kommen. Wien, 22. September 1809.
Er finde keine 'Gelegenheit' ihn nach Eisenstadt zu bringen, außerdem bewohne Demoiselle Stotz sein Zimmer und er wisse auch gar nicht wo seine Möbel sich jetzt befänden.
Diese Gründe ließ Szent Gály alle nicht gelten. Der Befehl des Fürsten müsse ausgeführt werden, sollte Möglich in der vom Fürsten bestimmten Frist nicht in Eisenstadt sein, werde das Gehalt einbehalten. Da die Reise nicht mit dem hochfürstlichen Dienst verbunden sei, habe Möglich die Reisekosten selber zu bestreiten. Der Güterregent ließ auch Vizekapellmeister Fuchs verständigen, daß die Sängerin Stotz unverzüglich das Zimmer von Sänger Möglich zu räumen habe. Eisenstadt, 28. September 1809.

No. 233 a-b
Philipp Ludwig Möglich writes to Regent Szent Gály why it is impossible for him to come to Eisenstadt in the given period. Vienna, 22 September 1809.
He finds no carriage that could bring him to Eisenstadt, moreover Demoiselle Stotz is living in his rooms and he has no idea where his furniture is at present.
Szent Gály does not allow any of these excuses. The orders of the Prince must be followed implicitly. If Möglich is not in Eisenstadt by the time appointed, his salary will be confiscated. Since the trip was not connected with the high princely service, Möglich has to pay for it himself. The Regent also informed Vice Capellmeister Fuchs that the lady singer Stotz is at once to vacate the rooms of the singer Möglich. Eisenstadt, 28 September 1809.

Acta Musicalia Nr.234 a-g

Barbara Tomasini soll ihr Holzdeputat gestrichen werden. Wien, 1. Januar 1809.

Acta Musicalia Nr.234a

Fürstliche Resolution. In Erledigung des Vortrags von Güterregenten Szent Gály vom 27. Oktober des Vorjahres verfügt der Fürst die Streichung des Holzdeputats, da die Tochter Elise nach Wien in die

Kost komme; gnadenhalber könne ihr noch eine einmalige Ration von sechs Klaftern gegeben werden.

Acta Musicalia Nr.234b

Güterregent Szent Gály gibt die fürstliche Verfügung an das Schafferamt weiter, doch werden nur mehr fünf Klafter zu liefern sein, da er, Szent Gály, der Witwe Tomasini bereits einen Klafter vorher angewiesen hatte. Eisenstadt, 8. Januar 1809.

Acta Musicalia Nr.234c

Barbara Tomasini ersucht den Güterregenten sich für sie zu verwenden und am 15. Dezember 1809 referiert dieser dem Fürsten, daß zwar die fürstliche Verfügung bestünde ihr nur mehr einmal Holz zukommen zu lassen, daß die Witwe sich jedoch auch diesen Winter auf das Deputat Hoffnungen mache. Ihre eine Stieftochter Elise käme zwar nach Wien, Josepha sei aber noch da. Szent Gály könne ihre Bitte nicht unterstützen, da der Holzverbrauch hier sehr hoch sei und der Preis des Holzes auch täglich ansteige. Er erwarte den fürstlichen Bescheid.

Acta Musicalia Nr 234d

Fürstliche Resolution vom 21. Dezember 1809 aus Eisenstadt: sechs Klafter Holz werden bewilligt.

Acta Musicalia Nr.234e

Szent Gály weist das Schafferamt an, das Brennholz auszufolgen (24. Dezember.

Acta Musicalia Nr.234f

Szent Gály berichtet dem Fürsten über ein neuerliches Gesuch der Witwe Tomasini ihr für 1810 ein Holzdeputat zu bewilligen.

Acta Musicalia Nr.234g

Gesuch der Barbara Tomasini vom 12; Dezember 1813 an den Fürsten um Bewilligung des Holzdeputats, da sie noch weitere drei unversorgte Kinder habe, abgesehen von den zwei Stieftöchtern. Der älteste Sohn lerne 'die Handlung' und brauche besonders viele Kleider und ihre Pension sei sehr klein.

Kommentar

Barbara Tomasini, geborene Feichtinger, eine Köchin aus Preßburg, war in einer besonders schlechten Lage dem Fürsten gegenüber, da sie ihren Mann, den Konzertmeister Tomasini 1799 ohne fürstliche Genehmigung geheiratet hatte, also ohne Pensionsanspruch. 1797 war ihr erstes Kind bereits auf die Welt gekommen. 1802 erteilt der Fürst die Heiratserlaubnis; 1808 starb ihr Mann, stark verschuldet. Die starke Teuerung, Erhöhung des Mietzinses, der leichtsinnige Lebenswandel ihrer beiden Stiefsöhne, machten ihr das Überleben schwer. Sie bat den Fürsten ihr Bilder und die Geige ihres Mannes abzunehmen, bat um eine Pension, alles wurde abgelehnt. Endlich erhielt sie 290, später 400 Gulden Pension und 80 Gulden für die beiden Stieftöchter Josepha und Elisabeth (Elise), die beide Sängerinnen waren. Ihr ältester Sohn Friedrich spielte die Violine und half beim Vizekapellmeister Fuchs aus, aber jedes Gesuch in der fürstlichen Verwaltung angestellt zu werden, wurde abgelehnt. Barbara Tomasini, die Fuchs für 'ein braves Weib allgemein anerkannt' hielt, starb am 24. Dezember 1821 an Typhus.

No.234 a-g
The firewood allotment for Barbara is to be cancelled. Vienna, 1 January 1809.

No.234a
Princely resolution, concerning the statement by Regent Szent Gály of 27 October last year. The Prince orders the cancellation of the wood allotment inasmuch as the daughter will go to Vienna and be given living expenses. In grace, however, one last ration of six fathom cords may be given to her.

No.234b
Regent Szent Gály forwards the princely order to the Administration but only for five fathom cords since he, Szent Gály, has already advanced widow Tomasini one fathom cord. Eisenstadt, 8 January 1809.

No.234c
Barbara Tomasini asks the Regent for his assistance and on 15 December 1809 the latter reports to the Prince that although there was a princely decision to give her only one more ration of firewood, nevertheless the widow hopes that she may have it this winter too. Her stepdaughter Elise went to Vienna, that is true, but Josepha is still with her. Szent Gály could not support her request since much wood is consumed here and the price of firewood rises daily. He awaits a princely decision.

No.234d
Princely Resolution of 21 December 1809 from Eisenstadt. Six fathom cords are permitted.

No.234e
Szent Gály informs the Administration to deliver the wood (24 December 1809).

No.234f
Szent Gály reports to the Prince about yet another petition by widow Tomasini for a firewood allotment for the year 1810.

No.234g
Petition by Barbara Tomasini to the Prince for permission to receive an allotment for firewood, since she still has three further children to care for, apart from her two stepdaughters. The eldest son is learning economics and needs many clothes, and her pension is very small.

Commentary
Barbara Tomasini, née Feichtinger, a cook from Pressburg, was in a dubious situation as far as the Prince was concerned, since she had married her husband, leader Tomasini, in 1799 without princely approval; therefore she had no right to a pension. Her first child had been born in 1797. In 1802 the Prince issued permission for the marriage, and in 1808 Luigi Tomasini died with heavy debts. The great inflation, the increase of rent money, and the irresponsible life style of her two stepsons made her life difficult. She asked the Prince to purchase the paintings and the violin of her late husband, and asked for a pension - all in vain. Finally, she did receive 290, later 400 gulden pension and 80 gulden for both stepdaughters Josepha and Elisabeth (Elise), both of whom were singers. Her eldest son Friedrich played the violin and helped Vice Capellmeister Fuchs, but his attempts to be engaged in the Princely administration were refused. Barbara Tomasini, who according to Fuchs 'was generally held to be a good woman', died of typhoid fever on 24 December 1821.

Acta Musicalia Nr.235 a-d
Acta Musicalia Nr.235a

Anton Polzelli schickt an den Güterregenten die Liste der Sänger, die von ihm unterrichtet werden. Eisenstadt, 8. Januar 1809.
Vom 1. Mai - 31. Oktober 1809 erhielten die Damen Schneider, Vadász, Sieber, Stotz, Dienelt, die beiden Schöringer und Herr Grell Unterricht- und Korrepetitorstunden.

Acta Musicalia Nr.235b

Bericht des Güterdirektors Szent Gály an den Fürsten, daß Polzelli die Korrepetitorstelle im Theater haben möchte. Eisenstadt, 16. Januar 1809.

Polzelli sei für den Unterricht von sechs Sängern verantwortlich und erhalte dafür 400 Gulden, auf Befehl des Fürsten habe er aber dann auch die Sängerinnen Stotz und Schneider ohne weitere Bezahlung annehmen müssen. Er würde nun vorschlagen - da kein Theater ohne Korrepetitor auskommen könne und er immer wieder von Sängern um Hilfe beim Einstudieren der Rollen gebeten werde - ihn als Korrepetitor anzustellen und ein Gehalt anzuweisen. Szent Gály habe darüber den Vizekapellmeister Fuchs befragt, der 1. der Meinung sei, daß die Sänger ihre Rollen selbst einstudieren sollten und dies hier immer so gewesen wäre. 2. Daß die besser bezahlten Sänger Korrepetitorstunden selber bezahlen müßten und man nur eine Ausnahme bei Sieber und Stotz machen könne, die noch nicht so sicher im Singen wären. Szent Gály habe in Eszterháza-Akten nachgesehen und das Amt eines Korrepetitors nirgends gefunden.

Acta Musicalia Nr.235c

Fürstliche Resolution, Wien 31. Januar 1809. Polzelli erhält seine 400 Gulden für 1808, wird in Zukunft nur mehr die Damen Stotz und beiden Schöringer unterrichten. Bei der nächsten 'Regulierung der Kapelle' werde an ihn (Polzelli) gedacht werden.

Acta Musicalia Nr.235d

Szent Gály weist am 8. Februar 1809 das Hauptzahlamt an, 400 Gulden an Polzelli auszuzahlen. Vizekapellmeister Fuchs wird unterrichtet, daß künftig nur mehr Stotz und die beiden Schöringer Stunden bekommen sollen und wegen der 'Verleihung' der Correpetitorstelle wird Suplikant Polzelli vertröstet.

No.235 a-d

No.235a

Anton Polzelli sends to the Regent a list of singers whom he teaches. Eisenstadt, 8 January 1809.
During 1 May-31 October 1808 the ladies Schneider, Vadasz, Sieber, Stutz, Dienelt, the two Schöringer and Herr Grell received teaching and coaching.

No.235b

Report of the Regent Szent Gály to the Prince that Polzelli would like to secure for himself the post of coaching in the theatre. Eisenstadt, 16 January 1809.
Polzelli is reponsible for teaching six singers and receives 400 gulden for this work. On the orders of the Prince he had to add the lady singers Stotz and Schneider without any further remuneration. He would suggest - since no theatre can exist without a coach and he is

constantly being asked by the singers to help them to learn their roles - to engage him as coach and pay him a salary. Szent Gály asked Vice Capellmeister Fuchs for his opinion; he thought: (1) the singers should study their roles themselves, as was always the case hitherto and (2) that those singers with the higher salaries should engage their coaches and pay for them out of their own funds; that one could make an exception out of Sieber and Stotz, who were not yet prepared as singers. Szent Gály looked in the files of Eszterháza and could find nowhere that there was a position of a coach.

No.234c
Princely Resolution, Vienna, 31 January 1809. Polzelli receives his 400 gulden for 1808, but in future will teach only the ladies Stotz and the two Schöringers. At the next reorganization of the Capelle, Polzelli will be considered.

No.235d
Szent Gály instructs the Chief Cashier's Office on 8 February 1809 to pay 400 gulden to Polzelli. Vice Capellmeister Fuchs is informed that in the future only Stotz and the two Schöringers are to receive lessons and as far as the position of coach, the supplicant Polzelli is to be considered.

Acta Musicalia Nr.236 a-b

Acta Musicalia Nr.236a

Güterregent Szent Gály wird vom Fürst Nicolaus II. angewiesen, dem Kammersänger Joseph Treidler die Fiskal Assistenz zu gewähren, außerdem wolle er Auskünfte über den Fiskal Regner, der Wimmer vertreten wolle. Wien, 18. Januar 1809.

Acta Musicalia Nr.236b

Szent Gály unterrichtet den Fiskalen Regner, daß er Treidler bei seiner Klage beim städtischen Magistrat zu vertreten habe, zugleich jedoch solle er dem Fürsten Bericht erstatten, ob er gedenke auch Wimmer zu vertreten. Eisenstadt, 23. Januar 1809.

No.236 a-b
No.236a
Szent Gály is ordered by Prince Nicolaus II to inform Chamber Singer Joseph Treidler to aid and abet the Deputy of the Exchequer, moreover he needs information regarding the Deputy Regner, who represents Wimmer. Vienna, 18 January 1809.

No.236b
Regent Szent Gály informs Deputy of the Exchequer Regner that he is to represent Treidler in his lawsuit at the town magistrate, and at the same time he should inform the Prince if he [Regner] intends to represent Wimmer as well. Eisenstadt, 23 January 1809.

Acta Musicalia Nr.237 a-c
Acta Musicalia Nr.237a

Nicolaus II. weist Güterregenten Szent Gály an den Sänger Treidler die Räumung der Wohnung am Berg zu befehlen. Wien, 13. Februar 1809.
Konzertmeister Müller und seine Frau werden Anfang April in Eisenstadt eintreffen und daher müsse Treidler sein Quartier, das sowieso nur bis Heilige-Drei-Könige (6. Januar) bewilligt gewesen sei, spätestens Mitte März räumen.

Acta Musicalia Nr.237b

Szent Gály gibt den fürstlichen Befehl an Treidler weiter. Eisenstadt, 18. Februar 1809.

Acta Musicalia Nr.237c

Schreiben des Regisseur Schmidt an Szent Gály vom 28. Juni 1809, daß Konzertmeister Müller und Frau am 29. Juni in Eisenstadt eintreffen werden. Auch er, Schmidt, wünsche nichts sehnlicher, als der allgemeinen Not und Teuerung zu entgehen.

No. 237 a-c
No. 237a
Nicolaus II indicates to Regent Szent Gály that the singer Treidler must evacuate the lodgings on the hill. Vienna, 13 February 1809.
Konzertmeister Müller and his wife will arrive in Eisenstadt at the beginning of April and Treidler must therefore leave his quarters by the middle of March at the latest; the quarters were in any case approved only until Twelfth Night [6 January].

No. 237b
Szent Gály transmits the princely order to Treidler. Eisenstadt, 18 February 1809.

No. 237c
Letter by Director Schmidt to Szent Gály of 28 June 1809, that Konzertmeister Müller and his wife will arrive in Eisenstadt on 28 June 1809; Schmidt, too, wishes nothing more than to avoid the present general want and inflation.

Acta Musicalia Nr.238

Güterdirektor Szent Gály referiert über das Gesuch des Bratschisten Treidler um ein anderes Quartier. Eisenstadt, 19. Februar 1809.

Treidler sei mit dem Quartier im Wimmerhaus nicht zufrieden, da die in den zweiten Stock führende Treppe direkt an sein Schlafzimmer angebaut und der Lärm für einen Kranken unerträglich sei. Außerdem sei das zweite Zimmer wegen der vier Fenster und seiner Größe unheizbar. Szent Gály gibt zu bedenken, daß Wohnungen knapp seien, der Winter ohnehin zu Ende gehe und Treidler in das größere Zimmer ziehen könne, falls er noch so lange leben würde. Sollte aber der Fürst dem Wunsche Treidlers nachgeben, so wäre die Wohnung des verstorbenen Baßsängers Specht bei Leopold Frank leer. Diese Wohnung habe vier Zimmer und zwei Küchen, könnte also ohne große Kosten zweigeteilt werden.

Kommentar

siehe A.M.239.

No.238

Regent Szent Gály informs about the petition of the viola player Treidler for another lodging. Eisenstadt, 19 February 1809.

Treidler is not satisified with his lodgings in the Wimmer house, since the staircase leading to the second floor goes directly past his bedroom and the noise is for a sick man unbearable. Moreover the second room is, on account of its four windows and generally large size, unheatable. Szent Gály warns that lodgings are scarce, the winter is coming to an end, and Treidler can move into the larger room, if indeed he lives that long. But should the Prince give in to Treidler's wishes the lodgings of the late deceased bass singer Specht at Leopold Franck's are empty. This apartment has four rooms and two kitchens, thus it could without great expense be divided in two.

Acta Musicalia Nr.239 a-d
Acta Musicalia Nr.239a

Hofrat Karner teilt Szent Gály mit, daß der neu engagierte Klarinettist Ignatz Skrabal verheiratet sei und eine Wohnung für ein Ehepaar gesucht werden müsse. Skrabal werde am 10. oder 11. März in Eisenstadt eintreffen. Wien, 25. Februar 1809.

Acta Musicalia Nr 239b

Güterdirektor Szent Gály berichtet am 6. März 1809, daß zur Zeit nur zwei Wohnungen für Skrabal in Betracht kämen, die des verstorbenen Specht oder des ebenfalls verstorbenen Bratschisten Treidler, die beide jedoch von den Witwen bewohnt werden.

Acta Musicalia Nr.239c

Fürstliche Resolution, Wien, 10. März 1809. Skrabal sei in der Wohnung des verstorbenen Bratschisten Treidler unter-zubringen.

Acta Musicalia Nr.239d

Szent Gály unterrichtet Vizekapellmeister Fuchs und Hausreferenten Vadatz vom Wunsch des Fürsten, Skrabal im Wimmerischen Haus, in der Wohnung des verstorbenen Bratschisten Treidler unterzubringen.

No.239 a-d
No.239a
Hofrat Karner informs Szent Gály that the newly engaged clarinettist Ignatz Skrabal is married and a flat for a married couple is needed. Skrabal will arrive on 10 or 11 March in Eisenstadt. Vienna, 25 February 1809.

No.239b
Regent Szent Gály reports on 6 March 1809 that at the moment only two flats for Skrabal can be considered, that of the late Specht or that of the late viola player Treidler, both of which are, however, occupied by the respective widows.

No.239c
Princely resolution, Vienna, 10 March 1809. Skrabal is to be installed in the flat of the late viola player Treidler.

No. 239d
Szent Gály informs Vice Capellmeister Fuchs and Lodging-master Vadatz of the Prince's wish to instal Skrabal in the Wimmer house where there is the flat of the late viola player Treidler.

Acta Musicalia Nr.240 a-b
Acta Musicalia Nr.240a

Fürst Nicolaus II. läßt den Sängern Grell, Cornega und Konzertmeister Hummel die Gehälter streichen. Eisenstadt, 10. Oktober 1809.

Am 16. September hatte der Fürst befohlen, alle in Wien befindlichen Mitglieder der Kapelle nach Eisenstadt zurückzubeordern. Szent Gály hatte ihnen zwei Wochen für die Anreise eingeräumt, aber weder Konzertmeister Hummel noch Tenor Grell oder die Sopranistin Anna Cornega leisteten dem Befehl Folge.

Acta Musicalia Nr.240b

Szent Gály berichtet Nicolaus II. über seine Maßnahmen. Eisenstadt, 12. Oktober 1809.
Er habe am 27. September Grell, Cornega, Hummel, Sieber, Möglich und Forti nach Eisenstadt zurückbeordert. Sieber, Möglich und Forti seien bereits in Eisenstadt, die anderen nicht. Cornega entschuldigte sich mit einer Krankheit der Mutter und auch damit, daß in ihrer Wohnung französische Offiziere einquartiert wären. Dies habe sie sich nur selber zuzuschreiben, da sie Eisenstadt verlassen habe. Der Hausbesitzer habe sich jedoch bereit erklärt, die beiden Offiziere in einem Zimmer unterzubringen, so daß ihr die beiden anderen Zimmer zur Verfügung stünden. Grell berufe sich auf einen Befehl des Fürsten sich bei dem Wiener Theater 'verwenden zu lassen'. So habe er mehrere Rollen einstudiert und sein Fehlen würde den Theaterbetrieb sehr stören. Hummel entschuldige sich auch mit französischer Einquartierung in seiner Wohnung, was Szent Gály nicht gelten lasse.

Kommentar

Hummel wohnte bei seinem Vater auf der Brandstätte in Wien und zeigte sich von den fürstlichen Befehlen so wenig beeindruckt, daß er erst 1810 nach Eisenstadt zurückkehrte. Er hatte eine neue Oper *Mathilde von Guise* komponiert, die mit mäßigen Erfolg am 26. März 1810 am k.k. Hoftheater aufgeführt wurde, da der Text 'höchst langweilig war'. Katalog 1978, *Johann Nepomuk Hummel und Eisenstadt*, S.18. Siehe auch A.M.230b, A.M.249

Nos.240 a-b
No.240a
Prince Nicolaus II orders the salaries of the singers Grell and Cornega and Conzertmeister Hummel to be docked. Eisenstadt, 10 October 1809.
On 16 September the Prince had ordered all the members of the Capelle who were in Vienna to return to Eisenstadt. Szent Gály allowed them a fortnight for the trip, but neither Conzertmeister Hummel, nor Grell, nor the soprano Anna Cornega obeyed the orders.

No. 240b
Szetn Gály informs Nicolaus II about his actions. Eisenstadt, 12 October 1809. On 27 September, Grell, Cornega, Hummel, Sieber, Möglich and Forti were ordered to return to Eisenstadt. Sieber, Möglich and Forti were already in Eisenstadt, the others not. Cornega excused herself because her mother was ill and French officers were quartered in her lodgings. But that was her fault because she left Eisenstadt. The house owner has suggested, however, to install the two officers in one room so that she could have the other two at her disposal. Grell maintains that he received a princely order to 'have himself employed' in the Vienna Theatre. He therefore studied several roles and his absence would disturb the

theatre's existence. Hummel also excused himself by saying French officers were quartered in his billet, which Szent Gály does not accept.

Commentary

Hummel lived with his father on the Brandstätte in Vienna and paid so little attention to the princely commands that he did not return to Eisenstadt until 1810. He had written a new opera, *Mathilde von Guise*, performed with middling success on 26 March 1810 at the I. R. Court Theatre in Vienna, the libretto having been considered 'very boring'. Katalog 1978, *Johann Nepomuk Hummel und Eisenstadt*, p.18. See also A. M. 230b, 249.

Acta Musicalia Nr.241 a-b
Acta Musicalia Nr.241a

Fürst Nicolaus II. erteilt seinem Kammersänger Otto Grell einen dreiwöchigen Urlaub, damit er bei den k. k. Theatern in Wien aushelfen kann. Sollte er aber nicht pünktlich wieder in Eisenstadt eintreffen, so sei ihm das Gehalt zu streichen. (Pest, 16. Oktober 1809).

Acta Musicalia Nr.241b

Güterdirektor Szent Gály beauftragt das Hauptzahlamt und den Vizekapellmeister Fuchs, den dreiwöchigen Termin im Auge zu behalten. (Eisenstadt, 20. Oktober).

Kommentar

Siehe A.M. 231, 240.

Nos.241 a-b
No. 241a

Prince Nicolaus II permits a three-week vacation for his chamber singer Otto Grell, to enable him to assist in the I. R. court theatre in Vienna. But should he not arrive punctually in Eisenstadt, his salary is to be docked. (Pest, 16 October 1809).

No. 241b

Regent Szent Gály orders the chief cashier's office and Vice Capellmeister Fuchs to keep in mind the three weeks' limit. (Eisenstadt, 20 October 1809).

Commentary

See A. M. 231, 240.

Acta Musicalia Nr.242 a-c
Acta Musicalia Nr.242a

Güterdirektor Szent Gály berichtet dem Fürsten über ein Gesuch des Violinisten Franz Lechner um Quartiergeld und Holzdeputat, sowie um die Bezahlung der Klavierstunden, die er der Tochter des Buchhalter Kühnel gegeben habe. Eisenstadt, 9. November 1809.

Lechner habe den Zins in Höhe von monatlich zehn Gulden 50xr aus eigener Tasche zahlen müssen, auch sei ihm noch einiges von seinem Holzdeputat nachzuliefern. Außerdem habe er auf fürstlichen Befehl der Tochter des Buchhalters Kühnel Klavierstunden gegeben und dafür wären ihm pro Jahr 100 Gulden versprochen worden. Nun sei aber weder Szent Gály noch dem Vizekapellmeister Fuchs darüber etwas bekannt, so erbitte er die gnädige Weisung. Zins und Holzlieferung seien bereits von ihm erledigt worden.

Acta Musicalia Nr.242b

Der Fürst antwortet am 24. November 1809 (Eisenstadt): Lechners Forderung bestehe zu Recht und es seien ihm für die Zeit bis August 175 Gulden zu bezahlen, in Zukunft müße er jedoch an Kühnel herantreten.

Acta Musicalia Nr.242c

Weisung des Güterregenten an die Hauptzahlkassa Lechner für die Klavierstunden vom 1. Dezember 1807 bis August 1809 zu bezahlen; in Zukunft aber wird Lechner mit Kühnel zu verhandeln haben. Kühnel wird ebenfalls von der Entscheidung des Fürsten unterrichtet.

Kommentar

Für Lechner siehe HJB XV, S.102, A.M.105

No.242 a-c
No.242a

Regent Szent Gály reports to the Prince concerning the petition of violinist Franz Lechner for board and lodging money, also for payment of piano lessons which he gave to the daughter of Bookkeeper Kühnel. Eisenstadt, 9 November 1809.

Lechner was obliged to pay the rent to the amount of ten gulden 50xr from his own pocket, also he is owed several of his firewood allotments. Moreover on orders of the Prince he gave piano lessons to Bookkeeper Kühnel's daughter and for that he had been promised 100 gulden. Neither Szent Gály nor Vice Capellmeister Fuchs was aware of this decision, however, so a gracious decision is requested. The rent and wood delivery have been taken care of.

No. 242b
The Prince answers on 24 November 1809 (Eisenstadt) that Lechner's request is quite justified and for the period until August 175 gulden are to be paid, but in the future he must turn to Kühnel.

No. 242c
Order of the regent to Chief Cashier Lechner to pay for the piano lessons from 1 December 1807 to August 1809, but in future Lechner will have to arrange matters with Kühnel, who is also informed of the Prince's decision.

Acta Musicalia Nr.243 a-b
Acta Musicalia Nr.243a

Weisung des Fürsten Esterházy an seinen Güterregenten, die Gruft in der Bergkirch in Ordnung zu bringen, da er seinen Kapellmeister Joseph Haydn dort beizusetzen gedenke. Eisenstadt, 25. August 1809.
Es sei ihm zu Ohren gekommen, daß die Gruft in der Bergkirche als Abstellplatz diene, die Särge willkürlich umgestellt würden. Die verant wortlichen Kirchenväter seien zur Ordnung zu rufen.

Acta Musicalia Nr.243b

Szent Gály beauftragt das Hofbauamt die Gruft zu säubern, und Probst Seitz, dann für die weitere Instandhaltung Sorge zu tragen. Eisenstadt, 30. September 1809.

Nos.243 a-b
No. 243a
Order by Prince Esterházy to his Regent that the grave vault in the Bergkirche [Mountain church] is to be brought in order, inasmuch as he proposes to bury Kapellmeister Joseph Haydn there. Eisenstadt, 25 August 1809.
It has come to his attention that the grave vault in the Bergkirche is used as a storeroom, and the coffins have been displaced at will. The church fathers responsible should be called to order about this.

No. 243b
Szent Gály orders the court works department to clean the grave vault and Provost Seitz is to be responsible for the future upkeep. Eisenstadt, 30 September 1809.

Commentary
For Lechner see HYB XV, p. 102, A.M. 105.

Acta Musicalia Nr.244

Fürst Nicolaus II. gewährt der Witwe des verstorbenen Tenors Thilo ein Holzdeputat. Eisenstadt, 30. November 1809.

Kommentar

Für Karl August Tillo (Thilo) siehe A.M.222, 231d.

No. 244
Prince Nicolaus II allows the widow of the late tenor Thilo to receive an allotment of firewood. Eisenstadt, 30 November 1809.

Comentary
For Karl August Tillo (Thilo) see A.M.222, 231d.

Acta Musicalia Nr.245 a-b
Acta Musicalia Nr.245a

Fürst Nicolaus II. erteilt dem Cancellisten Johann Raichen die Heiratserlaubnis. Eisenstadt, 6. Dezember 1809.
Johann Raichen darf Elisabeth Schöringer ehelichen, doch treten die normalen Bedingungen in Kraft. Diese Bedingungen verwehren der Witwe den Pensionsanspruch.

Acta Musicalia Nr.245b

Szent Gály hält am selben Tag noch die fürstliche Einwilligung aktenmäßig fest und bereitet die Pensionsverzichtserklärung der eventuellen Witwe vor.

Kommentar

Die Schöringers (Schiringer), eine begabte Musikerfamilie, war als 1767 in fürstlichen Diensten, seit Carl als Violonespieler und Flötist angestellt wurde; 1772 heiratete er seine Frau Katherina. Zwei seiner Töchter, Josepha und Magdalena wurden zu Sängerinnen ausgebildet. Den Unterricht erteilten Johann Haydn und Anton Polzelli. Josepha war bis zur Aufhebung der Kapelle im Opernensemble.
Fürst Nicolaus I. schätzte Schiringer als guten Kirchenkomponisten, dessen Werke sich jetzt in der Domkirche und im Esterházy Archiv in Eisenstadt befinden. HJB IX, 109, 113; XIII, 7; XIV, 74; XVI, 172;

XVII, 178, 187, 192. Über die Töchter siehe A.M.136, 137, 138, 156, 159, 235.

Nos.245 a-b
No. 245a
Prince Nicolaus II allows clerk Johann Raichen to marry. Eisenstadt, 6 December 1809.
Johann Raichen is permitted to marry Elisabeth Schöringer but under the usual circumstances, i.e. that she cannot receive a pension.

No. 245b
Szent Gály places a notice of the princely permission in the files and prepares a statement that as a widow she renounces all claims to a pension.

Commentary
The Schöringers (Schiringers), a gifted family of musicians, were in the princely service from 1767, Carl as violoe (double bass) player and flautist. In 1772 he married his wife Katharina. His two daughters, Josepha and Magdalena, were both good singers. Their teachers were Joseph Haydn and Anton Polzelli, Josepha was in the opera ensemble until it was disbanded. Prince Nicolaus I appreciated Schöringer's good church-music compositions, whose MSS. are now in the Cathedral Church and Esterházy Archives in Eisenstadt. HYB IX, 109, 113; XIII, 7; XIV, 74; XVI, 172; XVII, 178, 187, 192. Concerning the daughters, see A.M.136, 137, 138, 156, 159, 235.

Acta Musicalia Nr.246 a-b
Acta Musicalia Nr.246a

Fürstliches Intimatum, die von der Herrschaft verliehenen Möbel in den Sängerwohnungen zu kontrollieren. Eisenstadt, 27. Dezember 1809.
Der Fürst hält fest, daß er der Altistin Hammer zwar die Möbel versprach, die die abgereiste Kammersängerin Croll-Tomasini in der Wohnung gelassen hatte, jedoch nicht Alkovenvorhänge, Fensterstaffeln und dergleichen, die zum eigentlichen Quartier gehören und unverzüglich wieder zurückgestellt werden müssen. In Zukunft seien die Möbel genau zu kontrollieren, und ohne schriftliche Passierung und fürstliche Einwilligung dürfen keine Möbel verstellt werden.

Acta Musicalia Nr.246b

Szent Gály benachrichtigt am 10. Januar 1810 die Hofbuchhaltung, den Eisenstädter Schloßverwalter Pointner, den Pfleger Lechner und den Musikgebäudepfleger Pack von der fürstlichen Resolution.

Kommentar

Für Josepha Hammer siehe HJB XIV, 126; A.M.97. Sophie Croll, A.M.246.

Nos.246 a-b
No.246a

Princely intimatum to have an examination of princely furniture lent to the singers. Eisenstadt, 27 December 1809.
The Prince maintains that he did in fact promise the alto singer Hammer the furniture that had been left in the quarters of the Chamber Singer Croll-Tomasini, who has since left, but not the curtain in the alcove, the window sills and such like, which are fixtures of the apartment and must be forthwith returned. In the future the furniture is to be controlled exactly, and none is to be removed without written indications and princely approval.

No.246b

Szent Gály informs the Count Bookkeeping Administration on 10 January 1810, the Eisenstadt Castle Administrator Pointner, the warden Lechner and the Administrator of the music building Pack of the princely resolution.

Commentary

For Josepha Hammer see HYB XIV, 126; A.M.97. For Sophie Croll see A.M.246.

Acta Musicalia Nr247 a-b
Acta Musicalia Nr.247a

Güterdirektor Szent Gály berichtet Fürst Nicolaus II. über das Gesuch des Sängers Rotter um Bezahlung der Gesangstunden im Jahre 1806 für Ferdinand Gsell. Eisenstadt, 3. April 1809.
Szent Gály ist der Meinung Rotter mit seinem Gesuch abzuweisen, da weder er noch Vizekapellmeister Fuchs von dem fürstlichen Versprechen einer Remuneration für den Singunterricht wissen und Rotter seinen Anspruch hätte sofort anmelden sollen.

Acta Musicalia Nr.247b

Dieser Meinung schließt sich der Fürst am 21. April 1809 an, Rotter wird abgewiesen.

Kommentar

Für Rotter siehe HJB XV, 99, A.M.102.

Nos.247 a-b
No. 247a
Regent Szent Gály reports to Prince Nicolaus II on the petition of the singer Rotter concerning the payment for vocal teaching hours given to Ferdinand Gsell in the year 1806. Eisenstadt, 3 April 1809.
Szent Gály is inclined to refuse Rotter's petition, since neither he nor Vice Capellmeister Fuchs knows of a princely promise concerning such vocal teaching and Rotter should have registered his wishes at the time.

No. 247b
The Prince agrees to this proposal on 21 April 1809 and Rotter's petition is refused.

Commentary
For Rotter see HYB XV, 99, A.M.102.

Acta Musicalia Nr.248

Güterdirektor Szent Gály an den Eisenstädter Prefekten Menicoy. Eisenstadt, 3. April 1809.
Um die Bittschrift des Mattersdorfer Schaffers Adam List bearbeiten zu können, muß er weitere Unterlagen haben und wissen, ob der Mann seine Kostenamtsrechnungen ordentlich führen kann.

Kommentar

Über Adam Liszt (ungar. Schreibweise), Großvater des Komponisten Franz, siehe HJB XVI, S.192 f.

No. 248
Regent Szent Gály to the Eisenstadt Prefect Menicoy. Eisenstadt, 3 April 1809.
In order to deal with the petition of the Mattersdorf steward Adam List, more information is required to judge if the man is capable of producing a budget for his office.

Commentary
For Adam Liszt, grandfather of the composer Franz, see HYB XVI, p. 192f.

Acta Musicalia Nr.249 a-c

Güterdirektor Szent Gály berichtet dem Fürsten über ein Bittgesuch des Joseph Cornega um Kostgeld. Eisenstadt, 5. April 1809.

Acta Musicalia Nr.249a

Joseph Cornega befinde sich bereits drei Monate in Pflege und Unterricht beim Sänger Joseph Rotter, und er glaube, seine Eltern hätten 'auf ihn vergessen'. Nun wurde Rotter zu Szent Gály zitiert und gab an, daß er den Knaben auf Weisung des Fürsten angenommen, aber gegen eine Remuneration von 225 Gulden (Kost, Wohnung und Unterricht) samt 1 1/2 Klafter Holz pro Jahr. Dieses habe er auch der Mutter mitgeteilt. Nun sei der Knabe seit 15. Dezember bei ihm, ohne daß er das geringste erhalten habe. Für den Singunterricht fielen pro Monat noch einmal fünf Gulden an, so daß nun 165 Gulden zu bezahlen wären. Szent Gály weiß von keiner fürstlichen Verfügung den Knaben in die Kost zu geben, und ist auch der Meinung, daß es die Pflicht der Eltern sei sich um ihre Kinder zu kümmern, sie auch 'keinerlei Verdienste um das hochfürstliche Haus' hätten; so könne auf eine so kostspielige Versorgung wie Rotter hier anmeldet, kein Anspruch bestehen. Verdienstvolle Untertanen erhielten für ihre Kinder nur 100 Gulden jährlich als Stipendium. Sollte jedoch der Fürst wirklich die Unterhaltung des Cornega befohlen haben, so könnte man Rotter für die Kost und Singstunden monatlich 75 Gulden bewilligen, sollte er jedoch einen solchen Befehl nicht gegeben haben, so müsse Rotter an die Eltern verwiesen werden.

Acta Musicalia Nr.249b

Fürstliche Resolution, Wien 13. April 1809: Rotter sei abzuweisen, doch würde er eine einmalige Abgabe von 1 1/2 Klaftern Brennholz gnädig bewilligen. Außerdem wird Rotter die angesuchte Remuneration für den Sängerknaben Gsell nicht genehmigt, wie auch der Eisenstädter Stadtbürger Leonhard Ehrensperger keinen Anspruch auf Vergütung des Kostgeldes für Monsieur Rosenhaim beweisschlüssig anmelden kann.

Acta Musicalia Nr.249c

Szent Gály unterrichtet Rotter von der Verfügung des Fürsten und gibt dem Eisenstädter Verwalteramt den Auftrag das Brennholz für Rotter bereitzustellen. Eisenstadt, 21; April 1809.

No.249 a-c
Regent Szent Gály reports to the Prince a petition of Joseph Cornega concerning board money. Eisenstadt, 5 April 1809.

No.249a
Joseph Cornega has been with the singer Joseph Rotter, who gives him lessons and board and lodges him, since he [Cornega] assumes that his parents 'have forgotten him', Rotter was now ordered to appear before Szent Gály and said that he took on the boy on orders from the

Prince but for a remuneration of 225 gulden (board, lodging and lessons) and 1 1/2 fathom cords of wood each year. He also informed the mother. The boy has been with him since 15 December without any remuneration. For singing lessons there were an additional five gulden per month, making a total of 165 gulden. Szent Gály knows of no princely decision regarding the boys boarding and is moreover of the opinion that the parents ought to be responsbile for their children, also that they have not earned any services from the princely house, hence they have no rights to any such expensive board as that which Rotter indicates. Worthy subjects receive only 100 gulden p.a. as a stipendium. But should the Prince really have ordered Cornega's board, one could allow Rotter 75 gulden per month for board and lessons, but should the Prince have given no such order, Rotter must turn to the parents.

No. 249b

Princely resolution, Vienna, 13 Apeil 1809: Rotter is to be refused but is to be allotted 1 1/2 fathom cords of wood as a unique act of grace. Moreover Rotter will not be given the remuneration for the boy chorister Gsell, and the Eisenstadt town citizen Leonhard Ehrensperger has no right to the claims for boarding Monsieur Rosenhaim.

No. 249c

Szent Gály informs Rotter of the Princely decision and indicates to the Eisenstadt Administration the order to prepare the wood for Rotter. Eisenstadt, 21 April 1809.

Acta Musicalia Nr.250 a-b
Acta Musicalia Nr.250a

Kurze Notiz des Fürsten Nicolaus II. für den Güterregenten Szent Gály, ihm mit Vizekapellmeister Fuchs 300 Gulden nachschicken zu lassen. Die Jäger am Leithagebirge hätten bereits gestern von zwei Uhr bis in die Nacht kleines Gewehrfeuer und Kanonen gehört. 20. Mai 1809.

Acta Musicalia Nr.250b

Szent Gály benachrichtigt das Hauptzahlamt vom Wunsche des Fürsten, und befahl die von Fuchs unterschriebene Quittung den fürstlichen Konten beizulegen. Eisenstadt (?), 21. Mai 1809.

Kommentar

Am 15. Mai waren bereits die ersten Franzosen in Eisenstadt eingetroffen, Wien hatte sich am 13. Mai ergeben. Der Fürst war schon vorher nach Ungarn abgereist.

Nos.250 a-b
No. 250a
Short note by Prince Nicolaus II to the Regent Szent Gály to give Vice Capellmeister Fuchs 300 gulden to take with him. The hunters on the Leitha Mountains heard small fire and canon from 2 o'clock until into the night. 20 May 1809.

No. 250b
Szent Gály informs the Chief Cashier's office of the princely wishes and orders the signed receipt by Fuchs to be added to the princely account. Eisenstadt [?], 21 May 1809.

Commentary
On 15 May the first French troops entered Eisenstadt. Vienna had capitulated on 13 May. The Prince had already left for Hungary.

Acta Musicalia Nr.251 a-b
Acta Musicalia Nr.251a

Güterregent Szent Gály verwendet sich bei Distriktingenieur Krantz wegen einer Schuldforderung der Sängerin Barbara Pillhofer. Eisenstadt, 17. Juni 1810.
Barbara Pillhofer habe ein Gesuch an den Fürsten gerichtet und um Hilfe gebeten, da ihr Ingenieur Lorenzo seit drei Jahren 30 Gulden, die sie ihm auf drei Monate geborgt hätte, nicht zurückzahle und außerdem sich ihr gegenüber unverschämt benehme. Krantz möge nun Lorenzo zur Rede stellen und, wenn er nichts Rechtskräftiges vorzubringen habe, zur Bezahlung der Schulden zu bewegen.

Acta Musicalia Nr.251b

Szent Gály schreibt am 24. August erneut an den Distriktiningenieur: bis jetzt habe Barbara Pillhofer noch kein Geld gesehen und Krantz möge ihm nun innerhalb von acht Tagen berichten, was er gegen Lorenzo unternommen hätte.

Nos.251 a-b
No.251a
Regent Szent Gály turns to District Engineer Krantz on account of a debt registered by singer Barbara Pillhofer. Eisenstadt, 17 June 1810.
Barbara Pillhofer sent a petition to the Prince with a request for help, since Engineer Lorenzo owes her 30 gulden for the last three years, which she lent him for three months. Not only was the debt unpaid but he behaves very rudely to her. Krantz should confront Lorenzo and if he has no legal recourse, he should be forced to pay the debt.

No. 251b
Szent Gály writes again to the District Engineer on 24 August that Barbara Pillhofer has not yet seen the money and Krantz should report to him within eight days on the matter.

Acta Musicalia Nr.252

Fürst Nicolaus I. reorganisiert die Kapelle nach dem Tod seines Bruders Paul Anton im März 1762.
Vollständige Liste im Facsimile veröffentlicht in Landon I, 375ff, *Haydn-Studien* IV, S.172, Valkó I, Nr. 5 und 4.

No.252
Prince Nicolaus I reorganizes the Capelle following the death of his brother Paul Anton in March 1762. The complete document in facsimile reproduced in Landon I, 375ff; *Haydn-Studien* IV, p. 172. Valkó I, Nos. 5 and 4.

Acta Musicalia Nr. 253

Anstellungsvertrag des Theatermalers Hieronymus Le Bon. Bereits veröffentlicht in *Haydn-Studien IV*, S.171f.

No. 253
Contract of engagement for the theatrical decorator Hieronymus Le Bon. Already published in *Haydn-Studien* IV, pp. 171f.

Acta Musicalia Nr.254 a-b
Acta Musicalia Nr.254a

Fürst Esterházy verlangt von seinem Güterdirektor Szent Gály einen Bericht über die Zustände im Sängerknabeninstitut. Eisenstadt, 30. Oktober 1810.

Acta Musicalia Nr.254b

Szent Gály beauftragt Sakristan Skeley und Vizekapellmeister Fuchs, ihm über die Vorgänge im 'Stift' genauesten Bericht zu erstatten. [Eisenstadt ?] 6. November 1810.

Nos.254 a-b
No.254a
Prince Esterházy requires from his Regent Szent Gály a report concerning conditions in the Boys Choir Institute. Eisenstadt, 30 October 1810.

No.254b
Szent Gály orders Sacristan Skeley and Vice Capellmeister Fuchs to inform him about conditions in the Institute in precise detail [Eisenstadt?] 6 November 1810.

Acta Musicalia Nr.255

Anstellungsvertrag mit dem Pauker Johann Adam Sturm 1737.
Anheünde zu End gesezten Jahr, und Dato haben wür den Hanß Adam Sturm vor einen Paukher an und aufgenommen, und mit ihme sowohl wegen seines Gehalts, alß auch Dienstleistungen halber auf zwey Jahr nachfolgender Gestalten accordirt und zwahr.
Erstlich verstehen wür, daß derselbe vor seine Kost, und Besoldung Monathlich fünffzehen Gulden an bahren Geld, nebst einen Quartier, Holtz fünff Clafter, Khörtzen 30. Pfund und Wein Eysensätter Hämb Neun Emer von Unserer Eysenstätter Herrschaft zu Empfangen haben solle. Zumahlen wür aber vor ihme das aufding, oder Lohngeld zu bezallen versprochen, gleichwie an solchen bereits 90F erleget seynd worden. alß wird Er Solches durch dieses Jahr abdienen, mithin von denen fünfzehn Gulden nicht mehr dan Monatl. Zehen Gulden zu empfangen haben. anbey wird ihme von uns jährl. ein ordinarj Klayd gegeben werden: Was aber das Extra Klayd betrifft, solle Er solches niemahlen ausgenohmen auf unseren Befehl anlegen, und dessen Sich gebrauchen, welches wür demnach vor unser eignen Willkhür, und Disposition denselben geben werden.
Andertens verobligirt Sich gedachter Hanß Adam Sturm Sich nicht nur allein auf unsern Chor zu Eysenstatt mit deren ihm kündigen Instrumenten, als Paukher, Violin, Violon und Violoncello zu was Er nembl. von unsern CapelMaister gestelt wird werden, gebrauchen zu lassen, sondern auch auf unser allmahliges Begehren, es seye hernach auf unsern Gütter, als andrer Örther /: wohin wür nembl. denselben Beruffen, und verlangen werden :/ doch mit unser Beygeschaffter Gelegenheit zu erscheinen und Sich alda selbsten zu verkösten.
Drittens Wird Er Sich in Bemelten Instrumenten öfters exerciren, damit Er sich desto mehr perfectionire, und hierdurch unß Ein grösseres Vergnügen und Contentum leiste. Endlich Viertens Hoffen Wür, daß derselbe nicht nur allein seinen Diensten auf ds Embsigste nachkommen, und verrichten, solche ohne gehabter Erlaubnuß, oder wichtiger Ursach niemahlen versaumen, sondern auch darbey einen ehrbaren, und Gottes Förchtig Lebens Wandl führen, umb Sich so wohl von allen üblen Gesellschaften, als auch was einer Ehrbahren Lebens arth zu wider ist, hütten, und solche Best möglichst vermeiden werde. Gleich wie mir dieses zu meiner Versicherung gegeben worden, also verspreche zu obstehenden Puncten nachzukommen, undt solche zu observiren. Geben in Wienn den 1ten Marty 1737.
        Johann Adam
        Sturmb fürstlicher Paucker

No.255

Contract of engagement for the timpani player Johann Adam Sturm, 1737.

On the date and year hereto appended we have engaged Hanß Adam Sturm as a timpanist for a period of two years, the details of his salary and requirements for service appended as follows:

First he is to receive for his maintenance and salary fifteen gulden per month in cash, together with lodgings, five fathom cords of wood, 30 pounds of candles and nine Eimer of wine Eisenstadt regulation, all to be distributed by our estate at Eisenstadt. Inasmuch as we have agreed to pay him an advance on this contract and to this end have given him 90f. already, he will pay this off in the course of one year in that he shall be paid not fifteen gulden monthly but only ten. Moreover he will be issued an ordinary suit of clothes every year. As concerns the extra suit, he shall on our orders receive one and use it, and it shall be at our disposition to decide when another one is issued.

Secondly, said Hanß Adam Sturm shall oblige himself to appear in our chapel, in Eysenstatt playing those instruments on which he is proficient, viz. timpani, violin, bass and violoncello. Thirdly he will take care to practise diligently on the afore mentioned instruments, thus giving us more pleasure and delight.

Fourthly, it is to be hoped that he will not only perform his services as diligently as possible, and will never absent himself without permission or without very good reason, but will conduct himself in an honourable and god-fearing fashion, distancing himself from all dubious company and everything contrary to a respectable way of life, taking care to avoid such. And just as this [contract] is issued for my protection, so do I promise to honour and obey the above-mentioned points.

> Given at Vienna this 1st March 1737
> Johan Adam
> Sturmb princely timpanist

Acta Musicalia Nr.256

Anstellungsvertrag des Feldtrompeters Christian Wolfgang Dobmeyer. Erste zwei Paragraphen identisch, nur erhält Dobmeyer 200 Gulden Bargeld im Jahr. Dritter Paragraph:

Andertens verobligiret Sich gedachter Wolfgang Dompmayr Sich nicht nur allein auf eunsern Chor zu Eysenstatt mit dene ihm kundig Instrumenten als Trompete, Violin, und Violoncello zu was Er nemblich alda von unsern Capel Maister gestelt wird werden gebrachen zu lassen, [weiterer Text wie Nr. 255]

Drittens. wird Er Sich in vorbemelten Instrumenten absonderlich der Geigen und Bassetl öfters exerciren, damit Er sich destomehr perfectioniere, und hierdurch unß Ein grösseres Vergnügen und Contentum leiste. Endlichen

Viertens. [weiterer Text wie Nr. 255]

[Ge]geben in Wienn den 1ten Marty [1]737.
   Wolfgang Dobmeyer
   fürstl. Hof- und Feldt Trompeter

No. 256

Contract of engagement for the field trumpeter Christian Wolfgang Dobmeyer. First two paragraphs identical with that of Sturm, except that Dobmeyer receives 200 gulden in cash p.a.
Third paragraph:
Secondly, said Wolfgang Dopmayr [sic] obligates himself not only to appear in our choir in Eysenstatt playing those instruments on which he is proficient, viz. trumpet, violin and violoncello, for which ever purpose the Capellmeister will require, but will also, as and when required, appear on our estates or in other places which the signory requires and orders (but we will provide the transportation); and he will provide his own board on these occasions.
Thirdly, he will take care to practise diligently on the afore mentioned instruments, especially the violin and cello, so that he will be the more excellent on them, thus giving even more pleasure and delight. . . [See A.M. 255].

   Given at Vienna this 1st March 1737.
   Wolfgang Dobmeyer
   princely Court and Field Trumpeter

Acta Musicalia Nr.257

Anstellungsvertrag des Trompeters Joseph Reisinger, identisch mit A.M.256.

Kommentar

Fürst Paul Anton war 1734 großjährig geworden und übernahm das Majorat von seiner Mutter Fürstin Oktavia. Sie hatte die ganzen Jahre ihrer Verwaltung die Kosten für die Musikkapelle niedrig gehalten, doch unter ihrem Sohn wurden neue Musiker eingestellt, 1737 fünf Bläser, die beiden Trompeter Reisinger und Dobmeyer, der Flötist Adam Schultz und die beiden Hornisten Johann Berhard Ehrenhardt und Albert Wildner.
Tank, 266.

No.257

Contract of engagement for trumpeter Joseph Reisinger, identical with that of Dobmeyer, A.M.256.

Commentary

Prince Paul Anton came of age in 1734 and assumed the majority from his mother Princess Oktavia. She had kept the costs for the music Kapelle low, but now, under her son, new musicians were engaged: five wind players in 1737 - the two trumpeters Reisinger and

Dobmeyer, the flautist Adam Schultz and the two horn players Johann Bernhard Ehrenhardt and Albert Wildner.
Tank, 266.

Acta Musicalia Nr.258

Anstellungskontrakt des Feldtrompeters Joseph Bayer.
Anheunde zu Ende gesezten Jahr und Dato ist der Antonius Bayr in Sr. Durchl. des Heyl. Röm. Reichs Fürstens Pauli Antony Esterhazy de Galantha Diensten vor einen Trompetter an- und aufgenohmen, und mit Ihme so wohl wegen seines Gehalts, alß auch dienstleistungs halber auf zwey Jahr nachfolgender Gestalten accordirt worden, und zwar
Erstlich wird Ihme Antonio Bayr versprochen, ds Er vor seine Kost und Besoldung auf ein Jahr zwey hundert Gulden an Bahren Geld, nebst einen Quartier, Holtz fünf Clafter, Khörtzen 30 Pfund, und Wein Eysenstätter Hämb feun Emer von den Räntambt der Fürstl. Eysenstatt zu empfangen haben solle. Anbey wird ihme von Sr. Durchl. jährlichen ein Compagnie Klayd gegeben werden das Extra oder Galla Klayd Betr. soll Er solches niemahlen ausgenohmen auf Sr. Durchl. Befehl anlegen und Sich dessen gebrauchen, welches Hochdieselben auch nach eigener willkühr und disposition Geben werden.
Hingegen
Andertens verobligirt Sich gedachter Antonius Bayr Sich nicht nur allein auf den Hochfürstl. Chor zu Eysenstatt mit denen ihm khündigen Instrumenten als Trompetten, Gaigen etc. zu was nemblichen alda von den Fürstl. Capell Maister, welchen Er als seinen Vorgesezten respectirn und in allen gehorchen solle, Gestelt wird werden gebrauche zu lassen, sondern auch auf Sr. Durchl. allmahliges Begehren, und Befehl, es seye hernach auf die Gütter oder andere Örther, wohin nemblichen derselbe Beruffen, und verlanget wird werden /:doch mit beygeschafter Gelegenheit:/ zu erscheinen, und Sich alda Selbsten zu verkösten. Anbey Drittens: wird Er Sich in denen Khündigen Instrumenten öfters exerciren damit Er Sich dadurch desto mehr perfectionire, und Sr. Durchl. Größeres Vergniegen, und Contentum Leiste. Endlichen
Viertens: verspreche sich Hochged. Sr. Durchl. von Ihme Antonio Bayr ds Er nicht nur allein seine Diensten auf das embigste nachkommen, und verrichten, solchen ohne gehabter erlaubnus, oder wichtiger Ursach niemahlen versäumen, viel weniger ohne vorhin geschehner anmeldung Bey den Fürstl. Capell Maister Sich verwaisen,

sondern auch darbey einen ehrbaren und gottesförchtigen Lebenswandel führen, und Sich so wohl von allen üblen Gesellschaften, als auch was einer ehrbaren Lebens arth zu wider ist, hütten, und solche Bestmöglichst vermeiden werde. Gleich wie mir dieses zu meiner Versicherung gegeben ist worden, also verspreche auch obstehenden puncten nachzukommen, und solche zu observiren. Wienn den Ersten Janus 1741

 Anton Joseph Bayer
  Ihro hoch fürstl. Gnaden von Hesterhazie Hoff und
 Feldt trompeter

No. 258

Contract of engagement for the field trumpeter Joseph Bayer.
On the day and year hereto appended Antonius Bayr [sic] is herewith engaged in the service of the Prince of the Holy Roman Empire Pauli Antony Esterhazy de Galantha as a trumpeter, and has been accorded, regarding his salary and the extent of his services, a contract of two years, as follows:
First it is promised to said Antonio Bayr that he receive for his board and salary each year two hundred gulden in cash, beside lodgings, five fathom cords of wood, 30lbs. of candles and nine eimer of wine, Eysenstadt measure from the princely Eysenstatt Rental Office. Moreover he shall receive from H. Highness yearly a company [dress] uniform, concerning the extra or gala uniform he shall receive one and use only at his Highness's request and make use of it, this to be allotted according to H. H.'s will and inclination.
Contrarywise
Secondly, said Antonius Bayr obligates himself not only to appear in our choir in Eysenstatt playing those instruments on which he is proficient, viz. trumpet, violin, etc [rest of the paragraph nearly identical with the same clause in A.M. 256].
Thirdly, [nearly identical with the same clause in A.M. 256].
Fourthly, [ditto] [given at] Vienna, this first day of January 1741.

        Anton Joseph Bayer
  Field Trumpeter to His Princely grace von
    Hesterazie [sic]

Acta Musicalia Nr.259

Anstellungskontrakt des Trompeters Stephan Sachs vom 24. März 1738, identisch mit A.M.256.

No.259

Contract of engagement for the trumpeter Stephan Sachs of 24 March 1738, identical with that of Dobmeyer, A.M.256.

Acta Musicalia Nr.260

Anstellungskontrakt des Trompeters Peter Hofbauer vom 1. Januar 1741, identisch mit A.M.258

No.260
Contract of engagement for the trumpeter Peter Hofbauer of 1 January 1741, identical with that of Bayer, A.M.258.

Acta Musicalia Nr.261

Anstellungskontrakt des Waldhornisten Franz Kohl.
An heunte zu End gesezten Dato und Jahr ist der aus dem Königreich Böheimb gebürtige Frantz Kholl Bey Ihro Durchl. und Herrn Herrn Paul Anton des Heyl. Röm. Reichs Fürsten Eszterhazy de Galantha ecc. vor einen Wald Hornisten außer der Livrée in die Dienste an- und aufgenohmen worden, und gleichwie 1mo Er Frantz Kholl als ein Officier angesehen und gehalten wird werden, alß tragen Se Durchl. das gnädigste Vertrauen in Ihme, dß Er Sich auch also und dergestalten aufführen und verhalten wird, wie es einem ehrliebenden Haußofficir wohl anstehet, und gebühret. Anbey
2do Nebst diesem anhoffenden guten und Lobwürdigen Lebens wandl wird Er Sich bestermaßen befleißen seinen schuldigen Dienst alltäglich accurat zu vollziehen, und mit diesen die Hochfürstl. Gnaden weiters zu erwerben Sich angelegen seyn lassen, Besonders alltaglich /:es seye in Wienn, od. auf denen güthern:/ nachmittag in der antecamera zu erscheinen, und alda Cammerdienst verrichten.
3tio. Wird Er gehalten und obligirt seyn, alltäglich so wohl zu Mittag als auch NachtEssenszeit Bey der Herrschaftlichen Daffel zu erscheinen, alda nach Befehl Sr Durchl. entweders wehrender daffel zu Blasen, od. andere Musique zu machen, oder nebst denen übrigen Haußofficirs die Herrschaft Bedienen zu helffen. Ingleichen
4to Ist Er gehalten zu Eysenstatt, Kütsee, oder anderen orthen, allwo nemblichen Sr. Durchl. Grenadiers Compagnie aufziehen, exerciren, oder paradiren wird, die Mondur deren Hautboisten anzuziehen, und die paradirung mit seinen Instrument ohne einzige Compagnie Gage zu machen. Ubrigens gleich wie man all seine schuldige Dienst auf das Papier zu Bringen umbso ohnnöthiger fündet, als man Hoff-nung hat, ds Er aus eigenen antrieb in allen Vorfallen- und Begebenheiten seine Schuldigkeit auf das Beste Beobachten und vollziehen wird; als Lasset man jenes seinen eigenen eyfer und emsigkeit über. Hingegen

5to. Werden Ihme von Seithen hochgedacht Sr Durchl. vor Kost und jährliche Besoldung zusammen Monathlich richtig zu empfangen zwanzig Gulden Rheinl. id est 20F. versprochen, mit welchen Er verbundten ist Sich in allen Orthen es seye zu Wienn, auf denen Güthern, oder auf der Reyße, wohin Ihme nemblichen Se Durchl. mit freyer Fuhr werden kommen lassen, Selbsten zu verkösten. So fern aber eine Rayße in ein entlegenes Land vorkommete, allwo theurer zu leben wäre, in solchenfahl werden Se Durchl. eine Beliebigen Beytrag machen. Nebst diesem Gehalt

6to verspricht Ihme die gnädigste Herrschaft alljährlich ein gantzes Kleyd, als nemblichen Rock, Camisoll, Hosen, Huth, Strumpf, und Schuh machen zu Lassen und zu geben. Nicht weniger auch alle zwei Jahr ein Baar Stüffel, und einen Mantl, oder anstatt dieser völligen Kleydungs Sorten in Bahren Geld /: jedoch nach willkühr der Gdigsten Herr-schaft:/ alljährlich 60 Gulden Rheinl. mit welchen Er verbundten ist Sich ein honettes Kleyd, und gleichförmig mit seinen Cameraden zu schaffen.

Gleich wie nun diesen Contract mit Ihme Frantz Kholl von heutigen dato an auf zwey Jahr lang errichtet, und geschlossen ist, als verspricht Er zugleich mit vorbeschribenen gehalt diese Zeit zu vollstrecken, gut und emsig zu dienen, auch Sich ehrbar und gebührend aufzuführen, in widrigen solle es der Hochen Herrschaft freystehen Ihme auch unter dieser zeit des Dienstes zu entlassen. Nach Verflössung aber dieser zwey jahren kan dieser Contract weithers verlängert, verändert od. gar aufgehoben werden. Datum Brussel den 1. April 1755

      Frantz Koll.

No. 261
Contract of engagement for the horn player Franz Kohl.
On the day and year hereto appended Frantz Kholl, a native of the Bohemian Kingdom, is hereby engaged as a hunting horn player out of livery in the service of His Serene Highness and Lord Paul Anton von Esterhazy de Galantha etc., Prince of the Holy Roman Empire, as follows:
Firstly, the Frantz Kholl is to be regarded as and treated like an officer, and is the recipient of His Serene Highness's gracious trust that he will thus conduct and behave himself as is befitting an honourable house officer. Moreover
Secondly, Apart from what is hoped to be a good and praiseworthy conduct he will at all times fulfil his daily duties accurately and to the best of his abilities, in this fashion to continue in the grace of his Serene Highness, and in particularly to appear, whether in Vienna or in the princely estates, afternoons in the antechambre, there to perform chamber service.
Thirdly, he is expected and obligated daily to appear at the princely table, at noon and for dinner. There, at the command of His Highness, either to play during table or to perform other music, or, together with the other house officers, to help in serving the signory. Likewise

4thly, he is obliged in Eysenstatt, Kütsee [Kittsee] or in any other place where His Highness reviews parades or exercises the Grenadiers' company, to put on thereby the uniforms worn by the hautboys and to take part in the parade with his instrument without any pledge to the company. Moreover, just as it is not considered necessary to put on paper every detail of the service required of him, it is expected that he, of his own volition, will exercise his duties at all times and occasions and to display his own diligence and zeal. Contrarywise

5thly his Serene Highness promises to pay him, for his board and salary, a monthly stipend of twenty gulden Rhenish, i.e. 20F., whether in Vienna or on the estates or during travels, whereby H. H. will on those travels supply free transport and he [Kohl] will provide his own board. But should the travels extend to a remote country, where living should prove to be dear, in such a case H. H. will provide a *per diem* sum of His Highness's choice. Apart from this salary

6thly the gracious signory promises to provide him annually wih an entire suit of clothes, viz. a coat, waistcoat, breeches, hat, stockings and shoes, which will be made and given him. Not less than every two years he will be given a pair of boots and a greatcoat, or instead of this complete outfit of clothes cash (according to the wishes of the gracious signory) to the amount of 60 gulden Rhenish, for which sum he is obligated to procure an honest set of clothes corresponding to that of his colleagues.

Just as this contract, valid as of today's date, with him, Frantz Kholl, is to extend to a period of two years, for his part he promises to observe the terms herein stated with diligence and zeal and likewise to conduct himself honourably and properly, otherwise the high signory is free within this period to dismiss him from their service. After this period of two years the conract may be further renewed, changed or even annulled. Given at Brussels 1 April 1755.

Frantz Koll

Acta Musicalia Nr.262

Anstellungskontrakt des Waldhornisten Mathias Wirth vom 1. April 1755, identisch mit A.M.261.

No.262

Contract of engagement with hunting horn player Mathias Wirth of 1 April 1755. Identical with that of A.M.261.

Acta Musicalia Nr.263

Anstellungskontrakt des Oboisten Carl Joseph Brauner (Wien, 1 März 1737), identisch mit A.M.255.
Dauer auf zwei Jahre, fleißig üben an seinen Instrumenten, der Oboe, Fagott und Geige. Er erhält monatlich 12 Gulden, Freiquartier und das übliche Deputat.

No.263

Contract of engagement with oboist Carl Joseph Brauner. Vienna, 1 March 1737. Identical with that of A.M.255.

For a period of two years, he is to practise diligently upon his instruments, the oboe, bassoon and violin. He receives monthly 12 gulden, free quarters and the usual goods in kind.

Acta Musicalia Nr.264

Anstellungskontrakt des Flötisten Johann Adam Schulz (Wien, 1. März 1737), identisch mit A.M.255.
Er wird jedoch nur für ein Jahr aufgenommen mit einem Gehalt von 150 Gulden jährlich, Freiquartier und Deputat. Muß sich vom 'Cappel Maister' als Flutraversier, Hautbois und Geige brauchen lassen, darf aber öfter nach Wien, um bei seinem Vater weitere Stunden im Flöten- und Oboenspiel zu nehmen.

No.264
Contract of engagement with the flautist Johann Adam Schulz, Vienna, 1 March 1737, identical with that of A.M.255.
For a period of one year only with a salary of 150 gulden p.a., free quarters and the usual goods in kind. He is to be available to the 'Cappel Maister' as flautist, oboist and violinist, but may travel to Vienna to continue lessons with his father in flute and oboe.

Acta Musicalia Nr.265

Anstellungskontrakt des Geigers Franz Garnier in französischer Sprache (1. Mai 1761) mit den üblichen Bedingungen und Punkten. Als Bezahlung erhält er 20 Gulden im Monat, Freiquartier, die Uniform. Es wurden zwei gleichlautende Kontrakte ausgeschrieben, dieser hier ist von Garnier unterschrieben, ohne Vornamen. Siehe Landon I, 349 für ganzen Text.

No.265
Contract of engagement with the violinist Franz Garnier in the French language [transcribed in Landon I, 349], 1 May 1761. He receives 20 gulden monthly; free quarters and uniform. Two identical contracts were written. This one is signed by Garnier without his Christian name. See landon I, 349 for complete text.

Acta Musicalia Nr.266

Anstellungskontrakt des Flötisten Franz Sigl (Wien, 1. April 1761), identisch mit den vorigen. (A.M.261). Siehe Landon I, 135 für ganzen Text.
Er spielt Flöte und Oboe, wirkt bei der Grenadiersbanda mit, darf weder bei Bällen, Comödien oder anderen Herrschaften spielen. Er

erhält monatlich 20 Gulden, die Uniform, aber kein Deputat. Vertragsdauer ein Jahr.

No.266
Contract of engagement with the flautist Franz Sigl (Siegl, Siegel). Vienna, 1 April 1761. Identical with that of A.M.261 (transcribed in Landon I, 348). He plays flute and oboe, performs in the grenadiers' band and is not allowed to play in balls or plays put on by other houses. He receives 20 gulden monthly, uniform but no goods in kind. 1 year contract. See Landon I, 134 for complete text.

Acta Musicalia Nr.267

Anstellungsvertrag des Violoncellisten Joseph Weigl (Wien, 1. Juni 1761). Zeitdauer drei Jahre, monatlich 20 Gulden bar, eine Uniform oder 60 Gulden Kleidergeld. (Punkte identisch mit den vorigen) Siehe Landon I, 352.

No.267
Contract of engagement with the violoncellist Joseph Weigl. Vienna, 1 June 1761. Contract for 3 years, monthly salary 20 gulden in cash, a uniform or 60 gulden. Landon I, 352.

Acta Musicalia Nr.268

Anstellungsvertrag des Geigers Johann Georg Heger (Wien, 1. Juni 1761). Vertragsdauer drei Jahre, jährlich 150 Gulden, aber keine Uniform, Quartier oder Deputat. Siehe Landon I, 352.

No.268
Contract of engagement with the violinst Johann Georg Heger. Vienna, 1 June 1761. Contract for 3 years, salary 150 gulden p.a., no uniform, no free lodgings, no goods in kind. Landon I, 352.

Acta Musicalia Nr.269

Anstellungsvertrag des Fagotisten Johann Georg Schwenda (Wien, 1. April 1761). Identisch mit A.M.261. Siehe Landon I, 348.
Anständig gekleidet erscheinen, in weißen Strümpfen und Haarbeutel, aufspielen bei Paraden der Grenadiere, auf die Instrumente aufpassen, als Gegenleistung erhält er monatlich 20 Gulden und eine Uniform. Vertragsdauer drei Jahre. Der Kontrakt ist sowohl von Sekretär Johann Stiftl als von Johann Georg Schwenda unterschrieben.

No.269
Contract of engagement with the bassoonist Johann Georg Schwenda. Vienna, 1 April 1761. Identical with that of A.M. 261. Must appear dressed in white stockings and hair-bag, must play in the parades of Grenadiers, must take care of the instruments, receives 20 gulden monthly and a uniform. Length of contract three years. Contract signed by secretary Johann Stiftl and Johann Georg Schwenda. Landon I, 348.

Acta Musicalia Nr.270

Anstellungskontrakt des Oboisten Johann Michael Kapfer (Wien, 1. April 1761). Text identisch mit den vorigen. Siehe Landon I, 348.
Kapfer muß bei Tisch und bei Paraden aufspielen, auf die Instrumente gut aufpassen; als Bezahlung erhält er monatlich 20 Gulden, alle Jahre ein Kleid. Außerhalb Wiens erhält er täglich 17 Kreuzer. Vertragsdauer drei Jahre. Der Kontrakt ist wieder vom fürstlichen Sekretär Stiftl und von Kapfer unterschrieben.

No.270
Contract of engagement with the oboist Johann Michael Kapfer. Vienna, 1 April 1761. Text identical with other contracts. He must play at table and in parades, take care of the instruments, salary 20 gulden monthly, a uniform yearly. When away from Vienna he receives a *per diem* of 17 kreuzer. Contract for three years, signed by Stiftl and Kapfer. See Landon I, 348.

Acta Musicalia Nr.271

Anstellungsvertrag des Oboisten Johann Georg Kapfer (Wien, 1. April 1761) identisch mit dem obigen. Siehe Landon I, 348.
Muß bei der Tafel und Paraden spielen, darf auf keinen Bällen aufspielen. Er erhält monatlich 20 Gulden, jährlich eine Uniform, und außerhalb Wien täglich 17 Kreuzer. Vertragsdauer drei Jahre.

No.271
Contract of engagement with the oboist Johann Georg Kapfer. Vienna, 1 April 1761. Text identical with the previous contract, A.M. 270. See Landon I, 348.

Acta Musicalia Nr.272

Fürst Paul Anton kauft den Oboisten und Fagottisten ihre Instrumente ab.
Das die endes unterschriebenen von Ihrer Hochfürstlichen Durchlaucht Herrn Paul Anthon des Heil. Röm. Reichs Fürsten von Esterházy und Galantha etc. unseren gnädigen hochgebiettenden

Fürsten und Herrn aus Handen dero Secretärii für unsere mitgebrachte Musicalische Instrumente nehmlich zwey Fagott, zwey Houbois, und drey Englische Horn, Sechzehn Ordinaire duggaten richtig empfangen haben, solches bescheinen wir mit unterthänigem Danckh, und reversieren uns hiermit, das wir zu oben beannten Instrumenten, kein mindesten anspruch werden machen wollen, noch können, sondern stellen sothane der Hohen Herrschaft gehorsamst anheim, als ein dero Eigenthum. Urkund dessen haben wir uns eigenhändig unterschrieben, so geschehen in Wienn den 8ten April [1]761.

Johann Michael Kapfer Houboist
Johann Georg Kapfer Houboist
Johann Georg Schwenda Fagodist
Johann Hinterberger Fagottist. [Siehe Landon I, 349]

Kommentar
(A.M.255-272)

Johann Adam Sturm, der auf fürstliche Kosten ausgebildet worden war, spielte außer Pauke noch Violine, Cello und Baß. Siehe HJB XVI, 110, A.M.153 [Landon I, 349]. Detto Carl Brauner (Braun, Praun). Für Garnier, Sigl, Heger, Schwenda und die Brüder Kapfer siehe HJB XVI, 123f; A.M.154. Dobmeyer blieb drei Jahre in der Kapelle, Reisinger ein Jahr, Schulz vier, Sachs zwei, Bayer sechs, Kholl und Wirth beide nur zwei Jahre in fürstlichen Diensten. Tank, 266f.

No.272
Prince Paul Anton purchases their instruments from the oboists and bassoonists.
Herr Paul Anthon, Prince of the Holy Roman Empire von Esterhazy and Galantha etc., our gracious Prince and Lord, from the hand of his secretary undertakes to purchase the instruments we have brought with us, viz. two bassoons, two oboes, and three *cors anglais* for which we have received sixteen ordinary ducats, and these we acknowledge with gracious thanks; and we further attest that we will never claim any rights whatever over the said instruments but acknowledge in submission that they now belong to the high signory and are its exclusive property. In witness of which we have set our signatures, given at Vienna this 8 April 1761.

Johann Michael Kapfer, hautoboist
Johann Georg Kapfer, Hautboist
Johann Georg Schwenda, bassoonist
Johann Hinterberger, bassoonist

Commentary to Nos.225-272
Johann Adam Sturm, who had been trained at princely expense, played, apart from the timpani also violin, cello and double bass. See HYB XVI, 110; A.M.153. [Landon I, 349].

The same applied to Brauner (Braun, Praun). For Garnier, Sigl, Heger, Schwenda and the Kapfer brothers, see HYB XVI, 123f.; A.M. 154. Dobmeyer remained in the Capelle for three years, Reisinger one year, Schulz four, Sachs two, Bayer six, Kholl and Wirth only two years each. Tank. 266f.
The sale of the instruments to the princely household was a way to help the musicians with some ready cash.

Acta Musicalia Nr.273

Anstellungsvertrag mit dem Baßsänger und Violonisten Melchior Griessler. Wien, 1. Juni 1767.
Vertragspunkte wie vorher, doch bereits dem Vicekapellmeister Haydn Gehorsam zu leisten. Dafür erhält er: 6.to. Es werden ihme Melchior Griessler als Bassisten alle Jahr 200. Gulden Rhein. von der Hohen Herrschaft hiemit accordirt, und beym Ober Einnehmer-Amt angewiesen alle Quartal zu empfangen. Als Violinist aber wieder folgendes Deputat in Natura empfangen, nehmlich:
 4. Metzen Weitz
12. Metzen Rogen
1/4 Metzen Gerstenbräu
1/4 Metzen Hirsebräu
1/4 Metzen Linßen

Rindfleisch	300. Pfund
Salz	50. Pfund
Schmaltz	30. Pfund
Kertzen	30. Pfund
Wein	9 Eimer
Kraut	1/2 Eimer
Rüben	1/2 Eimer
Schwein	1 Stück
Brenn Holtz	6 Klafter

Der Vertrag galt für drei Jahre.

Kommentar

Für Griessler siehe A.M.36-38, 59, 70, 154, 200. Landon II, 58f.

No.273
Contract of engagement for the bass singer and violinist Melchior Griessler. Vienna, 1 June 1767.
[Terms as before, but stipulated that he is to be obedient to the Vice Kapellmeister [Haydn]. For this he] 6th, Melchior Griessler as bass singer shall receive 200 Rhenish gulden p.a. as agreed by the high signory, and the Chief Cashier is hereby empowered to pay out this sum

quarterly. As violinist, however, he is to receive the following list of goods in kind [*Deputat*].

4 Metzen [see glossary] of wheat
12 Metzen [see glossary] of rye
1/4 Metzen [see glossary] of barley-pap
1/4 Metzen [see glossary] of millet-pap
1/4 Metzen [see glossary] of lentils

Beef	300 pounds
Salt	50 pounds
Lard	30 pounds
Candles	30 pounds
Wine	9 Eimer
Cabbage	1/2 Eimer
Turnips	1/2 Eimer
Pork	one piece
Firewood	6 fathom cords

The contract ran for three years.

Commentary

For Griessler see A. M.36 - 38. 59. 70. 154. 200. Landon II, 58f.

Acta Musicalia Nr.274

Anstellungskontrakt des Fagottisten Johann Hinterberger.
Wien, 1. April 1761.
Vertrag indentisch mit Nr.273. Vertragsdauer ebenfalls drei Jahre. Als Fagottist war Hinterberger verpflichtet, bei den Grenadiersparaden mitzuspielen, wie alle anderen Bläser auch.
'8.vo. Für solche Dienst Leistung werden ihme Johann Hinterberger alle monath zwanzig Gulden Rhein .... angewiesen.
10.us. Werden ihme Fagottisten von der Herrschaft /: jedoch nur ausser der Stadt Wienn :/ alle Tag 17. Xr Resolviert .....'

Kommentar

Für Hinterberger siehe A.M.8, 70, 154, 185, 186, 272. Landon II, 72, Tank 153, 209, 272, 311. Wir haben beide Verträge, einen von Hinterberger unterzeichnet, den anderen vom fürstlichen Sekretär Johann Stiftl.

No.274

Contract for the bassoon player Johann Hinterberger. Vienna, 1 April 1761.
Contract is identical with No.273. Length of engagement also three years. As bassoon player Hinterberger was obliged to play during the grenadier's parades, as was the case with all the other wind instrument players.
'8[vo] For such services he Johann Hinterberger will be paid twenty Rhenish gulden per month . . .

10us He, as bassoon player, will be granted by the signory (but only when he is away from the city of Vienna) a daily allowance of 17xr.'

Commentary

For Hinterberger, see A. M.8, 70, 154, 185, 186, 272. Landon II, 72. Tank 153, 209, 272, 311. We have both contracts, one signed by Hinterberger, the other by the princely secretary Johann Stiftl.

Acta Musicalia Nr.275

Anstellungsverträge der Waldhornisten Franz Pauer und Joseph Oliva vom 1. Juni 1769. Siehe HJB XIII, A.M.5; dieses Exemplar ist jedoch von den beiden Musikern unterschrieben.

Kommentar

Für Pauer siehe A.M.50, 190-92, 218. Oliva A.M.22, 69.
Landon II, 76.
Harich HJB VIII, 32. Tank, 285, 288, 290, 296, 300, 302, 311.

No.275

The contracts of engagement for the hunting-horn-players Franz Pauer and Joseph Oliva dated 1 June 1769. See HYB XIII, A.M.5. This copy however is signed by both musicians.

Commentary

For Pauer see A.M.50, 190-92, 218. For Oliva see A.M.22, 69. Landon II, 76. Harich HYB VIII, 32. Tank 285, 288, 290, 296, 300, 302, 311.

Acta Musicalia Nr.276 a-d

Anette Dorner möchte das bezogene Kostgeld für den abwesenden jungen Cornega nicht zurückzahlen. Eisenstadt, 19. November 1810.
Durch ein Versehen der Buchhaltung war Madame Dorner Kostgeld für den jungen Cornega, der nicht mehr im Chorknabeninstitut sondern in der Lehre bei einem Wiener Goldschmied war, von Mai bis Oktober weiterbezahlt worden. Dem Güterregenten war zwar gemeldet worden, daß die Kammersängerin Cornega ihren Bruder aus dem Institut nehmen würde, er hatte jedoch vergessen, der Buchhaltung den Sachverhalt zu melden. Am 19. Dezember erstellte er ein Gutachten für den Fürsten und empfahl angesichts der großen Teuerung, Frau Dorner dieses Geld zu belassen, da sie sich sicher nicht bereichert, sondern die Knaben damit verpflegt habe. Der Fürst genehmigt am 26. Dezember Szent Gálys Vorschlag und dieser be-

nachrichtigt am 30. Dezember das Hauptzahltamt von der fürstlichen Resolution.

No.276 a-d

Anette Dorner wishes not to refund the board money she has received for the absent young Cornega. Eisenstadt, 19 November 1810.

Through a mistake in the bookkeeping department, Madame Dorner continued to receive, from May to October, board money for the young Cornega; who was no longer in The Boys Choir Institute but was in Vienna as apprentice to a goldsmith. The Regent had been informed that the Chamber Singer Cornega wished to remove her brother from the Institute but forgot to explain the circumstances to the bookkeeping department. On 19 December he prepared a statement for the Prince and recommended that in view of the enormous inflation the additional money be left with Frau Dorner, who certainly did not profit from the transaction but used the money to feed the boys. The Prince approved Szent Gály's proposal on 26 December, and on the 30th informed the Chief Cashier's office of this decision.

Acta Musicalia Nr.277 a-c

Friedrich Tomasini ersucht um ein Stipendium.

Dieses Gesuch wird am 1. Dezember 1811 von Güterdirektor Szent Gály begutachtet, der Fürst Nicolaus vorschlägt, den Bittsteller abzuweisen, da seine Mutter für ihn bereits seit 1808 100 Gulden erhielt, und im Juli 1810 eine Zulage von 40 Gulden bewilligt wurde; so würde eine neuerliche Erhöhung nur alle anderen Stipendienbezieher zu Bittschriften verleiten. Fürst Nicolaus lehnt daher am 18. Dezember das Gesuch ab (A.M.277b) und Szent Gály gibt am 31. Dezember den fürstlichen Bescheid weiter (A.M.277c).

Kommentar

Friedrich Tomasini war der Sohn des alten Konzertmeisters Luigi Tomasini, siehe A.M.231.

No.277 a-c

Friedrich Tomasini requests a stipendium.

This request was judged by Regent Szent Gály on 1 December 1811, who suggests to Prince Nicolaus to refuse the supplicant, since his mother already received 100 gulden for him in 1808 and in July 1810 received a supplement of 40 gulden. In this fashion all other recipients of stipendia would be encouraged to write similar requests. Prince Nicolaus therefore refuses the petition on 18 December (A.M.277b) and Szent Gály forwards the refusal on 31 December (A.M.277c).

Commentary

Friedrich Tomasini was the son of the old leader Luigi Tomasini, see A. M.231.

Acta Musicalia Nr.279 a-c

Barbara Tomasini bittet den Fürsten, ihren Sohn Friedrich bei einem Wirtschaftsdepartement als Praktikant einzustellen. Eisenstadt, 6. September 1811.

Szent Gály berichtet dem Fürsten, daß der 14jährige Knabe noch zu schwach und zu unreif sei für eine Praktikantenstelle, daß er in der Schule aber brav und fleißig sei, so daß zu einem späteren Zeitpunkt enventuell an eine Anstellung gedacht werden könne. Am 10. September schlägt der Fürst daher die Bitte der Barbara Tomasini ab (A.M.277b). Szent Gály leitet am 30. September die Resolution weiter (A.M.279c).

No.279 a-c

Barbara Tomasini begs the Prince to engage her son Friedrich as a practitioner in one of the economic departments. Eisenstadt, 6 September 1811.

Szent Gály reports to the Prince that the 14-year-old boy is too weak and immature for a position as a practitioner, but that he is good and diligent in the school and can be perhaps considered for such a position in the future. On 10 September the Prince therefore refuses Barbara Tomasini's petition (A.M.277b), Szent Gály forwards the refusal (*Resolution*) on 30 September. (A.M.279c).

'Nothing can exceed the Pleasure and Happyness of this Place...' An Englishman in Vienna and Eisenstadt Castle in 1748 and 1749

Transcribed and Edited by H. C. Robbins Landon

The Lewis Walpole Library in Farmington, Connecticut, owns a valuable correspondence between Thomas Steavens and Sir Charles Hanbury Williams concerning life in Vienna in the years 1748 and 1749, as well as an amusing description of Eisenstadt Castle in 1749, from which the quotation in the title is taken. The correspondence is catalogued as CHW St. 10909 and we are much indebted to the library for permission to publish extracts in the *Haydn Yearbook*.

Haydn was, of course, a penniless student in Vienna in the late 1740s, just expelled from St Stephen's Cathedral and this was the period when he composed his *Missa brevis* in F and early harpsichord sonatas. He was also about to work for Felix Kurz-Bernardon, with whom he collaborated in *Der (neue) krumme Teufel* in the Kärntnerthortheater.

At this period, Haydn's later patron, Prince Paul Anton Esterházy was the reigning prince at Eisenstadt Castle. His wife was Marchesa Lunati-Visconti, for whom Haydn would later compose *L'infedeltà delusa* in 1773.

Thomas Steavens arrived in Vienna in December 1748 and immediately reported to Sir Charles, who was the British envoy in Dresden and hence closely involved in diplomatic politics.

Vienna, Decr. ye 9th, 1748,

Mr Dear Sr Charles

I arriv'd here last Tuesday se'night after a terrible Journey from Prague to the Borders of Bohemia, where the Roads began to mend, grew still better in Moravia; & in Austria were so very good that I came the last six mile [*sic*] in a little more than four hours. by good Luck I immediately found very good Lodgings here, tho I pay very dear for them; I have four very handsome Rooms, besides my Servants, for all which I pay 110 florins a Month, exclusively of fire & Candle. The victuals they give me is very good, they make excellent Soop [*sic*], & have admirable sower Grout, in short I eat very well, tho seldom under three dollars a meal, so that, if my Bill had been to pay instead of to receive, you may imagine how unwellcome it would have been. The Letter you sent me surpriz'd me very much, it was from Monsr Splitgerben at Berlin to inform me that he had receiv'd from Mr Pello a fresh Credit for me, which tho' I cannot possibly account for, I am by no means dissatisfy'd with.

 I must now tell you what I have been doing ever since my Arrival here, but before I begin, I must say that I never knew a more agreable Place than Vienna, nor met with a more polite, obliging, affable, easy People than those I have found here. I am as well & as agreable here as at Berlin which you know is a great deal for me to say, & what is stronger is that the greatest Civilitys I have receiv'd have not been from the People I had letters to, tho' I can by no means complain of their having been wanting in them, for C.^{t} Uhlfeldt, C.^{t} Kevenhuller, Baron Firmian have all three been extreamly polite & obliging to me. -- the day after I came here & din'd with Mr Keith [Robert Murray Keith, British Ambassador in Vienna], who carry'd me in the afternoon to VeldtMar.^{l} Konigsegg, you may imagine I was well receiv'd there for the second time I was to wait on him he offered to give me Letters for Prince Kinski at Venice; the next morning I was to wait on C.^{t} Uhlfeldt & C.^{t} Kevenhuller & left my Letters; I met Baron Firmian at the opera after which Mr Keith carry'd me to Count Colloredo^s Assembly. The Assemblys begin here at half an hour after eight & last till half an hour after ten. there are never any Suppers in this Place. C^t Colloredo^s Assembly is as numerous as Count Bruhl^s & as fine except that there is no musick here[.] I met C^t Kevenhuller, & was presented by Mr Keith & Baron Firmian to all the first People of the Place. The morning after I waited on Prince Lichtenstein, Prince Trautzen [Trauttmannsdorf?], Mareschall Bathiani, Count Kinsky, General Pallavicini etc etc in the Evening I was presented by Count Kevenhuller to their Imperial Majestys, whose hands I kiss'd, who received me in the most gracious manner, & did me the Honour both to ask me several questions; after this I was presented to the eldest Arch Duke and Arch Dutchess. I never saw a handsomer Man than the Emperor, a more beautifull woman than the Empress, nor more lovely Children than the Arch Dukes and Arch Dutchesses. The Day after I din'd at Count Colloredo^s, where there was the finest Dinner I ever saw of above twenty Covers, & under every Plate a List of four & thirty sorts of wine, & all this without being the least gené or uneasy. the next day I saw the Emperor dine in publick with the

Knights of the Toison d'or in their Robes, which was indeed very magnificent. the day after I was presented to Prince Charles; I was carried into a Room where he was alone, I was there with him near ten Minuets [sic], nothing can be more gracious & amiable than this Prince.

You may imagine by what I have already said that I have pass'd my Time very much to my Satisfaction here. There is generally a Regiment (of those that Come from the low Countries) review'd every morning where all the Royal Family is present, at night there is a German Comedy with an Intermetzo between the Acts, and an Italian Opera, one night serious, another Buffa. Leucippo [by Hasse, first given at Hubertusberg in 1747, repeated at Vienna on 5 September 1748] has been play'd twice since I have been here, poor ombra Amante & Abbastanza were most cruelly Treated by the Tazi [Vitoria Tesi-Tramontini, contralto, engaged in Vienna on 3 May 1748], but Monticelli [the castrato Angelo Monticelli] sang Carestini[s] [Giovanni Carestini, who had created the title role when Steavens had heard him in Saxony] Songs charmingly; you know I suppose that he has been at Law with my L.[d] Middlesex for three hundred Pound; L.[d] Burlington supported him, & he has won his Suit. there is to be a Burletta in England this Winter, & my L.[d] Middlesex has undertaken it.

M[r] Keith has been as kind & civil as possible [;] he is very well here, *that you may depend upon*; & I believe lik'd by the People of the Place (I say no more) better than his Predecessor.

On Sunday last I din'd at Count Canal's, the Sard.[n] Minister, who is one of the most agreeable Men I ever knew. to day I din'd at Count Uhlfeldt[s], & have since been at Prince Augsbourg[s] [Auersperg], the Grand Ecuyer from whence I am come home to finish this Letter...

...I must tell you that Mareschal Bathiany was the day before yesterday declar'd Governour of the Archduke Joseph; The Marquis de Botta is appointed Grand Maitre to Prince Charles, & the Duc d'Aremberg commander of the Troops in the low Countrys, and Gen[l] Pallavicini of those in Italy.

It was not I assure necessary to remind me of the Coffee; my first enquiry here was for that & some Buda Wine; I have got you ten Pounds of the best Turkish Coffee; & I sent you with it 45 Bottles of Buda wine they assure me is the very best...

* * * * * * *

Vienna, Decr ye 21st 1748

My Dear Sr Charles

. . .if my Letters are very frequent, They cannot be very long, for I am engag'd here from Morning till Night; Interest must sometimes get the better of Inclination, & the Attention I am oblig'd to pay to the People of this Place prevent that I owe & shall always think I owe to you.

on Wednesday se-night I din'd at C^t Uhlfeldt where we had a most magnificent Dinner, & indeed all the Entertainments at his Place are so, for you seldom set down to Table with less than eighteen or twenty People. their wines are excellent, & without Number. at the beginning of Dinner they bring about vin d'Absynthe which is a fine bitter, & makes you eat like the Devill; but they have a wine here which exceeds all others I ever tasted. this is vin de Cerises, which is made of the Cherrys steep'd in Tokay, & is the most exquisite Liquour that can be Drunk. Thursday se'night I din'd at Baron Firmians, Friday at Keith^s, saturday at Monsr de Burmannia^s, where the strength & quantity of the Hungary wine got the better a little of my outward Man. Sunday I din'd at Home, & went at night to Prince Esterhasy^s. Monday I din'd at C.^{t} Kevenhuller^s, Tuesday at C.^{t} Colloredo^s, Wednesday at C.^{t} Kirchenberg^s, Thursday at Count Paar^s, and etc as at night at C.^{t} Colloredo^s Assembly. Yesterday din'd at Keith^s, & was at C.^{t} Kinsky^s & C.^{t} Uhlfeldt^s, at night to day I dine again at Keith^s, & shall go to Monsr Bartinstein^s, in the evening, & to morrow I dine at C.^{t} Podewils^s, 'tis impossible for any body to be better than I am here. I have rec'd the greatest Civility, & am Carress'd by all the People of the Place which is the most agreable I ever knew. The woman are extremely affable, & excessively handsome, the Men perfectly, polite, and easy, without any of that Reserve which one would expect to find in Persons of their high Birth & illustrious Descent. They do not only endeavour to make their own Fitz agreable to you, but study to make the Places where you are going so too; 'tis with great Regret that I shall leave this Place; but I shall do it in about ten days, for my Health is very indifferent, & as I have no Time to nurse myself, I am much out of Order at present. was not this the Case I assure you I would not stirr from hence till your Arrival at Turin...

* * * * * * *

Vienna, Jan:ʸye 4ᵗʰ. 1748 [*recte* 1749]

My Dear Sʳ Charles,

...Before I go on in my Letter it is necessary to say that last night I drunk too much Wine for my Head to be clear, or my Hand steady this morning if therefore I dont write strait, if my English is false, & my Letter half nonsense, you must excuse it, & having given you this warning I shall proceed to tell you all I know & can think of.

about ten Days ago I receiv'd the News of my mother's death, which shock'd me very much, & was a real & unfeign'd Affliction...I have order'd that all my Mother's Servants should be put into mourning at my Expence, & that my Steward should be allow'd for handsomest compleat Mourning also. I have put myself & all my servants into as deep mourning as possible...on Sunday last I met the Tazi [Tesi] at Comte Esterhasiˢ, I immediately made acquaintance with her, & took the opportunity of going away when she did to hand her to her Coach. I think she is perfectly agreable, & well-bred. She acts in the new opera (Siroé) [by Wagenseil, libretto Metastasio, first performed Vienna, 8 December 1748] in Man's Cloaths, & I think one Scene as well as Mʳ Garrick could do it. Amorevoli [Angelo Amorevoli] is gone to Italy for his Health, & they have got a Man from Thence, who sings much better, the Opera is really vastly fine, the Theatre for the German Comedy [Kärntnerthortheater] very pretty. They have a Terezzini there who does not dance well but is a perfect Beauty. -- The Day I receiv'd the News of my Mother's Death, I was to have din'd at P. Esterhasi's, but excus'd myself; the Prince in the afternoon to divert me send me two Monkeys, one of which fought with Poro, & bit his Ear; the day before yesterday I was invited to P. Esterhasy's, Prince Augsbourgˢ [Auersperg] & the Venetian Ambassadour but din'd with the former & a most magnificent Dinner we had, with a Custom which I never saw before but like extreamly, when the Dinner was over Every body rose from Tables, & went into the next Room where there was a Desert which they sat down to in the same order as before. in the Evening I went to the Masquerade which was the first we have had. the Room [Redoutensaal] is excessively large & very finely illuminated you pay a Ducat for Entrance, & for wine etc, you pay besides. I never was better diverted. I went first in a Woman's Dress & had the finest fun imaginable, several Ladys took me for a Whore, & abus'd me terribly, at last my Voice discover'd me, & I was obliged to go out for Another Dress which I had ready & which I made on Purpose. this was that of a Madman, which was the best & Compleatest Mask I ever saw. among many other ridiculous Things I had a gingerbread order about my neck. my Mask pleas'd so extreamly that I had a Crowd at my Heels, till the Masquerade was over. but this was the least of my Exploits of this Day. I spent above 80 ducats without having what I wanted, but I shall have it, tho' not without spending as many more. it will cost me altogether around hundred Pound, & if it was to cost me five I would give them; it is impossible for any Body to be more thoroughly captus or more compleatly mad than myself; I dare not enter into the Particulars of this Affair, I can only tell you that it is a dulce saltans La lage, -- Etrusco de Sanguine, yesterday I din'd at Keith^r, & went in the Evening to Monsr Bartinstein, & Count Colloredo^s Assembly. to day I din'd at home & to morrow at V: M: Koenigsegg^s who has been infinitely kind & obliging to me. . .

* * * * * * *

Vienna Feb.y ye 15th 1749

My Dear Sr Charles,
 . . .in three days it [the Carnival] will be ended & then I intend that Reason, who has been utterly banish'd for two months, shall take her turn to rule. you will easily believe that I am very indiscreet, but you will not easily believe that I am ten times more indiscreet than ever. I live almost without sleep, & when I do sleep it is only to dream of the Rosa. I believe I did not tell you that she is one of the sweets of Aeno^s Vale: she has all the warmth of them, but she has an infernal Dipsas about her, who tortures me with Disappointment, & makes me do very rash & inconsiderate things, that Beauty beyond Description, & Fondness without bounds can drive a Man upon. I have already spent 100 £. here & have sent for my eigth [*sic*] this morning. I tell this to you because I know it is deponere tutis Auribus. You may imagine I am very Popular among the Trades People of this Place, as for the others I am in as great favour as ever. the night before last I had a private Audience of the Empress Dowager, who has been ill ever since I have been here. I was with her for ten Minutes, she did me an infinite deal of Honour, &, had I been a foreign Minister, she could not have behav'd in a more gracious Manner to me. I shall always think with the greatest Satisfaction of the Time I have pass'd at this Place, for, besides the Civilitys I have receiv'd from the Nobility here, I have had the Honour to be greatly taken notice of by the Imperial Family. You will have seen in the Gazette that C: Choteck has got C: Kinsky^s Place. I din'd with him on Monday at Prince Esterhasy^s, & on tuesday at V: M:

Bathiany^s. we have had the most magnificent Courses de Traineau [sleigh-ride] here, I was in one at Schonbrun two days ago, but at present the Frost is gone, & I am afraid I shall find the Roads to Venice very bad. . .

* * * * * * *

Vienna March ye 19.th 1749

. . .Genl Colloredo the Vice Chancellor^s Brother has been long talk'd of to go to England, &, I believe, is at present as good as nam'd. He is Ambassadeur de Malte at present, but that will be over in three Weeks. Count Esterhasy & Genl Breitlach sollicited both to go to London, & the latter was warmly supported by the Emperour, who is very much his Friend. Breitlach has dissappear'd lately. People think he is sent to negotiate some private Affair in the Empire, but tis more probable that he is gone away in a Pout at his Disappointment.

Keith knows nothing yet of his Destination, he is perfectly well here. the People of the Place like him better than S.^{r} T: Robinson, whose Merit they did not know, & whose manners they did not like, & Firmian, who is as sensible & knowing a Man as ever liv'd, told me that Robinson never was well here but at Court, & that he ceas'd being well there immediately after the Peace of Breslaw. He was however certainly a most proper Minister for this Court, for He dealt with the Austrians in Terrore, & there is no so sure way to make People do right, as by making them afraid to do wrong. I do not think Keith a very bright Man, but he has certainly very good Sense, Knowledge, & Judgment. Caley says in a Letter I receiv'd from him some time ago that he believes Keith will go to Berlin.

I cannot pretend at present to give you any Account of this Court. I can only tell you in general that Bartinstein governs for foreign Affairs, & Mon.^{r} Cohl for domestick ones. the first is a Mountebank, the second a Bigot. Haugwitz^s Scheme is cryd down by all thinking People, C^t Harrach the honestest, sensiblest, & ablest Man here, has beg'd leave to have it inregister'd in the Records of Bohemia that he oppos'd to the utmost of his Powers so destructive a Measure. Count Choteck is to be replac'd at Berlin by General Grune. . .I have already recommended Stanhope to Firmian, if I should be gone from hence, I will send Stanhope a Letter for him, which will be of more service to him than any other Letter he can have. if you knew Firmian you would adore him. He has parts, Judgment, infinite Reading & Knowledge, with boundless Worth & Good nature. We are inseperable. it is impossible to say how much I am oblig'd to him,

& how much I love him. He is no more a Roman Catholick than I am, & no more a German than you are. I think of getting away from hence as soon as possible, but God knows when that will be. I have already spent about a thousand Pound [sic] here, I am (as Jack Maggot says) mad, very mad, exceeding mad. --- . . . Count Canal is the most agreeable man living, but He has a Wife that is a mad woman. --- I had almost forgot to tell you that about a fortnight ago, a few days after Rosa had left this Place, for Venice, I took it in my Head to follow her, accordingly I set out & travell'd four & thirty German Miles (Night & Day) to have the Pleasure of passing one half hour with her in a beastly Ale-house, & this Journey, which was all perform'd in a day & a half & two nights, cost me near fourscore Ducats.

I am oblig'd to open my Letter, which was seal'd & given to Sr James Caldwell, to tell you that this Evening I saw Monsr Sternberg at Court, who, in talking of his Journey to Dresden, said that nothing could have made him so happy as to have gone to England, but that that was now determin'd otherwise, & that he imagin'd that Monsr Richecourt, who was nam'd to go there, had already taken leave at Turin. I am sorry for this on General Colloredo^s Account, who would have done very well at London, & who, I am persuaded, thought himself so sure of going there, that this will be a Coup de Foudre for him, but the Vice Chanc.^{lr} his Brother is not a personal Favourite of the Emperor^s, as you imagin'd. It is probable that as Breitlach, whom the Emperor supported strongly, was not approv'd of they have pitch'd on a Lorrainer to make amends for not sending him. Monsr Sternberg said he was very sorry he should have so little of your Company at Dresden, I said I knew nothing of your Departure from thence. He said Count Perron was nam'd to go to England in Orsorio.^{s} Stead, pray let me know if this is true. . .

* * * * * * *

Thursday Morning, ye 20.th of March
. . .I beg pardon for this confus'd Letter, which will certainly make you think me distracted, but, before I seal'd up my Letter for the second time, I was determin'd to tell you all I could; for this reason I went to Keith this Morning, who told me, that the Reason why Richecourt was recall'd from Turin was because he had marry'd a Piedmontese Wife, & this Court were afraid of his growing too much a Subject & Friend of the King of Sardinia^s, that General Grune, who

is very well known to, & very much esteem'd by the Duke of Newcastle, was certainly intended to be sent to London, but that, as this Court has determin'd not to leave Monsr Richecourt (who has pleas'd extreamly by his Behaviour at Nice) unemploy'd, & as Monsr Richecourt is personally disliked by the King of Prussia, they were oblig'd to send him back to England, & to send Genl Grune, who has the Honour to be very well with his Pr May^s, to Berlin. (Monsr Richecourt is not a Gentleman) after this Keith show'd me a Letter he receiv'd yesterday from Villettes in which he says he is that Minuet [*sic*] inform'd of his Sard.ⁿ May^s Resolution to send Monsr de St Germain to Paris, & Monsr d'Orsorio to Madrid, that a Courier was dispatch'd with orders to Monsr d'Orsorio to prepare for his Embassy, & another to Dresden, with orders to C^t Perron to set out for England as soon as possible in order to have the Benefit of Monsr Orsorio.^s Instructions before he leaves London. Villettes says not a word about his leaving Turin, which makes me hope there is nothing yet determin'd about that affair. God bless you. if you can understand this letter excuse it, it is not my fault that it is not more intelligible -- once more adieu.

* * * * * * *

Vienna March ye 22.nd 1749

Mr Dear Sr Charles;

. . .I believe I shall be oblig'd to go next week to Prince Esterhasy^s Seat in Hungary but shall avoid it if possible, as it will make my stay here the longer. -- . . .

* * * * * * *

Eysenstadt near Edinbourg [*sic*] in Hungary
April ye 2.d N: S: 1749

My Dearest Sr Charles,

I write to you at present for three Reasons; first for the Pleasure of writing to you, secondly for the Pleasure of writing to you from Hungary, & lastly to give you some account of this Place, where I told you, in my last from Vienna, I was going.

This Chateau is situated on an Eminence, at one End of the Village of Eysenstadt, & was built by Prince Paul Esterhasy, Grandfather of the present Prince. It is a vast large House, built round a Court, & surrounded by a Mote, which you cross over a great Stone

Bridge, to enter into the Court. -- as for the Inside of the House, the only fine Room (I mean as to Size,) is the finest I ever saw. It is a great Hall that takes up almost one Side of the House, which is square. I never saw so large, & well proportion'd a Room; It takes in two Floors like the Hall at my Ld Pomfret^s at Eston. at each End of this Hall is a statue of a naked Man much bigger than the Life, and Ceiling is painted with Storys of the Heathen Gods, & on each Side are the Pictures of all the Kings of Hungary at full Length, & in one corner is the Picture of Prince Paul, who built the House, in a Woman's Dress. This Room has not been alter'd since the Building of the House, no more than a few more [?] which are furnish'd chiefly with Pictures of the Esterhasy Family, but the present Princess, *who is of Lorrain,* & who, among many other Accomplishments, has an admirable Taste, has now furnish'd almost all the Chateau, & these Apartments are as handsome & commodious as possible, Every Stranger has his Bedchamber, Dressing-room, Gaderobe, & Servants Room. I was astonish'd to be as well lodg'd here, as I could have been at Houghton or at Coldbrook, & did not expect to find in Hungary the finest Tapestry, the prettyest Silks, the prettyest Indian Paper etc for it was not the Magnificence but the elegance that surpriz'd me. ---The Chapell here is extremely handsome, &, as it is Passion Week at present, is made no small use of. The Room where we dine is very large; & it ought to be so, for we never set down to Table under two or three & twenty Covers & dine in a Croud of the Prince's Servants, Vassals etc. --- out of the great Hall you go into the Garden, which is one of the prettyest I have seen since I left England, but not large.

I must now give you some Account of the Manner in which We live. I arriv'd here three Days ago about Dinner Time. I was too much tir'd & the weather was too bad for me to get up this Day after before ten o'clock; but yesterday Morning I went in one of the Prince's Chaises to a prodigious Lake about a German Mile from hence, which is call'd the Lake of Cheyhl [Neusiedlersee]; they tell me it is fourteen French Leagues in Length, & twelve in Breadth, & swells or diminishes every seven years, that it was some years ago nothing like so large as it is at present, & that several Villages have been destroy'd by It's Increase. I saw several large Boats upon it, but the People of the Country are afraid to venture far from the Shore on account of the Sand Banks. Prince Esterhasy's Grandfather had some Dutchmen here to build a Vessel for him, but, when the Dutchmen were gone, the Vessel succeeded no longer. They had a Design not long ago to cut a Canal from this Lake into the Danube; but it was dropt on account of the Trouble & Expence it would have caus'd. --- in returning from the Lake I pass'd thro' a very large Wood about an

English mile from hence; which is thoroughly stock'd with Wild Boars, Deer, Hares, & all Sorts of Game. The Wood is of Oaks, but not such as grow in Althrop & Asbridge Parks. The Trees are small but, notwithstanding that, the Wood must in Summer be very beautiful; there are in it most magnificent Ridings of a prodigious Length.

Nothing can exceed the Pleasure & Happyness of this Place, every Man does exactly the Thing he likes best, & nothing but that. there is an Ease & a Profusion that are enough to make a Cynic turn Admirer of the good Things of this World. People eat, drink & sleep, as They please, & when They please. for the Morning Diversion there are Dogs, Hawks, & Guns; you order what Chasse you like best, & have always at Command the Prince's Servants & Horses among which are eighteen of the finest English ones I ever saw. but I cannot give you a better Idea of the Magnificence & Luxury of this Place, then by telling you that the Prince has forty Post Horses, with Chaises & Postilions accordingly for the Use of those who are not Sportsmen --- the Princess does not appear till eleven o'clock, soon after which she goes to Mass. at one the Dinner is serv'd, & it is imposssible to set down to a better Table; I am the only Person here that eats [foie] gras, & therefore have a little Dinner to Myself, which makes the Chops of some water, & the Blood of others rise, at Me. during the first Course the Prince has Musique de Chasse, & during the second there is a Concert by the best Hands from the Orchestra at Vienna. after Dinner People play at Cards, or at Billiards, or sleep, or read, or walk, till eight o'clock, when We sup & have another Concert. yesterday after Dinner We had a Hungarian Dance, which was the most extraordinary thing I ever saw. When we had risen from Table there came into the Room eight Hungarian Peasants, with their Sabres drawn, & with them a Merry Andrew, who began dancing in the following Manner, the first Man held his naked Sabre over his left shoulder, the second took this by the Point in his right Hand, holding his own Sabre over his shoulder with his Left, which the third held in his right, & so the Rest accordingly, in this Manner they continued dancing near an Hour, forming a string with their Sabres as I have describ'd, & running under one Another's Arms, & thro' one another's legs with the greatest Nimbleness & Dexterity, to my infinite Astonishment who expected to see them cut their Legs, & Hands to Pieces every Minuet [*sic*], you cannot conceive any Thing so clever & active as these Fellows, nor imagine what difficult Things They perform'd.

Besides Servants without Number Prince Esterhasy has a Regiment of Guards who do duty at all the Doors of the House, & at the Top & Bottom of every Staircase. Hungary is quite an open country, every thing in this many Miles round this Place belongs to the Prince, who is without doubt the first Man in Hungary. All the People here speak Latin & yesterday at Dinner I held a Discourse with an Officer of Hussars in Contempt of Cicero, & Sallust [Gaius Sallustius Crispus, 86-34 B.C., Roman historian], of all Case, Number & Gender.

If I have been too particular in my Account of this Place, I offend from a Desire to please you, who have often bid me be very long & very particular. . .

If I can leave this Place, I shall set out for Vienna to morow. I am afraid I shall not be able to go to Munich; a Million Pardons if you have taken the Trouble to get a Letter for me. be persuaded My Dear Sr Charles of my Sincere Love & Affection for you, & that I am

Entirely yours
T. Steavens

* * * * * * *

Vienna, April ye 23.rd 1749

Mr Dear Sr Charles ---

. . .I have been seiz'd with a violent Rhumatism which render'd me incapable of writing to you till now. I consulted Van Swieten the ablest Physician here, I am at present much better . . .

I was this morning at the Review of the Regiment of Anderhasi [Andrássy], of Hungarian Infantry, I never in my Life saw a Regiment of finer Men, & I do assure you that their Exercise very near equall'd that of the Prussians. . .the Vienna China is beastly stuff but you may depend on having what you desire. . .

* * * * * * *

Venice, Novr ye 28.th N: S: 1749

My Dear Sr Charles,

. . .Monsr Tron has lately left this Place with the Character of Venetian Ambassadour at the Court of Vienna, He is a very silly Fellow, & what is worse, he has a great opinion of Count Podewils the Prussian Min.^{r} at Vienna, which you will think an Article of some Consequence, when I tell you that Monsr Diedo the late Venetian

Amb.ʳ at Vienna was the Instrument that Count Podewils made use of to get his Intelligence by, & He was not a bad one, because, as all Venetian Ambassadours send Duplicates to one another of the Letters They write to their Republick, They are generally better inform'd of what is going on in the different Courts of Europe that any other Ministers. . .

* * * * * * *

A Short glossary of Names in Vienna and Elsewhere.

Augsburg	Auersperg, probably Heinrich Joseph Fürst von Auersperg, Obriststallmeister (Master of Equerry).
Bartinstein	Johann Christoph Freiherr von Bartenstein, Staatssekretär (Secretary of State)
Batthiany	Carl, Count, General of the Cavalry, later Feldmarshall
Breitlach	Johann Franz Freiherr von, General, Imperial Ambassador in St Petersburg 1746-8
Bruhl	Heinrich Count Brühl, Saxonian Minister
Burmannia	Bartholo Count Burmania, Dutch Ambassador in Vienna
Canal	Ludovico (Lodovicio) Count Canale-Malabaila, Sardinian Minister in Vienna
Charles, Prince	Charles (Carl) Alexander (1712-1780) Brother of the Emperor. In 1744 he married the Archduchess Maria Anna, sister of Maria Theresa. Oberbefehlshaber der Österreichischer Truppen (Commander in Chief of Austrian Troops) 1756-63.

Choteck	Johann Carl Count von, Obrister Kriegskomissar (War Commissioner), later Imperial Ambassador
Cohl (Colro?)	Rudolph Colloredo, Vice Chancellor *(q.v.)*
Colloredo	Rudolph Joseph, Count von, Reichsvizekanzler (Vice Chancellor of the Reich). His brother (Anton), was a Balio (District Commander) of the Knights of Malta, later Imperial Ambassador to Turin.
Diedo	Antonio, Cavalliere, Venetian Ambassador in Vienna
Empress Dowager	Elisabeth Christine von Braunschweig (Brunswick), widow of Emperor Charles VI.
Firmian	Carl Joseph, Freiherr von (Baron), later (1753) Imperial Ambassador in Naples. The family had furnished Salzburg with an Archbishop, an uncle of Carl Joseph - Leopold Anton, Freiherr von Firmian, reigned 1737-1744 -- and the Mozart family found in Carl Joseph a warm patron and friend in when he was later, as Count, Governor General of Lombardy.
Grune	Grünne, Nicholas Franz Joseph, Count, General
Kevenhuller	Khevenhüller-Metsch, Johann Joseph Count von (since 30 December 1763 Reichsfürst), Obersthofmeister (Imperial Major Domo)
Kinsky	Prince at Venice, a celebrated Austro-Bohemian family with two lines, princely and count, many members of whom lived in Vienna.

Konigsegg	Königsegg, Joseph Lothar Dominik Count von, Konferenzminister (Minister of Conference) and Obersthofmeister (Major Domo) of the Dowager Empress.
Lichtenstein	Liechtenstein, probably Joseph Wenzel Prince von, who assumed responsibility for the family administration's Fideikomiss after the death of the young reigning Prince Johann Nepomuk Carl at the age of 23 in 1748.
Paar	Wenzel Count von, Reichshof - und General-Erblandpostmeister (Postmaster General)
Pallavicini	Johann Lucas Count von, General, stationed in Italy
Podewils	Otto Count von, Prussian Ambasador in Vienna
Richecourt	Heinrich Hyancinth Count von, Imperial Ambassador in Turin, later in London
Robinson	Thomas, British Ambassador in Vienna
Stanhope	Philip, first Earl of Chesterfield, British Secretary of State
Sternberg	Franz Philipp Count von, Kurböhmischer Gesandter am Reichstag (Bohemian Minister at the Regensburg Reichstag), later Imperial Ambassador in Dresden (Saxony)
Swieten	Gerhard van, Personal physician of the Empress. His son Gottfried was a diplomat and musician.

Trautzen	Trauttmannsdorf (?), if correct, probably Franz Norbert Count von, Cammerherr, married (second) to Countess Maria Anna von Herberstein.
Tron	Andreas von, Venetian Ambassador in Vienna
Ulfeldt	Confiz Anton Count von, Hof - und Staatskanzler (Court and State Chancellor)
Villettes	Monsieur de Villette, attached to Court of Sardinia (Turin)

RHETORIC AND EXPRESSION IN HAYDN'S *APPLAUSUS* CANTATA

WILLIAM A. KUMBIER

> For applause or the clapping of hands is the natural
> action of a man on the descent of the glory of God.
> -- Christopher Smart, *Jubilate Agno*, 1759

> I therefore have produced a variety in every line, both
> of cadences and number of syllables. Every word and every
> letter is studied and put into its fit place: the terrific numbers
> are reserved for the terrific parts - the mild and gentle, for the
> mild and gentle parts, and the prosaic, for inferior parts:
> all are necessary to each other.
> -- William Blake, 'To The Public', *Jerusalem*, 1804

I

The composition of the cantata *Applausus* (Hob. XXIVa:6) and the circumstances surrounding it comprise a unique, if somewhat isolated, chapter in Haydn's career.[1] Haydn composed the cantata in the early months of 1768 for the *Professjubiläum*, or commemoration of the fiftieth anniversary of the taking of vows, of Rayner Kollmann (1699-1776), who was Abbot of Zwettl Abbey in Lower Austria from 1747 to1776, but who also was much more than an abbot. Kollmann has been described as an 'echt barocke Hofprälat' who played a prominent role in Austrian politics and, among other things, enjoyed the special confidence of Maria Theresia.[2] Accordingly, the monks at Zwettl had decided to look beyond the musical talents of the abbey - which were not inconsiderable - to find a composer of some stature to set a celebratory text that one of their number had written. How Haydn received the commission is not known, but possibly it was

---

[1] For background information on the *Applausus* see H.C. Robbins Landon, *Haydn: Chronicle and Works,* (Bloomington: Indiana University Press, 1976-80), II, 145-148, 236-239; the Preface to the Haydn-Institut edition of the *Applausus*, ed. Irmgard Becker-Glauch and Heinrich Wiens, *Joseph Haydn Werke* [*JHW*], (Munich: Henle, 1969), XXVII/2, vii-x; and Leopold Nowak, *Joseph Haydn: Leben, Bedeutung, und Werk*, (Zurich: Amalthea, 1951), 206-207. All references to the score of Haydn's *Applausus* are to the *JHW* edition.

[2] Pater Stefan Holzhauser, 'Die Melodie eines Klosters: zur Musikgeschichte der Zisterzienserabtei Zwettl', *Singende Kirche*, IV (June-Sept. 1966), 208, and Nowak, 205.

through Johann Nepomuk Paul Werner, who, besides being the son of Gregor Werner, Haydn's predecessor as *Kapellmeister* at the Esterházy court, was a monk at Zwettl and, until February 1766, the *Regenschori* there.[3] Of the 600 gulden that the monks had set aside for the celebration, what H. C. Robbins Landon called the 'handsome fee' of 100 gulden was paid to Haydn for his work.[4] At the time of the cantata's composition, however, Haydn did not know exactly for whom or for what occasion the work was intended, since the transactions involving his commission were handled entirely through the abbey's dependence, the Zwettler Hof, in Vienna, and the details of what was to be the occasion for the cantata apparently were concealed from him.[5]

Haydn sent the completed cantata by messenger to Vienna in March 1768. The autograph of the cantata survives in the archives of the Gesellschaft der Musikfreunde, Vienna; it is signed with a chronogram by Haydn that gives the year of composition: HVNC APPLAVSV M FECIT IOSEPH HAI DN (1768 = MDCCLVVVIII). Landon suggests this device would have pleased the 'learned monks'.[6] A famous letter by Haydn, which Landon and others have presumed accompanied the cantata and which gives detailed directions for its performance, requests those performing the work, for the sake of the composer's reputation and their own, 'to be as diligent as possible'. Haydn writes that 'if I have not guessed the taste of these gentlemen, I am not to be blamed for it, for I know neither the persons nor the place, and the fact that they were concealed from me really made my work very difficult'.[7] Haydn nevertheless goes on in the letter to express his hope that the cantata will please the 'poet, the worthy musicians, and the honourable reverend *Auditorio*'. Landon reports that Haydn kept a copy of the

---

[3] 'Vorwort', *JHW* ed., vii.
[4] Landon, *Chronicle*, II, 145.
[5] See the letter of Haydn quoted below. As an old man, Haydn believed that the cantata had been written for Kremsmünster and added a note to that effect over the *incipit* of the work in his *Entwurf-Katalog*: 'in lateinischer Sprache bey Gelegenheit einer Prälats Wahl zu Crems Münster', i.e., for the election of a prelate at Kremsmünster (Landon, *Chronicle*, II, 145). C. F. Pohl showed that this could not have been the case, since no installation took place at Krems in 1768, and concluded instead that the cantata was composed for Göttweig Abbey (C.F. Pohl, *Joseph Haydn*; (Leipzig: Breitkopf und Härtel, 1882 [repr. 1970-71]), II, 40). Nowak was the first to point out that the *Applausus* was written not for an installation but for a *Jubiläum*, and demonstrated that the cantata was written for Zwettl (Nowak, 206).
[6] Landon, *Chronicle*, II, 145.
[7] H. C. Robbins Landon, ed., *The collected Correspondence and London Notebooks of Joseph Haydn*, (London: Barrie and Rockcliff, 1959), 11.

Applausus at Eisenstadt; later *contrafacta* were made, either by Haydn or with his 'blessing'.[8] The cantata was performed on 15 May 1768, four weeks, actually, after the Profess was celebrated, and not performed again as a cantata until 1958.[9]

In addition to the other obstacles he faced in composing the *Applausus*, Haydn was compelled to work with an often arcane and challenging, if not utterly intractable text in Latin, or more precisely, eighteenth-century Austrian Latin. The cantata's text may not be stylistically unique among surviving texts of the *Applausus-Festkantate* genre, but it has little in common with other texts Haydn set, and in many respects its Latin is unlike that of the mass.[10] Otto Vincenzi, who provided a German translation of the text for Landon's Doblinger edition of the cantata, drew attention to a number of stylistic features. He pointed out the prominence in the text of strophic structures with strong trochaic meter and end rhyme and the author's reliance on rhetorical devices such as parallelism and antithesis, which Vincenzi claimed linked the text's style to that of early and medieval hymns, the medieval poetry of the 'wandering scholars' and the Old Testament poetry of the Psalms. Vicenzi asserted that the text was doubtless the work of a 'very learned' writer.[11] Certainly the text's pervasive allusiveness and the wide range of its diction would support this claim.

Examination of Haydn's setting of this curious text reveals that he developed a musical rhetoric for the cantata that responds, in a variety of ways and on several levels, to the rhetoric of the text. This paper will attempt to show that Haydn's rhetoric is at once conventional and innovative, even iconoclastic: though Haydn's

---

[8] Landon, *Chronicle*, II, 148, 236. For a catalogue of the *contrafacta* made from the *Applausus* and an evaluation of their authenticity, see the *Kritischer Bericht* to the *JHW* ed., 16-27.

[9] Landon, *Chronicle*, II, 146, 236.

[10] To my knowledge, the text of the *Applausus* has yet to be compared with the reportedly numerous libretti for such occasional pieces that survive from Zwettl and other abbeys. Holzhauser, op. cit., refers to 'zahlreiche Textbucher von Gelegenshietskantaten' still at Zwettl. On contemporary Applausus librettos at the nearby monastery of Melk, see Robert Norman Freeman, *The Practice of Music at Melk Monastery in the Eighteenth Century*, Ph. D. diss; University of California at Los Angeles (1971), especially 42-43, 263-267, and 369-388. See also Freeman's more recent *The Practice of Music at Melk Abbey* (Vienna: Österreichische Akademie der Wissenschaften, 1989). The Applausus cantatas listed by Freeman include several with music by J. G. Albrechtsberger. Landon (*Chronicle*, I, 95) refers to a catalogue at Herzogenburg Abbey listing dozens of eighteenth-century Applausus cantatas. One of these was composed in 1746 by J. G. Zechner for the golden anniversary of the ordination as priest of the abbot of Göttweig Abbey, Gottfried Bessel.

[11] Otto Vicenzi, 'Zum Text', in Joseph Haydn, *Applausus*, H. C. Robbins Landon, ed. (Vienna: Doblinger, 1969), n. p.

setting, to a certain extent, relies on or exploits the mannerisms of word-painting and musical-rhetorical figuration that had been part and parcel of vocal music since the Renaissance, it also transmutes them into instruments often called on to play more than one part. In the *Applausus,* musical figurations or 'paintings' stimulated by the text may have local, conventional significance, but they also, it seems, often elicit the cantata's latent implications. These devices could be regarded as formulaic or merely decorative, as stock reflexive or expected gestures, but in the *Applausus* they are more accurately apprehended as the vehicles through which the cantata conveys its subjects and structure.

It is important to note that by the time Haydn was composing his early sacred works in the 1750s and early 1760s, the reading of music in terms of rhetoric (or, as some would say, the reading into music of rhetorical terms) had long been practised.[12] This tendency was rooted in the rediscovery of Quintilian's *Institutio Oratoria* in 1416 at the monastery of St Gall, but it flowered with Joachim Burmeister's *Musica Poetica* (1606), in which numerous musical strategies and turns were marked as exemplifying one or another rhetorical trope.[13] The enterprise of understanding music and rhetoric in terms of each other followed obviously enough from the premise that the ends of well-ordered speech and of well-made music were one, namely, to stir and direct the listener's passions. The relation urged between music and rhetoric that Burmeister had codified finally reached its culmination over a century later in the writings of Johann Mattheson. Mattheson's encyclopedic treatise, *Der vollkommene Capellmeister* (1739), enthusiastically, unhesitatingly promotes music as a *Klang-Rede* ('sound-speech' or 'sound-discourse') and contains extended demonstrations of how the elements of music, like those of a carefully planned oration, can be variously and ingeniously worked to move the listener as the composer desires.[14] Remarkable passages

---

[12] For background in the relationships of music and rhetoric, see George J. Buelow, 'Rhetoric and Music', *The New Grove Dictionary of Music and Musicians* (London: Macmillian, 1980), XV, 793-803; James Anderson Winn, *Unsuspected Eloquence: A History of the Relations between Poetry and Music* (New Haven: Yale University Press, 1981), chapters 4 and 5; John Neubauer, *The Emancipation of Music from Language: Departure from Mimesis in Eighteenth-Century Aesthetics* (New Haven: Yale University Press, 1986), 22-41; and Brian Vickers, 'Figures of rhetoric/Figures of music?' *Rhetorica* 1/2 (Spring 1984), 1-44.

[13] On Burmeister specifically, see Buelow, 'Rhetoric', and Claude Palisca, '*Ut Oratoria Musica*: The Rhetorical Basis of Musical Mannerism', in F. W. Robinson and S. G. Nichols, Jr., eds., *The Meaning of Mannerism* (Hanover, New Hampshire, 1972), 37-65.

[14] Johann Mattheson, *Der vollkommene Capellmeister* (Hamburg, 1739 [repr. Basel: Barenreiter, 1954]), especially part II, chapter 14. Mattheson's treatise is available in English translation under the title *Johann Mattheson's Der vollkommene Capellmeister: A*

of Mattheson's work, such as that on musical 'punctuation', show the thoroughness and specificity with which Mattheson conceived point-by-point correspondences between musical structures and verbal structures such as the clause and the sentance.

Questions have been raised recently concerning this confluence of music and rhetoric. Though critics such as George Buelow have argued that the 'union of music with rhetorical principles is one of the most distinctive characteristics of Baroque musical rationalism' and have written at length to support that claim, others, such as Brian Vickers, have doubted that 'composers deliberately imitated specific figures of rhetoric' and have concluded that reading music in rhetorical terms was an 'enterprise. . .of more use to critics that creators'.[15] Undeniably, Vickers has presented evidence showing that verbal rhetorical figures have a semantic specificity that is lost in attempts to give them musical application: the definitive, subtle movements of verbal rhetorical figures can only be traced in music, melodic and harmonic turns imitating, at best, merely the form of the verbal trope. Vickers, though, does not confront convincing recent evidence that composers like J. S. Bach had in mind, followed, and exploited rhetorical principles while composing; evidence, for example, presented by Ursula Kirkendale in her study of Bach's *Musical Offering* and what she calls its 'origin' in Quintilian's rhetoric.[16]

Nor, more important, does Vickers treat at any length the 'hypotypotic' rhetorical figures, those 'pictorial' figures designed to create musical vividness and imbue the text with a lifelike quality. Paraphrasing Burmeister, Claude Palisca describes *hypotyposis* as 'that ornament by which the significance of a text is so delineated that the music near the text is seen to acquire life'.[17] Ungar, translating the same text in his seminal study of music and rhetoric, refers to *hypotyposis* as a *Belebung* or *Verdeutlichung* of the text.[18] Arguably, the hypotypotic figures may be more closely related to the visual arts than to speech, but vividness certainly was valued in classical rhetoric - as Vickers points out - and the hypotypotic figures abundant in

---

revised Translation and Critical Commentary. Ernest C. Harriss, ed. and trans., (Ann Arbor: UMI Research Press, 1981).
[15] Buelow, 'Rhetoric', 793; Vickers, 'Figures', 41.
[16] Ursula Kirkendale, 'The Source for Bach's *Musical Offering*: The *Institutio oratoria* of Quintilian', *JAMS* 33 (1980), 88-141.
[17] Palisca, 47.
[18] Hans Heinrich Unger, *Die Beziehungen zwischen Musik und Rhetorik im 16.-18. Jahrhundert* (Würzburg, 1941 [repr. Hildesheim: Georg Olms 1969]), 81.

Baroque music - *anabasis, catabasis, saltus,* and *circulatio*, for example - were in the air when Haydn composed his early work (Ex.1 see pp.248-49). As I hope to show, they play an important part in determining the character of the text-setting in the *Applausus*. A judgment of the force of rhetoric in Baroque music simply must take this body of figures into account and, indeed, give it prominence.

Finally, Vicker's persuasive argument that 'musical' rhetorical figures cannot help but lack the semantic resources and suppleness their verbal counterparts have to crystallize meaning at any given point in the text should not prevent the reader or listener from perceiving the power of musical figures, especially those bound to a text in the first place, to aim beyond any local significance and instead compel significance over the course of a musical work, contextually. I hope to show that this, too, happens in the *Applausus*, even though the work does not, I shall argue later, display 'organic' unity.

Critical discussion of Haydn and musical rhetoric so far has been limited. An analysis by Gernot Gruber of the text-setting and use of figures in Haydn's early sacred works suggests that Haydn probably encountered traditions of musical rhetoric in the sacred vocal music, especially the masses, performed in Vienna in the first half of the eighteenth century.[19] Gruber presents many examples of figurations in the text-setting of Haydn's early masses - e.g. the *Cäcilienmesse* (Hob. XXII:5) and the 'Great Organ Solo Mass' in E flat (Hob. XXII:4) - and the Stabat Mater. He attributes the figurative saturation these works display to the conservatism of sacred music in general and of sacred music composed by Fux, Caldara, and especially the younger Georg Reutter (1708-1772), music director at St Stephen's Cathedral in Vienna where, of course, Haydn sang and studied as a choir boy. Gruber argues that it would have been hard for Haydn to miss the complex of musical figures that apparently had become clichés for setting certain mass texts, notably the Credo.[20] Gruber notes, for instance, the repeated use of an *anabasis*, or rising, melodic figure to set 'Et resurrexit', and of chromatically descending melodic figures to set the pathetic portions of the 'crucifixus' and the 'passus et sepultus' passages.

The question of Haydn's exposure to the rhetorical tradition generally and to the conventions of musical rhetoric in particular has

---

[19] Gernot Gruber, 'Musikalische Rhetorik und barocke Bildlichkeit in Kompositionen des jungen Haydn', in Vera Schwarz, ed., *Der junge Haydn* (Graz: Akademische Druck - und Verlagsanstalt, 1972), 168-191.

[20] See, for example, the Credo of Reutter's *Missa S. Caroli, DTÖ* 88.

been explored further in a more recent analysis by A. Peter Brown of the structuring principles in the 'Representation of Chaos' in Haydn's *The Creation*.[21] Brown proposes that the 'appropriate generic title' for Haydn's 'Chaos' is *ricercar*, a label that has been applied to compositions whose style and structure can be richly read as musical exemplifications of the rhetorical *exordium*. Brown's analysis, in addition to offering a concise overview of Haydn's ties to the musical/rhetorical tradition, presents a detailed reading of the numerous rhetorical figures in 'Chaos' which indicates the considerable degree to which the *Figurenlehre* continued to influence Haydn's compositions well into the 1790s. Together, the studies by Brown and by Gruber strongly suggest that though questions remain regarding the nature and extent of the role played by musical rhetoric in a given composition and regarding the presence or significance of a given figure in a particular context, the force of the *Figurenlehre* in any composition by Haydn - vocal or instrumental - has to be taken into account, even if the risks of eisegesis and over-interpretation are always at hand.

II

The text of the *Applausus* is allegorical, consisting entirely of exchanges between four personified Virtues - Temperance (soprano), Prudence (alto), Justice (tenor) and Fortitude (bass) - and Theology (bass). The virtues are those which, according to numerous pronouncements in the text, the monastic life cultivated and which the cantata implicitly celebrates as being exemplified in the life and service of Rayner Kollmann. The Virtues and Theology justify their presence at the festivities, during the course of the cantata's eight sections, which are as follows.

I. Orchestral Introduction, Recitative and Quartet, 'Virtus inter ardua' (Temperance, Prudence, Justice, Fortitude)

II. Recitative and Aria, 'Non chymaeras somniatis' (Theology)

---

[21] A. Peter Brown, 'Haydn's Chaos: Genesis and Genre', *The Musical Quarterly* 73 (1989):18-59

IV.	Recitative and Aria, 'O pii Patres Patriae!' (Justice)
V.	Recitative and Aria 'Si obtrudat ultimam' (Fortitude)
VI.	Recitative and Aria, 'Rerum, quas perpendimus' (Temperance)
VII.	Recitative and Aria, 'O beatus incolatus' (Justice)
VIII.	Recitative and Chorus, 'O Caelites, vos invocamus'

With the exception of the recitative that opens No. II, which is sung by Theology alone, the recitatives consist of dialogue among three or more of the Virtues, each recitative preparing the listener for the topic of each section's main number.

The text is thematically unified by its preoccupation with metamorphosis and celebration, or, rather, with the celebration of metamorphosis. As Haydn observed in his letter of instructions for performing the cantata 'der gantze Text aplaudirend' (the whole text applauds), from its opening words, 'Quae metamorphosis?' on. Haydn must have sensed the importance of the word 'metamorphosis' in the text; apparently, he consulted Eisenstadt's Latin scholars about its pronunciation, and comments in his letter on how the word should be accented. He set the word prominently, after an abrupt halt in the rhythmic drive of the orchestral introduction. The metamorphosis celebrated by the *Applausus* is twofold. First, there is the metamorphosis presented as the fruit of the *usus*, or *consuetudo,* the habitual exercise or practice fostered by monastic discipline, which transforms all things. In the recitative of the second section, Theology states:

> Metamorphosis ista de sursum, est,
> dos rari pretii, a Patre luminum.
> Quae enim natura respersit amaritudine,
> haec consuetudo per gratiam replet dulcedine.
> Hac via mundi deliciae in nauseam transeunt,
> et ardua usu continuo mutantur in solatia.

> This metamorphosis is from on high,
> a gift of rare value from the Father of light.
> For that which is besprinkled with bitterness,
> this habitual practice replensishes by grace with sweetness.

In this life the pleasures of the world are changed to disgust, and difficult, unremitting practice into solace.[22]

    Later in the recitative to the sixth section, Theology remarks that by this 'discipline, both the most salutary conclusions were brought forth, and the wisest thoughts were born'. The metamorphosis of which the text speaks, therefore, has more than practical, mundane consequences. It is connected to an ultimate metamorphosis, whereby truth stands apart from deception, and clear vision and thinking from confused perception. The cantata opens with the Virtues' expressions of disbelief at the rejoicing and the gratification of their desires that have suddenly appeared in their 'halls' (*atria*), and Fortitude says that 'either we are deceived by a phantom of truth, or we dream of chimeras'. Theology responds, informing the Virtues that 'you do not dream of chimeras, but you think clearly: no deception hides here, but true things come to light' (*non chymaeras somniatis, sed perfecta cogitatis: nulla fraus hic later, sed res vera patet*). Thus, the cantata's occasion is not only the transformation of (a) human life, exemplified in the profession of Rayner Kollmann, but also what that transformation reveals of Truth and, one might say, the Heavenly Kingdom. For the 'Palatium' of the text, which the Virtues call their home and which is equated with the *atria*, is at once the abbey, the location of the *convictus* or feast of fellowship through which, Theology says, burdensome things become sweet; the abbot; and, generally, the space where divinity is perceived to be acting. One gradually senses an apocalyptic aura in the text, which comes forth very strongly in the fifth section when Fortitude, singing of the calamity forced by the 'final destiny' proclaims: 'Let all things be turned upside down' (*cuncta licet invertantur*). This dimension of metamorphosis perhaps corresponds to the transformation of which Christian scripture speaks, when Paul writes that 'we shall not all sleep, but we shall all be changed, in a moment, in the twinkling of an eye, at the last trump: for the trumpet shall sound, and the dead shall be raised incorruptible, and we shall all be changed (*allagēsometha*)' (I Corinthians 15: 51-52).

---

[22] Translations for the *Applausus* text provided here are based on translations found in Kathryn M. Talalay, *A Literal Translation of Joseph Haydn's Cantata Applausus* (Bloomington: Indiana University Music Library, 1977).

III

Haydn's setting of the *Applausus* responds to the text's central topics and preoccupations. I should like to show this by looking at the cantata's opening quartet, 'Virtus inter ardua', in some detail, and then, somewhat more briefly, at the subsequent numbers.

A. 'Virtus inter ardua' (No. Ib)
The quartet, an Andante (2/4) in G, sets the following text.

Virtus inter ardua
quaerit habitare.
Ignorat delicias,   } a
contemnit cupedias,
amaritudinis fel,
fragans virtutis est mel.
Inter haec assidua   } b
cupit latitare.

Virtue seeks to dwell
on steep heights.
[She] ignores pleasures   } a
contemns allurements.
The fragrance of virtue is sweet,
of acrimony, bitter.
Amidst these places constantly } b
she desires to hide.

Although the text is structured as an eight-line unit, Haydn seperates the lines I have labeled 'b' from the rest and sets then as the middle section of the quartet, in standard *da capo* area A-B-A form, with punctuation supplied by a ritornello, as follows.

Orchestral introduction/ritornello	(bb.1-23)	
First setting of text (a)	(bb.24-61)	A
Ritornello	(bb.62-71)	
Second setting of text (a)	(bb.72-133)	
Ritornello	(bb.134-147)	
Setting of text (b)	(bb.148-173)	B
Ritornello	(bb.174-182)	
Da capo, repetition of bb.25-147		A

As the soloists enter at b.24, Haydn focuses his setting on the aspects of the *ardua* in which virtue seeks to dwell (Ex.2, see pp.250-51). *Ardua* denotes 'steep heights' and, more abstractly, that which is difficult to negotiate, hence 'arduous'. As the dwelling-place of virtue it can also be identified with the abbey and with the halls of heaven. (The recitative preceding the quartet affirmed that the 'Creator of the Universe has put our halls (*artria*) in a steep place (*in arduo*)'.) Indeed, the *contrafactum* that exists for the quartet substitutes the line 'Christ intends to keep open the halls of heaven' (*Christus coeli atria tendit reserare*) for the first line of the text at hand. For this line Haydn uses hypotypotic figures, which, as suggested in the first section of this paper and as Warren Kirkendale has pointed out, are more closely related to the visual arts than to speech.[23] The vocal line in the eight bars in which the text is introduced (bb.24-31) describes a rough-sloped peak, which Temperance (soprano) and Justice (tenor) ascend together in tenths. The ascent is marked by an *anabasis* figure of three bars, rising in the soprano part an octave from g' to the g" of the sextuplet in b.26. The descent consists of an extended *catabasis* figure of five bars, the course of which actually runs only from d" to g', but which perhaps seems greater with the interruption of a brief rise back up to d" (b.29) followed by a quaver rest and notes tied over the bar at bb.29-30 before the descent is completed. At b.31, the strings continue the figure, *forte*, down another octave.

The ascent and descent here are distinguished from each other not only by melodic contour but also by rhythmic contrast. Dotted crotchets (bb.24-25) and the crotchet tied to the sextuplet of b.26, resting prominently on the tonic and the fifth, as well as on the downbeat and the accented syllables of the text, are offset by the irregularities in surface rhythm of bb.27-31, with their tumbling semiquavers and triplets, halted by the notes tied over the bar for 'quae' at bb.27-28 and bb.29-30. Haydn employs the strong caesura of the text (after 'ardua') to form two halves, virtually equal in weight, of a period firmly grounded at each end in the tonic. Harmonic change during these bars is almost imperceptible; the tonic seems to persist throughout, emphasized by the pulsation in the viola and bass, and this relatively uniform harmonic rhythm allows the melodic and rhythmic inflections of the vocal line to impress themselves clearly and memorably. In this case, Haydn has no need to repeat the text immediately or to extract and re-set, turn and re-turn, its individual

---

[23] Warren Kirkendale, '*Circulatio*-Tradition, *Maria Lactans*, and Josquin as Musical Orator', *Acta Musicologica* 56 (1984), 71.

words. The association of 'virtus', 'ardua' and 'habitare' is made concisely in these eight bars, and the image of the heights as the space where the heavenly and the human intersect through virtue is conveyed.

Following bb.24-31, four bars are devoted to setting the couplet 'Ignorat delicias,/contemnit cupedias', which displays the parallelism that Vicenzi noted. Haydn differentiates the two lines by setting the first for Prudence (alto) and the second for Fortitude (bass), and by setting the bass's responses with a sort of inversion (bb.32-26). At the same time, he highlights the symmetrical structure of the couplet by repeating the lines once and in the repetition giving each line the setting the other was first given, in an exchange between the soloists. Haydn's setting thus moves here from evocative, or mimetic, figuration to a figuration that draws attention both to the stylistic features of the text and to the musical syntax. The setting bridges the close, two-part vocal texture of the preceding bars and the full, four-part texture that will follow, yet it stands apart from both. At bb.99-100, a similar setting of the same lines has the same function. It is only with the third presentation of the lines (bb.122-124) that the setting's mimetic potential predominates, when the lines are almost shouted out by the soloists in unison octaves, with diatonically stepping descents from d to g and octave drops from d to d, in concerted 'contemnation' (i.e., 'stamping upon') of 'delicias' and 'cupedias'.

As the bass completes his second reponse at b.36, Haydn turns to 'amaritudinis fel, fragrans virtutis est mel'. Although the setting for this text takes up many more bars than did that for the preceding lines - it has the formal function of establishing the quartet's secondary tonal area - the main elements of its structure can be seen in its first seven bars (bb.36-42). Here the basic movement is from the home tonality, D, through a minor tonality, B minor, to a sharp dissonance (A-C-F sharp-D sharp) for 'amaritudinis fel', and then leading back through E minor, A, and then D for 'fragrans virtutis est mel'. Though this progression is not repeated exactly in subsequent settings of this text, frequently in the quartet 'amaritudinis fel', the bitterness of acrimony, is set with a piercing harmony. At bb.103-106, for example, this movement through exotic harmony is extended, as the words are set three times in succession and the setting, begging with the declamation of 'amaritudinis' on b flat' in the alto and on d" in the soprano, moves through two minor harmonies at b.104 that are made dissonant by the addition of a penetrating e flat" in the soprano, before resolving at b.105 to G minor, only to digress then to another dissonance (E flat-B flat-G-C sharp) for one bar before resolving finally to D at b.107.

Haydn's use of comparatively stark dissonances to set 'bitterness' is certainly conventional and not surprising. Though *amaritudo* does not appear in the list of Latin words that the musical rhetorician Nucius in 1613 recommended receive special expressive treatment, its German equivalent, *scharf*, does appear in a comparable catalogue compiled by Daniel Speer in 1691.[24] Both 'amaritidunis fel' and 'mel' fall within the category of sensually charged words Renaissance and Baroque theorists considered apt for musical 'painting'. The setting for 'amaritudinis fel' is also used, again not surprisingly, for the *contrafactum* text, 'Christ invites the mournful to him' (*tristes invitat ad se*), with 'mournful' receiving the force of the dissonance. Somewhat more interesting in this *Applausus* setting is the way Haydn uses the harmonic excursion and return that he builds into the couplet's setting to represent at once the oppositions of the text (sweetness/bitterness, virtue/acrimony), the rhyme of 'fel' and 'mel' and the *transformation* of one opposite into the other through virtue *and*, literally, *through the word* 'virtutis': a concise expression of one of the metamorphoses the cantata applauds.

One could say that Haydn, in passages like this, makes the text perform itself, act out its meaning(s). Such passages - vividly, almost jarringly concrete yet highly allusive to the cantata's more abstract concerns - suggest Haydn's profound interest in combining words to create a textuality where figures not only evoke what they may obviously and conventionally signify, but also turn to comment on the progress and manner of the musical discourse itself. The figuration enacts what Roman Jakobson has called the 'poetic' function, drawing attention away from the context, or what is signified, and calling attention to the signifier, focusing 'on the message for its own sake'.[25] Jakobson suggests that this poetic function, 'by promoting the *palpability* of signs, deepens the fundamental dichotomy of signs and objects' (emphasis added). We shall see in other instances in the *Applausus* how this poetic, or what I have elsewhere called *metamimetic,* function tends to assert itself precisely where the

---

[24] Unger, 38. Unger provides the lists of both Nucius and Speer.
[25] Roman Jakobson, 'Linguistics and Poetics', in Thomas A. Sebeok, ed., *Style in Language* (Cambridge, Mass.: M. I. T. Press, 1960), 356. See also the discussion of Jakobson's essay in Robert Scholes, *Structuralism in Literature: An Introduction* (New Haven: Yale University Press, 1974), 22-27.

figuration would *seem* to lead toward the purely representational.[26] Haydn's use of hypotypotic figuration seems to activate the musical text beyond the 'things' to which it refers.

A brief ritornello at bb.62-71 leads to a second setting of the first five lines of the text, in what could be called the development of the quartet's 'A' section, though the label 'development' is perhaps not as appropriate as 'intensification' or 'complication' of the traits of the first setting. Haydn takes the discrete musical periods that had been bound to their correspondingly discrete textual units in the first setting and elaborates them, still keeping them separate from each other, in a decidely paratactic composition. Perhaps this structuring seems primitive, but it certainly serves the didactic function of impressing the text on the listener. This is not to say that some instances of setting in this portion of the quartet are not remarkable. There is, for example, the setting of the first line, with altered word order ('Virtus quaerit inter ardua habitare') in bb.80-98, which develops and supplements the figuration of ascent and descent of the text's original setting (Ex.3, see pp.252-53). Soprano, alto and tenor interlace for thirteen bars on the 'a (r)' shared by '*ar*dua' and 'habit*are*', in a texture marked by (1) the figure of *polyptoton*, the repetition of a melodic idea in a different part, in this case, the passing of a small *circulatio* figuration from soprano to tenor (bb.85-86, 87-88); (2) the alternation of notes sustained for several beats with semiquaver triplets in the alto; and (3) the parallel movement of soprano and alto in thirds for two bars (bb.90-91), an instance of musical *paronomasia*, or the repetition of an idea on the same notes but with additions or alterations for emphasis.[27] These few bars of ethereal polyphony are underscored by *saltus* (leaping) figures of octave drops in the bass (bb.85-91). The paronomastic trope of bb.90-91 works to heighten the passage but also syntactically to signal a turn in the musical texture, as the three upper parts begin to move more homophonically over a sustained G in the bass, until the period's climax is reached with the soprano's g" to f" at b.95.

The parenthetical 'B' section of the quartet sets the seventh and eighth lines of the text, 'Inter heac assidua/cupit latitare'. After the initial setting of the lines (bb.148-153), which echoes the melodic contour of the earlier setting for 'Virtus inter ardua', Haydn sets the lines completely twice more (bb.154-163 and bb.164-173), in both

---

[26] For a fuller discussion of metamimesis in Haydn's work, see William A. Kumbier, 'A 'New Quickening': Haydn's *The Creation*, Wordsworth, and the Pictorialist Imagination', *Studies in Romanticism* 30/4 (Winter 1991): 535-563.

[27] On *polyptoton* and *paranonmasia*, see Buelow, 'Rhetoric', 796, and Unger, 86-87.

settings inventing musical counterparts for 'amidst' and 'hiding' (Ex. 4, see p.254). At b.154, the tenor embarks on an 'assiduous', perservering chromatic ascent from c' to f', rendering the text once straight through, which is, however, embedded in or masked by an interrupted presentation of the text by the other soloists. This 'covering' presentation is marked by the simultaneous use of *suspiratio*, 'sighing' or 'breathing' figures produced by the insertion of pauses; *gradatio*, or step figures (each segment of the text being pitched higher than the preceding); and verbal *anadiplosis*, the repetition of the last word of a segment at the beginning of the next. Then, when the soloists begin to declaim the text homophonically at b.165, their accents frame figures of hemidemisemiquavers in the first violins and violas, which themselves frame, or 'hide', similar figures in the second violins. The entire section is marked *piano* and *pianissimo*, contributing to the hushed concealment of virtue that the passage effects until, at b.173, the parenthesis closes and 'virtus' again bursts out in the ritornello.

B. 'Dictamina mea' (No. IIIb)

The figuration associated with elevation in the opening quartet reappears in 'Dictamina mea', the duet between Temperance and Prudence in the cantata's third section. The text begins:

Temperance:	Dictamina mea doceri qui gestit,
Prudence:	et dogmata scire sollertiae cupit,
Both:	accedat hoc Palatium...

[The one] who desires to learn my speeches,
and wishes to know the dogmas of wisdom,
shall enter this Palatine...

Haydn sets the approach to the Palatium with increasingly elaborate *anabasis* and *catabasis* figures (bb.18-19; 23-27; 29-32; and 51-61). The last written-out elaboration of this setting prior to the cadenza that closes the 'A' section of this *da capo* duet (bb.51-61) ascends to a peak, *forte*, in the solo parts and then descends an octave and a fourth in the first violins by way of semiquaver *circulatio* figures, forming a broad arc, or what appears to be half the sine curve of a much broader *circulatio*. These *circulatio* figurations, in conjunction with the duet's dramatic ascents, may have the exalted, regal connotations of crown and halo that Warren Kirkendale has detected; this would be borne out by other features of the setting, most notably the *clarini* fanfares with timpani;[28] also to be considered is the text of the very popular *contrafactum* for this setting, which speaks of approaching 'ad solium', to the throne. Haydn uses similar figuration in other works displaying what Landon has called Haydn's 'C major pomp' (for example, in the first movement of Symphony No. 48), and it is linked within the *Applausus* to the rushing fanfares with which the cantata opens. In the 'B' section of the duet, the line 'haec studia tollunt ad gradus honoris' (these studies raise [him] to the step of honour) is set as a *gradatio* (bb.83-88). Taken together, the various figurations of the duet form a complex of tropes that raise the accession to the Palatium to the level of an apotheosis.

C. 'O pii Patres Patriae' and 'Rerum, quas perpendimus' (Nos. VI and VI)

The tenor aria 'O pii Patres Patriae!' from the cantata's fourth section and the soprano aria 'Rerum, quas perpendimus' from the sixth section extend the praise of the celebrated abbot that was implied in the quartet and the duet. The arias meditate, respectively, on themes of enduring fame and prosperity. In the tenor aria, Justice exclaims:

> O pii Patres Patriae!
> Vos manet fama gloriae,
> quae nunquam finietur.
>
> O pious Fathers of the Land!
> The fame of glory, which is not yet ended,
> stays with you.

Haydn sets this text with two rhetorical flourishes, one on 'fama' and one on 'quae nunquam finietur'. 'Fama' is given increasingly ornate figuration that displays both *gradatio* and *circulatio* (bb.31-33; 42-48; and 73-80). Incorporation of these figures suggests, as in the preceding duet, the abbot's ascent to the 'fame of glory' the *circulatio* figures implying both 'never-endingness', or 'eternity' and the crown and laurel wreath.[29] Also noteworthy is the leap from a to a' in the third setting, at b.74, an instance of *saltus* or perhaps even *hyperbole*, accompanied by an upward rush of semiquaver and demisemiquaver notes on the harpsichord. These figures may suggest that the abbot's pre-eminence and the 'height' of his fame; they are

---

[28] W. Kirkendale, '*Circulatio*', 80.
[29] Gruber (174) notes these figures but refers to them as 'eine lange Koloratur'.

associated with a heroic topos that can be found in other 'regal' works by Haydn (again, see Symphony No. 48), and in passages of the mass celebrating the omnipotence of the King of Heaven.[30] Haydn then supplies a setting for 'quae nunquam finietur' that, appropriately, does not end, or postpones its ending, in several ways (Ex. 5, see pp.255-56). At the first 'finietur' - Haydn presents the text three times - the vocal line is underscored by descending thirds on the harpischord that move toward resolution on the dominant, B major, and, in fact, pause there on the third beat of b.51. On the fourth beat of that bar, though, Haydn switches to the dominant of the dominant (F sharp major), leading the listener to expect a final resolution on the dominant on the subsequent downbeat, but then, instead, repeats the figure that has just transpired, and not once but twice (bb.52-53). Brief harmonic resolution is eclipsed by the impression that the 'logical' anticipated conclusion has been evaded. In fact, the effect approximates that of *ellipsis*, as the contemporary theorist Scheibe described it: 'an unexpected new direction taken by a passage that has led up to an expected conculsion'.[31] After this chain of false endings, the setting further delays its close by moving into an extended *circulatio*, which, in turn, weaves into a recapitulation of the harpischord solo with which the aria opened (the ritornello). This intricately worked keyboard writing, though generically, according to Landon, an 'Austrian speciality', has a specific contextual function here, spinning off the figuration previously tied to the text and carrying it forward with its particular significance, which is, as Gruber put it, the *Weitläufigkeit* of fame.[32]

Similar figurative strategies characterize the soprano aria 'Rerum, quas perpendimus', which sets the following text.

Rerum, quas perpendimus,
et temperate agimus,
eventus, eventus properatur;
incessus est securior,
casus proinde rarior
si lente festinatur.

---

[30] See the discussion of the 'Et resurrexit' section of the Credo of Haydn's 'Great Organ Solo Mass' in Gruber, 180-182.
[31] Buelow, 'Rhetoric', 797.
[32] Landon, *Chronicle,* I, 87; Gruber, 174.

> To things which we weigh,
> and execute with temperance,
> events, events are given a favourable outcome.
> The gait is more sure,
> the fall, accordingly, more rare,
> when it is hastened slowly.

Haydn plays on 'prosperatur' here very much as he did on 'fama' in the tenor aria, giving it increasingly elastic, elaborate figurations that run from two to twenty bars in length (Ex. 6, see p.257). The patterning and embellishments of the soloist's part echo those of the tenor aria, but one could argue a slightly different significance for them here. They seem in this context to enact the *eventuality* or temporality of which the text speaks, the prolonged anticipation of a favourable outcome. The highly varied duration and range of notes in the vocal line at the texts 'quas perpendimus' and 'prosperatur' plays against the metrically regular setting in three that Haydn uses repeatedly for 'et temperate agimus' and 'eventus' (bb.37-42) and the force of the persistent beat-marking in the bass. Melodically, the vocal line seems 'suspended' between regular, stepwise ascents and descents for 'temperate' and 'eventus, eventus', on the one hand, and frequent leaps of an octave or more on 'quas' (b.35, b.47) and unpredictable forays for 'prosperatur', on the other. In fact, the tension between relatively simple and relatively complex melodic patterning, and the tension between the irregular surface rhythm of the vocal line and the steady, pedestrian 3/8 metre, heighten the uncertainty of the aria's 'eventual outcome', persisting into the aria's middle section (which begins at b.196).

The verses 'incessus est securior' and 'casus proinde rarior' are set as traces of the initial setting for 'Rerum, quas perpendimus', much as one would expect to find with thematic restatements at the opening of a so-called development section. But Haydn interrupts the verses twice with obtrusive pairs of bars of quavers sounded uniformly in all the voices, marked emphatically with Haydn's characteristic staccato notation (♪). In a hypotypotic context, where the listener is well-accustomed to having mountains and valleys palpably set before the eye and ear, these unison interruptions may be perceived as the aural equivalent for a firm tread (*incessus*) upon a rough slope. Yet, as previously in the *Applausus*, such pictographic bars also function structurally: here they strengthen the force of the subdominant as the tonal centre of the middle section by effecting a transition from E flat major through F minor to A flat minor, and also by preparing the listener for the chromaticism with which the text 'si lente festinatur' will be set. For the remainder of the middle section, the vocal line's melodic range constricts and its rhythmic activity wanes, until, at the last setting of 'si lente festinatur' the melody ranges, essentially, only from c" to e flat". At bb.220-234, the soloist throbs through a chromatically descending *catabasis* of dotted crotchets, finally coming to a standstill, or musically 'making haste slowly'.

The aria can thus be seen as structured by carefully worked out oppositions, oppositions both among melodic and rhythmic elements within each of the two main sections and oppositions between the sections themselves. Moreover, the polarities established in the aria of speed and slowness, and, eventually motion and stillness, are perhaps exactly what one would expect for the setting of a text that ultimately derives from the Latin motto 'festina lente' (make haste slowly). Ursula Kirkendale has noted a similar juxtaposition in the *thema regium* and canons of Bach's *Musical Offering*, where, she argues, Bach finds musical equivalents for walking, running and standing still (or 'idleness').[33] She brings together the music's rhythmic movement, the Latin motto, and interestingly, a bit of Renaissance animal symbolism, reminding the reader that slowness was conventionally emblematized by a crab and speed by a butterfly (Figures 1 & 2). Such an association might be made even more appropriately in connection with this movement of the *Applausus*, when it is a case of the motto's literally reposing in the line 'si lente festinatur'. It is possible that for the idea of hastening slowly Haydn invented musical emblems for animal motion, as he later was to do so unabashedly in *The Creation* and in *The Seasons*. If he did, the device probably would have impressed some of the erudite monks who performed or heard the cantata; and, in so far as any listener was aware of the more ancient association of the crab and the butterfly with mortality and immortality, with the 'dead' and the 'quick', the device also would have alluded once more to the metamorphosis that dominates the *Applausus*.[34] The flittings of the soprano line in the aria's 'A' section could well contrast with the torpidity of the solo line in the 'B' section to have this force. Again, this particular musical conceit also would exemplify the cantata's habit of enacting or drawing attention to the frame of latent musical structures or structurations by the most manifest figuration.

---

[33] U. Kirkendale, 111.

[34] W. Deonna; 'The Crab and the Butterfly: A Study in Animal Symbolism', *Journal of the Warburg and Courtauld Institutes* 17 c.1954), 47-86.

Figure 1. Emblem with crab and butterfly, displaying the motto 'festina lente'. (G. symeoni, *Le sententiose imprese*, Lyons, Rouille, 1561. Cited in W. Deonna, 'The Crab and the Butterfly: A Study in Animal Symbolism', *Journal of the Warburg and Courtauld Institutes*, 17 (1954), where this emblem is reproduced along with several other similar ones.)

Figure 2. Engraving with crab and Butterfly. Jacob Hoefnagl (1575-1630), *Archetypa Studique Patris Georgii Horfnaglii* ('Ampliat aetatis spatium tutissima . . .'), The Minneapolis Institute of Arts.

D. Bass Arias: 'Non chymaeras somniatis' and 'Si obtrudat ultimam' (Nos. IIb and Vb)

The distinct figurations of the *Applausus* in the numbers discussed so far can be understood as related to each other, generally, in a figural complex that has to do with the heroic, the celebratory, and, ultimately, with apotheosis. In this setting of the cantata's two arias for bass, Haydn draws on a different figural complex. The central oppositions of Theology's aria 'Non chymaeras somniatis' (see the text cited above), the opposition of false, chimerical dreaming to clear thinking, of concealment to revelation, stimulate, first, an opposition of tonal stability and instability in the setting. A twelve-bar segment (Ex. 7, see p.258; bb.34-35) sets the first two lines of the text. Here the emphatic declaration of a B flat major chord in octaves in the first two bars is immediately weakened by the wavering between the pitches f and e in the following two bars, and then by the restatement of essentially the same melodic idea, starting in F minor. Melodic contrast within each of the first two four-bar units also comes into play: the leaps (*saltii*) of the first two bars, ranging over an octave and a third, retract into the oscillation between tones with which each statement evaporates. Haydn's insertion of a crotchet rest in all the voices immediately before the theme resumes, *forte*, makes the two statements discontinuous with each other, an *abruptio*, or interruption of the movement by an unexpected silence.[35] Haydn was to repeat and develop this effect in other instances, for example, in the 'false' starts of the first movement of Symphony No.39 or of the quartet, op.33 no.3. It is only in the last four bars of the segment (bb.42-45), with their agitated surface rhythm and their more regular progression toward harmonic resolution, that tonality and direction are finally determined, when Haydn sets the text for 'perfect' thinking. As they are heard, the opening eight bars create a musical equivalent for the blurred, double vision, for St Paul's seeing things as enigmatic reflections rather than directly, face to face.[36]

On a smaller dimension in the same aria, the text 'non chymaeras somniatis' (Ex. 7; see p.258) is set much as 'amaritudinis fel' was set in the quartet, with a brief excursion to a diminished seventh chord for the monstrous chimera, and in this case there is even more harmonic tension, given the persistence of the C pedal beneath (bb.65-69). This treatment reappears many times throughout the aria, each time *forte*, and Haydn counters it with settings of 'sed

---

[35] On *abruptio*, see Unger, 70.
[36] I Corinthians 13:12. Or perhaps the figuration is merely the chimera's roar and flailing tail.

perfecta cogitatis' that are built on 'perfect' intervals, diatonic progressions and scales (for example, at bb.69-70 and bb.147-149).

Another striking contrast in the aria is sustained by Haydn's manipulation of the vocal line for the text 'sed res vera patet', bringing it into relief against the generally agitated texture of the accompaniment, letting it fall back into that texture and then resurrecting it. Here, after the plain, long notes on c (Ex. 7; see p.258, bb.51-54) the solo picks up the surface rhythm that the second violins and the bass had initiated,

(♪) ♫ ♬

similarly, in the aria for Fortitude ('Si obtrudat', No. Vb; Ex.10, see pp.259-62) where the text speaks of the fortitude of great minds (*magnae mentis*) in the face of calamity, the surface rhythm of the vocal line accelerates and the descending melodic intervals become smaller as the solo plunges into the word 'calamitatem'. The reverse (or inverse) of this tendency occurs several bars later, as the surface rhythm in the solo parts moves, on 'cuncta licet invertantur' (let all things be inverted) from movement parallel to that of the quavers of the accompaniment, to minims, and then to a trilled semi-breve before rising to a minim on the tonic to end the sequence. The drama of this resolution increases with the reintroduction of tremolo semiquavers in the first violins precisely at the point (b.34) when the notes sung by the soloist double in length to minims, and by the drop of a thirteenth from f' to A in the vocal line. Though, as Gruber noted, there is a prevalence of *saltus* figures in this line, to signify greatness, one could say that here the figure bounds beyond *saltus* into *hyperbole* in a leap that exceeds the boundaries of the scale.[37]

The bass arias are interesting not only for their settings in and of themselves but also because of the figurative *topoi* they bring together. Warren Kirkendale, in his analysis of the rhetorical traditions behind the text-setting of Beethoven's *Missa Solemnis*, comments on the frequent juxtaposition in eighteenth-century masses of long notes and tremolo figures in setting of 'judicare'.[38] Kirkendale argues that the repeated long notes evoke the King of Heaven as judge who cannot be swayed, who remains immovable, while the

---

[37] Gruber, 190n38. On *hyperbole*, see Buelow, 'Rhetoric', 798. Buelow cites Burmeister's definition of *hyperbole* as a melodic passage exceeding the normal ambitus of a mode, either above or below.

[38] Warren Kirkdendale, 'New Road to Old Ideas in Beethoven's *Missa Solemnis*', *MQ* 56 (1970), 669 and 671.

tremolo figures evoke the trembling of those awaiting judgment, by way of the *Dies irae* text, 'Quantas tremor est futurus, judex est venturus'. It is therefore not surprising that a precedent for the *Applausus'* bass arias exists in the bass solos of Haydn's Stabat Mater, particularly in No. XI, on the text 'Flammis orci ne succendar, per te, virgo, fac defendar, in die judicii'. The brief Stabat Mater aria anticipates the setting of the 'Si obtrudat' in its melodic contour (note the drop of a fourth followed by sucessively smaller intervals), in the play of the vocal line with the accompaniment's surface rhythm, and in the use of *hyperbole* (Ex. 8, see p.258).[39] These stylistic elements seem to appear together when Haydn writes of great or ultimate, 'last' things, whether that eschatology is explicit, as in the text of the Stabat Mater, or only suggested by textual implications, as in the *Applausus*. Another related instance of the confluence of these traits is in the bass solo that survives from Haydn's *Motetto de Beata*, 'Magna coeli Domina' (Hob.XXIIIa:c7), which parallels the other bass arias in rhythm and melodic contour, though it is in C major rather than a minor key and though its subject is divine omnipotence rather than the effect of God's power in the Last Judgment (Ex. 9, see p.258). At any rate, the bass arias all seem to respond to an apocalyptic strain in the texts they set and, in the case of the *Applausus*, the figural complex of the bass arias complements the figures of apotheosis that characterize the soprano and tenor arias, the duet, and the quartet.

E. 'O beatus incolatus!' (No. VIIb)

Generally Haydn keeps separate the two figural complexes that have been identified so far, but as the cantata begins to draw to a close, he begins to draw them together. In the cantata's penultimate number and last aria, 'O beatus incolatus!' they are juxtaposed quite clearly. The text of the this aria, sung by the tenor, is as follows.

> O beatus incolatus!
> Meritis qui laureatus } a
> superum de gratia;
> juste nobis vendicatur,
> et laetanter celebrantur } b
> Jubilaei gloria.

---

[39] Joseph Haydn, Stabat Mater, H. C. Robbins Landon, ed., piano reduction by Roderick Bliss (London: Faber Music, 1977), 56-60. Stylistic similarities between the arias for bass in the *Applausus* and those in the Stabat Mater have been noted previously by Landon, *Chronicle*, II, 237.

> O blessed residence!
> which, through noble strivings,
> is crowned with laurels   } a
> of grace from above;
> rightly it is due to us
> to celebrate with great joyousness } b
> the glory of this Jubilee.

The 'residence' (*incolatus*) of which the text speaks may be understood to refer, first, to Rayner Kollmann's residence at Zwettl and his 'residence' in the priesthood, the career that is the occasion for the awarding of laurels of grace and for the Jubilee. As Prudence says in the recitative introducing the aria, the 'celebration of this Jubilee is as dignified as is the glory of many years [i.e., old age]'. Haydn illustrates the decorum (*ornatu*) of the celebration by introducing the first section of the setting (labelled 'a' above) with a highly ornamented violin solo that unwinds into an extended full *circulatio* figure (bb.3-16). Shortly after the tenor solo begins, the motivation for this figure in the words 'beatus' and 'laureatus' becomes clear. Haydn here embroiders a cliché for the setting of the halo of beatitude and the laurel wreath.[40] The text 'superum de gratia', as one might expect, is set with variations on a graceful *catabasis* figure, first heard in bb.20-21. Three of these variations also display figuration for 'gratia' using both *circulatio* and *gradatio* (one of which (bb.39-44) *may* even echo the steep figuration for 'ardua' of the ritornello of the opening quartet). Haydn weaves the violin solo into the tenor's first presentation of the text (at bb.30-36), sustaining the significance and mood of the opening figuration, and unites the two voices, beautifully but pointedly, at bb.46-47 (Ex. 11, see p.263).

Such figuration may strike one as effective, but because of the commonplace nature of the figures in Baroque music generally and their many previous appearances in the *Applausus*, not at all unexpected. The middle section of 'O beatus incolatus!', however, takes a more surprising turn (Ex. 12, see p.263). This section's opening bars, Allegro di molto in D minor, compress and echo the opening of 'Si obtrudat', though the passage is marked *piano*, perhaps to enhance its echo-like quality. Immediately after this statement, other elements of the apocalyptic figural complex appear: agitated string accompaniment in quavers and semiquavers, leaps in the vocal line (bb.75-77), and repeated long notes on 'Jubilaei' (bb.70-72). But Haydn then combines this figuration with figures traditionally

---

[40] W. Kirkendale, '*Circulatio*', 80.

associated with majesty: corona-like *circulatio* figures (bb.72-75) and upward-rushing scales (bb.68-71). Gruber has cited another confluence of these figures, a passage from the Credo ('Et resurrexit') segment of Haydn's 'Great Organ Solo Mass'. That mass setting, too, displays both agitated string accompaniment and repeated long notes, but on 'judicare' rather than 'jubilaei'.[41] Like Fortitude's aria and the bass aria from the Stabat Mater, this section of the tenor aria appears to borrow its figuration from the Judex Christus or Christ Pantocrator *topos* of eighteenth-century mass settings exemplified in the 'Great Organ Solo Mass', so much so that one can almost hear the 'judicare' of the mass beneath the 'jubilaei' of the *Applausus* text.

The juxtaposition of such apocalyptic figuration with the beatific figuration of the aria's primary section suggests that the *incolatus* not only is to be awarded and applauded but also is to be exalted and, ultimately, judged and vindicated before the enthroned divinity. 'Incolatus' in both Medieval and Classical Latin denoted a *temporary* residence or sojourn, the status, in antiquity, of being a resident alien, perhaps a type of residence analogous to the monastic ideal of being in but not of the world.[42] At any rate, the figuration of the aria's middle section lends the 'justification' for the celebration this cosmic dimension, and at the *da capo*, with the return of the first section, the *incolatus* may be seen in a transfigured light, as the place where divine and human meet. Hence Prudence's subsequent prayer in the eighth recitative that the *incolatus* be prolonged.

IV

The proximity in 'O beatus incolatus!' of the *Applausus*' two main figural complexes suggests, I think, a more general context for understanding what is at stake in the aria and in the whole cantata. Seen and heard so closely together, Haydn's figures of apotheosis and apocalypse recall, respectively, the two aesthetic categories so often opposed to each other in the eighteenth century: the 'beautiful' and the 'sublime'. These two labels, it is true, were used by Haydn's contemporaries more often in relation to the visual and the verbal arts than to music, but they had their place in music criticism as well.[43]

---

[41] Gruber, 180-182.

[42] Art 'incolatus', *Medie Latinatis Lexicon Minus*, J. F. Niermeyer, compiler, (Leiden: E. J. Brill, 1976), 522.

[43] For a recent, far-reaching discussion of the sublime and the beautiful in music, see Claudia L. Johnson, "Giant HANDEL' and the Musical Sublime' *Eighteenth-Century*

A. The Beautiful and the Sublime

During the course of the eighteenth-century, the 'beautiful' in music came to be associated with smooth melodic contours, regular harmonic rhythm and, generally, unimposing sound patterns that could be apprehended easily or effortlessly. In his *Philosophical Enquiry into the Origin of Our Ideas of the Sublime and Beautiful* (1757), Edmund Burke refers to the 'softness, the winding surface, the unbroken continuance, the easy gradation of the beautiful' and remarks that the 'beautiful in music will not bear that loudness and strength of sounds, which may be used to raise other passions; nor notes, which are shrill, or harsh, or deep; it agrees best with such as are clear, even, smooth, and weak'[44]. Drawing on Burke but more directly on the 'Analytic of the Beautiful' in Kant's *Critique of Judgment*, Christian Friedrich Michaelis (1770-1834), in one of a number of articles on the beautiful and the sublime published in the *Berlinische musikalische Zeitung* just a few years before Haydn's death, wrote that the 'beautiful relates to *form, outline, limitation,* the easily apprehended melody, the gentle harmonic and rhythmic play of emotions in time', and further that if the 'emotions are easily integrated in audible expression and fuse into a whole; if the sounds relate fluently to one another, constituting by their rhythmic symmetry a melody that the imagination can grasp without difficulty, then true *beauty* manifests itself in music'.[45] One might observe that critical understanding of the beautiful in music was, to a great extent, spatially determined: given the terms Burke and Michaelis use to speak of it, it does not seem too great a step from the 'serpentine line' that many years earlier William Hogarth promoted as the basis of the beautiful in the visual arts to the extended *circulatios* of the *Applausus* arias, or to the curves and cascades of the vocal lines in 'Virtus inter ardua' and 'Dictamina mea'.[46]

By contrast, sublimity in music was marked by 'boldness of design, masses of harmony, extremes of contrast' and 'profuse invention'.[47] Burke associated with aural sublimity 'sudden and

---

Studies 19 (1986), 515-533. Much of the discussion of these two aesthetic categories here relies on sources cited in Johnson's study.

[44] Edmund Burke, *A Philosophical Enquiry into the Origin of Our Ideas of the Sublime and Beautiful*, J. T. Boulton, ed., (Notre Dame: University of Notre Dame Press, 1968), 172.

[45] Christian Friedrich Michaelis, cited in Peter le Huray and James Day, eds., *Music and Aesthetics in the Eighteenth and Early Nineteenth Centuries* (Cambridge: Cambridge University Press, 1981), 289-290.

[46] William Hogarth, *The Analysis of Beauty* (London, 1753 [repr. Hildesheim: Georg Olms, 1974]).

[47] Johnson, 533.

unexpected' and 'excessively loud' sounds, and he implied that 'great variety, and quick transitions from one measure or tone to another' may be conducive to sublimity since they are 'contrary to the genius of the beautiful in music'[48]. Michaelis provided a more extensive and resonant description of musical sublimity, which I will quote here at some length.

> ...when the sounds impinge on the ear at great length, or with complete uniformity, or with frequent interruptions, or with shattering intensity, or where the part-writing is very complex, so that the listener's imagination is severly taxed in an effort to grasp the whole, so that it feels in fact as if it is posed over a bottomless chasm, then the sublime manifests itself. The feeling of sublimity in music is aroused when the imagination is elevated to the plane of the limitless, the immeasurable, the unconquerable. This happens when such emotions are aroused as either completely prevent the integration of one's impressions into a coherent whole, or when at any rate they make it very difficult. The objectification, the shaping of a coherent whole, is hampered in music in two principal ways. Firstly, by uniformity so great that it almost excludes variety: by the constant repetition of the same note or chord, for instance; by long, majestic, weighty or solemn notes, and hence by very slow movement; by long pauses holding up the progress of the melodic line, or which impede the shaping of a melody, thus underlining the lack of variety. Secondly, by too much diversity, as when innumerable impressions succeed one another too rapidly and the mind being too abruptly hurled into the thundering torrent of sounds, or when (as in many polyphonic compositions involving many voices) the themes are developed together in so complex a manner that the imagination cannot easily and calmly integrate the diverse ideas into a coherent whole without strain. Thus in music the sublime can only be that which seems too vast and significant, too strange and wonderful, to be easily assimilated by it. Sublime notes, figuration and harmonies stimulate the imagination, which must exert itself and expand beyond its normal bounds to grasp, integrate and recall them. They offer it, not flowing melodies with gentle cadences, but something that appears intractable to rhythmic laws; they have no immediately pleasing effect on the personality and the imagination, but an almost violent one of frightful anf terrifying aspect. To the extent that music can depict greatness exceeding the normal capacity of the imagination, thrilling the listener with horror and rapture, it can express the sublime.[49]

The immediately obvious, superficial features of Michaelis's musical sublime are shared by, to borrow William Blake's adjective, the more 'terrific' figures in the *Applausus*. Sounds impinging 'on the

---

[48] Burke, *Enquiry*, 82-83, 122.
[49] le Huray and Day, 290.

ear at great length, or with complete uniformity' recall, for example, the long notes Haydn used to set 'judicare' and 'Jubilaei'. The display of 'too much diversity, as when innumerable impressions succeed one another too rapidly' and the mind is 'too abruptly hurled into the thundering torrent of sounds' seems not only to describe the semiquaver figuration of the bass aria 'Si obtrudat' but also to coincide precisely with Fortitude's sinking there into the frenzied accompaniment. Haydn's repeated used of *Saltus* and *hyperbole*, too, perhaps can be seen as a means of creating, musically, the impression of a great height or immensity that 'stimulates the imagination...to exert itself and expand its normal bounds', to create, so to speak, musical equivalents for the vertiginous heights, precipices and cliffs that figures so prominently in sublime vistas. Clearly, the violent 'frightful and terrifying aspect' of the sublime that Michaelis stresses peers out from the bass arias of the *Applausus* and the Stabat Mater, just as it will later in the storm and hunting sequences of *The Seasons* and the 'Military' symphony (No. 100, a work actually noted by a contemporary critic for its 'horrid sublimity').[50]

As Michaelis suggested, while the sublime moment may immediately have provoked pain, fear, frustration and terror, stimulation of these affects was also conceived of as preliminary to the sublime's ultimate force: the elevation of the imagination. As it was put recently, the 'sublime experience is typically presented as a three-fold moment : an encounter with the stimulating object, an episode of discontinuity (usually described as vertigo or blockage or bafflement), and a sudden and ecstatic exaltation'.[51] Claudia Johnson has pointed out in regard to the sublime in Handel's music that while the 'esthetics of the sublime in the eighteenth-century in some senses became the esthetics of the ugly' or even of the grotesque, the same esthetics promoted vastness and the sense of awe and wonder that immensity and incommensurability provoked.[52] Musically, Johnson argues, this vastness imposes itself through volume, the 'staggering multiplicity of sounds', density of contrapuntal texture, and exceptionally large vocal and instrumental forces, all displayed in the great choruses of Handel's oratorios. Judging from the contemporary critical accounts of performances Johnson presents, one would not be

---

[50] Review of a London performance of Haydn's Symphony No.100 in the *Morning Chronicle* (9 April 1794), cited by Johnson, 528.
[51] V. A. De Luca, 'A Wall of Words: The Sublime as Text', in Nelson Hilton and Thomas A. Volger, eds., *Unnam'd Forms: Blake and Textuality* (Berkeley: University of California Press, 1986), 218.
[52] Johnson, 528-529.

wrong to speak of Haydn's choruses, especially in the two late oratorios, in the same terms. What should not be undervalued in any case is the force of the aesthetic category of the sublime for understanding Haydn's work, and especially the *Applausus*. The 'sublime' and the 'beautiful', as they were understood by the composer's contemporaries, can and should be heard as such, and as much in Haydn's music as other supposedly characteristic features, such as humour and irony.

B. The chorus (No. VIIIb)

As far as the *Applausus* is concerned, one can speak of sublime, musical 'vastness' only in relation to the final chorus, 'O Caelites, vos invocamus', or, more correctly, *the* chorus, since Haydn's *Applausus* follows the tradition of the Applausus cantata genre by 'culminating . . . in a large climactic chorus intentionally reserved for the end of the work'.[53] The final number is the only one in the cantata scored for four-part chorus as well as for the four soloists and full orchestral forces, including the *clarini* in C and timpani. In some respects, this chorus does not distinguish itself from the great number of Haydn's other triumphant C major choral or orchestral works. Yet certain details of the text-setting here are remarkable for the way in which they involve and resume the cantata's figural and rhetorical tendencies.

The text of the chorus is as follows:

O Caelites, vos invocamus, ac perardenter flagitamus: petita non negate.	a
Multorum in solatium servate hoc Palatium dulci benignitate.	b
O gods on high, we invoke you, and we entreat you most ardently: do not deny our requests.	a
For the many in solace guard this Palatine[;] confer goodness, with your love.	b

The text is set in *da capo* form, with setting of the 'a' section comprising most of the chorus (bb.1-102) and that of the 'b' section occupying not much more than a musical 'parenthesis' (bb.103-130).

---

[53] Freeman, *Melk Monastery*, 229-230.

Within the 'a' section, the initial setting of the first two lines differs markedly from that of the third line, and in fact stands apart from the setting of the remainder of the chorus. It consists of eight bars, emphatically in triple time, with all voices sounding together from the outset. It is stamped with two prominent figures: *saltus*, in the soprano and bass lines at b.3 (and again in the soprano at b.7), and *abruptio*, the stunning, almost total breaking off of vocal and orchestral lines at bb.4 and 8 for one beat. These two figures, along with the initial outburst of all the voices and their brief, homophonic movement, convey both the massiveness and the discontinuity associated with the experience of the sublime. In the compression of these opening bars, it is as if the voices are constrained within two monoliths of sound.

The setting of the rest of the chorus contrasts clearly with that of this brief, initial setting: it is much more expansive and during it, the voices move much more freely in relation to each other, in and out of homophonic bindings. From b.9 on, the setting seems to explode in figurations resounding from earlier appearances in the cantata. Again, there are giant *saltus* figures, notably at b.11, where, in the course of one bar the bass must soar from G to d'; rushing semiquaver writing for strings throughout; and declamatory settings in the tenor and soprano lines of 'petita non negate' (e.g. at bb.13-16 and bb.22-24), recalling the earlier settings of 'jubilaei' (Ex. 12, see p.263, bb.70-72) and, from the first bass aria, 'sed res vera patet' (Ex. 7, see p.258, bb.51-54). Indeed, one could say that the impulsion of the setting, with its bounding triple metre and broad melodic range in each voice, spins off from the apocalyptic 'Non chymaeras somniatis', if in fact it has a direct antecedent anywhere in the cantata.

Yet there are two figurations here that seem not to have appeared before in the *Applausus*. The first of these is the *abruptio* setting of 'non, non, non...' at bb.18-20, and the second is the setting of 'negate' - and later 'invocamus' and 'flagitamus' - with quaver arcs, as in the tenor and bass lines at bb.22-25 'Ex. 13, see p.264). The latter figuration is commonplace in Haydn's choral settings, expecially in the masses, and in that context there is at least one other instance where these two figurations appear in proximity: the 'Et resurrexit' section of the Credo of the 'Great Organ Solo Mass', where *abruptio* is used to set the 'non, non, non' and arcs of quavers the 'regni' of 'cujus regni non, non, non erit finis' (i.e. his Kingdom shall never end). The broad compass of the vocal arcs in the cantata's chorus parallels the melodic and rhythmic contours that, for Haydn and others, were received devices for setting the text of the Credo that speaks of Christ's regeneration, his judgment, and the eternity of his reign; obviously an occasion, also, for an epiphany of the musical sublime. The quavers of the *Applausus* chorus, though, can also be heard as loosenings and expansions of the tightly threaded *circulatio* figurations of 'O beatus incolatus', rather like a similar *circulatio* figuration Beethoven was to use much later, reportedly to evoke the music of the spheres (Example 1(j), see p.249);[54] a *circulatio*, that is, with cosmic resonances. The setting for chorus, by taking up and unwinding, releasing the figuration that, a few moments earlier was so closely bound with the *incolatus*, urges and enhances the invocation and prayer of Prudentia and the other virtues for prolonging the 'residence' the cantata celebrates. The mediation between the earthly and the heavenly that the *incolatus* embodies is affirmed, climactically, literally 'recapped', in a setting of 'servate hoc Palatium' (Ex. 14, see p.265) that arises almost midway through the chorus, when the soprano line arcs from e" up to a" and back down to a' in a contour that recalls the settings of 'Palatium' in 'Dictamina mea' and the steep heights of virtue's dwelling from the quartet. The soprano ascends to a" several times in the chorus - it is the highest note in this vocal part - but here the note seems preeminent, functioning as if it were the keystone joining both the vaults of the chorus and the various trajectories of the cantata's figurations.

This is not to say that this moment of the chorus or even the chorus as a whole establishes or captures some kind of organic unity. If it is at all appropriate to speak of 'unity' in the *Applausus*, one should speak of a unity of decorum, or more precisely, of *ornatu*, the rhetorical term designating the decorations or illustrative elaborations embroidered on a discourse. One might say that the soprano line's curve at bb.121-127 (Ex. 14, see p.265) occurs precisely where it should, to bridge, provisionally, the discrete figural complexes that have predominated throughout the cantata. It meditates between the *ornatu* of the cantata's properly apocalyptic moments and the *ornatu* of what I have called its moments of apotheosis, moments which, as was stressed above, are discontinuous until the opening of the chorus. The soprano's arc works as a lock that can be perceived as *either* binding or releasing the figurative chains of the work, and the effect or the impression that they have been released at this point in

---

[54] Kirkendale, *Circulatio*', 82.

the cantata may be as strong or stronger than the impression that they have been 'unified'.[55]

If the *Applausus* has 'unity', and if its figurations contribute to any kind of unified impression, it is probably because Haydn's text-setting is so meticulously and consistently worked out. The cantata displays an ordering very much like that which the poet William Blake claimed for his epic *Jerusalem* (1804), whereby 'every word and every letter is studied and put into its fit place, with the terrific numbers. . . reserved for the terrific parts - the mild and gentle, for the mild and gentle parts, and the prosaic, for inferior parts'.[56] One does not leave listening to the cantata without a sense of an absence of overt integration of, or the difference and distance between, its rhetorical *topoi*. Arguably, this gap opens up most tellingly in 'O beatus incolatus', ironically just before the chorus, during which, if at any time, one senses that the figurative strands of the music are moving toward synthesis. Yet any 'synthesis' one *finds* in the cantata remains precisely that: found, discovered, negotiated, by seeing and hearing *in between* ostensibly discrete entities: by hearing between parts of each aria, especially by hearing connections that figuration urges among members and, especially, between the framing and middle sections of each number, as between the tacitly 'beautiful' main section of 'O beatus incolatus!' and its turbulent but hushed middle section. Finding the 'truth' of the cantata is like finding the dwelling-place of virtue that the soloists of the quartet affirm is 'among' (*inter*) the heights: it is not so much embedded or located in one or another of the figural complexes as it is suspended in the relations Haydn contrives within and among them throughout the work. It is as if, to get a clear sense of the cantata's direction, and of its contours, one has to stare at its figuration not directly but slightly from one side. For it is often just when the figuration seems most concrete, determined, or manifestly filled with mimetic content that the music, through the figuration, may articulate its discursive, formal, metamimetic tendencies. From what is arguably the most 'superficial' aspect of the music's texture, the potently, mimetically

---

[55] On the significance of release in art, see Irving Massey, 'The Effortless in Art and Ethics: Meditations on "The Frog King, or Iron Henry"', *The Georgia Review* 37 (1983), 640-658, especially 645-647. A version of this essay appears also in Irving Massey, *Find You the Virtue: Ethics, Image, and Desire in Literature*, (Fairfax: George Mason University Press, 1987), 113-130.

[56] William Blake 'To the Public', *Jerusalem*, in David V. Erdman, ed., *The Poetry and Prose of William Blake*, rev. ed. (Berkeley: University of California Press, 1982), 146. On Blake's prosody and its meanings, see William Kumbier, 'Blake's Epic Meter', *Studies in Romanticism* 17/2 (Spring 1978), 163-192.

referential melodic and rhythmic figuration, one begins to hear the non- or polyreferential resonances of the cantata's textuality. In the *Applausus*, a characteristic instance of figuration, such as the 'betweenness' of the tenor line at b.154 of the quartet (Ex. 3, see p.252-53), may turn out to have profound semantic implications as the cantata completes its course.

Despite the insights offered by those figurations in the *Applausus* that appear translucent and lend themselves to interpretation, many important questions remain. First, what did Haydn actually make of the idiosyncratic Latin of the text in those numerous passages that are most obscure - some would say corrupt - than the passages I have cited? Where an obvious meaning suggests itself, Haydn often seems to have proceeded as the Baroque theorist Heinichen recommended in his writing on the *loci topici*, or musical commonplaces, by focusing on a striking or seminal word and deriving the music's turns from it, disseminating the word's meaning(s) throughout an aria or musical number.[57] Indeed, much of the cantata's obvious figuration springs from unusual or highly charged words, or words traditionally suited for 'painting' or other special setting. Yet what did Haydn do when such words were not at hand, during those extensive passages of the text that are, to use Geiringer's words, of a more 'dry' and 'abstract' quality?[58]

Then, there is the problem of reading figurations that seem to lure the listener, that because of their unusual character or situation seem about to bear significance but do not appear to be motivated by nearby text or clearly tied to other figures in the cantata. A haunting example occurs near the opening of 'O beatus incolatus!' (bb.17-18), when the soloist intones (as would be intoned the first line at the outset of a segment of the mass) the text's first line, in a setting that also preceded the *circulatio* figurations of the opening violin solo, like a motto. Perhaps this setting, with its prominent hesitation and drop to d' on '-latus', and its solo violin accompaniment, has its counterpart or source in some part of the mass-setting tradition, as do so many of the cantata's figures, and we simply lack the key to unlock its significance. The figurations of the *Applausus* that *can* be read or deciphered, it seems, are like arrow loops in the work's

---

[57] George J. Buelow, 'The *Loci Topici* and Affect in Late Baroque Music: Heinichen's Practical Demonstration', *MR* (1966), 161-176. See also Buelow's *Thorough-Bass Accompaniment According to Johann David Heinichen*, rev. ed., (Ann Arbor: UMI Research Press, 1986), which contains translations of portions of Heinichen's writings on thorough-bass and commentary on them.

[58] Karl Geiringer (in collaboration with Irene Geiringer), *Haydn: A Creative Life in Music*, 3rd rev. ed., (Berkeley: University of California Press, 1982), 244.

walls: only by continuing to pursue a musical exegetics, by exploring the 'conceptual dictionary for this language of notes' that Jean-Jacques Rousseau and, lately, Warren Kirkendale called for,[59] can we hope for a more comprehensive view of Haydn's giant jubilation.*

---

*This paper was conceived, and the first draft of it written, during a National Endowment for the Humanities Summer Seminar, 'Patterns of Stylistic Development in Joseph Haydn's Music', held in 1984 at the School of Music, Indiana University, under the direction of Professor A. Peter Brown. I thank Professor Brown for his suggestion of the topic and for his encouragement and guidance during and after the seminar. I also thank Professor Irving Massey of the Department of English, State University of New York at Buffalo, whose invitation to present some of the material in this paper in a seminar at Buffalo in 1985 helped focus my ideas and whose comments at that seminar proved fruitful for me, as always.

---

[59] W. Kirkendale, 'Circulatio', 91.

Ex.1 Hypotypotic musical figurations

So ste - he denn, du gott - er - geb - ne See - le, mit Chri - sto geist - lich auf!

a) J.S. Bach, Cantata No. 31, *Der Himmel lacht, die Erde jubiliert*, No.5, bb.1-3. *Anabasis* figuration.

Et a - scen - dit in coe - lum:

b) Georg Reutter (the Younger), *Missa S. Caroli* (1734), Credo, bb.65-68. *Anabasis* figuration. (Source: *DTÔ* 88 (1952))

de - scen - dit de coe - lis.

c) Reutter, *Missa S. Caroli*, Credo, bb.33-35. *Catabasis* figuration.

Et re - sur - re - xit ter - ti - a di - e, se - cun - dum scri - ptu - ras, et a - scen - dit in coe - lum,

d) Joseph Haydn, *Missa in honorem B.V.M.* (Hob.XXII:4), Credo, 'Et resurrexit', bb.1-10. *Anabasis* figuration on 'Et resurrexit' and 'ascendit'.

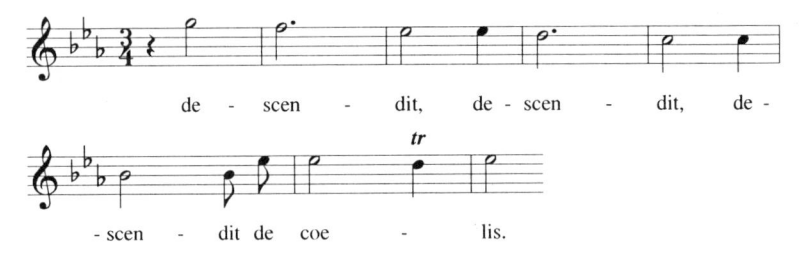

de - scen - dit, de - scen - dit, de - scen - dit de coe - lis.

e) Haydn, *Missa in honorem B.V.M.* (Hob.XXII:4), Credo, bb.66-73. *Catabasis* figuration.

the round_____ world

f) Henry Purcell, 'The Lord is King', (1688).
   Sine curve *circulatio* on 'round'.

al - le - lu - ja____

g) J.S. Bach, Cantata No.51, *Jauchzet Gott in allen Landen*, No.4, bb.217-224.
   Anabasis and *circulatio* figuration on 'alleluja'.

glo - - ri - am

h) Heinrich Biber, *Missa S. Henrici* (1701), Gloria.
   'Halo' *circulatio* on 'gloriam'.

glo - ri - fi - ca - - -

- - mus te

i) Reutter, *Missa S. Caroli*, Gloria, bb.75-77.
   Circulatio figuration on 'glorificamus'.

j) Beethoven, Quartet Op.59, No.2, 2nd movement.
   Circulatio figuration for 'music of the spheres'.

Ex.2

Joseph Haydn, *Applausus*, 'Virtus inter ardua', bb.24-32.
(Reproduced from the *JHW* edition)

Ex.3

Haydn, *Applausus*, 'Virtus inter ardua', bb.80-98.
(Reproduced from the *JHW* edition)

Ex.4

Haydn, *Applausus*, 'Vitus inter ardua', bb.154-163.
(Reproduced from the *JHW* edition)

Ex.5

Haydn, *Applausus*, 'O pii Patres Patriae!', bb.48-59.
(Reproduced from the *JHW* edition)

Ex.6

a) bb.43-44. a) bb.83-85.

a) bb.54-68.

d) bb.127-147.

Haydn, *Applausus*, 'Rerum, quas perpendimus'. Figurations on 'prosperatur'.
(Reproduced from the *JHW* edition)

Ex.7

Non chy - mae - ras so - mni - a - tis, non chy - mae - ras so - mni - a - tis, sed per - fe - cta co - gi - ta - tis: nul - la fraus hic la - tet, hic la - tet, sed res ve - ra pa - tet,

Haydn, *Applausus*, 'Non chymaeras somniatis', bb.34-54.

Ex.8

Flam - mis or - ci ne suc - cen - dar, flam - mis ne suc - cen - dar, per te, vir - go, fac, de - fen - dar, fac, de - fen - dar

Haydn, *Stabat Mater*, No.XI, bb.13-22.

Ex.9

Ma - gna coe - li Do - mi - na sum - ma or - bis glo - ri - a, or - bis glo - ri - a!

Haydn, *Motetto de Beata*, 'Magna coeli Domina', (Hob.XXIIIa:c7)

Ex.10

men - tes non tur - ban - tur,
- do - res ap - pro - ban - tur,

cun - cta li - cet in - ver - tan - tur,
San - cti at - que co - ro - nan - tur,

cun - cta li - cet in - ver - tan -
San - cti at - que co - ro - nan -

Haydn, 'Si obtrudat ultimam' bb.9-38.
(Reproduced from the *JHW* edition).

Ex.11

Haydn, *Applausus*, 'O beatus incolatus!', bb.45-48.
(Reproduced from the *JHW* edition)

Ex.12

Haydn, *Applausus*, 'O beatus incolatus!', bb.62-79.
(Reproduced from the *JHW* edition)

Ex.13

Haydn, *Applausus*, 'O Caelites', bb.18-28.
(Reproduced from the *JHW* edition)

Ex.14

Haydn, *Applausus*, 'O Caelites', bb.121-127.
(Reproduced from the *JHW* edition)

Joseph Haydn Werke, Reihe I, Band 3. Sinfonien 1761-1763.
Edited by Jürgen Braun and Sonia Gerlach xii + 223 pp. Munich: G. Henle Verlag 1990

Joseph Haydn Werke, Reihe XI, Band 1. Streichtrios 1. Folge.
Edited by Bruce C. McIntyre and Barry S. Brook. xii + 210 pp. Munich: G. Henle Verlag 1986.

Of this volume of the first seven Esterházy symphonies, Nos. 6 ('Le Matin'), 7 ('Le Midi'), 8 ('Le Soir'), 9, 40, 12 and 13, four (Nos. 7, 40, 12 and 13) exist in autographs, the rest in MS. copies and the occasional print of varying textual reliability. A detailed study of the sources and the principal textual divergencies are included at the end of the volume. The major problem concerns the timpani part of No.13, added to the autograph in a foreign hand but also included in various MS. copies and in the first French edition by Silly in Paris c.1777-8. The new edition includes the part but recommends that it be omitted in performance. The problem appears, however, more complicated than the editors suggest, both from the standpoint of eighteenth-century performance practice as well as from the sources (it appears in half-a-dozen). The editors are persuaded, moreover, that no harpischord continuo was intended, despite the fact that the autograph of No.7 has 'Basso Continuo' at the beginning of the work and later too (Adagio). This now hotly disputed problem has become a major factor in performing early Haydn symphonies. On the question of the horns in C for Symphonies Nos. 7 and 9, the editors are on safer ground when they recommend that the instruments must be in C *basso* and not *alto* (Haydn *never* writes c''' for *alto* instruments, and that note appears in No. 7, first movement and in the Trio of No. 9, while in No. 7's first movement there is even d''').

The engraving and printing are absolutely first class, and the proof reading, as we have come to expect with the Haydn Institute, is astonishingly free from error. A model production, then, in every respect.

The volume of string trios is the first of two, which will contain all the works which the Haydn Institute considers genuine. The first volume, here under discussion, contains those works which are listed in the *Entwurf-Katalog* and/or the Elssler Catalogue of 1805 -- a sensible decision with which no one can take exception. The actual edition of the trios arose from a seminar at the City University of New York, where a whole group of students worked on these works under the supervision of Bruce MacIntyre in 1975. (A similar project had in 1969 produced a new *Urtext* score, based on the then rediscovered autograph, of Mozart's 'Haffner' Symphony, subsequently published by Faber Music in London). There are no autographs of these trios whatever, and all of them had to be produced from manuscript sources, some of which, however, are from Haydn's own group of copyists. The critical report, included at the end of the volume, is a fine achievement, inviting the interested reader to share the ghastly textual problems facing the Haydn scholar. The first page of Violino Primo in every known source for the Trio V: 12 in E major has been reproduced in facsimile: 21 sources, one blank because the page in question is missing. This is the kind of situation that the Haydn scholar often has to face, and this admirable team of students and teachers has solved the problem, and many of the others, with great insight.

As always, the printing is a model of such things. Clear, large, easy to read and uncluttered by editorial warnings, every musician will welcome this handsome volume.

H. C. R. L.

Webster, James. Haydn's 'Farewell' Symphony and the Idea of the Classical Style: Through-composition and Cyclic Integration in his Instrumental Music.

Cambridge: Cambridge University Press, 1991. xx + 402 pp.

Even to the most casual observer, almost every aspect of Haydn's Symphony in F sharp minor grabs the attention. It is one of the composer's most astonishing and bizarre works, standing out admist the remarkable series of pieces that he wrote in 1772. Its tonal centre is unique amongst eighteenth-century symphonies. And - not least - it has a near-contemporaneous (but inauthentic) nickname, and (on Haydn's testimony) a memorable programmatic dimension. Yet these features seem to have conspired against its receiving serious critical attention. Conventional notions of the 'Classical style' being 'achieved' in the 1780s have consigned Haydn's earlier music to the ghetto of stylistic immaturity. The radical style of the 'Farewell', less suave than Haydn's later symphonies, might superficially confirm such critical preconceptions. Analytical and aesthetic ideologies that proclaim the superiority of abstract instrumental music have also exerted a profound effect. Critics have tended to patronize or trivalize the work's programme, with the implication that extra-musical associations somehow weaken the music's inherent strengths; or worse, that programmatic music is not a worthy object of analysis. In this substantial book, James Webster triumphantly overturns these prejudices. His challenging analytical account of the 'Farewell' is followed by a contextual exploration of related issues in other works by Haydn, and a pithy historiographical conclusion.

Webster's central thesis is that the 'Farewell' Symphony is an integrated, through-composed cycle. The notion of cyclic form was, of course, not unknown in the eighteenth century: in Austrian masses of the period, the Agnus Dei often reprises the music of the opening Kyrie; and composers sometimes concluded variation sets with an undecorated reprise of the theme, thus bringing the music full circle. Such overt thematic recall is much more rare in multimovement instrumental music of the time, (Haydn's Symphony No. 31, 'Hornsignal', is an obvious example). Nor, given the analytical preoccupation with *thematische Arbeit*, is the investigation of motivic links between movements foreign to twentieth-century criticism of this repertoire. Yet attempts to demonstrate the motivic integrity of entire works have met with mixed success, and none has been entirely convincing. Cyclic forms can be generated by a far wider range of compositional strategies than the '*ma fin est mon commencement*' type. Gestural and structural parallels can be drawn between movements, and musical processes can span over several movements to form a cohesive bond. On a broader level, there may be a single psychological progression running through an entire work. Although a few isolated analyses have tentatively explored these features (notably Hans Keller's 'functional analyses' of Mozart's String Quartet K.421 and String Quintet K.515), the issues have hardly been investigated in any depth.

Webster here examines integrative aspects of the 'Farewell' Symphony that are more fundamental than a commonality of motives in all five movements. He perceives a structural and rhetorical dynamic in which the symphony progresses from extreme instability with a denial of adequate closure in the first movement, through a 'promise' of resolution (still unachieved) in the central movements, to an 'apotheosis of ethereality' in the finale. Sceptics might protest that the succession of movement types in any eighteenth-century symphony will create the impression of a psychological progression of some sort. But Webster undermines any doubts with his brilliant demonstration of the many integrative features found in the work: for example, the gestural parallels at the end of the minuet and the end of the finale, unusual voice-leading patterns that recur throughout the piece, and the through-composition of the double finale. He describes the tonal organisation of the symphony as a double cycle:

Movement	F	S	M	fn_1/	fn_2	
Tonal centre (F sharp)	i	III	I	i	III	I

(p.13)

Webster is also at pains to demonstrate that cyclic integration in Haydn's music is not confined to the 'Farewell' and that through-composed elements appear in works throughout his long career. Clearly, this attribution of features traditionally associated with nineteenth-century principles, and often cited as some of Beethoven's most original innovations, is a startling piece of historical revisionism:

> Instead of seeing Beethoven (to put it crudely) as 'the man who freed music', we may view Haydn as the central figure in the 'First Viennese Modern School', the inventor of a rhetoric of

> through-composition, the composer of the first paradigmatic
> works of this type . . . and Beethoven as his follower
> (and eventually his equal).

That Webster can argue his historical case so convincingly is in large measure due to his impressive analytical technique. Following recent trends in operatic studies, a 'multivalent' strategy is pursued. Instead of engaging in a single-minded demonstration of organic unity, he uses an array of methodologies to explore independently several musical parameters (such as form, voice-leading structure, texture, motivic patterns, and topoi). While it carries the advantage of producing a multifaceted reading of a complex piece, there are dangers in this approach: as Webster admits, it 'runs the risk of mindless eclecticism' (p.5). He sidesteps this pitfall by several means. By presenting a resumé of his conclusions before embarking on the detailed analysis, he gives his readers a clear interpretive framework within which to evaluate his comments. His is also particularly patient in eplaining the shifting focus of his analysis as it progresses. To this end, the clear sectionalisation of the analysis, coupled with a liberal use of subheadings in the text, is particularly useful. Webster draws on a wide spectrum of methodologies, ranging from implication-realization models (from Cone and Meyer) to narrative theory and recent studies in eighteenth-century semiotics (Agawu) and topoi (Allenbrook). But the main thrust of his analysis relies on only three critical traditions: Schenkerian voice leading, Schoenbergian motivic principles, and a Toveyan respect for the music's phenomenology.

A potentially more damaging risk lurks within the multivalent approach. For a book which outlines a significant historical argument, and is presumably aimed at music historians and analysts alike, the debt to such a multifarious theoretical background threatens to alienate those with limited experience of, or little patience with, analytical literature. Like any good analysis, Webster's is intellectually challenging, but on a technical level it is, also, quite user-friendly. Statements that make their point by requiring from the reader a detailed theoretical knowledge are usually accompanied by succinct definitions and references; and the analysis as a whole is refreshingly free of jargon. The only place at which readers might become frustrated is the complex discussion of motives in the finale (pp.96-99 and pp.104-108), where Webster refers to a long catalogue of alphabetical symbols given on pages 24-8.

The analysis itself (Chapters 2 and 3), is persuasive. For example, in his discussion of the first movement, Webster is alert to the dangers of reductive processes and sensitive to the limitations of conventional Schenkerian graphic techniques in the study of such unpredictable, restless music:

> In analyzing [Haydn's] music one ignores 'what happens', in the most literal, tangible sense, at one's peril; perhaps even more than with other composers, *one must observe the integrity of the foreground.*
>
> (p.53; Webster's italics)

He frequently supplements orthodox graphs with alternative, 'literal' readings that maintain more fidelity to Haydn's 'difficult' voice leading. This undoubtedly enriches his analysis, and is particularly successful in highlighting the registral discontinuities and destabilising pitches that contribute so much to the movement's character. Even Webster's most striking theoretical unorthodoxy - the first movement's uninterrupted background structure (p.53), - is authentically Schenkerian in its analytical creativity and in the value of its insight.

Webster is admirably thorough, but one disconcerting omission from his discussion of the first movement is the effect of the development-recapitulation repeat (see *JHW* 1/6 [Sinfonien 1767-1772], Munich, 1966, p.82). This is particularly surprising, given his interest in Haydn's rhetoric, specifically the rhetoric of closure. Does the formal repeat intensify or compromise the lack of adequate closure? What are its larger formal implications? The brief F sharp minor prolongation at the end of the movement is first followed by the movement's stormy opening theme in A major, and - second time around - by the more tranquil adagio theme, which is *also* in A major. Do these two F sharp minor to A major juxtapositions strengthen the sense of through-composition? Or, at a more fundamental level, does large-scale formal repetition pose a serious obstacle to the sense of through-composition in this music? It is regrettable, given the superlative quality of his other insights, that Webster does not address these questions. (See, however, Michael Broyles 'Organic Form and the Binary Repeat', *The Musical Quarterly*, 46 (1980), p.339; and Johanthan Dunsby, 'The Formal Repeat', *Journal of the Royal Musical Association,* 112 (1986-7), p.196.)

Webster's analyses of the Adagio and the Minuet and trio serve to demonstrate how the first movement's most outlandish features are gradually eliminated from the musical discourse, and stylistic 'normality' is partially restored. The Adagio's restlessness results less from its middleground voice-leading structures than from the syntax of its foreground. For the first time in the work, conjunct melodic shapes become prevalent; but their constituent motives articulate cadences weakly, there is a disorienting flexibility in phrase lengths, and tonal resolution is postponed over long time-spans by major:minor chromaticism. The F sharp major tonality of the Minuet and trio completes the first of the work's two tonal cycles. Webster argues, however, that enough disruptive features remain to prevent any feeling of resolution. In a movement-type as stylized as the minuet and trio, destabilizing details have a disproportionate effect. Thus the major mode is challenged by bass interjections on *D natural*, and the movement's binary shape is blurred by the violin appendix in bars 11-12. Webster is surely right to suggest that the tag produces a lack of correspondence between the minuet's voice-leading structure and its form. Nevertheless, with their clear cadence structures and repeated melodic descents in the treble, the Minuet and trio anticipate the finale's resolution.

A consistently impressive aspect of the analysis is Webster's refusal to arrive at easy, satisfying conclusions. He never loses sight of the music's ironies. This is most apparent in his reading of the Farewell finale: although the movement is a culmination, with the symphony ultimately attaining closure, it has the effect of a 'negative climax'. *Pianissimo*, for two solo violins, and (the greatest irony) concluding with a 6-3 chord: 'as an ending, it is not 'easy'; it hovers between the apparently opposed values of structural closure and insubstsantiality; our attempted synthesis of them into a reassuringly unified state will be fragile at best, not easily sustained' (p.112).

Overall, Webster's approach to the relationship between hermeneutic and technical analysis treads a careful path between Kermanesque criticism, and the supposedly positivistic activities of much post-war analysis. At an early stage of the book, he writes that the symphony 'demands not merely to be analyzed, but to be interpreted' (p.5); and he concedes that its 'difficult' ending 'almost forces us to move 'outside' the work 'as such' -- which is to say, to reinterpret it on the basis of the external program' (p.112). Yet he admits that even the simplest and most dry analytical choices involve interpretation, just as the most fevered interpretation is based (however subconsciously) on analysis. His method is to set up a self-consciously symbiotic relationship between analysis, interpretation, and historical musicology, taking account of eighteenth-century attitudes towards the extra-musical dimension of instrumental music. We know that the symphony's programme achieved its desired aim, but a puzzle remains: how did Prince Nicolaus Esterházy get the point? On the evidence of the earliest sources, it seems unlikely that an early simple piece of music theatre was involved. Webster sensibly resists the temptation to solve the riddle of the prince's response, but asks instead how the symphony might project a programme? As a preliminary exercise, he surveys the work's reception history: critical reaction ranges from near-slapstick to Mendelssohn's more perceptive comment that 'it is a curiously melancholy little piece' (p.115). Schering's interpretation of the programme is dismissed as 'banal, . . . depressingly literalistic' (p.115). Webster does not make the same mistake. Rather than linking isolated musical details with specific extra-musical events in a picturesque narrative, his sophisticated (and broadly convincing) interpretation grows out of the analysis, and correlates the work's broad musical ideas with notions of a frustrated longing for home.

Magnificent though the analysis is, the heart of this book lies in Chapters 5 to 8, where Webster contemplates in the larger context of Haydn's instrumental music many of the stylistic issues raised by his analysis of the 'Farewell'. He explores progressive form and the rhetoric of instability; the role played by thematic integration, tonal organisation, run-on movement pairs and through-composition in the construction of instrumental cycles; and the attitutes of musicians and audiences in later eighteenth-century Austria towards the extra-musical dimension of instrumental music. While Webster does not aim to be comprehensive, he gives a well-balanced account of this side of Haydn's creative personality. This part of the study is a towering demonstration of his profound knowledge of the repertoire, and is well served by his virtuosic organisation of material. Large-scale comparative issues are usually processed in (digestible) tables, and detailed points of style are discussed with a marvellous series of analytical vignettes. The only quibble is that readers are likely to be left wanting more. Webster is not averse to spurring them into further enquiry. For example, regarding the opening movement of the String Quartet Op.50 No.4: 'afficionados of tonal instability will enjoy working out the consequences of its violent unison opening motive' (p.332). As well as conducting seperate investigations of musical gestures and processes that can contribute to through-composition, Webster draws the various strands together in brief case-studies of cyclically integrated works. These all create an interesting gloss on his analysis of the 'Farewell', but the most relevant case-study is of the contemporaneous Symphony No.46. Towards the end of its *Alla breve* finale, Haydn inserts a reprise (beginning *in media res*), of the second part of the minuet, before concluding with the movement's original tempo and material. By this stage in the book we are alert to the structural and extramusical implications of the reminiscence. Webster, drawing on recent musicological studies in narratology to interpret Haydn's astonishing process, is led to speculate that this symphony and the 'Farewell' might have been conceived as a larger two-work cycle. Although unexpected, this view seems reasonable in the light of Haydn's earlier symphonic trilogy, *Le Matin - Le Midi - Le Soir* (1761).

The book's analytical section is rounded off with a consideration of the dialectic of 'type' and uniqueness in Haydn's instrumental music. Having briefly scrutinized the philosophical basis of our notion of style, it seems natural that he should conclude with a more wide-ranging discussion of 'Classical style' itself. The final part of the book contains a brilliant deconstruction of the historical narratives (Sandberger, Adler, Kiesewetter) that gave rise to our lazy conception of 'Classical style'. (Curiously, Webster confines discussion of *Sturm und Drang* -- also ripe for deconstruction, one would have thought -- to a bibliographical footnote on page 3.) He presents a particularly devastating critique of those, including Rosen, who have underestimated the quality of mid eighteenth-century music. Unlike the period designation 'Baroque', 'Classical' has never managed to thow off its (positive) value connotations. As an alternative, Webster suggests that the 'Classical' repertoire might be labelled 'First Viennese-European Modern Style'. However historiographically plausible and suggestive, this tag seems too wordy to catch on with musicologists (let alone the public).

Historiographical tradition - based on teleological concepts of artistic development and fruition, and concentrating on a few favoured genres that date from Haydn's perceived 'maturity' - has been unkind to the majority of his works. The book ends with a detailed, powerful plea for their re-evaluation:

> In place of [the] notion of Haydn's development, I would argue that experimentation was a fundamental aspect of his musical personality, throughout his life . . . The corollary is that, in principle, all his works are mature. The qualification 'in principle' acknowledges that a few are not in every respect above criticism . . . [b]ut his music was never in any intrinsic sense 'immature' - but least of all his programmatically through-composed masterpieces of 1772
>
> (pp.365-6)

In sum, Webster has written a study worthy of classic status. It exhibits all the finest qualities of his previous work: an uncompromising intellectual rigor, an awesome command of sources, and an infectious enthusiasm. It is to be hoped that, with its rich multivalent strategy and its symbiotic approach to both analysis and historical musicology, the study will become paradigmatic for future work in eighteenth-century instrumental music. The book is handsomely produced by the Cambridge University Press: the layout is clear, music examples are numerous and given a generous amount of space within the text, the large bibliography and index are extremely useful. There are few production errors: an incorrect key signature in Example 6:6 (p.216); the footnote for page 214 is confusingly placed at the bottom of page 213; and there is a slip in the labelling of Example 2:8b (p.54).

T. R. J.

ROBERT N. FREEMAN, *The Practice of Music at Melk Abbey. Based upon the Documents, 1681-1826* (Österreichische Akademie der Wissenschaften, phil.-hist. Klasse, Sitzungsberichte, Band 548. Veröffentlichungen der Kommission für Musikforschung 23, hrsg. von Othmar Wessely). Wien (Verlag der Österreichischen Akademie der Wissenschaften) 1989; 524 S.

Eine Stein gewordene Trompetenfanfare - so mag dem Musikfreund das goldgelb strahlende Stift Melk erscheinen, wenn er vom Donautal aus den majestätischen Baukomplex Jakob Prandtauers hoch über dem Fluß erblickt. Unmöglich, sich vorzustellen, daß das Leben der seit 1089 hier ansässigen Benediktiner sich ohne Musik abgespielt haben könnte. Im Gegenteil: ein Blick in die Stiftskirche mit der prachtvollen Sonnholz-Orgel (1732) und auf die musizierenden Engel der Kuppelfresken, ein Verweis auf die aus der Melker Schule hervorgegangenen Musiker wie Johann Georg Albrechtsberger, Marian Paradeiser, Robert Kimmerling und Maximilian Stadler überzeugen bereits davon, daß die Tonkunst in Melk in höchstem Ansehen stand - nicht zu reden von den Beständen des Musikarchivs, das gerade der Haydn-Forschung reiches Material zu bieten hat. Eine umfassende Veröffentlichung zur Musikgeschichte des Stiftes fehlte jedoch bislang.

Robert N. Freeman, der schon in seiner Dissertation das Thema *The Practice of Music at Melk Monastery in the 18th Century* (University of California, Los Angeles 1971) behandelte und weitere Schriften über die Melker Organisten Franz Schneider, Robert Kimmerling und die *Austrian Cloister Symphonists* folgen ließ, hat rechtzeitig zum 900jährigen Stiftsjubiläum nach mehrjähriger Archivarbeit die erste Darstellung des Melker Musiklebens vom späten 17. bis zum frühen 19. Jahrhundert nach den in Melk erhaltenen Dokumenten vorgelegt. Die Wahl des Zeitraums 1681-1826 wurde dabei einerseits durch die Quellenlage, andererseits durch den Umfang des Forschungsvorhabens bestimmt: von 1681 stammt eine aufschlußreiche 'Instruction Pro Regente Chori' und vom folgenden Jahr an existieren Rechnungsbücher des Stiftes. 1825, das letzte Dienstjahr des Chorregenten Adam Krieg, brachte mit einer großen Zahl von Messen- und Oratorienaufführungen einen Höhepunkt des Musiklebens in Melk, soll aber nicht als Grenzlinie zum Niedergang betrachtet werden - eine Ausweitung der

Veröffentlichung auch auf die hochinteressante Tradition des 19. Jahrhunderts hätte den Rahmen gesprengt.

Im ersten von fünf Kapiteln stellt Freeman die Geschichte des Stiftes und seine Bedeutung sowie die von ihm untersuchten Archivalien vor. Zu den wichtigsten Quellen gehören neben den Manuskripten des Musikarchivs die 'Priorats-Ephemeriden', d.h. das von 1682 bis 1876 geführte Tagebuch des Priors, und die Ausgabenlisten des Wirtschafts-Archivs. Zitate aus den lateinischen oder deutschen Dokumenten hat Freeman für den Textteil seines Werkes generell ins Englische übersetzt, und zwar mit einem so ausgeprägten Gefühl für die Eigenheiten der Sprache des 18. Jahrhunderts, daß man die Übersetzungen für Originalzitate halten könnte. Der Wortlaut kann in jedem Fall überprüft werden, da immer auf die Dokumenten-Exzerpte im Appendix C (s.u.) verwiesen wird. Wenn Freeman aus Texten zitiert, die in diesem Anhang nicht enthalten sind, wird das Original in einer Fußnote beigegeben.

Das folgende Kapitel ist der Organisation des Musiklebens und der Stellung aller daran Beteiligten gewidmet, wobei Freeman nicht allein musikhistorisch relevante, sondern auch soziologische Ergebnisse mitteilt. Er konstatiert in Melk eine eigenartige, durch die Praxis bewährte Kombination von Organisationsformen nach monastischen Regeln und nach dem Modell weltlicher Hofhaltungen, die zur Beschäftigung von Klerikern und Laien nebeneinander führte. Das musikalische Personal des Stiftes umfaßte im untersuchten Zeitraum ständig etwa 20-30 Personen, zu denen die Chorknaben, der Organist (immer ein Laie), der 'Thurnermeister' mit seinen Untergebenen (Blechbläser und Pauken), einige Berufsmusiker und natürlich die musizierenden Mönche und Novizen gehörten. An der Spitze stand, dem weltlichen Hofkapellmeister vergleichbar, der Regens chori. Jede dieser Gruppen wird in einem eigenen Abschnitt vorgestellt; dabei tragen die neuerschlossenen Dokumente zahlreiche Details zu den Biographien der Chorregenten und Organisten bei und liefern auch kleine Überraschungen - etwa die Beschreibung der farbenfreudigen Chorknaben-Livreen, die in eine eigens angefertigte Illustration umgesetzt worden ist. Daneben erfährt man vieles über die Baugeschichte der Melker Orgeln und die Instrumentensammlung des Stiftes, zu der teilweise exzellent erhaltene Streich-, Blas- und Tasteninstrumente des Barock und der Klassik gehören.

Im dritten Abschnitt zeichnet Freeman ein ungemein vielfältiges Bild der musikalischen Aktivitäten innerhalb des Jahreslaufes in Melk. Dabei geht es nicht nur um die regelmäßig wiederkehrenden Feiern der benediktinischen Liturgie, sondern ebenso um

Prozessionen, 'Music for Recreation' (Anlässe boten die Faschingstage und ein 'Erbauungstag' im Mai), musikalisch untermalte Ausflüge zu befreundeten Klöstern und Kirchen, Abtswahlen und -einführungen, Aderlaß-Tage oder den Empfang von Gästen. Was anläßlich der Besuche der Kaiserfamilie in Melk dargeboten wurde, gehört zum großen Teil in das fünfte Kapitel, worin erstmalig eine Untersuchung der Theaterspielstätten des Stiftes, ihrer Ausstattung und des Repertoires geboten wird. Da Schauspiel und Musiktheater im Lehrplan benediktinischer Schulen ihren festen Platz besaßen, verwundert es nicht, Nachweise für 51 Produktionen aus den Jahren 1686-1785 in Melk zu finden, von denen leider nur sechs Kompositionen überliefert sind. Es handelt sich in vielen Fällen um 'Finalkomödien', die am Schuljahrsende aufgeführt wurden; Theateraufführungen standen jedoch auch auf den Programmen von Feiern zur Investitur eines neuen Abtes und zur Unterhaltung hoher Gäste. Im Gegensatz zu anderen Klöstern wurden für die Melker Produktionen überwiegend hauseigene Kräfte herangezogen: Textdichter wie P. Beda Schuster arbeiteten mit Komponisten wie Johann Georg Albrechtsberger, Marian Paradeiser oder Maximilian Stadler zusammen, und die Ausführenden stammten aus den Reihen der Chorknaben und Studenten (die dabei auch Tanzeinlagen zeigten!), unterstützt von den professionellen Sängern. Nach einer Betrachtung der musiktheatralischen 'Sonderformen' des klösterlichen Repertoires - Singspiel, Applausus, Singgedicht - gelangt Freeman zu dem Resümee, daß sich im Melker Theaterwesen progressive und konservative Elemente nebeneinander feststellen lassen, insgesamt aber das Stift in diesem Bereich eine außergewöhnliche Unabhängigkeit von anderen Zentren des Musiktheaters zeige.

Um die musikalischen Beziehungen des Stiftes geht es im letzten Kapitel, d.h. um Kontakte zu Institutionen und Persönlichkeiten in Wien, Passau, St. Pölten, Stift Göttweig, und - in unserem Zusammenhang besonders wichtig - um die Verbindung zwischen Melk und Joseph Haydn. Zwar hat auch die Durchsicht der Dokumente noch keinen Hinweis auf einen Aufenthalt Haydns im Stift geben können, doch betont Freeman die bedeutende Rolle, die der Haydn-Schüler und ab 1761 als Musikdirektor in Melk wirkende Robert Kimmerling als Vermittler und Sammler von Haydns Musik spielte. Bereits 1787 besaß das Stift mindestens 44 Sinfonien Haydns; daneben existieren im Musikarchiv Abschriften zahlreicher Kirchen- und Kammermusikwerke und etlicher Konzerte, von denen das bis 1965 einzige bekannte Manuskript des Violinkonzerts A-Dur (Hob. VIIa:3) als 'Melker Konzert' berühmt geworden ist.

Etwa drei Fünftel des Buches nimmt der auswertende und beschreibende Textteil ein, der Rest gehört den bescheiden als 'Appendices' auftretenden Registern und Dokumenten. Appendix A listet alle zwischen 1676 und 1789 in Melk nachweisbaren Chorknaben auf und liefert soziologisch interessantes Material, da (soweit bekannt) die Berufe der Väter angegeben sind. Appendix B besteht aus einem Katalog der in Melk aufgeführten Theater- und Gelegenheitswerke (1686-1785), in dem neben Titel, Nachweisen und Signaturen, Textdichter und Komponist auch Aufführungsanlaß, Rollen- und Sängernamen und Literaturverweise zu finden sind - ein unentbehrliches Werkzeug für jeden, der sich mit dem klösterlichen Theaterwesen des 17. und 18. Jahrhunderts befaßt. Auf 150 Seiten folgt schließlich Appendix C mit allen von Freeman festgestellten musikhistorisch bedeutsamen Textstellen aus den Stiftsdokumenten in der Originalsprache, wobei auf die Wiederholung von bereits zuverlässig edierten Texten verzichtet wurde. Die Zitate (nach den Richtlinien des Deutschen Geschichts- und Altertumsvereins übertragen) sind chronologisch angeordnet und tragen eine aus Jahreszahl und laufender Nummer zusammengesetzte Verweisnummer, an deren Gebrauch der Leser sich schnell gewöhnt. Dank der Vielfalt der Exzerpte, die sowohl Honorarabrechnungen wie Augenzeugenberichte von großen Festlichkeiten, Briefe wie Rechnungen über neu angeschaffte Instrumente umfassen, ist dieser Anhang kein 'totes Kapital': Auch nach der Lektüre von Freemans sorgfältiger Aufarbeitung und Interpretation dieses immensen Fundus bereitet es großes Vergnügen, in den Texten zu stöbern - besonders, wenn der Leser des Lateinischen mächtig ist und die Auszüge aus den 'Priorats-Ephemeriden' bewältigen kann. Daß eine unter den Auspizien der Österreichischen Akademie der Wissenschaften veröffentlichte Schrift ein Quellen- und Literaturverzeichnis sowie einen Personen- und Ortsindex enthält, braucht kaum erwähnt zu werden; hingewiesen werden sollte aber darauf, daß die Ausstattung des Buches mit 2 Farbtafeln und 41 Schwarzweißabbildungen bzw. Noten beispielen auch optisch dazu beiträgt, ein geschlossenes Bild von Stift Melk und seinen musikalischen Bewohnern zu vermitteln. Insgesamt lassen Druckqualität und Layout keine Wünsche offen.

Mit Freemans Arbeit liegt eine beispielhafte Studie zum Musikleben eines der bedeutendsten österreichischen Klöster in seiner Glanzzeit vor, die nicht nur Musikhistorikern, sondern auch Theaterwissenschaftlern, Soziologen und Volkskundlern eine Fülle von Informationen bietet. Es wäre zu wünschen, daß auch in anderen Klöstern ähnliche Darstellungen entstünden, um Vergleiche auf breiterer Basis als bisher zu ermöglichen. Eine Institution wie Stift Melk ist, das zeigt Freeman an vielen Einzelheiten, immer noch eine Schatztruhe für die Musikwissenschaft.

D. S.

Vignal, Marc. *Joseph Haydn.* Paris: Librairie Arthème Fayàrd (*Bibliothèque des Grands Musiciens*), 1988. 1534 pp.

During Haydn's lifetime his music was remarkably popular among French audiences. The earliest Haydn prints, though not authentic, appeared from the Parisian house of Chevardière in 1764. His Stabat Mater was received with special approbation by the Parisian public. Concert series in Paris and the provinces performed Haydn's music, and Claude-François-Marie Rigoley, Comte d'Ogny, a sponsor of 'Le Concert de la Loge Olympique', commissioned the six so-called 'Paris' Symphonies (Nos. 82-87) as well as Nos. 90-92, which the composer simultaneously sold to the Prince Krafft-Ernst of Oettingen-Wallerstein. The French took to Haydn's late works with the same enthusiasm found throughout Europe. With the establishment of Haydn's student Ignaz Pleyel as one of the leading Parisian publishers, a complete edition of the so-called 'eighty-three' string quartets was engraved and, despite its bibliographic problems, remained the standard for determining the composer's contribution to this repertoire until after the Second World War.

French scholarship and criticism of Haydn's output have hardly reflected the composer's popularity. Granted, there were the diplomas presented to the old Haydn by the French Institut and Paris Conservatory (1805) and there were two posthumous tributes at the Institut: on 6 October 1810 Joachim Le Breton gave his lecture, which was subsequently published, based mainly on Dies and Griesinger, and the same year Nicolas Étienne Framery gave a similar speech, which presented new information supplied by Pleyel. The well-known biography (1814) by Stendhal (Marie Henri Beyle) was plagiarized from Giuseppe Carpani's *Le Haydine* (1812), a work oriented more toward aesthetic matters than a clear and orderly presentation of the life and works. It was not until 1839 that François Joseph Fétis synthesized this material for his Haydn article in the *Biographie universelle*; he considered both French and German (Griesinger, Dies and Gerber) sources. After a hiatus of three decades, Hippolyte Barbadette's Haydn survey (1874) provided new information on the commissioning of the 'Paris' Symphonies.

The hundredth anniversary of Haydn's death in 1809 prompted two studies that were to have international influence: 1) Michel Brenet, a first-class scholar, presented a new biography of modest length that was subsequently translated into English (1925) and provided with a laudatory preface by Sir Henry Hadow; and 2) Théodore de Wyzewa writing in the *Revue de deux monde*, established the idea that those symphonies in a minor key from the late 1760s and early 1770s were manifestations of a 'romantic crisis' in Haydn's life. It came to be called his 'Sturm und Drang' period. For almost eighty years since this centenary, neither a major study of Haydn's life and works, nor any compelling critical essay appeared from a French writer until Marc Vignal's book under discussion here. Thus, this volume is a landmark in French Haydn studies and one that bids favourable comparison with any of the available books on the composer.

Vignal's book is the product of an involvement with Haydn for more than three decades beginning with a 1961 essay in the keyboard music and a 1964 short life and works. In the interim, he has published a series of articles and reviews, the latter often penetrating in their observations. *Joseph Haydn,* as the book is directly titled, is the biggest and most thorough exposition in a single volume and the most extensive survey ever to appear in French. It also ranks among the most solid and detailed of any one-volume Haydn study. More than fifteen hundred pages are divided into two nearly equal parts, the first dealing with the life and the second with the music. The life is laid out in fourteen chapters:

1. Haydn à Rohrau, Hainburg et Vienne (1732-1761)
2. Les Esterházy avant 1761
3. Haydn à Eisenstadt (1761-1766)
4. Eszterháza
5. Haydn à Eszterháza (1766-1775)
6. La diffusion des œuvres de Haydn jusque vers 1780
7. Haydn à Eszterháza (1776-1784)
8. Haydn à Eszterháza (1784-1790)
9. Haydn à Londres (1791-1792)
10. Haydn à Vienne (1792-1794)
11. Haydn à Londres (1794-1795)
12. Haydn à Vienne et à Eisenstadt (1795-1799)
13. Haydn à Vienne et à Eisenstadt (1800-1803)
14. Haydn à Gumpendorf (1804-1809)

Though no biography after Landon's *Haydn: Chronicle and Works* can avoid a deep debt to his compendium of documents, Vignal chooses his material carefully and cogently in order to focus directly on Haydn, as compared with Landon's more expansive treatment of the composer and his time. Additionally, Vignal uses and integrates all of the post-Landon research into his narrative, which results in a biography that more than any other reflects (as of 1988) the current state of knowledge. All of these additions are documented in marginal notes, which are also for identifications of other characters and for further explanations that would otherwise clutter the main text.

The most notable aspect of the biographical part concerns the dissemination of Haydn's works up to c.1780 (Chapter 6). Here, Vignal provides a notable overview of not only the copies and their distribution, but also the music's reception in North and Central Germany, France, England and Spain. In the following chapter, the author cites the new contract that Haydn signed with the Prince Esterházy on 1 January 1779, deleting the provision of the 1761 agreement that Haydn was to compose exclusively for his patron. This began a new phase in Haydn's life; he could now sell his music on the open market. Vignal fails to emphasize the significance of this change; beginning in 1780, Haydn sold his music in Vienna to Artaria and quickly expanded his dealings to publishing houses in other centres.

Vignal's other non-biographical chapters in part one are simply titles 'Les Esterházys avant 1761' (Chapter 2) and 'Eszterháza' (Chapter 4). The latter begins with an appropriate appellation 'Le Versailles de Nicolas le Magnifique'. Included is much of the material Landon took up in his chronicle, except that Vignal's is, by necessity, a tighter presentation of information about the princely household and its operation. The chapter concludes with a series of eyewitness views of this marshland castle by Baron Riesbeck (1783), Johann Friedel (1784) and the extended description by Johann Ferdinand Schönfeld (1784), *Excursion à Esterhaz en Hongrie en Mai 1784*.

The biographical chapters are consistently strong in their presentation of essential documents and the standard outline of Haydn's life, whether it be the early years in Hainburg and Vienna, the three decades in the Esterházy employ, the two London sojourns, or the Viennese final years. Advocates of the new historicism will want more embellishment of the facts and will certainly be disappointed. However, Haydn is not a figure easily subjected to psychological interpretations, or what Dika Newlin, perhaps more appropriately, has called necropsychiatry. Unlike Mozart or Beethoven, Haydn was not subjected to the stresses of a *Wunderkind*, was not exploited or nagged by overbearing parents, and did not have any perceived adolescent crisis. Haydn's letters, except for a few, do not reveal any stresses, much less psychological abnormalities. It would be difficult to cultivate him as a fertile field for a psychoanalytical biography. Perhaps the only area open for discussion was the composer's unfulfilling marriage and the lack of a family unit. Nevertheless, the author might have placed more emphasis on the sort of anti-Papa Haydn revisionism found in Georg Feder's admirable 1972 article, 'Joseph Haydn als Mensch und Musiker'.

Part two, 'L'œuvre', is one of the most complete surveys of the works found in any single volume. Its organization approximates that of the biography, but the boundries are by necessity not so firmly defined because of the less than secure dates for many of Haydn's composition (e.g. 'L'œuvre de Haydn jusque 1765'). Vignal does not try to formulate a cross-genre chronology, but instead within each period takes up each category in a roughly chronological order. Pratically every work is discussed at some point and often with some acumen; only a few of the baryton works do not find a place. Otherwise, every composition seems to have at least a statement or paragraph, whether it be a barebones accounting of songs or insertion arias or the more extended comments allotted to the symphonies, overtures, quartets, and solo and ensemble keyboard sonatas. Vignal refrains from a number by number account of the operas; instead, he provides a summary of the action, and highlights the more notable moments.

Any potential user of this tome who already owns Landon's five volumes would ask how Vignal's discussion of individual works differs. Surprisingly, the author duplicates little of what Landon pursues, so that any reader can use both books and gain a fuller sense of the music and its background. This can be demonstrated by reproduing their paragraphs on the so-called *Divertimento à Tre* (Hob.IV:5). First to Landon (pp.348-49):

> By some miracle, this work has survived in autograph (the only known source), dated 1767 and now in British private possession. Its two movements are, of course, intended primarily as a virtuoso vehicle for the horn player, and the roles of the violinist and cellist are secondary. It is now thought that the cruelly difficult horn part - ascending to sounding *a flat* " in the first movement - was written for Carl Franz, who was the principal first horn in the band from 9 April 1763 to November 1776. This theory, advanced by Paul Bryan, gains plausibility if we examine Franz's own copy of the Quintet (X:10) which is discussed *infra* (p.355), and where the technical demands on the

player are equally formidable and very much of the same kind. On the whole, Haydn in this Trio utilizes the bright side of the horn's multi-faceted nature, though there are also pedal notes (in the bass clef) which require a rapid shifting of the embrochure.

And then Vignal (p.937):

> Cette œuvre nous est parvenue par une seule source: son manuscript autographe, daté de 1767 et intitulé *Divertimento a tre per il Corno di Caccia.* Actuellement de possession privée en Angleterre, cet autographe fut offert par Haydn à la fin de sa vie au corniste princier Michael Prinster, qui lui-même en fit plus tard cadeau à un ami de Györ (Raab) en précisant: ". . .trio pour cor, violon et violoncelle que notre bienheureux Haydn-Papa a écrit pour un de mes prédécesseurs" (sans doute pas Thaddäus Steinmüller, comme le crut Pohl, mais plutôt Carl Franz). Inscrite en bas de la page 14 de l'*EK* sans incipit et sous l'indication *Trio per il Corno* di Caccia (plus tard rayée et remplacée par *Trio per il Corno*), l'œuvre fut publiée pour la première fois par Landon en 1957, d'après l'autographe. Cet autographe était allé peu avant 1877 de Györ à Vienne, où Pohl avait pu le voir, puis en 1901 en Angleterre, où Tovey, dans son important article sur la musique de chambre de Haydn paru en 1929, avait atirré l'attention sur lui. Deux movements se succèdent, marqués respectivement moderato assai (thème suivi de trois variations) Tovey écrivit d'un ton admiratif dans l'article susdit qu'elles contenaient "des passages pour cor faisant apparaître presque faciles les envolées les plus redoutables de Bach."

The replications and contrasts found here as well as their complementarity reveal Vignal's resourcefulness. In many instances he does take over ideas from the existing literature, but he effectively absorbs and recycles them.

As in the biographical first section, the author introduces several chapters that depart from the mainly descriptive and analytical aspects. 'Les Origines' is an overview of eighteenth-century musical historiography. Vignal takes up such issues as the Baroque/Classical dichotomy as represented by J. S. Bach and Haydn, and the theories about the origins of the so-called Classical style and the 'predecessors' of Haydn as argued nationalistically by Riemann for Mannheim, Adler and Fischer for Vienna and Torrefranca for Italy. He examines

Viennese developments using Larsen's model of Baroque, Mid-century and Classical phases. The author correctly views Haydn on a grand scale as personally and dynamically coming between the end of the Baroque and the beginning of Romanticism. Viewed most expansively, Haydn generated a tradition extending to the beginning of the twentieth century.

Another critical chapter is an intermezzo titled 'En guise d'intermède': la haute maturité de Haydn'. Using this reviewer's 1976 *Musical Quarterly* article as a point of departure, Vignal expands his remarks to a survey of critical opinion of the music from the 1780s and beyond. Cited here are views as diverse in time, place and perspective as Johann Friedrich Reichardt, Wilhelm Heinrich Riehl, Robert Schumann, Richard Wagner, Johannes Brahms, Donald Francis Tovey and Carl Dahlhaus. Again, the author's resourcefulness is in evidence; Vignal complements rather than duplicates the parallel section at the end of Landon's *Haydn: Chronicle and Works*.

Physically, this is a thick book, nearly two-and-a-half inches, and it has been produced with a sewn binding to withstand the stress of its weight. The bibliography is thorough, and much of the material within it is cited in the text. Likewise, the index seems carefully executed, and Vignal wisely combines the work-list with the index of works. A number of typographical slips should be corrected in subsequent printings. A major disappointment is the absence of illustrations, not even a frontispiece portrait of the composer; once the dust jacket is worn out with its handsome colour reproduction of the Hardy portrait, the reader will have no pictorial means of identifying the person who elicited such a flood of discussion.

Vignal's audience is first and foremost the French reader, whether he or she be the amateur musical connoisseur or the non-specialist musical scholar. But to consign this book to a circle confined by language is unfair to its author and the prodigious effort that went into its research and writing. It is bigger and more complete than the Landon/Wyn Jones single-volume presentation (1988), which is admirably aimed at the educated amateur, and certainly more up-to-date than Geiringer's (1982) overview, which found its first inception in 1932. And Vignal often has something different to say from his competitors, making it worthy of regular consultation. For those who will own only a one-volume life and works, Vignal offers more than any other.

A. P. B.

La Création
Discographie

Elisabeth Grümmer (Gabriel, Eve), Josef Traxel (Uriel), Gottlob Frick (Raphael, Adam). Choeur de la cathédrale Sainte-Hedwige et Orchestre Symphonique de Berlin. Wolfgang Meyer (clavecin). Direction: Karl Forster. 2xCD EMI 7 62595-2. Enregistré en janvier-février 1960.

Gundula Janowitz (Gabriel, Eve), Fritz Wunderlich & Werner Krenn (Uriel), Walter Berry (Raphael), Dietrich Fischer-Dieskau (Adam), Christa Ludwig (solo du n° 34). Wiener Singverein et Orchestre Philharmonique de Berlin. Joseph Nebois (clavecin), Ottomar Borwitzky (violoncelle). Direction: Herbert von Karajan. 2xCD DG 435 077-2. Enregistré de 1966 à 1969.

Norma Burrowes (Gabriel), Sylvia Greenberg (Eve), Rudiger Wohlers (Uriel), James Morris (Raphael), Siegmund Nimsgern (Adam). Choeur Symphonique et Orchestre Symphonique de Chicago. David Schrader (clavecin), Frank Miller (violoncelle), Joseph Gustafeste (contrebasse). Direction: Sir Georg Solti. 2xCD Decca 430 473-2. Enregistré en novembre 1981.

Edith Mathis (Gabriel, Eve), Francisco Araiza (Uriel), José van Dam (Raphael, Adam). Wiener Singverein et Orchestre Philharmonique de Vienne. Jean-Pierre Faber (clavecin), Robert Scheiwein (violoncelle), David Bell (orgue). Direction: Herbert von Karajan. 2xCD DG 410 718-2. Enregistré en 1982.

Krisztina Laki (Gabriel, Eve), Neil Mackie (Uriel), Philippe Huttenlocher (Raphael, Adam). Collegium Vocale de Gand. La Petite Bande. Direction: Sigiswald Kuijken. 2xCD Accent 58228/9 D. Enregistré en octobre 1982.

Edith Gruberova (Gabriel, Eve), Josef Protschka (Uriel), Robert Holl (Raphael, Adam). Choeur Arnold-Schönberg et Orchestre Symphonique de Vienne. Herbert Tachezi (pianoforte), Walter Schulz (violoncelle). Direction: Nikolaus Harnoncourt. 2xCD Teldec 8.35722 ZA. Enregistré en avril 1986.

Judith Blegen (Gabriel), Lucia Popp (Eve), Thomas Moser (Uriel), Kurt Moll (Raphael), Kurt Ollmann (Adam). Choeur et Orchestre Symphonique de la Radio de Bavière. Hedwig Bilgram (clavecin). Direction: Leonard Bernstein. 2xCD DG 419 765-2. Enregistré en juin 1986.

Kathleen Battle (Gabriel, Eve), Gösta Winbergh (Uriel), Kurt Moll (Raphael, Adam). Choeur de la Radio et Choeur de Chambre de Stockholm, Orchestre Philharmonique de Berlin. Frank Maus (clavecin). Direction: James Levine. 2xCD DG 427 629-2. Enregistré en décembre 1987.

Emma Kirkby (Gabriel, Eve), Anthony Rolfe Johnson (Uriel), Michael George (Raphael, Adam). Choeur du New College d'Oxford, Choeur et Orchestre de l'Academy of Ancient Music, (Kym Ampf, mezzo soprano solo). Direction: Christopher Hogwood. 2xCD Oiseau-Lyre 430 397-2. Enregistré en février 1990.

Arleen Auger (Gabriel, Eve), Philip Langridge (Uriel), David Thomas (Raphael, Adam). Choeur et Orchestre de la ville de Birmingham. Harry Bickett (pianoforte), Ulrich Heinen (violoncelle), John Tattersdill (contrebasse). Direction: Simon Rattle. 2xCD EMI 7 54159-2. Enregistré en mars-avril 1990.

Parmi les grandes oeuvres vocales, *La Création*, est de celles ayant fait l'objet d'un nombre très élevé d'enregistrements. Elle est dépassée sur ce plan par le *Requiem* de Mozart, mais on en compte bien une quarantaine depuis la version de Clemens Kraus diffusée en 1949 par la Haydn Society (l'exécution proprement dite remonte à quelques années plus tôt). Plus de vingt sont actuellement disponibles en CD. Cette discographie abondante est due à la très bonne réputation dont jouit l'oeuvre actuellement (il ne se passe guère d'année sans qu'une ville comme Paris n'en entende deux ou trois exécutions, et la province française ne demeure pas en reste), mais aussi au fait qu'elle n'est pas trop longue et ne présente pas de grosses difficultés. *La Création* a eu, en général, de la chance au disque. Les versions franchement détestables sont pour ainsi dire inexistantes.

Certaines n'en sont pas moins particulièrement précieuses. Les deux derniers enregistrements de *La Création* critiqués dans ces colonnes ont été ceux de Dorati (HYB vol. XI) et de Marriner I (HYB vol. XIII). Je n'y reviendrai pas, sinon pour rappeler que H. C. R. L.

considérait alors (1982) Marriner I (Philips) comme sa version favorite, et que l'une et l'autre ont été rééditées en CD (Dorati chez Decca). En l'année Haydn 1982, les éditeurs n'ont pas craint d'ajouter à celles qui existaient ou avaient existé (environ une vingtaine) cinq versions supplémentaires: celles d'Armin Jordan (Erato), de Gustav Kühn (Harmonia Mundi), de Solti (Decca), de Karajan II (DG) et de Sigiswald Kuijken (Accent). Il s'agissait encore de microsillons, mais ces cinq versions sauf celle de Gustav Kühn ont été rééditées en CD. Depuis, au moins neuf versions nouvelles ont paru: celles de Kubelik (Orfeo), Harnoncourt (Teldec), Hogwood (Oiseau-Lyre), Bernstein II (DG), Marriner II (EMI), Atzmon (BIS), Rattle (EMI), Levine (DG) et Robert Shaw (Telarc), toutes bien sûr en CD. Trois d'entre elles (Hogwood, Rattle, Shaw), comme jadis celle de Willcocks, sont en anglais. Ont été rééditées en CD, outre les six mentionnées ci-dessus, celles de Clemens Kraus (Preiser), Günter Wand (Accord), Karl Forster (EMI), Karajan I (DG), Münchinger (Decca), Jochum (Philips), Bernstein I (Sony), Markevitch (DG), Gönnenwein (Vox) et Willcocks (EMI). D'autres, comme celles de Helmut Koch (Eterna), Horenstein (Vox) ou Frühbeck de Burgos (EMI), ont disparu. Cette énumération comporte certainement des lacunes, et il est évident que dans le cadre de cet article, il est impossible de tout traiter.

Sur les vingt-cinq versions recensées en CD, je n'en conserverai que dix, citées en tête de cet article dans l'ordre où elles ont été enregistrées. Parmi les quinze autres, deux restent cependant hors concours. Je ne saurais pour ma part m'en passer. Ce sont celles de Clemens Kraus, au parfum de légende (la première jamais réalisée), magnifiée notamment par Julius Patzak et Georg Hann, et d'Igor Markevitch (enregistrée en 1957) avec Irmgard Seefried, Richard Holm et Kim Borg. Les treize autres ont été rejetées pour diverses raisons dans les détails desquelles on ne saurait entrer ici. Jochum (1966) est assez lourd, et Gottlob Frick est moins convaincant avec lui qu'avec Foster. Chez Wand (1964), les solistes sont pâles, et la prise de son confuse. A la réaudition, Müchinger (1967) déçoit. Bernstein I (1966), assez brutal, n'atteint pas (et de loin) les dimensions spirituelles de Bernstein II. Le même reproche peut être adressé à Antal Dorati (1977), qui, comme Jordan (1981), d'ailleurs de nouveau supprimé, réussit davantage *Les Saisons*. Kubelik (1984) et Atzmon (1990) sont oubliables, Shaw (1992) souffre de ses solistes, et Marriner II (1989) reste sagement "classique".

Les dix versions retenues l'ont été pour leurs qualités, mais aussi, pour quelques-unes, parce qu'elles sont récentes et dues à des chefs faisant leurs débuts en la matière. Karl Forster, chef de choeur plutôt que chef d'orchestre, a signé vers 1960 de remarquables enregistrements de pages sacrées de Bach, Mozart, Haydn, Bruckner et autres. Sa *Création* n'a rien perdu de son impact. On admire tout d'abord un des plus beaux trios de solistes jamais réunis pour cette oeuvre, Josef Traxel et Gottlob Frick ne le cédant en rien à la merveilleuse Elisabeth Grümmer, et l'on ne peut que se montrer convaincu par Forster lui-même, un de ceux qui surent rendre justice à la dimension sacrée de la partition. Sa version, rééditée en série économique, se situe parmi les meilleures.

Aux deux versions "commerciales" de Karajan, réalisées à une quinzaine d'années d'intervalle, s'en ajoute sous sa direction une troisième, plus ancienne (*live* à Salzbourg en août 1965, parue chez Hunt en 1989). Elle bénéficie d'excellents solistes (Janowitz, Wunderlich, Borg, Prey), mais est mutilée par plusieurs coupures (choeur final, où les solistes n'apparaissent pas). Des deux versions commerciales, la première fut réalisée en studio, mais étalée sur plusieurs années en raison de la mort de Fritz Wunderlich, remplacé dans certains numéros par Werner Krenn. La seconde est un *live* salzbourgeois. Cette version Karajan II confirme les profondes affinités du chef avec *La Creation*. La conception n'a pas fondamentalement évolué depuis Karajan I, et il serait vain de vouloir comparer ici les mérites respectifs de la Philharmonie de Vienne (Karajan II) et de celle de Berlin (Karajan I), l'une et l'autre permettant tout autant que la formation réduite d'un Kuijken d'admirer la science prodigieuse que possédait Haydn de l'instrumentation. Les différences tiennent en partie à celles existant entre le concert et le studio. Dans Karajan II, 'Die Himmel erzählen' est d'une véhémence à couper le souffle, on voit déjà Verdi - compositeur d'élection de Karajan - se profiler à l'horizon. Le début du dernier choeur ('Singt dem Herrn alle Stimmen') est d'une grandeur indicible, mais pour des raisons opposées, Karajan adoptant un tempo extrêmement large ouvrant toutes grandes les portes de l'éternité. Cela dit, les solistes satisfont davantage dans Karajan I (où ils sont cinq, et même six), sauf peut-être en ce qui concerne José van Dam. La version Karajan I, plus que toute autre sans doute, réussit à donner à chaque numéro de *La Création* un éclairage unique. Elle s'impose en priorité.

Outre *La Création*, Karajan a enregistré, de Haydn, *Les Saisons* en 1972 ainsi que, après quelques symphonies isolées, les six *Parisiennes* et les douze *Londoniennes* de 1980 à 1982. Solti a enregistré quant à lui *La Création* en 1981, et les douze *Londoniennes* de 1981 à 1991. Il est intéressant de voir ces deux chefs s'intéresser à Haydn, en le présentant sous des jours très différents il est vrai, en fin de carrière (Claudio Arrau lui aussi envisageait de se consacrer à lui). On n'oublie pas pour autant les quelques symphonies gravées par Solti dans les années 1950. On a reproché à Solti de présenter *La Création* avec des véhémences exagérées et des gestes trop péremptoires. Ces reproches sont injustifiés étant donné le contexte historique et artistique dans lequel l'oeuvre fut écrite et exécutée, cela sans oublier l'attitude et les gestes de Haydn quand il la dirigeait (cf. Griesinger dans l'*AMZ* du 15 janvier 1800). *La Création* de Solti est ample, puissante, grandiose, avec des tempos étonnamment retenus dans certains airs ('Leise rauschend'), plutôt rapides dans certains choeurs ('Die Himmel erzählen'). Mais Solti ne travaille pas qu'à grands traits. On admire aussi un accompagnement orchestral souvent d'une extrême finesse, due aussi bien à la virtuosité des membres de l'Orchestre Symphonique du Chicago qu'à la volonté du chef. Un bon exemple en est l'air 'Rollend in schäumenden Wellen', avec d'extraordinaires poussées incisives des violons. On est pris également par le remarquable *pianissimo* des violoncelles et des contrebasses lors de la naissance de la lune. Il est impossible, après avoir entendu cette version très vivante, d'accuser Solti de manquer de subtilité et de ne s'intéresser qu'aux effets de masse. Les solistes sont bons, sans se situer au tout premier rang.

Comme celles de Jordan et de Kühn (supprimées), la version Kuijken est à effectifs réduits. Des trois, c'est la plus radicale. Elle seule fait penser, par exemple, aux premiers enregistrements de Bach par Harnoncourt, en particulier à sa *Passion selon saint Matthieu*. Je comprends qu'on puisse s'enthousiasmer pour cette réalisation, lui trouver un pouvoir décapant, et estimer que *La Création* en sort transfigurée pour le mieux. Et de fait, bien plus que les versions Jordan et Kühn, elle donne une impression de jamais entendu. Il n'y a que quinze violons, cinq altos, quatre violoncelles et une contrebasse. Comme chez Kühn, on est déçu par le récitatif 'Seid fruchtbar alle . . . Mehret euch', à cause de manque de cordes graves, et on regrette également que dans le duo avec choeur 'Von deiner Güt' de la troisième partie, les cordes jouent de façon si détachée (typique des 'baroqueux', mais ne convenant pas à ce passage précis). Le "Chaos" manque de mystère, mais les timbales, là comme ailleurs, sont percutantes à souhait, et les choeurs débordent de vigueur et d'enthousiasme. Parmi les solistes, Philippe Huttenlocher apparaît plus à l'aise qu'avec Jordan. Une version qu'en tout cas il faut connaître.

Kuijken est *live*, Harnoncourt et Bernstein II également. Harnoncourt n'a pas réalisé une version archaïsante avec instruments anciens, mais utilise un orchestre "moderne" à assez grands effectifs, avec comme résultat une *Création* puissante, mais pas écrasante. Certains détails surprendront, liés ou non à l'exécution *live*, comme les silences avant les interventions de l'orchestre dans 'Und Gott machte das Firmament', ou enore les débuts de fugue dans la nuance *piano* ('Stimmt an die Saiten'). Même l'accord final de l'ouvrage est légèrement retenu. On s'y fait, mais on aurait aimé, pour les quatre accords finaux de la première partie, voir Harnoncourt conserver le rythme. Contrairement à ce que l'on pouvait redouter, il n'y a jamais de précipitation dans les tempos, le 'Chaos' est un des plus impressionnants de l'histoire du disque, et peu de versions font aussi nettement ressortir les couleurs si variées de l'orchestre haydnien. Les récitatifs "secs" sont accompagnés au pianoforte, comme déjà chez Kraus. Des solistes, le meilleur est Robert Holl, les deux autres peinant parfois quelque peu, Edita Gruberova dans les aigus et Josef Protschka par son timbre.

Je ne suis pas du tout d'accord avec mon collègue du 'Gramophone' de Londres, qui lors de la parution de la version Bernstein II, l'a "descendue en flammes", la trouvant trop lourde, trop romantique, etc. Certes, on a là une interprétation puissante et à gros effectifs, mais Haydn n'y était pas opposé, bien au contraire. Surtout, il se dégage de l'interprétation de Bernstein une force de conviction à nulle autre pareille, tant sur le plan spirituel que purement musical. On peut dire la même chose à propos d'Harnoncourt, mais Bernstein pousse cette synthèse encore plus loin. Il évite tout maniérisme, même lorsqu'il se permet - par exemple avant le fugue finale de la première partie - un ralentissement "expressif". Et il n'a pas son égal, aidé en cela par la prise de son, pour faire sonner comme il convient trompettes et timbales, presque "à la Verdi", mais sans brutalité, de façon parfaitement intégrée à l'ensemble sonore. Les tempos sont plutôt larges, ce qui n'est pas un mal, sauf dans 'Die Himmel erzählen', qui traîne un peu. Seul le choeur final de la troisième partie 'Des Herren Ruhm, er bleibt in Ewigkeit' est franchement "enlevé", et on ne s'en plaint pas. On peut dans certain épisodes préférer Karajan ou Harnoncourt, mais le souffle qui parcourt Bernstein II ne se retrouve nulle part ailleurs ('Der Herr ist gross in seiner Macht'). C'est splendide, et l'on regrette que ce chef ne nous ait pas donné aussi (comme Karajan, Harnoncourt et Kuijken) *Les Saisons*.

La version Levine, parue quatre ans après sa date d'enregistrement, s'inscrit dans la tradition des Karajan et autres Bernstein, et avec elle, DG possède cinq versions de *La Création* à son catalogue CD. Une comparaison de Levine avec Bernstein donne nettement l'avantage à ce dernier. Levine n'est pourtant pas sans qualités, et d'aucuns seront comblés par un "Chaos" impressionnant de lenteur et mystérieux à souhait, des choeurs puissants et aux plans larges, des solistes satisfaisants. Mais Bernstein, dans la même optique, offre encore davantage: des accents incisifs (l'orchestre dans 'Rollend in schäumenden Wellen'), un élan, une vitalité projetant littéralement la musique en avant (choeur final) et une dimension spirtuelle très prenante. En outre, les plans sonores resortent mieux chez Bernstein (trompettes dans le choeur final), et les solistes sont plus présents (il suffit de comparer à lui-même Kurt Moll, qui chante dans les deux versions). Bernstein est de loin préférable à Levine.

Les versions en anglais de Rattle et Hogwood n'utilisent pas exactement le même texte musical, le point important étant que Hogwood, utilisant la nouvelle 'performing edition' de A. Peter Brown, se conforme selon les passages soit à l'édition de 1800 (à laquelle se réfèrent exclusivement tous ses concurrents), soit au matériau en provenance des exécutions dirigées par Haydn en personne à partir de 1798. Pour le livret, l'un et l'autre reviennent à l'édition de 1800 (avec chez Rattle de minimes retouches dues à Nicholas Temperley), abandonnant les diverses "améliorations" qui ultérieurement lui furent apportées en Angleterre. Des deux interprétations, celle de Rattle n'est sans doute pas la meilleure en soi, mais elle subjugue davantage. Rattle tire de son orchestre des effets spectaculaires mais toujours en situation, par exemple lors des sept *ut* martelés vers le fin du "Chaos", ou lors de l'évocations du tonnerre (roulement de timbales *crescendo*) dans le récitatif n⁰ 3. Il s'agit d'une version "de chef", avec des choeurs splendides, plus puissante mais parfois moins allants ('Achieved is the glorious work') que chez Hogwood. L'orchestre est également magnifique dans les airs 'Now heaven in all her glory shines' et 'In native worth and honour clad'. Seule ombre au tableau: la basse David Thomas, qui suscite de nettes réserves. La version Hogwood fait appel à 120 instrumentistes et 80 chanteurs, pour recréer les sonoritées, l'échelle et la disposition spatiale des exécutions dirigées par Haydn à Vienne". Par rapport aux versions concurrentes entrant en considération, il n'en résulte pas une puissance accrue, mais (étant donné le type d'instruments utilisé) davantage de transparence, une texture sonore à la fois claire, articulée et voluptueuse. Paradoxalement, une certaine impression d'austérité se dégage également, en particulier en ce qui concerne les vents et les solistes vocaux dans les numéros à grands effectifs. La version Hogwood et de celles qui ne livrent tous leurs secrets qu'après plusieurs auditions, mais il est sûr qu'elle indique une direction qu'il faut continue d'explorer.

Au printemps 1989, j'ai participé pour la première fois à la fameuse émission "Disques en lice" de la Radio Télévision Suisse Romande, où sont comparés les mérites respectifs de divers enregistrements d'une même oeuvre. Le sujet était *La Création*, et deux versions se sont alors détachées (parmi celles existant en CD): Forster et Bernstein II, au détriment notamment de Harnoncourt, de Karajan II et de Kuijken. Karajan I et d'autres (Solti) n'étaient pas encore réédités, et on ne connaissait encore (entre autres) ni Hogwood, ni Rattle, ni Levine. Les deux versions anglaises mises à part, le seul événement de première importance qui se soit produit depuis est la réédition de Karajan I. Cette version domine la discographie, et c'est elle qui, avec celle de Forster, bénéficie du meilleur groupe de solistes. Bernstein II les rejoint dans le peloton de tête. Suivent à des titres divers, et sans qu'un ordre s'impose, Harnoncourt, Solti, Kuijken. Mais comment oublier Kraus? Ce bilan me semble honnête, mais je sais qu'il n'a rien d'obligatoire et qu'il peut, à tout instant, être remis en question.

M. V.

Haydn News

In a joint auction held at Basel on 19 September 1992 between J. Stargardt (Marburg: Berlin) and Erasmushaus - Haus der Bücher (Basel), an unpublished Haydn letter was sold as lot 461. It is a small note (one-third of a 4° page) to Charles Burney concerning a query about a textual problem in Metastasio, whose memoirs Burney was writing and for the publication (in 1796) of which Haydn had brought some engraved portraits of the Italian poet from Vienna. The letter seems to date from 1794 or 1795 and reads in part, '. . . Lei troverà poco differenza, mà la replica della 2da parte è tu chi sa se mai chi sa se mai. Son sicuro che Metastasio non ha fatto, poiche con questa repetizione il Rhytmo saria disuguale . . .' (You will see little difference, but the repetition of the second part is 'tu chi sa se mai chi sa se mai'. I'm sure Metastasio did not do that, because as a result of this repetition the rhythm is rendered unequal). The letter shows Haydn's profound knowledge of the Italian language. It was sold to an Austrian buyer for the astonishing price of Sfr. 20,000.

In the same auction was sold (lot 502) a letter from Haydn's pupil Ignaz Pleyel to Muzio Clementi dated 25 September 1801. Pleyel offers some violin pieces to Clementi and adds, 'Si vous pourriez m'envoyer quelque chose de vous, or de viotti vous me ferez bien plaisir, mais envoyez moi le proprieté bien en Regle, j'ai perdu mon proces envers le duc pour les quators d'Haydn parce que dans votre acte il se ne [*sic*] trouve pas copie de l'acte ou cession que Haydn vous a fait. . .'. This long affair regarding the Opus 76 Quartets has been only recently brought to light. One such document was published in the *Haydn Yearbook* VII (1970), pp.313ff. concerning Sieber's publication of the set in Paris in 1799. This letter fetched Sfr. 1900 and went to the music antiquarian Hans Schneider in Tutzing.

* * *

Haydn's *La vera costanza* was performed at the Garsington Festival near Oxford in the summer of 1992. *L'infedeltà delusa* at the Albi Festival in southwest France, a co-production with the Széged Opera in Hungary conducted by Tamás Pál in the summer of 1992, was completely sold out and the subject of much favourable comment in the Press. In 1993, Zomeropera of Holland is to produce *La fedeltà premiata*, which will tour in Holland, and parts of France, including the Besançon Festival in September 1993. Zomeropera have meanwhile recorded their successful production of *Die Feuersbrunst* on the Paladino label, conducted by Frank van Koten. *Il mondo della luna* (produced by Bernard Broca, conducted by Diego Masson) was performed several times at the Paris Conservatoire in June 1992. *Lo speziale* was given at the Festival of Périgord Noir in July 1992.

* * *

The sketch to Haydn's last string quartet, Op. 103, which was discussed by M. Jennifer Bloxam in the *Haydn Yearbook XIV* (1984), pp.129ff., was sold by

Christie's in London on 24 June 1992 (lot 1) and fetched £19,800. Haydn's letter to Artaria of 3 February 1784 was sold by Sotheby's in London on 29 May 1992: the autograph, sold on behalf of the National Trust, was reproduced in facsimile in the catalogue (lot 556), as was another Haydn letter in the same sale (lot 554) to Giovanni Battista Viotti dated 'Bury Street' (London), 19 December 1794, first transcribed and reproduced in *Haydn Yearbook IV*, p. 202. The latter was purchased by the Burgenländische Haydn Festival.

* * *

Sony Classical will continue its series of Haydn symphonies performed by the Canadian period orchestra, Tafelmusik, conducted by Bruno Weil, with Nos. 45, 46, 47, 50, 64, and 65, in other words with works of 1772 and 1773. Sony has also begun a series of CDs containing sacred music by Haydn, performed by the Tölzer Knabenchor and recorded in the Parish Church of Bad Tölz in Bavaria conducted by Bruno Weil. The first record, which will be issued in the spring of 1994, contains the hitherto unrecorded *Missa* 'Sunt bona mixta malis' of 1768, the *Ave Regina* in A (XXIIIb:3) with the French soprano Marie-Claude Vallen, the *Salve Regina* in E (XXIIIb:1), also hitherto unrecorded, the *Quatuor Responsoria de Venerabili* (XXIIIc:4 a-d), the *Libera (Responsorium ad absolutionem*, XXIIb:1), the *Offertorium* 'Non nobis, Domine' (XXIIIa:1) and the *Missa brevis S. Joannis de Deo*. A special recording consisting of the *Missa* 'Sunt bona mixta malis' and the Offertorium will be issued to the Press in the autumn of 1993. The same combination - Tölzer Knabenchor, Tafelmusik, Bruno Weil - will perform *The Creation* in the new edition by A. Peter Brown (Oxford) at the Irsee Festival in September 1993 and will subsequently record it at Bad Tölz. The last four piano trios by Haydn, Nos.42-45 (XV:27-30), performed by Robert Levin (fortepiano), Vera Beths (violin) and Anner Bylsma (violoncello) were issued by Sony in the spring of 1993.

* * *

The two series of Haydn symphonies on period instruments by the Academy of Ancient Music under Christopher Hogwood (Decca) and the Hanover Band under Roy Goodman (Hyperion) continue regularly and have received favourable reports in the international Press. Both series make it a rule to record the earliest versions of each work concerned (e.g. without the trumpets and timpani in No.90). There is a prominent continuo harpsichord in the Hyperion series but none in the Decca. A third series of all the Haydn symphonies, which has also been very favourably received, is that issued by Nimbus Records: the Austro-Hungarian Orchestra is conducted by Adam Fischer and the series is recorded in the Great Hall (Haydnsaal) of Eisenstadt Castle. Over half the works have already been issued. No continuo harpsichord is used.

* * *

The Haydn-Tage in Vienna, now in its tenth year, runs from 6 to16 March 1993. The programme includes sacred music in the Church of the Hospitallers conducted by Friedrich Lessky (*Schöpfungsmesse*, Michael Haydn 'Laudate populi', Offertorium, and Leopold Hofmann, whose bicentenary we celebrate this year, 'Beatus vir', Motetto; a concert of the Wiener Kammerphilharmonie conducted by Claudius Traunfellner (Brahmssaal, Symphonies Nos.34 and 44, piano concerto in D XVIII:II, György Ligeti 'Ramifications'); an organ recital with violin in the Salvatorkirche (Marianne Rönez, Baroque violin, Ernst Kubitchek, Baroque organ c.1750, the music by Haydn and his contemporaries and precursors); *The Seven Words* in the vocal version, Augustin Church, conducted by Friedrich Wolf; a church concert in the Piarist Church conducted by Gerhard Kramer with works by Wenzel Zivilhofer, the Requiem in G minor and other works by Gregor Joseph Werner and the Haydn *Te Deum for the Empress*; another service in the Hospitallers with the *Missa* 'Sunt bona mixta malis' and Reutter's 'Domine miserere'; another in the Augustin Chruch with Michael Haydn's *Missa Sanctae Crucis* and 'Tenebrae factae sunt'; a concert with the Arnold Schönberg Chor and the Concentus Musicus Wien conducted by Nikolaus Harnoncourt in the Musikverein, Großer Saal, Symphony No.59 ('Feuer') and the *Missa in tempore belli*; and a concert of baryton trios played by Christoph Coin on a baryton by Stadlmann, Vienna 1732, reported to be Haydn's own and since 1838 in the collection of the Gesellschaft der Musikfreunde, Vienna.

* * *

An enterprising record company called 'Opus 111' (based in France) have made the first commercial recording of Haydn's *Applausus* in co-production with the Conseil Régional de Picardie (OPS 61-9207/8, 2 CDs). The conductor is Patrick Fournillier. The project was also supported by the Fondation France-Télécom and the Ministry of Culture. There is a tri-lingual booklet of 48 pages with the album.

* * *

A new and highly important manuscript of Haydn's *Armida* has been discovered in the Italian antiquarian market and is now safely in private possession. It consists of the full score in two volumes of oblong format, written by an Esterházy copyist and with hundreds of holograph corrections in Haydn's own hand. In this respect it is similar to the authentic score of *La fedeltà premiata*, of which two further volumes have recently been discovered (see Haydn News in the previous *Haydn Yearbook XVII,* p.193). We are happy to reproduce here the beginning of the only complete copy of the the Aria 'Non vi sdegnate, mia signorina' from Act II of *La fedeltà premiata* as found in this new score - it was inserted into the main body of the score by a different copyist but before the whole was translated into German, since the German translation, added to the whole in red ink, is also present in 'Non vi sdegnate'. And to this we may add specimen pages of the new *Armida* score, showing a page with corrections in Haydn's hand, as well as the title page, written by copyist no. 63.

2 Corni in F.
Oboe 1mo
Oboa 2da
Viola 1ma
Viola 2da
Viole
Non vi Degnate
Basso.

Armida
Dramma Eroico
per Musica
Atto 1.mo

Del Sig.r Maestro Giuseppe Haydn

Corni in B fa
Oboe Imo
Oboe 2do
Flauto
Fagotti
Col Basso
Violino Imo
Violino 2do
Viola
Violoncello
Contra Bassi
Vivace
Cantabile
tenuto
pia:

Recitativo
2 Corni in E mol
Oboe 1mo
Oboe 2do
Fluuto
Fagotto
Violino 1mo
Violino 2do
Viola
Scena 21.
Ubaldo
Valorosi compagni nuovi perigli a superar vi guido. andiam....
Bassi
Presto
Allegro

* * *

In the *Sunday Times* Review of 27 December 1992, there was an interesting survey of Radio 3 and Classic FM in England by Paul Donovan. The most frequently played works in Radio 3 were, as usual, Beethoven, Brahms, Mozart and Tchaikovsky. 'For the fourth year running, no Bach, Vivaldi or Haydn manages to make it into the top 20. Haydn, however, is gradually gaining more exposure: 409 performances of his works in 1990, 435 in 1991 and 443 this year [1992], a figure likely to continue to increase when Radio 3 starts broadcasting all 104 of his symphonies on the breakfast show . . . Meanwhile, what of Classic FM, the cheap and cheerful interloper? It was unable to provide a similar record of all its musical output since it began on September 7, but . . . in that month there were 58 performances of Haydn works and 154 of Mozart which, extrapolated over a year, would add up to 696 and 1,848 - compared with Radio's 3's 443 and 823. In general, therefore, Classic FM is playing more than twice as many Mozart pieces as on Radio 3 and 64% as many Haydn pieces. . .' Classic FM now has some five million listeners (BBC's Radio 3 has about half that number), but the choice of music on Classic FM is determined by the reaction of the listeners, which reflects interestingly on Haydn. *Vox populi?*

* * *

Jordi Savall, whose new recording of the original (instrumental) version of *The Seven Words* with period instruments has been causing widespread positive reaction, has now decided to record Haydn's *Stabat Mater*. All three of Haydn's late oratorios have been receiving much attention from record companies: there are currently twenty versions of *The Creation* listed in The Classical Catalogue (published by *The Gramophone*) and even *The Seasons* has been much recorded of late (spectacularly by John Eliot Gardiner in a version prepared for the first time from the authentic performance material in the Vienna Rathaus which was discovered after the War). A new version is also being prepared by Roger Norrington for EMI).

* * *

Marc Vignal has discovered a ms. copy of Haydn's letter to Georg August Griesinger of 13 March 1803; it is owned by a private collector in Berlin and we reproduce it here is facsimilie. It was sold by J. A. Stargardt of Berlin on 26 November 1869 to a Herr Minden in Königsberg (now in Poland) and was described as an autograph, which it is not. Stargardt acquired it at an auction by List & Franke in Berlin as item 165 on 28 June 1869. As will be seen, the wording differs from that found in *Joseph Haydn Gesammelte Briefe und Aufzeichnungen* (ed. Dénes Bartha, 1965, p.421). The principal differences are: line one, remove 'von', line six, add, after 'tausendfachen' the words 'Verbundensten Danck' and the signature should read 'Ihr / gehorsamster d^r [Diener] / Jos: Haydn mpria / den 13^t Mertz 803'. The ms. is obviously a copy of the lost autograph.

Hochgeehrt. würdigster Herr Griesinger!

Aus unserem wohl überdachten Versprechen nehmlich die Übersendung meiner Gesänge an die Rußische Kayserin, kraut Herr Hartel durch baldige Herausgab seiner Nahmen desto geschwinder beförderen kan, ich bitte dennoch es Ihm sobald möglich zu bereiten.

Ihnen aber allerbester Herr v. Griesinger sage ich durch nachfolgen verbundensten Dank für alle mühe, so sie sich meinetwegen gegeben haben, und bin mit Vorzüglichster

Hochachtung

Ihr
gehorsamster dr.
Jos: Haydn

Jan 13t März 803

***

In the new Burney correspondence, Alvaro Ribeiro (ed.), *The Letters of Dr. Charles Burney* vol.1 Oxford: Clarendon Press, 1991, there are some hitherto unknown gems about Haydn both by Burney and by his friend the Rev. Thomas Twining, who on 5-6 July 1783 wrote

'Haydn & Boccherini spoil me for all other fiddle music. Haydn, I think, is much *oftener* charming than Boccherini. Yet when Boccherini *is at his best*, there is a force of *serious* expression, a pathos, that is not so much Haydn's fort, I think. I never see a *smile* upon Boccherini's face; he is all earnestness, & Tragedy. Haydn leans to Comedy: even in his adagio he is wanton, playful, & never forgets his *tricks*. -- It is, now & then, *serious* comedy, but seldom, I think, amounts to Tragedy, or even to the Comedie *larmoyante*. -- Not that I mean to find fault; he is, to me, delicious, & I wish for nothing better while I am playing him. For variety, & endless *resources*, I know no composer like him.'

Dr Burney, Haydn's stoutest champion, replied in a letter as follows:

'--I love Boccherini, as I have told you before very -- very much, but I think I shall live to make you eat your words about his pathetic being superior to Haydn's, whose fort you say is not pathos. I will undertake to prove, however, when we meet, that you have not seen his merit in adagio & Cantabile movements, for want of reading more of his music.'

to which Twining replies on 22 October:

'Sir? -- *eat my words?* -- "make me eat my words," I think you said? -- I fancy, Sir, you will not find that so easy. . . "When we meet" you say? -- But alas! when shall we meet? . . . as to my *words*, I scarce know what they were; - but I think I am yet upon firm ground; for I *do* not say, nor, I verily think *did* say, - that Haydn was *never* pathetic, or that he was *always* leaning to the comic - but only that, in his *general cast & manner*, Boccherini is a more serious, *earnest* composer.'

Referring to some quotations of Haydn's movements which we can no longer identify, Twining continues in the same letter:

'All the movements of Haydn you mention, I know very well; I allow them to be very fine, -- serious, & pathetic: -- but I spake of *general* style & character only; & it still appears to me that Boccherini's genius is Tragic, & that in Haydn the graceful, the fanciful, the enjoué, the playful &c. -- prevails upon the whole. -- Such is my idea still - not from obstinacy, Dieu scait -- but from the impression which these two charming composers make upon my ear & mind.'

In an extraordinary letter from Burney to Twining of 10-12 November 1783 we read a comparison of Haydn and Purcell, then little studied:

'-- do tell me, dear Friend - are you much aquainted wth Purcell? If you are not, for heaven's sake! get every note you possibly can of his, *curled* or *uncurled* -- why 'tis another Haydn. In the midst of barbarians, in savage times, before an opera, an opera singer, or the works of Corelli had been heard on the Island, to have such resources of force and expression, is more wonderful than that Haydn, who with his own property has incorporated the best of all others during the present century, sh^d be so perfect, so bewitching & Charming!!! - I shall speak of Purcell from an *actual survey*, or *review* of all his works. . .'

There is also an unknown description of Haydn by Clementi, preserved in Dr Burney's hand and which reads as follows; to it Burney attached another from the great singer Mara:

'Clementi, who saw him in Hungary at Prince Esterhausi's [*sic*] says he is a little, brown complexioned Man, turned of 50 -- wears a wig -- and when he hears any of his own Pieces performed that are capricious he laughs like a fool . . . The Mara says when any one praises him to his face, he runs away & hides himself. He is so modest & humble as to fear to quit the Prince of Esterhausi, lest he sh^d starve' (MS 'Materials Towards the History of German Music & Musicians', Osborn shelves c 100, p. 7).

To conclude this interesting series, there is the following exchange between Burney and Twining about Haydn and Boccherini:

Dr Burney to Twining, 10-12 November 1783:

'I'll allow that Boccherini is more constantly serious than Haydn -- nay that he is serious & Charming -- but in Haydn's works, more serious Compositions in the true gran Gusto, may be selected, than Boccherini has ever produced -- & then you will have all his fun, fancy, extravagant if you will & Capricious, for Gigantic players, *di plus* -- God bless 'em both, I say; but if I were forced to part with one of them -- I sh^d not hesitate a moment in locking Haydn fast in my Arms, & only sending a sign after the other'.

Twining to Burney, 22 October 1783:

'His [Haydn's] Quartetts spoil me for almost all other kind of music of the kind. There are, in *them* too, some very fine, *serious* Cantabiles; -- yet now & then in the midst of them, he takes a freak up to the top of the finger-board -- & then, (to *my* ear, at least) the charm is dissolved -- trick, caprice, & the difficulté vaincue, take place of expression & pathos. - It seems to me as if no composer, or player cou'd be in earnest, in *altissimo*: - it is not the climb-at/climate for it.'

Burney to Twining, 10-12 November 1783:
'What you say of high Notes is as true as it is punnish & Comical -- My Accomp^{ts} to Haydn are not yet out, though engraved -- but though I wrote them in a very short time, without a Score, except the two p^{ts} of the Lessons to look at -- I have left out bars, & blundered so much that some of the plates must be broken & newly engraved'.

Dr Burney tried to persuade Haydn to come to London for the Opera. In that letter of 10-12 November 1783 from Burney to Twining we read:
'Did I tell you that Gallini's agent shewed me a Letter from Haydn, in wch he was in treaty to come over for the opera -- all is in such Confusion now that there remains no hope, for this Winter -- but -- who knows, when I have mounted my *Ballon*, but he may yet come?'

To this we may add the following report from Burney's hand:
'In 1783, Gallini wrote to him [Haydn] to come over as Composer to the opera: I saw his answer, he asked £600. Gallini was then in Italy. Since that according to Fischer he had asked him £1000 for coming over expressly for the opera'. (MS 'Materials Towards the History of German Music & Musicians', Osborn shelves c100, p.7).

In a letter to Sir Robert Murray Keith, British Ambassador in Vienna, Burney writes on 8 November 1784 as follows:
'I had last year hopes that the admirable Haydn the chief ornament of the Vienna School & of the Age, w^{d} have made us a visit; If the universal admiration & performance of his works w^{d} be a temptation to visit us, I can as[s]ure him of that claim to his favour; but as to the opera, at present, its regency is in such confusion that it is hardly certain whether its existence will be ascertained during the ensuing Winter.'

* * *

The Orchestre National du Capitole of Toulouse, conducted by Michel Plasson, is to mount a large-scale Haydn Festival in Toulouse during the second half of October 1993. There will be several orchestral concerts, several devoted to chamber music, and a concert of sacred music in the Cathedral St. Étienne, with the *Te Deum for the Empress*, the *Missa* 'Sunt bona mixta malis' and the *Missa in tempore belli*. The other concerts will take place in the Théâtre du Capitole, where *Le pescatrici* will be staged. For tickets and information, write to Orchestre National du Capitole de Toulouse, Halle aux Grains, Place Dupuy, 31000 Toulouse. Telephone 61 22 24 40.

* * *

In February 1993, the Centre Culturel de l'Albigeois, in conjunction with the city of Angoulême, mounted a concert to celebrate the bicentenary of Carlo Goldoni's death in 1793. The concert was given several times, culminating in Albi, where it took place in the theatre and was recorded by Radio France. The Orchestra was Opus 16 from Angoulême, conducted by Jacques Pesi, with Florence Launey (soprano) and Didier Nicolle (flute). The programme included extracts from the three Goldoni libretti set by Haydn -- *Lo speziale* (1768), *Le pescatrici* (1770) and *Il mondo della luna* (1777), Mozart's Aria 'Voi avete un cor fidele' (Goldoni), the Flute Concerto in D by Piccinni (Rome 1769) and Boccherini's Symphony *La casa del diavolo*.

* * *

The Radio Suisse Romande in Geneva presented a series of five programmes devoted to the music of Johann Michael Haydn. The series was produced by Luc Terrapon and devised by Marc Vignal, and was the largest radio series on Michael Haydn's music ever broadcast (it was transmitted in five hourly programmes in January 1993). The music included concertos, symphonies, smaller church music, two Requiems, masses, string quartets and quintets, and other chamber music.

* * *

In the March 1993 issue of the new *BBC Music Magazine*, there is an article (p.86) entitled 'Classical countdown', in which the most popular composers of Radio 3 are listed, both for 1992 and for 1991. The first top six are, in order of the numbers of works broadcast, Mozart (812), Beethoven (588), Schubert (571), Bach (550), Haydn (448), and Brahms (375), followed by Handel, Dvorak, Chopin, etc. The first six composers remained unchanged in 1991 and 1992 (in 1991 the order of the following composers had been Debussy, Liszt and Stravinsky, while Handel had, in 1991, been 20th).

* * *

The Haydn Tage 1993 at Eisenstadt will take place between 10 and 19 September 1993 and will include concerts by the Canadian orchestra Tafelmusik under Bruno Weil as well as the Hanover Band under Roy Goodman. For further details please write to; Büro der Burgenländische, Haydnfestspiele, Schloss Esterházy, A7000 Eisenstadt. Tel: (43) (0)2682 618660 Fax: (43) (0)2682 61805

* * *

In the 1993/4 season of the Gesellschaft der Musikfreunde, Vienna, the programmes include thirteen performances of twelve Haydn symphonies, one concerto (cello in D), extracts from *L'anima del filosofo* (Harnoncourt), eight string quartets and one piano trio -- a much increased percentage of Haydn over what one would have expected even ten years ago. These programmes do not include the items to be played during the Haydntage 1994.

* * *

The world's largest collection of letters by Haydn was recently offered for sale at Sothebys in London. The Burgenland Haydn Festival.managed to acquire the letters before the auction took place, preventing the letters from being auctioned separately. The letters, which date from 1780 to 1805, were all written to Haydn's publisher Artaria. The collection contains several previously unknown writings and letters that have never been published. The letters are going to be kept in the Eisenstadt Haydn Museum, where of course they will be made available to scholars.

H. C. R. L.